The Portable Bunyan

TRANSLATION / TRANSNATION

SERIES EDITOR   EMILY APTER

ISABEL HOFMEYR

The Portable Bunyan
A Transnational History of *The Pilgrim's Progress*

PRINCETON UNIVERSITY PRESS

PRINCETON AND OXFORD

Library of Congress Cataloging-in-Publication Data

Hofmeyr, Isabel.
    The portable Bunyan : a transnational history of The pilgrim's progress / Isabel Hofmeyr.
        p.   cm. — (Translation/transnation)
    Includes bibliographical references (p.) and index.
    ISBN 0-691-11655-5 (acid-free paper) — ISBN 0-691-11656-3 (pbk. : acid-free paper)
    1. Bunyan, John, 1628–1688. Pilgrim's progress.   2. Bunyan, John,
1628–1688—Translations into African languages—History and criticism.   3. English
language—Translating into African languages.   4. Bunyan, John,
1628–1688—Appreciation—Africa.   5. Christian fiction, English—History and criticism.
6. African literature—English influences.   7. Bunyan, John, 1628–1688—Influence.
8. Translating and interpreting—Africa.   9. Christianity and literature—Africa.
10. Books and reading—Africa.   I. Title.   II. Series.

PR3330.A9H64 2004
828'.407—dc21

                                                                        2003044491

British Library Cataloging-in-Publication Data is available

This book has been composed in Minion

Printed on acid-free paper. ∞

www.pupress.princeton.edu

Printed in the United States of America

10   9   8   7   6   5   4   3   2   1

CONTENTS

LIST OF ILLUSTRATIONS

ACKNOWLEDGMENTS

A major theme of this study is that texts are made across time and space. This book is no exception and was forged on two continents and across nearly a decade. Its making depended on the kindness, comradeship, and forbearance of many.

I am fortunate in having a vibrant intellectual community in the Faculty of Humanities at the University of the Witwatersrand in Johannesburg. I am indebted to numerous colleagues who commented on papers, recommended readings, chased up details, undertook translation, scanned pictures, prepared tables, offered encouragement, and scanned the horizon for bits of "Bunyaniana." My thanks to Michelle Adler, Muff Andersson, Dinesh Balliah, Rayda Becker, Molly Bill, Philip Bonner, Belinda Bozzoli, David Bunn, David Coplan, Bill Domeris, Paul Germond, Carolyn Hamilton, Simonne Horwitz, Judith Inggs, Cynthia Kros, Tawana Kupe, Karen Lazar, Mark Leon, Tom Lodge, Mufunanji Magalasi, Kgafela Magogodi, Achille Mbembe, Libby Meintjes, Phaswane Mpe, Pam Nichols, Anitra Nettleton, Gerrit Olivier, Deborah Posel, Yvonne Reed, Colin Richards, Dumisani Sibiya, Pippa Stein, Jane Taylor, Michael Titlestad, Ulrike Kistner, and Susan van Zyl. A special word of thanks to my colleagues in African Literature, Merle Govind, James Ogude, Dan Ojwang, and Bheki Peterson, who provide a collegial and intellectually engaged environment, which makes such books possible.

Beyond the university, other colleagues offered assistance and support. Catherine Burns and Keith Breckenridge invited me to Durban on several occasions to present papers. Greg Cuthbertson was always willing to discuss his rich grasp of Nonconformist missions with me. Jeff Opland generously sent me his outstanding translations of Xhosa poems. Terry Barringer was an indefatigable tracker of information on Bunyan in the mission world as was Louise Pirouet. Liz Gunner invited me to speak in Pietermaritzburg and furnished friendship and academic comradeship. Catherine Woeber provided enthusiasm and many points of detail on mission history. Jeff Guy shared his voluminous knowledge on Zulu history and the Colenso family with me. Stephanie Newell generously read the entire manuscript and commented perceptively on it, as did Sarah Nuttall, whose friendship and insight meant much during the final stages of the project. Michael Bath, Margaret Soenser Breen, Bernth Lindfors, Karen Middleton, Rosemary Guillebaud, Jack Thompson, Jim Grenfell, Las Newman, Patricia Sills, and Luise White went out of their way to provide me with information.

When I first started this book, many interlocutors, on hearing that my research had to do with evangelical missionaries, edged away nervously. A small handful, however, grasped the project's importance immediately. Tim Couzens first made me realize, many years ago, that such a project was possible and continued to send me material on Bunyan. Tony Morphet's magisterial knowledge of many things, including the English Revolution, was always illuminating. John Peel saw to the heart of the project and offered key insights from his deep understanding of African Christianity. Stephen Gray volunteered interest and insights from his catholic knowledge of African literature and forwarded me examples of Bunyan in Africa. Simon Gikandi showed a generous interest in the book and helped it along its path in significant ways. Karin Barber's fine grasp of textual anthropology contributed much to sharpening my understanding of what I was doing.

Much of the research was undertaken on a sabbatical trip to England in 1998. The unstinting intellectual and material generosity of Shula and Isaac Marks made this trip, and indeed much of this book, possible. Shula's continued interest in this, and all other southern African Studies research, remains an inspiration to us all. In Britain and Europe, a community of Africanist and other scholars offered friendship, seminar opportunities, and support. Thanks to Jo Beale, William Beinart, Anna Davin, Wayne Dooling, Saul Dubow, Deborah Gaitskell, Deborah James and Patrick Pearson, Paul la Hausse, Jennifer Law, John Lonsdale, John McCracken, Ato Quayson, Jenny Robinson, Hilary Sapire, Stan Trapido, Flora Veit-Wild, and Brian Willan. The School of Oriental and African Studies (SOAS), University of London, hosted me for the duration of the sabbatical. There, David Appleyard, Graeme Furniss, Akin Oyetade, Graeme Rosenberg, and Ridder Samson answered questions and provided information. Annie Coombes was a transcontinental friend and comrade without peer.

As with all research, this book was enabled by wonderful librarians and archivists. Carole Holden, whose work at the British Library is so important for scholars of Africa, offered interest and assistance. Susan Mills and Jennifer Thorp at the Baptist Missionary Society Archives at the Angus Library, Regent's Park College, Oxford, where I did the bulk of research, were consistently helpful. Alan Cirket at the Bunyan Meeting House Museum allowed me access to their collection despite building operations. Margaret Acton at the Centre for the Study of Christianity in the Non-Western World, University of Edinburgh, helped with reproducing photographs. Sandy Fold and the staff of the Cory Library were outstanding. Brian Whitewick from Camden Road Chapel in London generously provided access to the church's papers. Rosemary Seton at SOAS was helpful throughout. Albert Brutsch and Stephen Gill of the remarkable Morija Museum and Archive in Lesotho were every researcher's dream archivists. At the University of the Witwatersrand, Carol Archibald, Fay Blain, Peter Duncan, Sefora Leeto, Pinky Matai, Jay Mathe, Margaret Northey, and Michelle Pickover patiently dealt with a decade worth of queries.

Family and friends assisted in numerous ways with this text. My parents, Syrith and Haldane Hofmeyr have provided a lifetime of unstinting support. Jan and Angela Hofmeyr and family and Elise and Kevin Tait and family are always there and readily answered biblical and theological questions. Jon Hyslop's family offered moral support: my thanks to Robert Hyslop and Mary Park. A great sadness is that Merilyn Hyslop did not live to see the book. Helen Struthers and Bridget and Rosamund Lamont provided friendship, holiday companionship, and fridge magnets. My final thanks are to Jon Hyslop whose care, companionship, and conversation are woven into every page of this book.

Generous financial assistance from various funders made this book possible. The opinions and conclusions expressed in this book are mine alone. My thanks to the Centre for Science Development (now the National Research Foundation) and the University of the Witwatersrand for funding. The Ernest Oppenheimer Memorial Trust provided a most generous Traveling Fellowship.

During the course of doing this research, I made use of different archives and I am appreciative of their permission to reproduce material. The Baptist Missionary Society (BMS) of Didcot, U.K. granted permission to consult and select my own quotations and visual material from their archive material that is housed in the Angus Library at Regent's

Park College, Oxford. Permission from the Council for World Mission to use material from the London Missionary Society (LMS) Papers housed at the SOAS, University of London, is gratefully acknowledged. Permission from the United Society for Christian Literature (USCL) to cite from the Religious Tract Society (RTS)/USCL Papers (also housed at SOAS) is acknowledged. The Church's Commission on Mission granted permission to quote from the papers of the International Committee on Christian Literature for Africa (ICCLA), which forms part of the Conference of British Missionary Societies/International Missionary Council collection housed at SOAS. The Regions Beyond Mission Union (RBMU), whose papers are housed at the Centre for the Study of Christianity in the Non-Western World, School of Divinity, University of Edinburgh, granted permission to reproduce material. The Lovedale Press granted permission to quote from material in the Lovedale Collection. I am grateful to the Bunyan Collection, Bedford Library, Bedford, for access to and use of material, likewise to the Joint Matriculation Board of the South African Universities, University of South Africa, Pretoria (JMB), for access to and use of examination papers. I am grateful for the assistance provided from the following archives, whose material I consulted but which I did not cite: Church Mission Society (CMS) Papers, University of Birmingham; Church of Scotland Foreign Mission Papers, Edinburgh; Historical Papers, University of the Witwatersrand; Morija Museum and Archive, Morija, Lesotho; Manuscripts Collection, University of Edinburgh Library; Natal Archives, Pietermaritzburg.

Sections of the introduction, chapter 2, and chapter 10 appeared in an article "How Bunyan Became English: Missionaries, Translation, and the Discipline of English Literature," *Journal of British Studies* 41, no. 1 (2002): 84–119, and are reprinted here with the permission of the publisher, University of Chicago Press (© 2002 by the North American Conference on British Studies. All rights reserved). An earlier version of chapter 6 appeared in *Journal of Religion in Africa* 32, no. 2 (2002): 1–17, and sections of that article are reproduced here with the permission of the journal. Routledge granted permission to reprint sections of the introduction, which appeared previously in "Bunyan in Africa: Text and Transition," *Interventions: International Journal of Postcolonial Studies* 3, no. 3 (2001): 322–55 (http://www.tandf.co.uk/journals/routledge/1369801X.html).

ANC	African National Congress
BMS	Baptist Missionary Society
CMA	Christian and Missionary Alliance
CMS	Church Mission Society
ICCLA	International Committee on Christian Literature for Africa
JMB	Joint Matriculation Board
LMS	London Missionary Society
NAD	Native Affairs Department
PEMS	Paris Evangelical Mission Society
RBMU	Regions Beyond Mission Union
RTS	Religious Tract Society
SCA	Students' Christian Association
SOAS	School of Oriental and African Studies
SPCK	Society for Promoting Christian Knowledge
USCL	United Society for Christian Literature

The Portable Bunyan

This book tells the story of the transnational circulation of John Bunyan's *The Pilgrim's Progress* (written in two parts, published in 1678 and 1684), one of the world's bestsellers. Bunyan's book was produced in seventeenth-century England in a period of political turmoil and persecution occasioned by the aftermath of the English Revolution. Bunyan himself was a target of such harassment and sections of the book were written in prison. Unsurprisingly for a work of prison literature, the book addresses itself to questions of social and religious inequality and, as Christopher Hill's seminal work on Bunyan has consistently argued, takes up the cause of the weak against the strong. Over the centuries, the text became a spectacular international success and was translated into some two hundred languages. Its migration can be plotted in three stages. The first emanated from England in the seventeenth century, where *The Pilgrim's Progress* had found many eager readers among the politically and religiously marginal. As these groups were hounded, many fled to Protestant Europe and across the Atlantic, taking their beloved book with them. The book's next major migration formed part of the nineteenth-century Protestant mission movement that adopted *The Pilgrim's Progress* as a key evangelical document. Via these mission channels, the book soon reached most corners of the globe. Its final migration was as part of the emerging discipline of English literature, where, from the mid-nineteenth century, Bunyan became canonized as the "father" of the English novel and as a figure in the "Great Tradition."

It is this image of Bunyan as English that has come to dominate the way he is remembered today. In both the popular and academic domain, Bunyan stands as an icon of Englishness. Indeed, existing Bunyan scholarship is almost obsessive in its focus on him as a national figure of seventeenth-century England. His broader transnational presence is largely excised from the critical record. The historiography of Bunyan consequently presents a paradox: an intellectual of the world with a transnational circulation is remembered only as a national writer with a local presence.

This book seeks to explain how this paradoxical set of circumstances has come about: How has a writer with a global reach been turned into a local writer of England? In fashioning an answer to this question, this book directs attention to the interconnections between missions, translation, and the discipline of English literature. Briefly put, the argument presented here suggests that British Protestant mission organizations translated and disseminated the text both "at home" and "abroad." This international circulation was in turn publicized by Nonconformists "at home" to improve the standing of their most revered writer, still regarded with class and denominational suspicion by the Anglican establishment. This mission publicity popularized the idea of Bunyan as a "universal" writer, an idea taken up by the emerging discipline of English literature. Its intellectual project, however, was less about "universality" than about constructing literature as a way of denoting the cultural and racial distinctiveness of Britons in the empire. Bunyan, long associated by missions with the black colonized bodies of empire, did not fit neatly into this grid. The solution to the "problem" was forged by changing the meaning of the word "universality." Instead of betokening the literal spread of a text to different societies, it became a more abstract word concerned with "human nature." The positive properties of universality could be retained while Bunyan was lifted above the societies of empire that threatened to "contaminate" him. In this way, Bunyan could be repackaged as a local writer of England.

This book also asks what happens if we reintegrate this divided terrain of Bunyan scholarship. What new insights might we derive if we resist the divisions of a "local" and "global" Bunyan and instead read him in one integrated field? Arising out of this agenda, this book asks how one might prosecute an analysis of a transnational and translingual text, like *The Pilgrim's Progress*. What made this particular text so translatable?

This book's method of answering this question is perhaps best captured in the implied pun of its title, *The Portable Bunyan*. Read strictly, the title suggests that this book could be a small volume of selected excerpts from Bunyan's work aimed at a popular audience. Such a volume would come into being by a process of textual selection and reconfiguration. It is, this book suggests, such processes, writ large, that make texts translatable. Put another way: when books travel, they change shape. They are excised, summarized, abridged, and bowdlerized by the new intellectual formations into which they migrate. These formations "select" novel configurations of older texts and make them accessible to new audiences. In addressing questions of translatability, this book foregrounds these procedures of intellectual reshaping. It also suggests that such methods of textual creation are stretched across time and space and unfold in different places, often at the same time. Such an approach requires us to consider the space of empire as intellectually integrated (rather than being segregated between "metropole" and "colony"). It also allows us to understand how a text like *The Pilgrim's Progress* becomes a transnational "archive" that opens up novel possibilities for international addressivity. As a transnational and translingual text, *The Pilgrim's Progress* furnished an arena in which various intellectual positions could be accommodated, while also providing a vehicle through which these positions could be dispersed into an international arena.

In addition to summarizing this book's method, its title also signals that not all Bunyan's work proved portable. Bunyan was a prolific writer and intellectual who produced volumes of sermons, tracts, and narratives. Of these, it was only *The Pilgrim's Progress* that proved portable (although there were a handful of mission translations of some of his sermons, *The Holy War*, and his autobiography, *Grace Abounding to the Chief of Sinners*).[1]

A final intention in the conceit of the title relates to the ability of a portable volume to travel and range broadly. Similarly, and of necessity, this book has a wide geographical and historical focus. Its primary focus is on Africa, the site of eighty translations. The continent is, however, understood as part of a broader diasporic and imperial history in the Protestant Atlantic. The story presented here consequently weaves together African literary and intellectual traditions, nineteenth-century British history, African Christianity and mission, Caribbean history, and debates on English literature. It shuttles between London, Georgia, Kingston, Jamaica, Bedford (Bunyan's hometown), and several regions of sub-Saharan Africa.

The Pilgrim's Progress is no longer widely read today. For those unfamiliar with the plot, we set out a brief synopsis. In the first scene, a man in rags, oppressed by a burden on his back, is reading a book. He is distressed and agitated because he knows the City of Destruction in which he lives faces certain damnation. While he maunders in the field, Evangelist approaches and advises him to flee, pointing him in the direction of the Wicket Gate and a distant shining light. Christian, for such is the hero's name, takes off in that direction, running hard with his fingers in his ears to block out the entreaties of his wife and family whom he leaves behind. Two of his townsmen, Obstinate and Pliable, follow to try and knock some sense into him. They are unsuccessful and Obstinate harrumphs home. Pliable, however, is won over by Christian's arguments and decides to join him. Soon, they stumble into the Slough of Despond. Disgusted, Pliable scrambles out and heads for home, leaving Christian to struggle on alone.

After being assisted from the Slough by Help, Christian meets one of the many false pilgrims who will try to mislead him. This one is Mr. Worldly-Wiseman, who advises him to leave the road and head toward the town of Morality where Legality can ease him of his burden. Christian follows his advice. However, the mountain that he has to pass has a dangerous looking overhang and emits flashes of fire. Christian stands undecided until Evangelist comes striding along and berates him for leaving the prescribed route. Christian recommences his journey and arrives at the Wicket Gate, where he is given entry and directed to follow the narrow way. Shortly afterwards, Christian arrives at the Interpreter's House, the first of several places of instruction. Here he is shown various visual allegorical tableaux that teach him key points of belief and doctrine.

The next leg of his journey takes him to the Cross, where the burden of sin falls from his shoulders. Three Shining Ones appear and fit him with new clothes, place the mark of election on his forehead, and give him a roll that he is to hand in at the gates of the Celestial City. Thus fortified, he sets off and, after various interludes, struggles up Hill Difficulty only to fall asleep at an arbor along the way and lose his precious roll, which he has to backtrack to retrieve. He then comes to his second place of instruction, the Palace Beautiful where he is outfitted with a sword and armor. These he soon needs as he is confronted in the Valley of Humiliation by the dragon Apollyon, whom, after a taxing battle, he puts to flight.

After stumbling through the horrors of the Valley of the Shadow of Death, he meets up with a companion, Faithful. They encounter further false pilgrims and then find themselves in Vanity Fair, a town of overheated commerce, greed, and political corruption. Here they are soon at odds with the venal townsfolk and are charged with sedition. Faithful is burned at the stake. Christian is imprisoned but manages to escape and shortly afterward encounters a second companion, Hopeful. Their journey goes well until Christian takes the wrong turn and they end up on the property of Giant Despair, who imprisons them in a dungeon that they eventually escape when Christian belatedly recalls that he carries the key to the prison cell. Their next port of call is the Delectable Mountains, where they are again instructed and given directions to their destination. They encounter additional smooth-tongued travelers, whom they put right on matters of doctrine, and after going astray once again, they pass through the Enchanted Ground and finally arrive at Beulah Land, heaven's waiting room from where one is summoned to heaven by crossing the River of Death. With some difficulty, Christian and Hopeful get across the waters and, after handing over their certificates, enter the gates of heaven. Ignorance, one of their overconfident part-time fellow travelers, arrives shortly afterwards, can produce no certificate, and is thrown straight down into hell.

In the second part of the story, Christian's wife, Christiana, receives a letter from heaven summoning her to join her husband. She sets off with her children and a neighbor, Mercy. They pass through the Slough of Despond, enter the Wicket Gate, and are entertained and instructed at the Interpreter's House. The chivalrous knight, Mr. Great-heart, a manservant of the Interpreter, is sent to accompany the party. They proceed at a much more leisurely pace than Christian, who makes his journey in a few days, and thus their journey takes several years. Their route generally retraces that of Christian—they go up Hill Difficulty, they come to Palace Beautiful, and they pass uneventfully through Vanity Fair, staying with a trusted friend. Much of the action comes from Great-heart who dispatches several giants and demolishes Doubting Castle, home of Giant Despair. In Beulah Land, Christiana and the co-pilgrims Stand-fast, Valiant-for-Truth, and Feeble-mind each in turn receive their summons and make their way across the River of Death to the Celestial City.

The story itself comes to us in a double frame. The first of these is "An Author's Apology for his Book" in which Bunyan, in rhyming couplets, justifies his story to a Puritan audience that may find it too worldly. (Part 2 likewise has an apology. This one, however, performs a slightly different task—it proclaims the authenticity of Bunyan's version as opposed to the "imitations" and "spurious continuations"[2] that flooded the market in the wake of the phenomenal success of part 1. Bunyan also urges his creation to travel widely and convert people, and this "talking book" enters a dialogue with its author.) The second frame is that of a narrator who sees the events unfolding in his dream and relays them to us. He, like Christian, is a vagabond sleeping here and there, and his dream comes to him as he lies in the "den" in the "wilderness of this world." As the text's side notes tell us, the "den" refers to the prison in which Bunyan wrote much of part 1 of the book. This image of Bunyan, the dreamer in prison, was taken up in the frontispieces of early editions, which show Bunyan asleep over his den, while in the top half of the picture, the dream unfolds and we see Christian embarking on his journey (figure 1).

This image of "the immortal dreamer" (known also as "the sleeping portrait")[3] was to become a staple of Bunyan commentary and iconography. The text's excursion to Africa was to change many things about the book, this image included. In one African edition, for example, the "classic" Bunyan frontispiece is reproduced but with significant changes (figure 2). We see Bunyan in the recognizable pose, head in the palm of his hand—he is, however, wide awake and is writing not dreaming. Having a white man asleep in a "public place" was not a propitious way to start a mission-sponsored text. The shifts in this one picture (see figure 3) which I will discuss further in chapter 8, suggest something of the profound ways in which the text altered as it entered the continent. As some have suggested, Bunyan certainly changed Africa. This study demonstrates how Africa changed Bunyan.

Figure 1. Bunyan frontispiece, 1679. Reproduced with
permission from the copy in the British Library.

Figure 2. Bunyan frontispiece by C. J. Montague from the
Ndebele edition of 1902. Source: John Bunyan, *Ugwalo lu ka
Bunyane ogutiwa uguhamba gwohambi* (*The Pilgrim's Progress,*
part 1), translated by D. and M. Carnegie (London: South
African District Committee of the LMS, 1902). Although every
effort has been made to trace and acknowledge the copyright
holders of this image and other images by Montague (figures 11
to 16), we have not been successful. If notified, the author will
be pleased to rectify any omissions at the earliest opportunity.

Figure 3. Bunyan frontispiece by W.F.P. Burton used in various African editions. Source: John Bunyan, *Leeto la Mokreste* (*The Pilgrim's Progress*, part 1), translated by Adolphe Mabille and Filemone Rapetloane (1896; repr. Morija: Morija Sesuto Book Depot, 1988). Reproduced with the permission of the trustees of the Central African Mission (CAM), U.K. charity no. 1049246.

Portable Texts
Bunyan, Translation, and Transnationality

On 31 October 1847, the *John Williams*, a ship of the London Missionary Society (LMS), left Gravesend for the Pacific Islands from whence it had come. Its cargo included five thousand Bibles and four thousand copies of *The Pilgrim's Progress* in Tahitian.[1] Like other such mission ships, the *John Williams* had been funded by the pennies and shillings of Sunday school subscriptions and had become a huge media spectacle. It was but one of the many international propaganda exercises at which mission organizations excelled.[2]

This picture of *The Pilgrim's Progress* as part of an international web is an appropriate one. Written in the wake of the English Revolution, the Puritan classic had spread across the Protestant Atlantic as its persecuted readers fled (or were transported) to Europe, North America, and the Caribbean. Its next major international fillip came courtesy of the Protestant mission movement, whose adherents, recruited from across the Atlantic, propagated their most beloved book wherever they went. By the late 1700s, it had reached India and by the early 1800s, Africa. Yet, some two hundred years later, this avowedly international image of *The Pilgrim's Progress* has been turned inside out. Once a book of the world, it has become a book of England. Today Bunyan is remembered as a supremely English icon, and his most famous work is still studied as the progenitor of the English novel. Roger Sharrock best exemplifies this pervasive trend of analysis in his introduction to the Penguin edition of *The Pilgrim's Progress*. He begins by acknowledging Bunyan's transnational presence, but this idea is then severed from the "real" Bunyan who is local, Puritan, and, above all, English.[3]

Sharrock's vision of Bunyan is avowedly national and it is this viewpoint that has dominated academic study of Bunyan.[4] The story of Bunyan as a transnational writer has attracted almost no serious scholarly research. With the signal exception of Tamsin Spargo's work, the career of Bunyan's work outside Britain has generally only been explored by antiquarian or evangelically related investigation.[5] There are some cases, like David Smith's *Bunyan in America*, where the influence of *The Pilgrim's Progress* outside Britain is seriously assessed.[6] Such studies, however, make no attempt to link that international circulation back to Britain or to inquire what it might imply for Bunyan's standing in England. The two topics—Bunyan in Britain and Bunyan "abroad"—remain sundered areas of inquiry.

In a situation where global integration has enfeebled national boundaries and where literary studies is increasingly postcolonial in orientation, this division today in the terrain of Bunyan scholarship is peculiar. Virtually every other major figure in the British canon, like Shakespeare, Milton, Austen, or Dickens, has been subject to reinterpretations that consider them in a transnational rather than simply a national domain. Similarly, readings of the novel as a form shaped in empire are now commonplace. As a writer translated into some two hundred languages worldwide, Bunyan's claims to such a reevaluation are even stronger and more pressing.[7] Yet, studies of Bunyan remain resolutely local.

This book attempts to reintegrate the divided terrain of scholarship on *The Pilgrim's Progress*, firstly, by reinserting Bunyan back into a transnational landscape and, secondly, by asking what the implications of such a move might be in theoretical and literary historical terms. This story is primarily explored in the context of Bunyan's circulation in Africa—the scene of eighty translations.[8] The narrative unfolds in three parts. The first section traces how *The Pilgrim's Progress* entered the continent as part of the evangelical Protestant mission movement. The second section examines how the book traveled into various African societies and how it was changed by the intellectual and literary traditions into which it migrated. The third section narrates how the African (and wider mission imperial) circulation of Bunyan changed his standing back in England.

This book, then, is an investigation of how a particular text was translated and circulated throughout much of the African continent (and indeed most of the Protestant world). Given its dissemination across so many different languages, societies, and intellectual contexts, *The Pilgrim's Progress* can be considered as an early example of a translingual mass text (leaving aside, of course, the sacred books of world religions). In telling the story of its dissemination, this book asks how this one text came (or at least appeared) to be translatable across such a vast realm. Its theoretical agenda aligns three domains—translatability and its limits; the material and social practices of translation; and circulation. The argument woven around these items is set out below—first in summary and then in extended detail.

My argument commences with translatability, an a priori assumption in the Protestant mission world. Driven by universalistic theories of language and evangelical ardor, mission organizations held that any and every text with the "right" message was translatable. The mission domain consequently presents an instructive instance through which to approach issues of translatability. Their presuppositions of translatability understood as a linguistic feasibility produced a flurry of texts. Yet, what became of those texts? Did they prove intelligible or meaningful to their new audiences? Did they prove as translatable to their readers as they did to their producers and under what circumstances?

One long-standing route for answering such questions has been to consider factors internal to the translated text and to speculate on what orders of understanding its linguistic and stylistic choices do or do not enable. More recently, however, translation theorists have widened their frame of inquiry to pose prior questions about how ideas of equivalence or nonequivalence come into being. As Lydia Liu asks, "Can the achieved or contested reciprocity of languages be plotted as the outcome of a given economy of historical exchange?"[9] Attention to these economies of exchange with their "struggles over the commensurability or reciprocity of meanings as values" may generate crisper insights into problems of intellectual and cultural translatability. Such an analysis, as Liu points out, would involve capturing the "radical historicity" and contingency of how such climates of intelligibility (or nonintelligibility) are created.[10]

In investigating this set of issues, this book suggests two related lines of inquiry. The first examines the broad context of ideas and discourses that made translation thinkable to both Protestant missionaries and African converts. Evangelical enthusiasm certainly played a critical role in propagating translation; however, translation alone could never ensure intellectual portability. Instead, this book focuses on how shared ideas of literacy as miraculous agent and books as magical objects grew up as a field of discourse between missionary and convert. These ideas were driven, on the one hand, by mission evangelical theories of language by which texts are empowered to seize and convert those they encounter, and, on the other, by African attempts to embed the new technology of print into a sacred domain where it became a vehicle for ancestral revelation. This field of discourse furnished an apparently shared set of motivations for undertaking translation, but one broad enough to provide a semblance of shared objectives while allowing for differing agendas to be pursued.

This book's second line of inquiry is to focus sustained attention on the material and social practices of translation itself. It argues that the social relationships, fields of power, methods of working, and technologies of production associated with translation are critical sites for understanding whether, and what kinds of, notions of equivalence might come into being. The basic unit of production in the mission arena was a "first-language" convert and a "second-language" missionary.[11] This intimate nexus became a crucial domain in which ideas of comparison and translatability were produced. This "production unit" consequently forms one of the themes of analysis in this book and brings into focus how texts were selected for translation, how the work of translation proceeded, how these translated texts were produced, and for whom and in what forums they were distributed. Once we take this as our analytical field, we are forced to describe much more precisely how, and in what form, texts are circulated; how they are translated, taught, and read; and how their meanings are determined, not prior to their circulation but in the social arenas of their dissemination.

The "methodological fetishism" of keeping our eye on the textual object is also extended to the question of circulation, and it directs our attention to the material routes of circulation along which texts were funneled. Both the actual and the imagined limits of circulation allow us to speculate on the forms of publicness that translated texts bring into being. What kinds of imaginaries, for example, coalesce when texts circulate across language boundaries? These forms of virtual solidarity can in turn throw light on the broader questions of how decisions around equivalence or nonequivalence are ceded or withheld.

The final segment of the argument concerns the limits of translatability. Under what circumstances did the text not prove portable? Under what conditions was it consciously rejected? Or, in what conjunctures did it simply evaporate? In addressing this cluster of questions, this book suggests that while these conditions are always contingent, they can usefully be thought of in relation to the role of African intellectual brokerage. It is such intellectual formations, and their internal debates between leader and led, that play a critical role in whether translated texts find acceptance or whether they are cast aside as politically tainted, as meaningless, or as unintelligible. Such instances of conscious political rejection generally spell the end of a translated text's life, although its outline can linger, often as an irritant against which arguments are framed. In such instances, the text can find a short-lived and spectral translatability. Yet, not all instances of untranslatability derive from rejection. Often a translated text disappears, either through boredom or, in some instances, by evaporating into nearly identical narrative forms where the translated text ceases to be itself. In such instances, untranslatability is brought about not by too little commensurability, but rather by too much.

The remainder of the introduction spells out this argument in more detail before turning to consider its implication for the literary historiography of Bunyan. The introduction concludes with comments on the geographical and historical scope of the book, its research procedures and sources, and an overview of chapters.

Translatability

The question of why *The Pilgrim's Progress* appeared so translatable or "universal" has long attracted speculation but produced little sustained research. This armchair surmise has produced two orders of answer: the first concerns itself with features internal to the text, the second with factors external to it, namely the imperial context in which it was disseminated. In the first line of argument, certain themes in the text are nominated as assuring its successes. For nineteenth-century Protestants, this secret ingredient was Bunyan's evangelical message; for those involved in English literature as a discipline, it was the book's enactment of a "universal" human nature. More recently, Christopher Hill has mooted that it is the text's political radicalism that attracts audiences in colonized societies.[12] The second line of argument moves outside the text and posits Bunyan's universality as being tied up with a relentless imperialism via whose structures a text like *The Pilgrim's Progress* is disseminated in order to "control non-Western, non-Christian subjects."[13]

Both lines of argument have limited validity. In some instances, the generic and episodic features of the text did play a part in winning popular audiences for the text. However, as the case studies in this book demonstrate, the sections of the text so foregrounded are different from those nominated by casual speculation and can only be brought to light via a serious engagement with the African intellectual formations into which such segments were enfolded.

The arguments about imperialism as an enabler of the text likewise have some salience: empire furnished a crucial context for missions and hence conditions for the text to be propagated in translated form. Furthermore, in disseminating this, one of their key ideological documents, missionaries invested extraordinary amounts of determination, labor, capital, and technology. These mechanisms were reinforced by an array of distributive institutions: mission schools and bookshops; mission-run literary, debating, and dramatic societies; journals and newspapers; and literature bureaus (joint mission/colonial state institutions set up to promote "appropriate" vernacular literatures). As sections of this book demonstrate, this mission doggedness resulted in environments saturated with *The Pilgrim's Progress* in at least two and sometimes three languages. The investment in the text also occasioned a determination to make it "catch on" at all costs. As one mission publisher observed, "It sometimes takes three to five years for a new book to become known so that people ask for it."[14]

Yet, at the same time, this explanation of mission and imperial doggedness is partial in several regards. Most obviously, it conflates the colonial state, white-settler interest, and missions and treats these as identical. Hence, white-settler appropriations of *The Pilgrim's Progress* in English (in which the story was frequently fashioned as an imperial allegory) are construed as similar to the translated versions sponsored by mission organizations.[15] Most importantly, however, such interpretations assume that missionaries (backed by imperial compulsion) can determine the field of debate for the audiences they encounter, a proposition that scholarship on missions has consistently disproved.[16] Instead, as this latter research demonstrates, mission agendas are always curtailed by the circumstances into which they are inserted. In relation specifically to mission translation, this scholarship has started to sketch a picture of how such constraints played themselves out in the contradictory processes of vernacularizing Christianity and of fashioning theological equivalences across languages. Birgit Meyer, for example, examines the field of biblical translation that took shape between Ewe Protestant and North German Pietist in Ghana. She focuses on the symbiosis between the witchcraft beliefs of the former and the devil theology of the latter and how these interactions registered themselves in the translation choices made for key terms in the Scriptures, such as "devil," "holy spirit," and "God." The semantic fields of these terms allowed Ewe-speakers and German missionaries to operate in an apparently shared field of understanding while continuing to attribute power to older beliefs like witchcraft by energetically disavowing them. Vicente Rafael's study of Spanish Jesuit interactions with Tagalog societies in seventeenth-century Philippines foregrounds ideas on language, signification, and translation as a primary domain for grasping the complicit contestations that characterize Christian colonialism. As he demonstrates, both Spaniard and Tagalog had "something else in mind" in the process of conversion—for the Jesuits, it was the universalization of a hierarchical Christian order; for Tagalog-speakers, it was an attempt to "manage" Christianity by keeping it at arm's length. For many Tagalog, the new religion was treated like a troublesome and unbidden spirit that required fitful appeasement. The result was "conversion in a state of distraction" and an almost absent-minded filtering and dismembering of Jesuit texts, producing a social order "premised not on consensus between ruler and ruled but on the fragmentation and hermeneutic displacement of the very basis of consensus: language."[17] Meyer and Rafael demonstrate that in two mission locations, the intellectual traditions of mission and convert jointly produced a semantic "haze," a field of strategic misreading that enabled a form of translation to became possible.

This book extends Meyer's and Rafael's lines of argument by examining the shared fields of discourse that Protestant mission and convert, in their early stages of interaction, bring into being around literacy as a miraculous technology and books as magical objects. For missions, this perception was driven by evangelical theories of language and conversion that entail magical notions of textual agency, since language is seen as a primary vehicle through which conversion (a form of magical transformation) occurs. For Africans, the perception was driven less by the novelty of the technology than by its embedding in existing understandings of the sacred. These allowed a new form of communication to be harnessed to speak to existing spiritual and ancestral worlds. It also allowed a bypassing of mission authorities since the technology was seen to come from God or the ancestors rather than the mission colonial world. Both traditions of interpretation, to some extent, construed the book as a magical object and, in this apparent agreement, could construct a discourse field that validated the propagation and translation of further texts, while simultaneously pursuing different agendas.

This intellectual convergence is captured as well in the term the "white man's fetish," which was used to describe books in general. The book can hence be seen as similar in its operation to the workings of the "fetish" as outlined by Pietz.[18] As he demonstrates, the term emerged from the trading entrepôts on the West African coast and became a way of managing contradictory ideas of value and of making trade possible. The operations of the "white man's fetish" can be understood in an analogous way. The term became a way of managing contradictory orders of value, this time in relation to the spiritual realm, and generated a field of discourse and meaning through which translation became possible.

One claim of this book is that *The Pilgrim's Progress* functioned as a privileged "fetish." This capacity derived from three features. The first was the emotional and compulsive power with which Protestant missionaries invested the text. Particularly for Nonconformist missionaries, it was a book of extraordinary appeal that had long been scripted into their theology and their conversion narratives.[19] Because of its power, and because it summarized the key message of evangelical Protestantism, the book was widely treated as a substitute for the Scriptures themselves. This latter attribute gave the text its second "fetish"-like property, namely its ambiguity. As a near-Bible, it was both secular and sacred; serious and pleasurable; fictional yet also "true." Its form as an allegory extended these ambiguous possibilities: it could support divergent interpretations while still apparently remaining the same book. Thirdly, the book has a structure that lends itself relatively easily to translation. It is episodic and could be translated serially as a sequence of freestanding installments. The text has little realistic detail. Its topography is vague and biblical in orientation and presents few impediments to translation.

For Protestant missions, there was consequently both a will and a way to translate the text and to disseminate it widely. As an object that had wrought their own conversion, missionaries imagined the text doing likewise to others and dispelling the darkness of heathendom. For African Christians working under constrained and supervised circumstances, the text offered a number of opportunities for experimentation. Not only was it an arena of allegorical possibility but its illustrations and the dramatic reenactments of *The Pilgrim's Progress*, which were routinely staged, provided a landscape in which converts could "try on" different characters and plot lines. For those in the mission domain wishing to produce their own writing in English or African languages or both, the story—one of the few semi-secular texts used by evangelical missionaries—offered a compendium of generic potentialities to explore and greater opportunities for intertextual rescripting than the Bible whose integrity was fiercely policed.[20] In these ways, Bunyan's text could become an object authorizing transactions while also absorbing the contradictory meanings generated in the mission domain.

In relation to mission translation, this book attempts to draw attention to evangelicalism, a topic that has been widely studied but whose implications for translation have not been fully grasped. Historically, the phenomenon has been extensively discussed as a major factor in the late eighteenth- and early nineteenth-century emergence of the Protestant mission movement. Likewise, its theological meaning as a doctrine of salvation by faith rather than by good works or the sacrament has been much debated. Also well understood are the phenomenological manifestations of evangelicalism that entail a particular style of conversion: a burdensome awareness of sin is followed by an overwhelmingly emotional experience of conversion.[21] Less understood, however, are evangelical ideas about language, text, and translation.

These are, of course, shaped by the compelling imperatives of proselytization. Not only was each Protestant obliged to preach the word and save souls but in some schools of thought this activity also served to hasten the second coming; when the word had been preached to all nations, Jesus was to return to earth. An individual's textual practice could consequently have millennial implications. Working in such pressing contexts, it became imperative to broadcast the word as widely as possible. Consequently, there was considerable technological and media inventiveness on the part of mission organizations that sought to render their messages as physical objects in order to extend their reach. These objects, in turn, could become proxy agents or prosthetic missionaries, "noiseless messengers" who could extend the missionary's range and penetrate into regions where missionaries themselves could not go.[22] The propaganda prerogatives attendant on foreign missions provided an additional incentive to making texts material. Audiences back home were often skeptical of, if not opposed to, foreign missions, whom they thought should stay put and attend to the "heathen" at home. Crusades of persuasion were hence required and one object often deployed in such campaigns was the translated text. Bibles, hymnbooks, tracts, and copies of *The Pilgrim's Progress* in foreign languages routinely formed part of missionary exhibitions and publicity. Home viewers generally knew the original of the translated texts well and could sustain the illusion that readers across the world imbibed the "same" message as they did.

Underlying these evangelical practices was a view of reading (and implicitly a theory of language) that invested texts with the capacity to seize and entirely transform those whom they addressed. This point is worth stressing as several current understandings of mission translation have highlighted only its universalistic assumptions in terms of which any language is a transparent and inert medium through which God's truth could shine. In such analyses, missionaries are portrayed as naive in their translation practices.[23] By holding that equivalence and translatability were divinely ordained and hence possible, a universalistic view of language was undoubtedly important in fueling the frenzied translation activity of Protestant missions. However, in order for these translated texts to be effective in the world, one required a supplementary theory of textual compulsion that conferred agency on texts to capture those they encountered. Mission translation in effect mobilized both theories—those of transparency and those of capture—in order to function and to sustain the belief that texts could cross languages and cultures so as to bring the "same" form of belief and consciousness into being. Or, put another way, such textual theories sought to propagate a "transnationally translatable monoculture."[24] In part, of course, missionaries failed in this intention as the message they bore was rescripted by its recipients. Overall, however, the mission project in Africa had a fair degree of success in propagating itself, a process that depended, in part, as Lamin Sanneh has argued, on the strategies of translation that it evolved.[25]

Translation as Material and Social Practice

As an exercise in evangelization, mission translation is shaped by a cluster of constraints that confer on it certain distinctive attributes. Firstly, as the purpose of translation is to recruit followers, missionaries constantly experiment with different textual configurations to see what will communicate best with the audiences they encounter. Secondly, as most missionaries are second-language speakers, they are dependent on first-language converts with whom they work closely. Thirdly, mission translation is always an avowedly transnational and transcontinental activity shaped, on the one hand, "at home" by the parent body's denominational objectives and funding capacities, and, on the other, "abroad" by the interaction of mission and convert. Each of these constraints prompts certain characteristic ways of working, patterns of funding, sets of social relationships, and material textual forms that together create both limits and possibilities for how translated texts will be interpreted.

As the first and second points indicate, mission translation is a system heavily dependent on convert audiences and expertise. African Christian thinking can consequently imprint itself on the final translated products at a number of junctures. The first of these relates to the broad parameters in which Christianity itself came to be understood. As a wealth of research has demonstrated, the tenets of the religion found differing degrees of acceptance in the continent. The doctrine of original sin, for example, with its presupposition of an unwilled, universal condition of evil, was often sidestepped by African Christians in favor of a more social understanding of sin. Other concepts, notably that of a supreme being, already existed and hence found general acceptance. So, too, did the idea of God having a son. Despite this being a novel notion, it generated an extensive African Christology in which the figure of Christ is reworked, generally as an intermediary rather than a son.[26] As this book demonstrates, these templates, often shaped in the "labor process" of translation itself, furnish a critical context for considering any translated text in the mission world. They consequently provide important boundaries when considering the translatability of *The Pilgrim's Progress*, a text heavily steeped in Protestant doctrine.

A second node at which African Christian thinking could intervene was in determining the material shape, form, and content of the translated text. The exigencies of proselytization mean that texts have to be experimentally disseminated in bits and pieces and in a variety of media (image, illustration, photograph, postcard, magic lantern slide, pageant, sermon, hymn). Popular taste consequently registers itself in how these media are configured. As chapter 8 shows, the decision of which European illustrations to include in mission editions was at times influenced by converts. The conventions employed in Africanized illustrations likewise reflected the opinions of African Christians. Equally, the segments of the book that proved most durable were determined by convert opinion. In short, popular judgment has a decisive impact on whether translated forms become portable.

It is also important to underline that mission methods of producing translation seldom involved a solo translator. As we have seen, the basic working unit comprised a second-language missionary and first-language convert. Virtually all mission translation was hammered out in such pairs. These "couples" worked long hours, were locked in tense and often intimate relations of dependence, and produced a style of translation that was coauthored. Adding further complexity was the convention of translation by committee, particularly in relation to anything biblical where doctrinal and theological questions had to be negotiated among the home organization, the members of the mission, the Bible Society, and mission colleagues from other denominations in the region.

This complexity of operation meant that any mission translation was shaped in a web of negotiation, disagreement, and contradiction. Mission translation is hence less about the "technologies of colonial domination" than about opening up fields of maneuver.[27] The possibilities for such maneuver were further enabled and limited by the complex linguistic landscape against which translation unfolded in Africa. Such arenas not infrequently involved more than one African language and more than one European language—a feature of the linguistic landscape routinely obscured by the idea that colonial encounters entailed two "sides" and hence, it is unquestioningly assumed, only two languages. Many precolonial African societies were "multilingual," a word that cannot fully capture the complex linguistic and dialect layering of a world where languages in the modern and strictly demarcated sense did not exist. Languages also overlay other forms of social status, such as royal and commoner, slave and free, indigene and latecomer. Into this complex linguistic landscape came missionaries, speaking different languages, and colonial forces of occupation, often speaking yet others. In these unequal arenas, missionaries claimed the right to "own" and codify African languages, turning them into the orthographical and grammatical subordinates of European languages. However, this domination did not prevent the linguistic domain from persisting as a critical political forum in which Africans continued their multiple battles against mission, colonial state, and their precolonial enemies. In such an environment, having one's language chosen for codification by missions could give one an edge over one's social betters (who sometimes spoke another language). It could also mean elevation into a "tribe," a form of social organization through which one could win recognition and some resources from the colonial state.[28] The cost, however, was a mission-made language not always fully recognizable to its speakers and a world of racially supervised literary and cultural production. Language politics in and around the mission provided a landscape of both possibility and constraint within which African Christians had to try and position themselves.

The case studies in this book seek to understand the translation process as wrought in such intricacies and complexities. One such instance, narrated in chapter 3, involves a minority language community, the Kele, on the Upper Congo and their interaction with the British Baptists. Kele was one of at least a dozen languages in the vicinity and was chosen by missionaries in order to "protect" its speakers from the ravages of modernity. In the process of translating Bunyan, Kele Protestants played a role in conferring a particular shape and form on an abridged translation of *The Pilgrim's Progress*. In this version, the theological explanations regarding original sin with which the story is larded were generally left out. This configuration of the text bears the imprint of Kele Protestant opinion. Firstly, in bypassing the sections on original sin, readers could sidestep this Protestant doctrine that proved untranslatable across most of Africa. They could also "prime" the story to make it more amenable to interpretation by removing the distracting second-guessing of the author who violates his own allegorical procedures by explaining what episodes mean. Through the translation process, the story is "cleaned up" and made more amenable to Kele interpretation.

Adding to this complex translingual environment was a third characteristic of mission translation, namely its transnational and transcontinental orientation. This arose both from the globalizing ambitions of Protestantism as an evangelical religion and from the sprawling transcontinental infrastructure (of committees, printers, warehouses, transport routes, and so on) that mission organizations established to support translation. These imperatives tend to produce Protestant texts that carry both an international mode of address (implicitly addressed to all actual and potential believers throughout the world) and more local agendas shaped in the individual nodes of the international network.

In traveling through these various circuits, a text like *The Pilgrim's Progress* accumulated traces of its prior journeys. In some cases, such signs could be the language/s into or from which it was translated. In other cases, it could be an introduction giving something of the text's history. In yet others, the text's illustrations could betoken its prior paths: African and African American editions, for example, showed black characters and so indicated that the text had acquired new "personnel" on its travels.

These various traces and reminders in turn conferred on the text a capacity to enable imaginative international addressivity. Put another way, it allowed people to think, read, and write *as if* they were addressing a vast international Protestant public (even if in reality they only reached a limited actual or potential audience). *The Pilgrim's Progress*, as a virtual international text, functioned as a set of "backdrops" against which one could imaginatively project oneself into an international arena.

Such texts acquire a layering that is important to their perceived translatability. The case studies in this book provide instances of this process by which different groups used this "doubleness" for a variety of political objectives. The novelist, Thomas Mofolo, for example, engages with *The Pilgrim's Progress* to rescript local ideas of masculinity by entering a broad debate on Protestantism, gender, and empire. The middle-class African mission elite frequently turned to Bunyan to articulate anti-colonial and, at times, antimission ideologies not only to themselves, white settlers, and the colonial state but also to an international audience. In the case of the Kongo translation in northern Angola, African mission notables used the opportunity opened by photographic illustrations of *The Pilgrim's Progress* to project themselves (as characters in the images) and, implicitly, their local ethnic micropolitics into an international arena, thereby passing around and over the Portuguese colonial state.

A focus on translation, then, requires us to grapple with the organization and implications of intellectual labor across the empire. This approach proves useful in putting into practice recent revisionist readings of empire. These posit empire as an intellectually integrated zone, instead of a divided terrain of "center" and "periphery." The imperial arena is a complex force field in which circuits of influence travel in than one direction. How to put such a vision into practice is, however, by no means self-evident. In essence, we are required to understand how events are made in different places at the same time. Such an approach necessitates a multi-sited methodology that can provide both breadth and depth. We are obliged to have a broad canvas, but, equally, each point on that canvas must have sufficient depth to plumb the local intellectual formations underlying that node. One also needs a method of telling the story that captures the movement in and between these various nodes. Given these difficulties, the temptation is often to adopt a proscenium approach where narration focuses primarily on one site. Ideas, influences, or intellectual currents from elsewhere feature, but only in walk-on parts. Such situations can be characterized by what Dipesh Chakrabarty terms "asymmetrical knowledge."[29] In this scenario, most scholars' knowledge weighs in at the metropolitan end of things with the local being read—if at all—only at the level of elite culture. The intellectual hinterlands informing this elite cultural production seldom come into focus. Attention to themes of translation can provide one route into solving these problems by forcing our attention on to intellectual production in varying sites and among an extensive cast of players. Such a framework also directs us to think about questions of textual circulation.

Circulation

With regard to questions of circulation, this book suggests that our task is twofold: firstly, we have to uncover empirically the complexity of circuits along which texts are marshaled and, secondly, we need to ask what the theoretical import of such journeys might be. In order to address the first point, we have to keep our eye on the text as a material object. This procedure is necessary in order to bring to light the intricate circuits along which texts are funneled rather than the routes we imagine or anticipate they might traverse. One such presupposition is that texts tread predictable paths, namely from "Europe" to "Africa," "north" to "south," "metropole" to "colony." With regard to *The Pilgrim's Progress*, the commonsense temptation is to imagine the text traveling this route, diffusing outwards from the imperial center to the furthest reaches of empire, with apparently little consequence for the context from which it emanated.

Instead of this "center"/"periphery" model, we place Bunyan's text in the broader space of the mission empire and trace its circuits within it. These routes along which the texts travel are varied. The text, for example, often travels "side-ways" between African languages. It loops back to the metropolis. It follows diasporic trajectories. In some cases, it travels between heaven and earth. This book attempts both to bring the empirical complexities of these textual journeys into view and to ask what their theoretical import may be. What difference might such empirical information make analytically? What significance might we divine from the routes along which texts migrate?

One answer to this question comes from Michael Warner's recent work on publics and counterpublics.[30] For him, questions of circulation, both real and imagined, lie at the very heart of how publics come into being, how they think about themselves, and hence how they script social imaginaries, in turn the template on behalf of which much social and political action is taken. For Warner, it is the limits and pathways of circulation that are critical. How these are imagined become the sinews around which publics take shape. A key methodological move in such an equation is to pay close attention to how texts dramatize the limits of their circulation. In Warner's words, "From the concrete experience of a world in which available forms circulate, one projects a public. . . . This performative ability depends, however, on that object's being not entirely fictitious—not postulated merely, but recognized as a real path for the circulation of discourse. That path is then treated as a social entity."[31]

One purpose of this book, in tracing the routes along which *The Pilgrim's Progress* was guided, is to bring into focus a variety of forms of publicness that these circuits make visible. Some of these are well known and have long been discussed in nationalist and diasporic analyses of Africa. These include the political congregations of the African mission elite, the crisscrossed diasporic networks of the black Atlantic, and the messianic worlds of popular African Christianity. The analysis offered here examines the role that one particular text performed in the discourse fields of these publics and how the text furnished intellectual and performative arenas in which these groups could workshop versions of themselves.

Yet, at the same time, this analysis also insists, in opposition to much of the nationalist historiography on Africa, that such groups spoke not only to themselves or their oppressors but equally to a worldwide public, albeit a type that has largely fallen from view. As we have seen, Protestant texts are always transcontinental in their mode of address, speaking implicitly to all actual and potential believers, even if such believers cannot understand the language in which the text is written. In looking at how such texts dramatize the limits of their circulation, we can detect the cosmic arena in which African Protestants placed themselves. Such arenas provided novel horizons against which forms of selfhood could be rehearsed to produce new modes of publicness. One of these, mentioned earlier, was a public sphere that straddled heaven and earth. In this divine order, texts circulated between this world and the next and in some instances, were produced in heaven and made their way to earth. In such an ancestral economy, the dead are interpellated retrospectively, via the mechanisms of print culture, as "honorary" members of modernity. The technologies of modernity, in this case print and literacy, are likewise made ancestral and are seen to emanate not from colonially aligned missions but from the spiritual realms of "tradition." As one boundary of projected textual circulation, the ancestral world represents a novel cosmic imaginary marked in part by the languages in which the ancestors are deemed to be competent. In most cases, the dead read and write in a named African language, but in some cases, they appear to be polyglot, able to deal with documents in any language. As Rafael remarks, paradise can "mark the end of translation" and so provide the threshold for a new imaginative formation.[32]

Another type of public was signaled by texts that are translated "sideways" between African languages, rather than moving, as the commonsense view would expect, from a europhone to an afrophone language. Such "lateral" moves were often registered in the introduction to editions that spelled out the African languages through which the text had already traversed and hence the African intellectual circuits and formations in which it had been inducted. In the few cases where *The Pilgrim's Progress* was translated solo by an African, the book became ensconced in the printed and oral literary culture of the language as well as in popular taste and perception. Such popularity had in part to do with the superior quality of translation, done by a first-language speaker, but also with the implied circulation of the text, which was seen to have been thoroughly "baptized" in the literary and intellectual traditions of the language. In some cases, the text even appears to enter its print version from a prior oral existence in an African language. The preface to the Zulu version of 1868, for example, states: "Here it is, then, the book of Christian. You have heard others talk of his existence, and that he has his own book . . ."[33]

In this quotation, the idea of the book occupies a para-literate zone in which texts become multimedia and multilingual portfolios. In such understandings, texts are configured across the printed and the spoken, image and text, and, at times, heaven and earth. This "portfolio" understanding of texts in turn inaugurates and forms part of an extensive field of African popular cultural production which plaits together intellectual traditions, media, genres, and languages in novel ways, as Karin Barber's seminal work has demonstrated. These formations in turn play a critical role in convening sub-elite reading, writing, and interpretive formations whose outlines are beginning to be traced by scholars like Barber and Stephanie Newell.[34] As much of this book demonstrates, *The Pilgrim's Progress* often functioned as a text around which models of reading, writing, and interpretive practices were negotiated. Its history can hence throw some light on the intricate ways in which African reading formations, both popular and otherwise, take shape. The history of Bunyan's text in Africa, often the model of what a book might or could be, likewise starts to throw some light on what a history of the book in Africa might look like. This book's contribution to that as-yet-unwritten story is to highlight the extraordinary possibilities that emerged from a situation in which print technology, for much of the nineteenth century at least, was mediated by the mission domain. As already indicated, this conjuncture of circumstances produced a realm of miraculous literacy in which the potentialities of the book (and hence how its history might be written) were grasped in novel and distinctive ways.

As a text that crossed so many languages and served so many

purposes, *The Pilgrim's Progress* came to function as a portmanteau text. In this guise, the book can be seen as an archive in which various intellectual positions could be billeted. As the case studies in this book illustrate, the text provided a shared landscape and set of reference points around and in which debates could be rehearsed. Whether these were about "progress," modernity, masculinity, the nature of heaven, the political possibilities of the diaspora, or the workings of a transcontinental Protestant arena, they were enfolded in readers' idea of the story. These interpretations were also supplemented by knowledge (which obviously varied from reader to reader) that one was encountering a text that had been "baptized" in a range of domains. As this book demonstrates, these were far-flung and as diverse as Jamaican slavery, the struggles of the Eastern Cape African elite in South Africa, and the dream-geographies of heaven. These temporalities likewise leave traces of themselves in the text and become part of its cumulative meaning. This archive in turn comes to play a significant role in African intellectual history when it is taken up as a sub-tradition in the African novel. As chapter 9 demonstrates, various African writers address themselves to Bunyan, not as an "imperial" writer but as a long-standing African presence with whom particular intellectual debates, particularly around modernity, have come to be associated.

These various circumstances, then, played a part in helping *The Pilgrim's Progress* to "get a life" in Africa. Yet, under what circumstances did the text not survive?

The Limits of Translatability

In assessing the limits of the text's portability, this book foregrounds the nature of the African intellectual brokerage that Bunyan's narrative encountered. As we have seen, African intellectual formations were central in ensuring the book's longevity. They were likewise critical in those scenarios where the text did not survive. The role that African intellectuals played in this regard was both witting (involving a political choice of rejection) and unwitting (where the text falls by the wayside not out of rejection but out of boredom or indifference).

An apt example of witting rejection concerns Simon Kimbangu, the leader of a prominent breakaway prophet movement that emerged as a "fall-out" of Baptist missions on the Lower Congo in the 1920s. Kimbanguists adapted quite a few features of the Baptist tradition, including aspects of church organization and bureaucracy as well as catechisms, sermons, and hymns. The movement, however, evinced no systematic interest in *The Pilgrim's Progress*, despite the fact that it had been so intensively propagated by the BMS.[35] While the situation is difficult to judge precisely, this decision to bypass Bunyan may, in part, have been driven by Kimbangu himself, who at times used elements of *The Pilgrim's Progress* while disavowing its provenance. One such instance emerges from Kimbangu's belief that the hymnbook he wrote came from the other world. In order to travel there and back to locate his hymns, Kimbangu had to pass through a great body of water. Despite his dunking, however, the book of hymns remained dry, proving its divine origin. The Kongo version of *The Pilgrim's Progress* in circulation on the Lower Congo at the time, showed an illustration of the hero, Christian being helped from the Slough of Despond. He is soaking wet. The book in his hand is dry. Persecuted by both British Baptists and Belgian colonial officials, Kimbangu presumably "poached" from the text but disavowed the source, making a political decision to reject the book while still maintaining it as a ghostly reference point. This soon faded. In the extensive body of material on Kimbanguism, there is no indication that *The Pilgrim's Progress* made any imprint.

In this Kimbangu scenario, the text withers, largely because of an active decision of disavowal. However, translated texts can also disappear through indifference and boredom. Consider, for example, the wider fate of the Kongo version of the book. Within the mission world it took strong hold, while in Kimbangu's secessionist movement, it made only a fleeting impression. Beyond the mission hinterlands, the text made no discernible impact whatsoever. One way to think about this issue would be to consider *The Pilgrim's Progress* against the background of existing Kongo narrative traditions. From this perspective, the story would seem quite unexceptional. Tales of a man with a bag on his back traveling from this world to the next were commonplace. Featuring a trickster protagonist who in some variations is called Moni-Mambu, the one with affairs and concerns on his back, the narratives follow a pattern whereby the protagonist sets off from this world to the next.[36] There he has a series of encounters with the gods and ancestors, and using his wit and the objects stored in his bag, he is able to bring back some desired items, such as ideas, solutions to problems, hunting luck, or treasures. The overall pattern of the story is a movement from this world to the next and back again. Against this background, Bunyan's story is a bit of a yawn. A man with a bag on his back sets off on a journey and has adventures along the way, often with creatures like Apollyon from the other world. What's the big deal? Not only is the story quite ordinary, but it is also incomplete. It starts off promisingly enough, but then stops abruptly halfway through just at the point where the protagonist reaches the next world and the story promises to get really interesting. As chapter 9 discusses, the early West African novelists Amos Tutuola and D. O. Fagunwa, who embed elements of Bunyan in their novels, could in effect be read as attempting to complete the story and reinsert it in a matrix of traveling to the next world and then coming back again.

In such situations, translated texts disappear via generic erosion or evaporation. A related process of disintegration is what one might call textual "randomization." As we have seen, the text was broadcast in bits and pieces via different media—postcards, wallcharts, magic lantern slides, sermons, or choir services. This mode of dissemination put into circulation atomized bits of the text that could be reconfigured in different ways. The postcard version of the story (figure 7), which comprised two packs of six cards, for example, allowed one to shuffle the plot units as one saw fit. This rearrangement of the plot in turn accords closely with how story episodes behave in certain oral narrative traditions. Here stories are open-ended and there is little sense of climactic closure, so that plot episodes have no strictly preordained sequence. The way in which episodes are knitted together depends much on the moment of performance and the performer's assessment of the interests and composition of the audience.[37] Within such a system, any randomized episodes deriving from *The Pilgrim's Progress* could become narrative fodder absorbed into a new generic field. This tendency for the story to be "digested" is further aided by the folkloric elements of the story. These include folktale motifs and plot outlines, dramatic dialogue, two characters to a scene, proverbs, riddles, formulaic phrasings, and onomastic strategies. These features are present in African literary traditions into which particles of the story could be elided. In these circumstances, texts disintegrate, not through political resistance or rejection but rather under systems unaware of, or indifferent to, their supposedly "correct" and "original" meaning.

In these ways, *The Pilgrim's Progress*, despite being so energetically propagated, in some instances, became "extinct." The text had indeed reached the limits of its circulation. Yet, what did the limits of its circulation mean for Bunyan's text back in England? And might we use the templates of translation and transnational circulation to revise the existing historiographies of Bunyan?

Rethinking Bunyan Historiography

One important objective of this book is to reformulate the divided terrain of Bunyan scholarship, currently split between a Bunyan "at home" and another, largely disavowed Bunyan "abroad." One way to reconfigure the field, as many others have done, is to refuse the division of "home" and "abroad," "metropolis" and "periphery." Instead, as Gyan Prakash suggests, we need a realignment that releases "histories and knowledges from their disciplining as area studies; as imperial and overseas histories . . . that seals metropolitan structures from the contagion of the record of their own formation elsewhere."[38]

The first move in such a realignment is to recognize Nonconformity, the heartland in which Bunyan was nurtured, as a transnational movement. Much existing Bunyan historiography has, of course, examined the role that Nonconformity played in Bunyan's rising national fortunes.[39] As Nonconformity became more respectable and powerful—so these studies suggest—*The Pilgrim's Progress*, as one of its most prized cultural possessions, appreciated commensurately. This work has, however, overlooked the international dimensions of evangelical Nonconformity. More recently there have been a number of attempts, most eminently in the work of Susan Thorne, to reconsider Nonconformity as a transnational phenomenon.[40] She demonstrates how Nonconformists, faced with social disabilities at home, harnessed the glamour of foreign missions as a means of raising their national profile and their political fortunes. Bunyan can usefully be inserted into this scenario. His dissemination via the Protestant mission movement presented an opportunity for Nonconformists to advertise to a "home" audience Bunyan's "universal" appeal to millions of readers throughout the world. In so doing, Nonconformists could display the virtues of their cultural preferences and "add value" to their cause. Bunyan could also strengthen support for foreign missions by providing a much-needed point of identification for "home" audiences, often unfamiliar with the obscure location of foreign missions. One vehicle for achieving this objective was through the circulation and display of translated texts. These, as we have seen, could be exhibited both to publicize mission work and to give substance to the conviction that everyone in the mission domain read the "same" texts and believed the "same" ideas. By consciously invoking the outer limits of Bunyan's circulation, Nonconformists were able to constitute an evangelical Protestant public sphere that took this text as one of its major reference points.

However, with vertiginous de-Christianization, particularly after the First World War, evangelicalism lost ground as a public intellectual force. One institution that came to occupy the space it vacated was the emerging discipline of English literature, which sought to constitute the field of literature as a way to confer racial and cultural distinctiveness on Britons "at home" and in the empire. The idea of Bunyan as a writer who appealed to converts across lines of race was initially attractive and could bestow value on him as a writer who demonstrated the universal appeal of Englishness. However, as more aggressive racist ideas took hold, Bunyan came to be "tainted" by his association with those on the imaginative peripheries of empire. Particularly for those wishing to see Bunyan (and English literature more generally) as a marker of racial distinctiveness, such ambiguity presented an uneasy problem. One response from within the literary field to this "problem" was to vigorously foreground Bunyan's white Englishness while shifting the definition of his universality from a concrete to an abstract realm. Instead of universality meaning the literal circulation of Bunyan's texts to numerous far-flung societies, it came to denote a concern with an abstract "human nature." Such arguments could salvage the value-conferring properties of universality while disconnecting Bunyan from his potentially "contaminating" association with colonized people. In this way, Bunyan could be reclaimed as white and English, while *The Pilgrim's Progress* could become a book of England.

What in effect is expunged in this process of canonization is the knowledge of *The Pilgrim's Progress* as a translated and transcontinental text. This global existence of the book must be retrospectively erased in order for it to emerge as monolingual and national. This retrospective view also creates the impression that Bunyan is first a national writer who is then broadcast to the world to become international. The story told here reverses this order. In brief, it argues that evangelicalism made Bunyan international, while English literature made him national. He is hence a transnational writer who was belatedly made national. The story of Bunyan's influence has been narrated back to front. Closer attention to questions of translation and circulation will help us put matters in the right order.

Given the imperatives set out above, this book, unsurprisingly, is broad in its scope. In terms of Africa, it takes in much of the sub-Saharan area of the continent. Its major focus is on southern and Central Africa, the zones of most intense Bunyan distribution. With regard to the first, southern Africa was the earliest and most intensively missionized area in Africa and it produced twenty-three translations of Bunyan in all. In a situation where British missionaries worked under British colonial rule (which was true for much of the subcontinent), the text became pervasive and far-reaching. Although the colonial state itself seldom took direct responsibility for African education—a task left to missions—its broad educational policies, which favored the promotion of British culture, often gave the text a helping hand. Somewhat counterintuitively, Central Africa, under French and Belgian rule, likewise produced twenty-three translations. These arose firstly from the presence of the BMS, which made the Congo River its primary mission field. Bunyan was strongly scripted into Baptist traditions. He was at times claimed as a founding father of the denomination and his theology had also played a key role in the Baptist evangelical revival, a major motor for the Baptist mission movement itself.[41] In all, the BMS was to produce nine translations, the highest tally for any mission society on the continent. A second group of ardent Bunyan fans in Central Africa were the fiercely evangelical faith missions, nondenominational organizations that had often broken from the bigger denominational societies whom they saw as over-bureaucratized and complacent. These groups swarmed into Central Africa, in their terms the most "untouched" part of the continent. Wherever they went they translated *The Pilgrim's Progress*, a book that exemplified their "theology" in forms accessible not only to their converts but to themselves (who generally had little, if any, serious theological training) and their supporters back home who likewise lived by a narrative and biblicist theology. Within the enclaves established by both the BMS and faith missions, the text had a powerful and deep influence. Beyond these small pools, however, the text had a feeble impact. British and other missions, notably Swedish and North American, separated by language, nationality, and denomination from the Catholic French and Belgian colonial authorities, had little influence on educational policy. As such, *The Pilgrim's Progress*, while influential in limited pockets, never gained the wide purchase of a text disseminated via a school system, as it often was under British rule.

The study also "visits," if more briefly, East and West Africa with twelve (thirteen if one includes Madagascar, the large Indian Ocean island off the continent's East coast) and twenty-one translations respectively. The East African translations, while few in number, were far-reaching in their influence. As with southern Africa, where settler-dominated states, like Kenya, made their influence felt on mission schools, the text was propagated by public institutions including the quasi-governmental East African Literature Bureau. In the West African case, the book was disseminated in mission schools, then subsequently in colonial and post-independent, state-run educational institutions. Government-funded literature bureaus also played a role in spreading the text. The ways in which the text was woven into the intellectual histories of these regions is explored through an examination of two early Nigerian novelists (Fagunwa and Tutuola) and the Kenyan, Ngũgĩ wa Thiong'o.

For readers interested in the nitty-gritty of where, when, and by whom the text was spread, I attach two appendices. The first lists all known African translations of The Pilgrim's Progress by language, present-day nation(s) where the language is spoken, place of publication, publisher, mission society, and translator (where this is known: mission societies, as we have seen, favored anonymous translation-by-committee and so individual names did not always appear). The second discusses the social profile of Bunyan translators.

The details of exactly where, when, and by whom mission translations of The Pilgrim's Progress were done are difficult to document with any exactitude. The book was produced in different places, and such transnational texts do not leave neat records in any one place, making it difficult to establish a comprehensive picture. Mainstream Bunyan scholarship has, moreover, never shown an interest in this area so little attention has been devoted to it. Available figures do indicate that overall there have been about two hundred translations of The Pilgrim's Progress (about twenty of these into European languages).[42] The geographical distribution of these figures accords with the spread of the Protestant mission endeavor.[43] Their most successful field was non-Islamic Africa, where Protestants made considerable headway, unimpeded by transethnic forms of organized religion and, particularly in southern and East Africa, assisted by colonial conquest. These inroads are apparent in the eighty translations that finally emerged from the continent. The next highest translation tally is in South Asia, where some twenty-four translations were done. This number is bigger than one might expect for a region where Protestantism made only a limited impact on Hinduism and Islam. Yet, as the most favored site of the British Empire, India held prestige in mission eyes and considerable resources were invested into work in this region, accounting in turn for the relatively high number of translations. Like India, China (five translations), Southeast Asia (nine), and the Middle East (eight) were dominated by transpolity religions that largely kept Protestantism at bay. Oceania (another area of considerable Protestant advance) produced eleven translations, while in North America, where Christianity made little headway amongst indigenous societies, there were three translations—into "Cree," "Dakota," and "Eskimo."

The key import of the first appendix is the extent to which it reflects the diversity of Bunyan translators, most notably by nationality, but also by race, class, and gender (a discussion of this point is included in the second appendix). With regard to nationality, mission societies came not only from Britain but from eight countries in all: the United States, Britain, Switzerland, France, Germany, Finland, Sweden, and South Africa. As the personnel of these missions was at times drawn from beyond the boundaries of the country in which the society was based, the nationalities of translators were more diverse than this list reflects. Joseph Jackson Fuller (figure 4), for example, who worked with the BMS, came from Jamaica. Other translators, while not themselves missionaries, included Charles Chinula in Nyasaland (currently Malawi in south Central Africa), who did the Tumbuka translation, and Moses Mubitana, who undertook the Ila translation in Northern Rhodesia (today Zambia in south Central Africa) on a LMS station.[44] Perhaps the most influential translation of all (in the southern African language Xhosa) was by the African Scottish-trained Presbyterian missionary, Tiyo Soga.

This diversity of translators reminds us again of the complexities involved in understanding the "textual zones" that inform any Bunyan translation. Clearly, this is not simply a story of the circuits between Britain and Africa but rather a story of the continent in, and as part of, the Protestant Atlantic. In this study, I have consequently attempted to highlight the complexities of movement within this zone. Inevitably, the focus has been mainly anglophone, partly because British mission societies did dominate the field of Bunyan translation, completing thirty-nine of the sixty-one translations to which we can attach specific missions.[45] Of the remaining tally, the U.S. mission societies produced seven, European Protestants thirteen, and South African mission organizations two. The book does touch briefly on mission translations emerging from

Figure 4. Joseph Jackson Fuller. Source: BMS Archives. Reproduced with the permission of the BMS.

other nationalities, such as the Sotho version sponsored by the Paris Evangelical Mission Society (PEMS). The Bunyan traditions emerging from northern European Protestant countries—where the book traveled from Holland (where it was translated in 1681) to Germany (translated in 1703 from the Dutch) to Sweden (translated in 1727 from the German)—are not broached here.[46] Neither are the U.S. mission-sponsored translations. Their inclusion would obviously have added to the book and would have underlined further the intricacies involved in any Bunyan translation. I hope that this book may encourage others to follow up these routes.

With regard to the timing of translations, establishing precise information is not always possible. However, from the available dates, one can divide translation activity into three clear "stages." The first involves a small but steady increase of nineteenth-century translations, which total seventeen in all. The second period runs from the 1900s to the 1940s, during which the bulk of translations (forty-seven) was done. The final stage, the 1950s and 1960s, witnesses a decline in translations (sixteen) as the continent moved toward independence. In their broad outline, these figures conform to the trajectory of Protestant missions in Africa. While the nineteenth century, in financial terms, was the heyday of mission activity, personnel numbers were restricted and the amount of translation work that could be done was limited. This profile changed markedly in the interwar years. Mission personnel increased and there were consequently more "hands" available to do translations.[47] During this time, overall funding did, however, decline. Yet, as regards mission translation and educational work, new sources of subsidy became available. These included government grants for mission-sponsored education in colonial territories[48] and the growth of several organizations promoting "Christian Literature," which made earmarked funding available for precisely such projects as translations of *The Pilgrim's Progress*.[49] The growth of a school market also pushed up the number of translations (particularly in the 1950s and 1960s when several editions by multinational publishers appeared). In the wake of the Second World War, many missions started turning themselves into local churches, a movement that gained considerable momentum as the continent moved to independence.[50] The number of translations consequently dropped off, although one or two evangelically inspired translations continued to appear after independence, while in many parts of the continent, the story itself remained in print and, by some accounts, migrated into other formats, such as video and photocomic.[51]

One question many readers will ask is how one researches a book involving eighty different translations (of which I have a reading knowledge of only Sotho and Afrikaans). In order to take account of this linguistic limitation, I have attempted to be as empirically exhaustive as possible and have been guided by a method of keeping one's eye on the book as a material object. I have consequently attempted to locate as many of the physical books as possible. In England, the Bunyan Meeting House Museum, the Bedford Bunyan Collection, the British Library, and the SOAS library all hold copies of translated editions. In South Africa, I located further copies in Johannesburg, Pretoria, Durban, and Cape Town. These books can teach one a surprising amount. In some cases, editions have short English forewords; in other cases, I have had forewords translated. The physical book also reveals whether the text has been abridged, what illustrations were used, and in some instances, the name of the translator. This information was supplemented with detailed research in mission archives in South Africa, England, and Scotland. Careful trawling through these sources revealed a considerable amount about the translated Bunyan texts. There were reports on how translations were done and how the book appeared—often, for example, it was first serialized before appearing as a whole volume. There was also information on how, where, and why the book was used. By drawing together this data, one can gain a fairly detailed sense of how the book was translated, circulated, and interpreted in various contexts. With regard to African uses and interpretations of the text, I have relied primarily on a wide selection of discourses by Africans, whether these be novels, sermons, tracts, letters, hymns, or diaries, mostly in English, in some cases in Sotho, in one case translated from Yoruba, and in another from Kikuyu. A careful consideration of these writings, placed in a broader context of African intellectual and religious traditions, has revealed how Bunyan was read and interpreted.

The book itself has three sections. The first section—Bunyan in the Protestant Atlantic—seeks to sketch the nature of the evangelical mission imperial domain, as it was in this zone that Bunyan translations were shaped. This section unfolds in four chapters. Chapter 1 establishes some broad characteristics of this mission imperial world. This task is accomplished by focusing on one particular mission circuit, namely the links between a Baptist congregation in Camden Road, London, and one mission station, San Salvador, situated in the heart of the Kongo Kingdom in what is now northern Angola (situated slightly below the equator on the continent's Atlantic seaboard). In examining this interaction, I focus on how Camden Roaders constructed a vision of the "Congo" and how these images were in part shaped by the social, intellectual, and cultural structures of the Kongo Kingdom that the Baptists encountered. Chapter 2 examines how Bunyan enters this field and in turn is "beamed" back for use in mission publicity. In telling this story, I first examine how *The Pilgrim's Progress* was deeply woven into Nonconformist life and how these missionaries attempted to reconstitute the text wherever they went. The chapter narrates how Nonconformists back in Britain were quick to pick up Bunyan's successes and publicize these to a home audience. The chapter also explores the convergence of textual practice that arose between evangelical views of *The Pilgrim's Progress* and those of African converts, both of whom saw the text as a quasi-magical charm or object capable of precipitating extraordinary transformations in its users and readers. For both mission and convert, the text became a type of "fetish," whose correct use could compel events in this world and the next. Chapter 3 moves on to consider how missionaries translated the text. In doing so, I understand translation not as a bounded event but as a process that unfolds across time and space. Once seen in this way, we can better understand how various interests in the mission domain—be they mission, convert, or home committee—help to determine the final shape and form of the translation. We examine two case studies: one to probe translation across time, the second across space. The first case study looks at the Kele translation in the Upper Congo. This translation stretched across several decades, and its final form was that of a series of highly abridged episodes. By considering the "biography" of the translation, the case study demonstrates how mission and convert interests registered themselves in the shape that the text ultimately took. The second case study looks at a Cameroonian translation undertaken by the Jamaican missionary, Joseph Jackson Fuller. In considering this story, we trace the various versions of the story that Fuller inherited from three sources—the black Baptist tradition (which had traveled from the American South to Jamaica), the British Baptists, and slave Christianities. We also consider how Fuller used these knowledges of the story in his precarious tightrope existence as a black missionary in a white-dominated world. Chapter 4 extends this analysis of Bunyan in the mission imperial domain by comparing and contrasting different interpretive strategies used by various readers. Seen from afar, the reading strategies of Protestants, whether in Africa or Europe, were similar and involved a didactic application of the text, often to one's own circumstances. However, through looking in detail at the interpretive methods used by Protestants, we trace the "African" contribution to this reading technique. This "African" method drew on the quasi-allegorical methods inherent in riddle and "folktale" and adapted these for reading Bunyan.

The Pilgrim's Progress traveled into the mission domain in complex and varied ways and established itself as a discursive arena or public sphere in which different audiences and readers could participate. The second section—Bunyan, the Public Sphere, and Africa—examines how African intellectuals and audiences entered their claims in this domain.

The first chapter in this section focuses on the African mission elite and how they re-allegorized Bunyan as a way of addressing their particular political concerns. The chapter is arranged around a case study of the African mission elite in the Eastern Cape in present-day South Africa and one of their prestigious institutions, Lovedale Mission Institution, a Scottish-run outfit saturated with Bunyan. We examine both the kinds of reading strategies that pupils brought with them to the school and the ways in which Bunyan was taught. The chapter then proceeds to examine in detail how *The Pilgrim's Progress* was deployed in the public pronouncements of the elite. In chapter 6 we turn to discuss more popular appropriations of the text and analyze how aspects of the story were taken up and changed by African Christians operating in a para-literate environment where documents were both a source of religious authority and a form of colonial control. Put another way, documents were both "passports to heaven" and "passes." *The Pilgrim's Progress* offers a very similar vision. The hero Christian carries various documents during the course of the story. One of these is his "pass," namely a permissory document that he, as a masterless man, has to carry. It is also a sign of his election and hence his "passport to heaven." When Christian and his companion, Hopeful, arrive at the gates of heaven, they are required to hand in these documents. Popular African Christian interpretations of the text often lighted on this set of scenes, which migrated into other forms like dreams, conversion narratives, and popular poetry.

In chapters 7 and 8 we examine how aspects of *The Pilgrim's Progress* were used as forums where issues could be discussed and debated in the mission imperial domain. Chapter 7 looks at the character Great-heart, the chivalric knight who accompanies Christiana and her party to heaven in the second part of the book. We analyze how this single, celibate figure became a site in which debates about gender relations in the mission domain could be discussed and experimented with. The vehicle for this analysis is two novels—one, an early nineteenth-century bestseller by Ethel M. Dell called *Greatheart* and the second, a Sotho novel by Thomas Mofolo called *Moeti oa Bochabela* (*The Traveller to the East*, 1906).

Chapter 8 turns to the illustrations of *The Pilgrim's Progress*, which, as with most European versions, became a standard feature of nearly all African editions. We focus mainly on twentieth-century editions, which generally adopted Africanized illustrations. We examine two sets of pictures: the first a sequence of line drawings, the second a "gallery" of photographic illustrations for the Kongo edition produced at San

Salvador, the BMS station in northern Angola. We examine how these pictures are enabled by the audiences they address and on whose generic competencies they draw. We also examine the use of mission photography and how it, along with the political interests of leading Africans at San Salvador, produced a form unthinkable in Europe, namely photographic illustrations for a fictional text. Chapter 9 turns to analyze how various African novelists have engaged with these Africanized traditions of reading Bunyan as well as with each other's uses of the text.

The final section—Post-Bunyan—takes the story back to Britain. In chapter 10 we examine the story of how Bunyan became English. We trace how he was taken up by the emerging discipline of English literature and how this grouping sidelined older evangelical and international views of Bunyan, which had initially "added value" to Bunyan by portraying him as universal. In the longer run, however, these views threatened to "contaminate" him by over-associating him with colonized societies. The project of the emerging discipline of English literature was to establish a racialized view of literature that could confer cultural distinctiveness on Britons. Bunyan, sprawled across the globe, did not fit into this framework, and so had to be "reeled" back in order to construct him as white and English.

The conclusion asks what would happen if we lift the "tollgate" separating a "national" and an "international" Bunyan and traces the implications of this move both for postcolonial studies and mainstream Bunyan scholarship.

Bunyan in the Protestant Atlantic

I

The Congo on Camden Road

Just as many other churches of the mid-nineteenth century, the Camden Road Baptist Chapel is dressed with Kentish ragstone. Quarried in southern England, this soft stone had long been used in church building, particularly in medieval times. With the nineteenth-century Gothic revival, ragstone was rediscovered and became a favored vernacular retro-idiom. New urban churches, like the one on Camden Road, mimicked their ancient prototypes, basking in the reflected glory of these medieval structures. That the London atmosphere ate into the soft stone did little to damage its popularity.[1]

Within its immediate neighborhood, Camden Road was the only Nonconformist church. Yet, in style, it closely resembled the two Established churches nearby. This Nonconformist embrace of Anglican architecture was not unusual. As Nonconformists became richer, and as they forgot the forms of civil disability suffered by their parents, they sought to transform the austerity of their inheritance and the barnlike meeting houses of their past.[2]

The Camden Road Chapel was built in 1854 and—after a gallery was added five years later—could seat more than a thousand people. On any day of the week, the church or its adjoining hall and classrooms hummed with congregants, Sunday school children, women's auxiliary workers, deacons in meetings, and the like. In these gatherings, there was a good chance of hearing discussion on a topic that was to become as English as ragstone, namely Baptist mission work on the Congo.[3]

This mission tradition had been propagated by the first pastor of the Chapel, Francis Tucker, who had himself worked in Calcutta with the BMS. Another twenty-two foreign mission workers were to emanate from

Camden Road, twelve of them destined for the Congo.[4] As the church fathers liked to claim with some pride, the sons and daughters of Camden Road stood in the "front rank of Christ's army."[5]

Today, the Camden Road Chapel is much curtailed. The ragstone building has been leased to an organization for the homeless and the congregation now meets in the hall behind the church. But, despite these changes, the mission past is still a theme in the life of the congregation. Once a year, pictures of the missionaries come out for an annual mission fête, which first began in 1878 as the Camden Road Congo Sale.[6] In the hall, a roll of honor records the "fragrant"[7] names of church members who peopled the Baptist missions in Congo, China, and India.

Two important names on this board—Thomas Lewis and Gwen Lewis (figures 5 and 6)—were associated with Camden Road, where they were married. Both went to the Congo region as missionaries and both were to translate parts of *The Pilgrim's Progress* into Kongo. In seeking to understand the broader field of African translations of Bunyan, the evangelical world of Thomas and Gwen Lewis becomes emblematic. Their lives shuttled between the Congo and Camden Road (as well as many other points), and provided an example, in miniature, of the complex transnational space in which mission cultural practices were wrought. One such practice was translation and, like all mission work, it unfolded in and across this global arena of mission imperialism. As a process stretched across time and space, translated texts are less bounded "events" restricted to one locale than webs stretched across this mission domain, synaptic networks along which currents of understanding travel back and forth. If we wish to analyze Bunyan in the nineteenth century, we need to situate him in this broader interactional field. This chapter begins this task by describing the nature of the international evangelical space into which his famous text flowed. By examining the Congo on Camden Road, we probe the imaginative filaments of this mission imperial world and ask how its infrastructures of the imagination were built and sustained. How did the congregants of Camden Road come to construct and internalize a picture of the Congo, especially one in which Bunyan could be accommodated? Our story proceeds in two parts—in this chapter, we examine how the Congo was constructed on Camden Road, and in the next, we examine how Bunyan was accommodated in this landscape.

Rev. Francis Tucker (B.A.), the first pastor of Camden Road, was an accomplished and popular preacher. His sermons, "finished in style, evangelical in tone,"[8] spoke to his modestly meaned but aspirant congregation. Like many of the Nonconformist would-be elite, the Camden Road congregants had moved to the rural edges of London. As Tucker reminded them, much had been given to them and much was expected in return.[9]

One way to settle such evangelical debt was to carry God's word into what Tucker termed the "dark places." As an area given over to cattle raising and slaughtering, Camden contained such "dark" pockets—of abattoir workers, dairymaids, haymaking hands, and their broods of ragged children. Dickens had grown up in the vicinity and recorded it in *Dombey and Son*: "frowzy fields, and cow-houses, and dung-hills, and dust-heaps, and ditches . . . broken crockery and faded cabbage leaves."[10]

Farther south lay the dark continent of the East End. This tract of heathendom offered up objects of charity such as George Henry Bertie, an eight-year old from Spitalfields, "redeemed" as a protégé of Camden Road Sunday school.[11] The East End also offered a boundary of self-definition. Against the mudlarks and costermongers, against the Russians, Poles, Jews, and Chinese, against the desperate and the destitute, Camden Road congregants could think of themselves as respectable, English, and Christian.[12]

In this thinking, they were aided by Tucker's sermons, which dwelt on the textures of heathenism, near and far. The figure of "the Greek," "the Jew," and "the Hindoo" were conjured up in the chapel along with their "degeneracy," "profligacy," and "vice." Even to those who were not "twicers" and "thricers" (those who attended two or three sermons a week),[13] the message was urgently clear. "Open their eyes and turn them from darkness to light and from the power of Satan to the power of God."[14]

Driven by Tucker's evangelical ardor, Camden Road became an active mission center whose arms reached both into the immediate surrounds of the church and much further afield into Africa, Jamaica, and India. Locally, the chapel underwrote two missions—one on Brewery Road, Belle Isle, just south of the Cattle Market, and a second not far off in Goodinge Road.[15] With regard to foreign missions, Camden Road focused heavily on Africa and the chapel was to support a number of stations in Cameroon and the Congo. For those involved, the local mission outreaches and the African stations formed part of one continuous evangelical field. As Gwen Lewis wrote from the Congo, "People in England seem to forget sometimes that I am as much interested in their work as they are in mine. It is the same work, only we are on distant service."[16] Like Gwen, Thomas Comber (another Camden Roader) did his apprenticeship in the local mission outreaches and then in 1875 departed for the

Figure 5. Thomas Lewis. Source: BMS Archives. Reproduced with the permission of the BMS.

Figure 6. Gwen Lewis. Source: BMS Archives. Reproduced with the permission of the BMS.

Cameroon and, subsequently, the Congo. From his new home, Comber, a charismatic figure ("his belt . . . buckled by the fingers of Almighty God")[17] wrote to a Camden parishioner: "Hand in hand we [work] for the dear children at Camden . . . hand in hand we [work] for the dear children of the Dark Continent."[18]

There was one garment of which Alice Hartland was particularly proud. It was a black and red striped Chesterfield dressing gown that she and her Camden Road sewing class had stitched for the King of the Kongo.[19] The King, Dom Pedro V, was known to English Baptists through their mission magazine. He had granted land to the first Baptist missionaries who arrived at his capital San Salvador/Mbanza Kongo in 1878 and hence featured in frequent articles.[20] For one shilling, readers could order his *carte de visite* from Messrs Debenham and Gould in Bournemouth.[21] Having read much about the King and his capital, Alice Hartland felt she knew both well. San Salvador "seemed quite a familiar place," and the King "a good natured old fellow."[22]

Whether the King ever received the dressing gown or what he thought of it, we do not know. As someone descended from one of the best-dressed dynasties, the homemade gown from Camden probably held little allure. Since the sixteenth century, the Kingdom had been one of the prominent slaving empires of the Renaissance Atlantic world, a monarchy of middlemen feeding the Portuguese slave trade. The Kingdom, which had quickly adopted Catholicism as a royal cult, supported ambassadors in Portugal, Spain, the Low Countries, Rome, and Brazil and was itself the seat of an episcopal see.[23]

Like all feudal states, the Kongo Kingdom excelled at sartorial spectacle and panoplied performance fed by a global wardrobe of fabrics and styles.[24] Locally, the area specialized in fine raffia cloth likened to damask, velvet, and taffeta by Portuguese visitors.[25] Such fabric could be enhanced with finely brayed civet skins, zebra tails, plumes, and feathers. Male courtiers could add European capes, tabards, buskins, and rapiers, while royal women adopted black velvet caps ornamented with jewels and gold chain necklaces.[26]

When the Baptists arrived in 1878, the Kingdom was much reduced from the height of its seventeenth-century powers, when it had been able to exploit its position as middlemen between kingdoms further inland and Portuguese slavers. The Kingdom, however, was unable to control the proliferating points of the trade and the pretensions of provincial chieftains. By the eighteenth century, it had splintered into a welter of warring fiefdoms, and industrial production in Europe deepened this fragmentation. As European factories churned out soap, piano keys, and billiard balls, markets for rubber, ivory, and gum proliferated in the Kongo region. The trade routes for these goods were quickly monopolized by the parvenu warlords who gnawed at the boundaries of the Kingdom driving it back into its original heartland in present-day northern Angola.[27]

As Britain and Portugal began to vie for control of the Congo River mouth, the King's authority rallied briefly as both powers recognized him.[28] When Thomas Lewis met him in 1878, the King was wearing a Portuguese military uniform, a feathered cocked hat, and the red, ermine-trimmed mayoral robes of Bristol, which had been given to him as a gift.[29]

The contrast between Alice's austere dressing gown and the King's lavish wardrobe captures something of the Baptist enterprise in northern Angola. Rather like the dressing gown, the Baptists were to be swallowed up into a larger political world of feudal intricacy and intrigue. The major players were initially the Portuguese and the Kongo court, and it was into this byzantine world that the Baptists entered in the 1870s. Their objective was to make inroads into the Kongo Kingdom, but, like most Protestants, they made little imprint on the upper reaches of African society and instead recruited slaves, orphans, and runaways. These converts were outsiders both to the Kingdom and, subsequently, to the encroaching Portuguese colonial state that demanded that they assimilate and speak Portuguese. The Baptists, by contrast, evangelized in African languages. Protestant missions consequently became strongly associated with "African tradition" as opposed to the assimilationist policies of the Catholic Portuguese. Because of these linguistic politics, the Baptists built up a substantial Kongo-speaking following and, over time, the BMS became a "tribal church" in which denomination and ethnicity overlapped to a considerable extent.[30]

Like all other mission organizations, the BMS aggressively publicized their foreign mission endeavors. With its two freighted syllables, the word Congo—associated with Stanley's explorations and Livingstone's travels—evoked immediate and intense public interest. The presence of Islam in the east and Catholicism in the west simply added a touch of piquancy for Protestants, many of whom believed that they could personally hasten the advent of the Lord by ensuring that the gospel was taught to all nations.[31] Staggering death rates for fever-prone visitors encouraged, rather than dampened, these millennial expectations.

Small wonder that the Congo became known as "the short-cut to heaven."[32] As the Baptists, aided by Leopold's annexation of the Congo Basin, made a push upriver from their base at San Salvador, they could exploit the ballyhoo around these spectacular events to promote their mission cause.

At some levels, it may appear that these accounts that exploited the "glamor" of the Congo had little to do with the actual societies and people being depicted. However, if one examines the narrative strategies that Baptist publicity adopted, the shaping imprint of the region being depicted becomes apparent. Most obvious is the geography of the Congo River itself, which determined a central BMS genre, namely that of traveling upriver by boat. Initially, these journeys were pursued in local canoes, but in 1884 the society acquired the steamer *Peace*, which plied the navigable portions of the river and formed part of its bustling traffic (which Joseph Conrad incidentally was to erase in order to depict the river as eerily deserted).[33]

In elaborating stories and publicity around the ship, the BMS did not have to look far for examples on which to draw. Most large mission societies—whose personnel spent long periods at sea—owned at least one sea-going vessel, like the *John Williams* with which we began this book. Such ships provided endless publicity opportunities in terms of funding drives, stories, pictures, hymns, poems, and spectacle.[34] Viewing the mission ship in dock prior to its departure, for example, was a popular pastime. Here spectators could observe the heart-wrenching parting of missionary and child on deck and linger to hear the very last refrains of hymns echoing over the water as the ship left harbor ("Bear me on, thou restless ocean! / Let the winds my canvas swell / Heaves my heart with warm emotion / While I go far hence to dwell").[35]

A second feature of Kongo life to imprint itself on BMS publicity was the group among which the Baptists found their first wave of converts, namely young boys who were often slaves and runaways. Letters and articles from missionaries personalized these converts for a home audience. The *Missionary Herald* ran frequent biographies and photographs of young male converts.[36] Their pictures were posted in the church and on mission collection boxes.[37] One of Comber's converts was christened "Camden Road" after the church.[38] From time to time, these converts would be brought back to London where they would be turned into spectacles and mobbed by over-enthusiastic congregants.[39]

This combination of the young male converts along with the Congo River provided a framework for much BMS promotion. The publicity around boats, for example, was aimed at young Baptist boys, and for them it became a major way of building up and occupying a concept of the "Congo."[40] These boys were also encouraged to identify with "Congo boys," whom they "mimicked" in a variety of ways. In 1910, for example, in a Baptist Sunday school in Bath, one could have seen groups of young boys standing on a large floor map of the Congo making rowing motions with canoe paddles.[41] At the same time, they would have been singing another homegrown Baptist genre, the "Congo boat song."[42] These boat songs were generally the first African forms that missionaries learned. They were originally in Lingala, a trade creole of the river that Baptist missionaries were subsequently to promote into a language.[43] Phonetic renditions of these songs in "Congo Language" were produced with music in mission publications for use by churches.[44] Elsewhere, English adaptations of the "Congo boat song" were made available. One version called "The Hymn of the Congo Convert" was sung to the tune of "Swanee River":

> Far off the Lualuba sings it
> Christ died for sin
> To us the tide of Congo brings it
> Jesus is sure to win.[45]

This "Congo mimicry" was common. Sunday school pupils, for example, were coaxed to internalize the mission geography of the Congo. In one lesson, the teacher traced out the course of the Congo River, focusing (like so many subsequent writers, including Conrad and Naipaul) on its prominent bend. "I want you to follow my finger as it follows the river straight into the heart of the continent. Here it goes in the shape of a rough arch. Now watch while I do it again—for I want you to remember it."[46] In another lesson, students had to memorize the mission stations along the river.[47] In London in 1916, Baptist Sunday school pupils pretended to visit or, at times, to be Congo villagers. ("Today we will visit a Congo village. Here we go along this narrow path in proper Indian file, up this steep hill and down the other side.")[48] One could sing "Congo" boat songs, inhabit "Congo" villages, and even memorize "Congo" idioms or "Congoisms" (like "he has a body," meaning he feels sick).[49]

While young boys created their own "Congos" in the Sunday school room, women stitched their versions of that far-away mission field. They made clothes for converts,[50] and they sewed for fêtes and for the famed Congo Sale, a three-day event at Camden Road that generated about £200 per year. They stitched hundreds of red and white squares for a huge Congo quilt measuring 11 by 12 feet. Each square was embroidered with the initials of its maker as well as with phrases like "Greet the brethren."[51]

The boat songs, the red and white squares, and the scrapbooks were all ways of inventing a Congo, of living imaginatively somewhere else. Mrs. Hartland, mother of Alice, dressing gown maker for the Kongo King, lived on Falkland Road, a few streets away from the chapel. Her son John joined Thomas Comber as a missionary in the Cameroon and died there after a few months.[52] The Hartland household ran according to a hectic Congo timetable. Alice and her sister Lilley (by their own description, in a state of "missionary excitement") attended at least six to seven mission engagements a week.[53] Her mother, with limited mobility, stayed at home and beamed spiritual energy toward the Congo mission field. Alice was devoted to the memory of her brother in life and death. She "curated" his objects that remained behind—a picture of him, his harmonium, the curios he sent back ("your room looks quite African now," she wrote). She acquired a parrot and trained it to say his name.[54] She kept up her Sunday school and home mission work among the children of the cattle market workers. She sewed frantically for various causes and produced untold numbers of antimacassars and white rosettes for the Congo Sale.[55] When her mother died, it was said that she lived more on the Congo than in Camden.[56] Much the same could be said of Alice.

While Alice Hartland pictured the Congo with ease, there were many others, hundreds of boat songs notwithstanding, who could not do so. Sunday school teachers complained that it was "difficult to keep the interest alive in Foreign Missions as our children cannot see who they are working for."[57] What made more sense to them were the plights of the children of the local cattle market missions and other underprivileged "waifs and strays"—people one could see and touch. One project that the mission society of Camden Road took on was to periodically entertain "cripples" from a nearby home. Young members in the mission society could then sit and "mother their little crippled visitors, trying to make them forget for a time their suffering." On another occasion, a group of blind children demonstrated their occupation of making cane chairs and baskets.[58] This climate of caring for the weak and dependent was extended to work undertaken for the Congo. After patting the "cripples," children prepared bandages, sheets, and pasted Kongo greetings into old Christmas cards for the Congo missions.[59]

In order to keep alive a picture of a mission far away, the Camden Road missionary initiative had to invent its own local "natives" upon whom the Sunday school children could practice their paternalism. In patting the "cripples," the children performed yet another miniature enactment of the Congo on Camden Road, but one in which they were the benefactors and those in the Congo the recipients of their charity. The appeal of this philanthropic pageant lay in its simultaneous local and global dimensions—an act of mission charity toward the neighborhood poor resonated with a distant and romantic mission field. In undertaking this linked activity, one became part of an evangelical drama that played itself out on an international stage. One's actions were situated in this bigger arena and had consequences in far-away places.

The habit of mind inculcated by such performances and practices can be likened to translation. To translate is to stitch together, to ferry between languages and genres. Mission work was exactly this—shuttling through time and space, knotting together different worlds, living imaginatively in many places at once but belonging to none. This uncertainty about "home" was a condition for which many had prepared themselves since childhood. As a child, Gwen Thomas (subsequently Lewis) with whom this chapter opened, used to sit under the dining room table of her Islington home with her brother Herbert reading stories about "Africa." Hidden behind the floor-length tablecloth, Gwen devoured mission biographies and inhabited the far-away places of the "heathen" with more intensity than her quotidian world.[60] In these daily apprenticeships, she was learning to create and inhabit the imaginative space of evangelicalism in which her adult professional life would unfold. Part of that life was to involve a translation of the second part of *The Pilgrim's Progress*, a text whose trajectory into the mission domain was made possible by the daily performances of the type we have examined. By bringing a distant world to their doorstep, Camden Roaders could act out relationships of philanthropic paternalism. In this way, they could imagine a world that was both familiar and structured in paternalism. It was a world into which one could easily envisage one's favorite text traveling and being gratefully received.

2

Making Bunyan Familiar in the Mission Domain

In Baptist terms, the Congo Exhibition in Bristol in 1928 was a great
success. Baptists made up only a small percentage of Protestants in England, yet the attendance figure of six thousand compared well with similar ventures by other mission societies. Part of the exhibition's appeal no
doubt lay in the tried and tested format that the organizers used. This
formula, which had been the hallmark of such events for at least three
decades, involved the visitor experiencing the exhibition as an explorer.
In the Bristol event, this format was given a Baptist spin and viewers
"navigated" the Congo River. The floor plan was horseshoe shaped. On
entering, visitors found themselves on the Lower Congo. They strolled
past "mission stations," "huts," "curios," and "tropical foliage" displayed
on the "banks" of the river. Midway, viewers passed under a rocky arch-
way, marking their movement from the Lower to the Upper Congo. At
the end of their journey, visitors encountered another distinctively Baptist feature, namely a Bunyan landmark in the form of the Interpreter's
House. The area was "gaily decorated" and in it the themes of the exhibition were repeated or, in the parlance of the *Missionary Herald*, "lessons
that should have been learned along the way were emphasized."[1]

    The exhibition, then, drew together two favored Baptist land-
scapes—that of the Congo River and that of Bunyan. The first constituted one of their most publicized mission arenas; the second, that of a
founding father of the denomination. The year 1928 was also auspicious.
It was the fiftieth anniversary of the BMS in the Congo; the tercentenary
of Bunyan's birth, and the 250th anniversary of the publication of *The
Pilgrim's Progress*, part 1. By combining these two settings, the BMS were
playing their two strongest cards.

W. Y. Fullerton, Home Secretary of the BMS from 1912 to 1927, improved the shining hour and produced two books, *The Legacy of Bunyan* and *The Christ of the Congo River*.[2] The first belonged to an army of tercentenary publications and offered a Baptist angle on "the immortal tinker"; the second book commemorated the BMS Congo half-century anniversary. Like the Bristol exhibition, it began by inviting readers onto the Congo River and concluded with Bunyan.

This closing Bunyan episode in Fullerton's book concerns Mpambu, a runaway slave who joins an American Baptist mission station, Lukenge, near the mouth of the river. The young convert soon shows himself to be most reliable and takes charge of a caravan to transport several large bags of salt ("eight day's journey through an unexplored cannibal country"). A day or two into the trip, his porters desert him. Mpambu is left stranded, sitting all alone on the bags of salt, until he is discovered by some villagers. "They were overjoyed: here was not only meat but salt to eat with it, and they made known their intention through unmistakable pantomime." The villagers retire briefly to summon the chief to sanction proceedings. Mpambu pulls out a book and starts reading to wile away the time. The book (need we add) "was a translation by Thomas Lewis of 'The Pilgrim's Progress,' and, interested in the joys and sorrows of the Pilgrim, Mpambu seemed scarcely conscious of his own." When the chief arrives, he is awed by Mpambu's reading and the boy's apparent lack of concern about his impending fate. The nervous chief decides to hold over his decision on the young boy's destiny until the next day. Mpambu, of course, continues to read and the villagers assume that his book has supernatural powers. "No doubt the stranger was acquainted with its power as a Fetish. If so, ought they not to be careful? Who could tell what dread consequences might come from that book?" In light of this concern, the chief releases him, but not before the indefatigable Mpambu compels the villagers to provide him with some carriers. Mpambu finally arrives at his destination, fatigued, but with his salt and his book intact.[3]

Read today, Fullerton's story sounds comically colonial with its cartoon cannibals and gawking chief, hypnotized by the technological objects of the white man. For nineteenth-century Baptist (and most Nonconformist) readers, such motifs had long been naturalized and, within this genre, they would have recognized a mission parable about *The Pilgrim's Progress*. In this genre, Bunyan's book acts as the hero of the story and has miraculous powers of redemption. It wards off evildoers, it intimidates the chief, it saves its owner and assists in removing his burdens, it proves itself the salt of the earth, and it "seasons" Mpambu and lays the ground work for the future conversion/"salting" of the villagers and their chief. We assume, as well, that it has played a role in Mpambu's initial conversion.

For Baptist audiences, encountering Bunyan in the Congo, as they did in the Bristol exhibition or Fullerton's story, was not unusual. Today, of course, such a combination may appear curious. For many, Bunyan will be remembered as an "English" writer, and the Congo as "un-English." The two consequently would seem almost as opposites. Yet, for Baptists like the Camden Roaders, who had "rehearsed" the Congo in such detail, the juxtaposition was easy to accommodate. In this chapter, we will pursue further how this association came to be "naturalized" and > how Bunyan was projected in the mission imperial domain. Our story proceeds in three parts. First, we will begin by outlining the seminal and revered place that Bunyan occupied in an evangelical Nonconformist world. Second, we will examine how and why Nonconformists seized the opportunity to publicize at home Bunyan's "universal" successes abroad. We will then trace the evangelical theory of texts underlying this Nonconformist publicity work and highlight its "magical" dimensions in terms of which texts were believed to be capable of causing dramatic transformations in those who encountered them. Third, we will analyze how these views come to converge with very similar "African" understandings of texts as magical objects or "fetishes" capable of precipitating events in this world and the next.

To nineteenth-century Nonconformists, *The Pilgrim's Progress* was a devotional text of extraordinary importance. Indeed, for many, it stood second only to the Bible. This special status of the text related, on the one hand, to the long presence of the book in Dissent and Nonconformity and, on the other, to the renewed importance that it gained through the Evangelical Revival. Published between 1678 and 1684, *The Pilgrim's Progress* had rapidly become a firm favorite and bestseller amongst lower-class Dissenters and Nonconformists. In E. P. Thompson's words, it was a book that belonged to the heart of "poor man's Dissent" and "humble Nonconformity."[4] The book's social reach was to be considerably extended by the enthusiasms of the Evangelical Revival.[5] Central to this movement was a stress on conversion, ideally an emotional event prefigured by a haunting awareness of sin. Much of Bunyan's work fits well into this schema.[6] His autobiography, *Grace Abounding to the Chief of Sinners* (1666) tells a gripping story of Bunyan's own dramatic conversion. In this story, Bunyan strives to render his internal spiritual torments and his subsequent victory over them. In narrating these "inner psycho-logical terrors," Bunyan relies heavily on personification to make his internal terrors real. In *The Pilgrim's Progress* this conversion process is spatialized and temporalized as a journey in which the protagonist, Christian, makes his way from earth to heaven.[7] The language of the text is strongly interwoven with biblical references, both in its cadence and in the marginalia that certain editions provided.

With its riveting plot, memorable tableaux, and powerful images, the story provided readers with a graphic and easily accessible biblicist theology. It also equipped them with a language to talk about the emotional and personal experience of religion. It was a book of "heart power," "branded in [the] imagination," a text "suited to every season of human life."[8] In short, *The Pilgrim's Progress* was woven into the emotional fabric of evangelical Nonconformity and became a type of shadow Bible, a text that captured the core verities of the Protestant message in memorable and user-friendly form. It was not unusual for Nonconformists to keep a copy of *The Pilgrim's Progress* alongside their bedside Bibles.[9]

As a book of such centrality, it was disseminated and broadcast from numerous sites. The first of these sites was the "mini-church" of the household. Here the book was favored for Sabbath day readings, where its exciting storyline provided some relief from the dour climate of such events.[10] Other styles of reading also prevailed. In addition to silent reading for pleasure, the book could be used as a devotional text with the assistance of study guides like *Half-hours with Bunyan's Pilgrim's Progress* (1856) and *Some Daily Thoughts on The Pilgrim's Progress* (1917).[11] Household performance and dramatization was not uncommon.[12] Robert Blatchford, editor of *The Clarion* (an early and important Labour newspaper), described Bunyan as "the friend and teacher of my childhood, *The Pilgrim's Progress* was my first book . . . in my tenth year I knew it almost by heart."[13] Like many other children, he amused himself by enacting scenes from the text. To do this, he equipped himself with a stage sword, a paper helmet, and a breastplate. Thus prepared,

> I went out as Greatheart and did deeds of valour and puissance upon an obsolete performing poodle, retired from Astley's Circus, who was good enough to double the parts of Giant Grim and the two lions.
> The stairway to the bedroom was the Hill Difficulty, the dark lobby was the Valley of the Shadow, and often I swam in

great fear and peril, and with profuse sputterings, across the black River of Death which lay between kitchen and scullery. The baby also, poor, unconscious mite, played many parts. Now it was Christiana, and had to be defended against the poodle at the point of the sword; now it was Faithful being tried for his life; now it was Ignorance crossing the Black River in a cradle boat rowed by myself as Vain-Hope; and anon it was Prudence and Charity buckling on my harness before I went out to fight and vanquish Carlo [the poodle] (as Apollyon) in the Vale of Humiliation.[14]

Yet another way of reading was through the illustrations that most texts invariably carried. Largely through popular demand, the book had been illustrated since its very earliest editions.[15] These images often become a crucial site of imaginative entry into the text. For many, pictures became mnemonics for episodes in the story. For others, these illustrations *were* the story. One nineteenth-century reader said: "If you had ever seen our 'Pilgrim's Progress' with its thumbed, tousled and tattered pages, you would have sworn that it had been read by generations of children, but all torn pages and creases did not really mean that we had read it; they only meant that we were never tired of looking at the pictures."[16]

Bunyan could also be "consumed" through an assortment of commodities with which fans could adorn their homes. One could drink tea from a Bunyan cup while contemplating a portrait of Bunyan on the wall, possibly acquired from an edition that included such pictures specifically for framing.[17] Children could make Bunyan jigsaws, while their parents displayed ever more elaborate and expensive volumes in their drawing rooms.[18] Bunyan volumes became treasured family possessions and were passed down across several generations, as inscriptions still show.[19] One of these, in a Welsh edition, was haltingly written: "Plece yo give this book to David John Beynon the son of John Phillip Beynon after is father and if David will die be fore Elizabeth his sister plece to give her."[20] Others were decisive: "Hannah Williams—the gift to her daughter Jane Froud on her dying bed Aug 21 1852 at her death it is to be given to Emma Froud daughter of the above."[21] Some readers turned their texts into little reliquaries that stored photographs, news cuttings, recipes, and letters.[22] One ardent Methodist, James Mellor, landscaped his Cheshire garden to resemble a Bunyan theme park.[23] A path snaking through rhododendron bushes, yew trees, and sycamores conducted visitors past various Bunyan scenes like the Slough of Despond (a dark part of the garden under gnarled ash and Wellingtonia). The by-way to Hell ran alongside a small pavilion with a wind and smoke machine to emulate the sites and sounds of perdition. In a departure from the original, a small bridge assisted pedestrians across the River of Death and then meandered on to the Celestial City, an elevated small stone chapel fronted by a spiral staircase.

Beyond the home, the book featured heavily in the weekly timetable of chapelgoers. Episodes from the book fueled talks at mothers' meetings, cottage lectures, and midweek sermons.[24] Choir services, cantatas, church pageants, and magic lantern shows shaped themselves around themes from *The Pilgrim's Progress.*[25] "Twicers" and "thricers" would in all probability have had multiple Bunyan encounters. Their children would have met Bunyan in Sunday schools and day schools and at times would have received his book as a prize.[26] These Nonconformist churches also functioned as centers of outreach to the very poor and destitute. In spreading Bunyan to them, chapels could rely on the simplified versions of the story charitably distributed by the Religious Tract Society (RTS), the predominantly Nonconformist tract organization that circulated material "at home" and abroad. The RTS provided the text in penny parts, in a Sunday school prize version, and in abridged editions that "featured among even the most meager of household libraries."[27]

The Pilgrim's Progess was woven into the warp and weft of Nonconformist experience. The book was a kind of second nature that was almost impossible, Blatchford said, to comment on or review: "I might as well try to criticize the Lord's Prayer." The book was also profoundly familiar. The characters were like friends and family, as reassuringly familiar as figures "on the Front at Brighton."[28] Dean Stanley, at the unveiling of Bunyan's monument in Bedford in 1874, said, "How deeply extended is the power of sympathy, and the force of argument, when the preacher or the teacher knows that he can enforce his appeal with a name which . . . comes home as if with canonical weight, by figures of speech which need only be touched on in order to elicit an electric spark of understanding, and satisfaction."[29] It was not so much a book as an environment, a set of orientations, a language, and a currency shared by most evangelicals.

The evangelical energy that drove the dissemination of *The Pilgrim's Progress* "at home" simultaneously led to the book's propagation and translation in other parts of the globe. In the early stages of the movement, missionaries received little professional training and so tended to mimic abroad the strategies they had used among the "home heathen."[30] In the view of John Brown, a biographer of Bunyan, the book had "always had a hold upon the toiling poor . . . the one book . . . well-thumbed and torn to tatters among them." As such, it suggested itself as the "first book to be translated by the missionary."[31] *The Pilgrim's Progress* was frequently chosen as a tool of proselytization and, in many Nonconformist missions, made it into the first ten titles translated.[32] This process likewise rebounded back in Britain. An historian of the RTS comments that "the impulse which drove [the RTS] to give the Christian gospel . . . to the heathen in distant lands drove them also to take counsel together about the heathen at home."[33]

In propagating the text, the missionaries took with them the gallimaufry of shapes and forms that the text's evangelical distribution "at home" had occasioned. These included the text itself and then its versions in choir services, pageants, dramas, tableaux, magic lantern slides, postcards (figure 7), posters, and the like. These were then used and adapted in sermons, hymns, classrooms, Sunday schools (figure 8), and talks.[34] These forms were further fragmented by methods of proselytization that required that missionaries experiment with bits and pieces in order to establish what would appeal to their new audiences.[35] These procedures promoted the fission of yet further Bunyan "molecules," which wafted out from mission stations at times like clouds of confetti. In the chapters that follow, I trace how these bits and pieces were received and interpreted by the African societies into which they floated. In the meanwhile, let us return to Britain to see how this dissemination of *The Pilgrim's Progress* was publicized back "home."

One of the major problems bedeviling the early mission movement was how to persuade followers to invest emotionally and materially in a venture thousand of miles away.[36] In a situation where British Protestants sometimes did not know the difference between China and the Congo,[37] and had little incentive to do so, it required considerable intellectual and imaginative effort to inveigle them into identifying with remote mission fields. As much scholarship has shown,[38] mission organizations evolved imaginative and effective solutions to these problems. By "colonizing" popular forms such as exhibitions, magazines, public meetings, picture technology, and revival gatherings, mission societies had tremendous success in attracting followers and glamorizing their pursuits. As we have seen in the previous chapter, these technologies, practices, dispositions, and methods of publicity were endlessly rehearsed and employed in congregations like Camden Road.

One strategy in this battle to create personal links across the

I.—CHRISTIANA AND HER CHILDREN.

Then said Christiana to her children, Sons, we are all undone.
I have sinned away your father, and he is gone: he would have
had us with him, but I would not go myself: I also have hindered
you of life. With that the boys fell all into tears and cried out to
go after their father. Oh (said Christiana) that it had been but our
lot to go with him! then had it fared well with us, beyond what
it is like to do now.

Figure 7. Example of RTS postcard version of *The Pilgrim's Progress*, part 2. Source: RTS/USCL Papers, the SOAS, University of London. Reproduced with the permission of the USCL.

"estranging seas"[39] was to create a picture with which people could identify. One such node of familiar recognition was *The Pilgrim's Progress*,
and many mission discourses evoke the text as a way of establishing a
shared field between themselves and their funding communities for whom
much mission publicity material was produced. Mission travelogues, for
instance, compared difficulties along the way to sections in the book like
the Slough of Despond or Hill Difficulty.[40] To a home audience, a foreign
landscape is rendered imaginable.

Mission material also likened converts to characters in the story.[41]

Figure 8. Use of Bunyan wallchart in Sunday school class, Upper Congo, 1920s. Source: *Regions Beyond*, 1928 (?), 89. (The dating of this journal is not clear. The image is taken from a volume dated 1927–1931.) Reproduced with the permission of the RBMU.

H. Sutton Smith, speaking of his experiences at Yakusu on the Upper Congo, wrote:

> Others who were once near the wicket gate, have been enticed away by Mr Worldly Wiseman; other have failed to climb 'Hill Difficulty.' But others have come to the Saviour and 'found rest by His sorrow and life by His Death,' and are treading hopefully and determinedly the road which leadeth to the Celestial City.[42]

This type of description creates the impression that converts in the Congo tread the same spiritual path as Protestants back in England. It also functions as a euphemistic form of explanation for success and failure in the mission field. The passage does not question why converts should or should not adopt Christianity; instead the story itself serves as an "explanation." Likewise, the characters in the book could be invoked to legitimate relationships of inequality between missionary and convert. Missionaries tended to be likened to leading characters in the book such as Evangelist, Interpreter, or Great-heart.[43] Converts were compared to weak and vacillating characters who need guidance.[44] Readers "at home" would have experienced the relationships between such characters as benevolent and a similar picture could be generated of the mission field thousands of miles away.

Mission magazines, a major plank in the media repertoire, invoked *The Pilgrim's Progress* in their articles. In cases where missionaries had translated the text, this information featured in their biographies and obituaries.[45] The book provided items of news, such as when a translation was completed, when it had been printed, or when new illustrations were made.[46] Snippets informed readers of how the book was taught in Sunday school and deployed in church services.[47]

The RTS, which funded many Bunyan translations, invariably featured some item on *The Pilgrim's Progress* in each of its annual reports. Most often this information took the form of a "league table" reporting the latest tally of non-European languages into which the book had been translated.[48] As one of the items for which the RTS most frequently provided funding, translations of *The Pilgrim's Progress* feature in the histories of the organization. The book almost takes on the status of a minor character and is discussed in a familiar tone. As a contemporary history of the Society noted in 1899, "Christian and the rest are represented in Japanese."[49]

One major strategy for popularizing the mission endeavor in Britain was the missionary exhibition, and these included exhibits of how Bunyan was being propagated in the mission field.[50] At times, this information featured in the RTS book display that generally formed part of these exhibitions. Included in their stalls would be a number of "foreign" Bunyan editions (figure 9).[51] In another instance, references to the book were integrated into displays. As we have seen, the Baptist exhibition in 1928 ended with the Interpreter's House.[52] In a 1909 exhibition, a "live" display showed a missionary translating *The Pilgrim's Progress* (figure 10).[53] Some of these techniques were reproduced at a local level at church meetings. Here indigenized illustrations from foreign editions also appeared in displays and magic lantern shows.[54] Fans of the book could buy African editions of the text that were advertised as showing "how Bunyan appeals to the African reader."[55]

With regard to Africa, these publicity ventures were immeasurably helped by the circumstances that unfolded in 1835 in Madagascar surrounding the first African translation of *The Pilgrim's Progress*. This translation took shape against a background of intense persecution of converts by the Merina royal court. The Merina king, Radama, had initially invited the LMS in 1820, with an eye to acquiring their Roman literacy (Arabic literacy existed in small pockets), technological capacity, and bureaucratic knowledge for his expanding kingdom. However, he died in 1828 and the new monarch, Queen Ranavalona, switched strate-

Figure 9. RTS book stall at missionary exhibition, 1911. Source: *Seedtime and Harvest*, Sept. 1911, 4. Reproduced with the permission of the USCL.

Figure 10. A display from a missionary exhibition, 1909. The man on the right is translating *The Pilgrim's Progress.* Source: *Seedtime and Harvest*, Sept. 1909, 7. Reproduced with the permission of the USCL.

gies. She ordered the missionaries to leave the island and embarked on a program of intense persecution against anyone who had taken up the new religion.[56] On the eve of their departure, one of the missionaries, David Johns wrote out a translation by hand of part of *The Pilgrim's Progress* (interleaved with illustrations cut from his edition). A further six to eight copies were written out by the converts and these were circulated.[57] The Malagasy Christians read and often memorized the text and found it a source of comfort in their persecution. They also used it to construct a framework to narrate their experiences and to make sense of their suffering.

One convert, for example, likened his persecution to Christian's fight with Apollyon:

> We read in the Pil[grim's] Progress that when Christian saw Apollion [*sic*] coming to meet him he began to be afraid and to hesitate whether to return or to stand his ground, but when he considered that he had no armour for his back he thought that to turn his back to him might give him greater advantage to pierce him with his darts, therefore he resolved to stand his ground, for, said he, had I no more in my eye than the saving of my life it would be the best way to stand. When Christian . . . entered the Valley of the Shadow of Death, he said, though it be a gloomy valley, yet it is the way to the Celestial City. These words of Christian and the passages quoted above express in few words our own feelings and views.[58]

Another convert wrote: "O God, do thou enable us to make the progress that Pilgrim made, and if thy kingdom in Madagascar is to be advanced by these means [persecution] be it so."[59] Elsewhere, a convert observed: "and those who received the word at first are not faint, but they are diligent in conversing together, on the favour of God towards them that believe, and the progress of Pilgrim, though he had much to annoy him."[60] When a group of converts managed to escape, and made their way to the coast, they narrated portions of their journey in terms of *The Pilgrim's Progress*. At one point, they took shelter in an empty house and "called it the 'Porter's Lodge,' for it seemed as if had been made for their relief and security."[61]

The story of the Madagascar persecution was extensively reported in the LMS and broader mission press.[62] In 1839, six converts who had managed to escape were brought to Britain where they addressed packed meetings.[63] Books and pamphlets on the persecution appeared in rapid succession, many of them accompanied by lurid illustrations of burning at the stake and other forms of execution.[64] These narratives in turn became powerfully woven into LMS accounts of itself and appeared in its subsequent histories, annual reports, pamphlets, tracts, books, plays, and pageants.[65] One strand in this broader story was that of *The Pilgrim's Progress* and the details of this saga were endlessly recounted: the fragile manuscript copies passed lovingly among converts; the public drive in England for funds to print copies; the resulting small tract-size books that could be easily carried and concealed and were at times bound in with bits of the Bible; the adoption of the story by the converts whose persecution evoked the early history of Dissent from which the text had first emerged.[66] These stories were taken up in publications across the Nonconformist world[67] and this first Bunyan translation in Africa emblematized the power that *The Pilgrim's Progress* might exercise in a mission context.

One feature of the Malagasy case that attracted attention was that the text appeared to cross the boundaries of race and language with apparent ease. This phenomenon was often noted in reports[68] and in turn became the basis for a standard piece of Bunyan discourse regarding the ability of the text to travel across frontiers of race and culture. Rev. W. Morley Punshon, in his popular lecture series on Bunyan, for example, maintained that *The Pilgrim's Progress* "calmed the fierce Malay; it has been carried up the far rivers of Burmah, and it has drawn tears from the dark eyes in the cinnamon gardens of Ceylon. The Bechuana in the wild woods have rejoiced in its simple story. . . . The Hindoo has yielded to its spell by Gunga's sacred stream; and, crowning triumph! Hebrews have read it on the slopes of Olivet."[69] Another report noted: "From the frozen snows of the Arctic Circle to the sunny lands of Tropical Africa, the story of Christian and his burden is widely read and known. . . . Many of our fellow-subjects in India are as familiar with Christian's flight with Apollyon, the Valley of the Shadow of Death, and the Land of Beulah, as we are at home."[70] The same idea was often phrased as the pilgrim speaking different languages, or the pilgrim assuming a disguise. In 1837, when Robert Moffat was completing the Tswana translation of Bunyan, he wrote, "I am at the present moment dressing Bunyan's Pilgrim in a Sichuana [Tswana] garb, and if he does not travel this land through and through I shall be much mistaken."[71]

One consequence of these invocations of Bunyan was the notion that everyone read the same book, which passed unchanged through the ether of language and culture. Yet, translation is, of course, more than cross-dressing, and each translation occasions a new text as even a brief look at some translated titles—*The Book of Bunyan*, *The Traveller*, *A Heaven's Pilgrimage* (the Zulu, Swahili, and Somali renditions of the title)—will tell us.[72] Nonetheless, the idea that everyone read the same story persisted. In 1928 the Dean of Winchester wrote in an article in the *Sunday Magazine* that anyone who had encountered the book would absorb its key meaning: "There are thousands of folk in obscure corners of the earth who will never meet an Englishman in this life, but in the next there will be one Englishman whom they will all greet as an old friend and companion—John Bunyan, the tinker of Bedford."[73]

Much of this sentiment is, of course, fueled by eurocentric vanity. Yet, some of its strands arise from a slightly different quarter, namely evangelical ideas regarding how texts and language work in the world.[74] In terms of these ideas, religion had to be a vital and emotional experience. One agent for sparking this emotion was a religious text that could have extraordinary power to "capture" readers and lodge its message firmly in their souls.[75] Evangelicalism placed particular emphasis on education and so didactic texts had an added importance.[76] Texts could also become surrogate evangelists, "noiseless messengers" traveling into those places where missionaries could not go or could not reach. In such instances, tracts could, for example, put on a "Chinese coat" and so "penetrate even to the chamber of the Emperor."[77] Against such a background, it did not seem strange to presume that people in different countries imbibed the same story.

Illustrations, too, reinforced this notion. From having such an intimate knowledge of the story and its illustrations, readers could recognize "foreign" pictures. Discussing a set of Japanese illustrations, one commentator said, "Apollyon giv[es] a truly Japanese conception of that great enemy." Another observer claimed that the Japanese pictures were "very characteristic, especially the portraiture of Mr. Worldly Wiseman who appears before us as the very ideal of a smug, self-satisfied Pharisee."[78] Such pictures signaled that everyone read the "same" story.

Embedded, then, in these mission messages was a picture of *The Pilgrim's Progress* as a text that had traveled to all corners of the world. Nonconformist congregational and denominational audiences encountered this message repeatedly. Within these "publics," the theme of Bunyan as a universal writer of the world became a "fact" and a piece of Nonconformist common sense. This "fact" in turn featured routinely in the plethora of ceremonies that clustered around Bunyan's name and memory. These events were arranged around his tomb,[79] relics, and realia.[80]

At the refurbishment of Bunyan's tomb in 1922 at Bunhill Fields in London, the revered Nonconformist graveyard, one speaker mentioned that *The Pilgrim's Progress* had been translated into "more languages than any book except the Bible and is read by all the races of mankind."[81] Introductions to the numerous editions of *The Pilgrim's Progress*, as well as lectures and commentaries on the book, mentioned his international popularity.[82] Bunyan's "universal" success featured prominently in popular illustrated lecture series. The authors of one of these lecture series claimed to have delivered their lecture with slides over three thousand times during a twenty-five-year period.[83]

While most of these events and activities were aimed at a Nonconformist public, they did extend beyond these boundaries. Commercially produced mission biographies were at times bestsellers. The massively popular missionary exhibitions reached a pan-Protestant and even pan-Christian public.[84] Influential Nonconformist commentators on Bunyan also spread his local and global achievements to a broader readership.

All these efforts were addressed to a world that Nonconformists felt was ignorant of or hostile to Bunyan's achievement. This point is worth stressing since if we turn to the periodization provided by Bunyan scholarship today,[85] we are given a different picture. In these accounts, Bunyan's fortunes were basically assured by the 1830s. Popularized by the Evangelical Revival and lauded by Romantic thinking for its "untutored genius," Bunyan's work was further crowned in 1830 by Robert Southey's influential edition of *The Pilgrim's Progress*. Laudatory reviews of this edition from Walter Scott and Thomas Macauley further promoted his standing.[86] A rediscovery of and enthusiasm for Puritanism,[87] along with the rising fortunes of Nonconformity are cited as further evidence for Bunyan's general acceptance by at least midcentury. To Nonconformists, however, such a periodization would have seemed overly optimistic. To one commentator, William Hale White (a childhood Nonconformist), Bunyan only really "arrived" in 1880 with James Anthony Froude's biography, which formed part of Henry Morley's prestigious English Men of Letters Series.[88] Until then Bunyan had continued to be hobbled by his association with Nonconformity and the vulgarity invariably imputed to it.[89]

Recognition where it probably mattered most for chapelgoers—from the High Church—was seen as belated and grudging. As a writer with a wide social reach, Bunyan was admittedly invoked at ceremonies with an agenda of reconciliation between church and chapel. Three such occasions were the unveiling of a statue of Bunyan in Bedford in 1874 and the inauguration of two stained-glass windows in memory of Bunyan, one in Southwark Cathedral (1900) and one in Westminster Abbey (1912).[90] Yet, to at least some Nonconformists, these ceremonies seemed belated and backhanded. Speaking of the 1874 unveiling of Bunyan's statue, one Baptist commentator added a telling aside—"so late!"[91] Furthermore, the Westminster Abbey window had not been freely given but had instead been "shamed" out of the Established Church when a petition was started in response to a group of visiting North American Baptists aghast that there was no national monument to Bunyan.[92] The petition to the Dean of Westminster put together by the World Evangelical Alliance for the window noted the international circulation of Bunyan as one of the reasons why he merited a monument of his own. One of the press reports on the unveiling of the window read: "Millions (not only in England, but even more in America and the colonies) [are] stirred by [the] announcement of [the] window in the Church that reviled Bunyan."[93] As late as 1928, in the midst of massive national tercentenary celebrations blessed by the King, a prominent Anglican cleric could still write an article explaining to his followers why it was important for them to read Bunyan.[94] By 1928, however, any such pockets of High Church disdain were rare, and the tercentenary events ensconced Bunyan as a writer whose status was firmly established and recognized.

Such an account of Bunyan's international circulation may create the impression that everything was determined from England. The projection of the text out into the evangelical world, in the first place, reflected Nonconformist taste and priorities. Furthermore, the book provided a shared point of focus for mission and home audience and propagated the idea that the text that Nonconformists so loved was equally revered and identically interpreted by converts throughout the mission world. Did the drive to publicize the book lie solely with the imperatives of Nonconformist politics and its attempts to use the foreign mission venture as a means to leverage concessions at home? Did the African locales in which Bunyan was circulated have any impact on how the book was publicized back home?

The Madagascan case provides an interesting answer to this question. It demonstrates that the African societies into which *The Pilgrim's Progress* traveled did play a part in shaping the book's fortunes in Britain. The regional politics of Madagascan society was critical, both in determining how the text was taken up and how it was represented back in Britain. As Piers Larson's recent analysis of LMS evangelism in Madagascar has shown, Christianity in Madagascar was vernacularized by its recipients, who determined the conceptual terrain into which mission belief and doctrine had to be translated. Conversion was not a shift from a Malagasy state to something alien but rather "the creation of a new religious consciousness and practice from various familiar and familiarized cultural resources and traditions."[95] Against this background, mission tracts and books, in keeping with extant sacred practice, became treated as protective objects and charms. Larson notes that this practice appears the most credible way of explaining the quite disproportionate desire for reading matter amongst converts, many of whom were not fully literate. By the early 1830s, the LMS press in the capital Antananarivo, was producing twenty thousand items per year for a "reading" population of, at most, five thousand. As Larson points out, this understanding of documents as protective objects influenced missionaries, who gained a renewed understanding of the Scriptures as a "charm of life."[96] The adoption by persecuted converts of *The Pilgrim's Progress* as a charm and guide must similarly have given missionaries, and the audiences to whom these stories were relayed, a revitalized grasp of the book's extraordinary powers and underlined, popularized, or, in some cases, possibly even inaugurated the idea of Bunyan's text as a second Bible (given the practice of binding *The Pilgrim's Progress* in with sections of the Bible, a fact that featured in Nonconformist publicity on the text). These mission depictions are inflected by Malagasy understandings of documents as protective charms or "fetishes." Such representations of the text far away rebound back on the text "at home" and resonate with evangelical audiences who themselves hold magical theories of textuality and texts that are capable of "seizing" and utterly transforming readers.

For further evidence of such "magical" practices, one need only look at the inscriptions and introductions to British editions that urged readers not only to read but also to act. The text is consequently something that, fetish-like, compels its readers to particular forms of action in the world. Instructions on how to read the text often take up this theme and advise the reader on how they might allow themselves to be compelled by the text. One inscription, for example, urged: "Reader! Whosoever thou art . . . before beginning the perusal of this book . . . offer up from thy heart, the following brief, but most comprehensive and necessary petition 'O God, for Jesus Christ's sake, give in the Holy Spirit that I may profit by whatever is good in this book.'" Another inscription (of 1869) outlined an action for its reader to follow: "Dear Annie, Be a little pilgrim to the Glory land." An introduction to a 1776 edition likewise spoke directly to the readers and advised them how to permit the text to compel them: "Let the Preface close with a word to the Reader's heart . . . The Pilgrim's Progress is a parable, but it has an interpretation in which you are . . . concerned. If you live in sin, you are in the City of Destruction. O hear the warning voice! Flee from the wrath to come!" An echo of these practices remains in a First World War edition that asked its readers to sign and date an enclosed bookmark as a token of having accepted Jesus as their savior. They were also requested to tear out, complete, and then send off a postcard to the Open Air Mission that had published the book.[97]

Similar themes of magical conversion emerge in the story of Mpambu with which we started. In that story, The Pilgrim's Progress exercises an astounding power over the villagers and changes them from would-be cannibals to awestruck observers, a mission trope frequently used in relation to Bunyan's text.[98] For the villagers, the book is a protective object or "fetish." Such items were widely publicized in BMS literature and exhibitions and functioned as a shorthand symbol of heathendom.[99] Baptist readers would consequently have interpreted Fullerton's parable as a story of the struggle between the fetishistic heathen beliefs of the Congo and the antifetish of The Pilgrim's Progress (a surrogate Bible), which could turn cannibals into converts. However, as with all such paired terms, the boundary between fetish and antifetish is at times uncertain. Both in how Mpambu uses the book and in other mission descriptions of The Pilgrim's Progress as a quasi-magical object, Bunyan's book has become a type of "fetish," namely a material object whose correct manipulation can compel events in the real or spiritual world. Most missionaries would have been appalled at such a suggestion— Mpambu probably less so. Like many other mission recruits of slave background, he had ameliorated his marginal position by becoming a convert and hence a guardian of the book, an object that was widely treated as a category of fetish.[100] In his encounter with the villagers and chief, all participants recognize that he has the authority to manipulate the book/fetish and it is this acknowledged power that probably ensures a happy outcome for Mpambu.

Early twentieth-century Baptists, of course, would not have countenanced such a reading of the Fullerton extract. For them, Bunyan's book (as a second Bible) radiates holy power and vanquishes the superstition and heathendom of the fetish-enthralled villagers. Yet, whatever one's reading, Fullerton's anecdote (as well the Madagascan case) serves to induct Bunyan's book into the symbolic field of the "fetish"—whether as a fetish in its own right or as an antifetish. In this guise, the text fulfilled a complex role—a "fetish-like antifetish"—with compulsive powers to possess and transform readers both "at home" and "abroad." This perception of the text is admirably illustrated in a comment from the introduction to a nineteenth-century edition of *The Pilgrim's Progress*:

> It seizes us in childhood with the strong hand of its power, our manhood surrenders to the spell of its sweet sorcery. . . . Its scenes are as familiar to us as the faces of home. . . . We have seen them [characters] all, conversed with them. . . . There was never a power which so thoroughly possessed our hearts.[101]

As long as readers subscribed to an evangelical, hence implicitly magical, view of Bunyan, such ideas could cohabit quite easily. However, once one attempted a secular reading of *The Pilgrim's Progress*, the magical component of evangelicalism became a problem. Alfred Noyes, who launched one of the first and most widely noted secular interpretations of Bunyan in 1928, ran into precisely this dilemma. He clearly recognized—and disapproved of—these magical powers. "When one looks at poor Caliban-Bunyan himself there are symptoms of a reversion to type which all students of primitive religion will recognize." Bunyan we are told is mad: "He wanted to pray to broom-sticks, to a bull, and to Satan" (in his preconversion phase, that is).[102] Bunyan consequently exercises a premodern power that Noyes finds, and constructs as, dangerous by equating it with African societies (the book "is on the lowest and most squalid levels of the primitive races of Africa"; Bunyan is described as having a "narrow and stunted brow").[103] Bunyan clearly "spooks" Noyes. Part of this antipathy arises from a lingering class prejudice against him. Part of it, as we shall see in chapter 10, has to do with Bunyan's "over-association" with colonized society and the difficulties that this posed for those who wanted to claim him as English and "white." Yet another (and related) dimension of this prejudice emerges from Noyes's own attempts to disavow a premodern superstitious British past and project it onto Africa. By racializing a past he does not desire, Noyes seeks to exile it into a realm that has no connection to him and that signifies primeval pastness. Through this maneuver, he seeks to position himself in a domain that has apparently always been secular, modern/rational, and white. Bunyan—superstitious, irrational, and long associated with Africa—falls outside these criteria and has to be exorcized. However, as with most such exorcisms, Noyes's attempts to "ban" Bunyan to the periphery cannot work. Instead, Bunyan lurks like a ghost around the corners of Noyes's articles, emerging as the specter of superstition each time secularism is invoked. He functions, then, as a necessary "familiar," the ghost-like twin without whom terms like modernity and secularism cannot function.

By being projected into the far-away field of the fetish and then reflected back to Nonconformists in Britain, Bunyan and his text become "familiar" in a number of senses. Firstly, everyday, and hence familiar, uses of the book as a magical "charm of life" are underlined and revitalized. Secondly, the book itself is made "familiar" to the world, which seems to read it in exactly the same way as Protestants back home. Finally, as evangelical ways of reading declined, Bunyan becomes the "familiar" of modernity, the ghost of the premodern and magical, inhabiting the borders of the modern and secular.

The year when Noyes wrote (1928) was a long time past the Madagascan translation of 1835, but this chapter has nevertheless suggested that these two events can be read together. By inaugurating Bunyan into the symbolic field of the talisman, the Malagasy translation and its reflections back in Britain inducted the book into a zone of magical practices to which evangelical audiences, who themselves read this way, could relate. However, as Noyes attempted to insert Bunyan into a secular domain, these magical practices, both "at home" and "abroad," became a "problem" that Noyes attempted to excise. These shifts indicate the complex transformations that awaited Bunyan's text "at home" as it traveled into new zones of intellectual and spiritual practice. One crucial bridge in this process of induction was translation and it is to this topic that we now turn.

3

Translating Bunyan

"Prophets," as John Whitehead noted, "are a nuisance."[1] Whitehead knew whereof he spoke. A self-styled prophet himself, he worked on the Upper Congo for fifty years and caused a considerable nuisance. His obduracy still survives in the euphemism of obituary: "hard, forthright, clear and firm in his views . . . a lone figure unable to work easily with his colleagues."[2] Indeed these colleagues soon abandoned the station rather than work with him. Eventually his wife left him, too. His employers (the BMS) and his children begged him to come home. In 1925 the BMS cancelled his contract. Whitehead—"the prophet of Wayika"—stayed on defiantly, returning reluctantly to Britain in 1946. "The Congo," he observed (rather like a Baptist Kurtz), "was a fine place to lose one's character in."[3]

Whitehead believed fervently that God had directed him to the Congo to work as a linguist and translator. Before leaving for the Congo, he had studied the Kongo grammar of Holman Bentley, the legendary Baptist linguist. Whitehead became convinced that "Bentley's Elijah cloak" had fallen on him and he envisioned his role of translator as that of a mighty ventriloquist. His gospel translation enabled him to speak "with 15,000 voices" ("I hope to add 8,000 more in the new year when more paper arrives," he mused). Whitehead imagined his "voices" reverberating across entire territories as his hymns traveled from the Upper Congo into Tanganyika.[4] As relations with the home committee deteriorated, Whitehead believed there was a conspiracy to silence his "voices." He ignored all directives to stop work and continued to order paper and equipment on the BMS account. When this channel too closed up, he begged and pouted: "For Christ's sake, send me that paper. . . . Abandon me, cross me out, but let me finish the work."[5]

In its extremity, Whitehead's career dramatizes two key features of the mission translation endeavor. The first of these is the extravagant stage—several countries with a cast of thousands—on which he saw his translation work unfolding. A second instructive feature of Whitehead's career is the constant tension between him and his home committee. Their differences were, of course, exacerbated by Whitehead's impossible personality. Yet, behind this personal discord, one can detect disagreements that were organizational and professional. Whitehead, for example, felt driven by an urgent apocalyptic mission to spread the word. By contrast, BMS structures (with their "bloodless obedience to dead rules," as Whitehead said) demanded caution, delay, and fiscal restraint.[6] Whitehead (rather unusually for a missionary) craved individual glory as a translator. Yet he worked in a mission society structure that did not favor "one-man" translations. Like all mission organizations, the BMS—particularly in matters of biblical translation—recommended translation by committee.

Judged from this encounter, mission translation was a vast and vexed field. Its avowedly international scale encompassed different and often competing interests, and ranged across the arena of mission imperialism. Translation is consequently not one "event" by which a text is lobbed from Europe into Africa. Translations stretch across the time, space, and ideological tensions of the mission domain. If we are to understand the complexity of such translation events, we have to follow their threads in detail. This chapter attempts such a task. In the first part, I examine the paradoxes inherent in mission translation and how *The Pilgrim's Progress*, as a second Bible, offered temporary relief from some of these contradictions. I then turn to narrate a "biography" of one Congo translation as it unfolds in time. Through this process, we gain insight into how various players in the mission arena imprint their interest on the translation's final form. In the third section, I trace one Cameroonian translation through space, the translation undertaken by the West Indian missionary, Joseph Jackson Fuller (figure 4). We follow the journey of the text from Bedford (Bunyan's hometown) to New England, to the American South, to Jamaica, and finally to West Africa. We examine how the story becomes "black" as it travels into a slave world and how Fuller, an ex-slave-turned-missionary, used this changed text to negotiate the contradictions of being a black missionary in a white-dominated world.

The contradictions besetting mission translation are numerous. Not only does translation have to steer a path between different languages, different denominations, and competing theological viewpoints,[7] but it also has to negotiate the problems of dialect (which of the many dialects around the mission station is to be written down as a language?), orthography (using what orthographical choices?), and local politics (taking heed of which sets of interests?).[8] Much translation is determined by first-language converts rather than second-language missionaries. Missionaries labor in others' linguistic vineyards without full control over how key ideas, concepts, and terms come to be rendered.[9] Indeed the core business of biblical translation itself rests uneasily on a set of theological fault lines. Can heaven's design be expressed in human idiom? Can God's message be transferred from one language to another? Can translation reproduce revelation?[10]

Mission translation is thus essentially about managing contradiction. As such, any translation could only ever be a temporary truce between clusters of warring demands. Each piece of translation was always provisional, one of many "rehearsals" in a process that had no final performance. Indeed, many early mission translations were interleaved with blank pages so that evangelists could jot down better phrasings or indicate where sentences were not clear.[11] Mission journals frequently reported mistranslations ("sitting on a stick" for "going to heaven," or "Jesus is in a snail-shell" rather than "in heaven").[12] The invariable blitheness of such accounts speaks not only of the contempt that some missionaries held for "savage" languages but also underlines the prevailing view of translation as necessarily hasty and provisional.

Within this ambiguous environment, *The Pilgrim's Progress* could play a useful role. For nineteenth-century Nonconformists, as we have seen, the book was a substitute Bible: the story of Christian and his burden that rolls from his shoulders at the Cross captured in vivid and dramatic form the essential kernel of Christianity. Through a series of syllogistic steps, this story could come to stand for the Gospel message and hence for the entire Bible. The deep interpenetration of Bunyan's language with that of the Bible, and the latter's pervasive influence on the text, strengthened this claim of *The Pilgrim's Progress* as a substitute Bible.[13]

As a near-Bible, the book could share in the importance of the Scriptures while being exempt from the rule-bound rigors of biblical translation. Translating the entire Bible often took decades. During this time, the Bible per se did not exist except as a scrappy handful of little booklets indistinguishable in most regards from tracts, catechisms, or primers.[14] Some parts of the Bible—particularly with regard to prophets and polygamy—carried mixed messages and certain missionaries refrained from translating them.[15] A small minority, taking up a peculiarly un-Protestant position, even felt that the Bible should never be written down in African languages.[16] While missionaries argued behind the scenes about these issues, *The Pilgrim's Progress* (or parts of it) could be held up as a synecdochal scripture. In this context, mission publicity material was quick to light on stories of converts who preferred Bunyan to the Bible. A missionary from the Punjab, for example, reported that one of his flock had turned down the offer of a Bible. "'I have got something much better than a Gospel.' And he pulled out a Pilgrim's Progress . . . 'This is wonderful. I can understand this. I cannot understand the Gospel.'"[17] Such pictures resonated well with a "home" audience who had, no doubt, from time to time, secretly harbored similar thoughts themselves. Such accounts also allowed British readers to believe that they and converts far away read the same book and believed the same set of ideas.

This complexity of the relationship between Bunyan and the Bible was at times apparent in the physical nature of the book itself and in the Madagascan case, bits of the Bunyan text were bound together with sections from the Scriptures.[18] In the minds of some, the two texts often swirled together. A Baptist medical missionary in China, for example, did some illustrations for evangelical purposes, and the pictures he chose ran together biblical and Bunyan scenes indiscriminately. They were the Prodigal Son; Noah and the Flood; the Horrible Pit and the Miry Clay; the Good Samaritan; and the Burden and its Removal.[19]

This intimate relationship of Bunyan and the Bible was, in some instances, figured in metaphors of gender. Bernard Cockett, the pastor of Bunyan Meeting House in Bedford, wrote: "[The] Pilgrim speaks 121 languages, and accompanies the Bible in Christian missions with the intimacy of Greatheart and Christiana."[20] In this image, the Bible becomes Great-heart, the chivalric knight who protects Christiana and her party on their journey to heaven. *The Pilgrim's Progress* itself is compared to Christiana and so becomes the Bible's female companion. *The Pilgrim's Progress* is hence likened to a feminized Bible, an image that usefully captures the ambiguous zone that the text occupied. The text was secular, yet also sacred; it was fiction, yet also "true" in that it carried the Gospel message. Translating it could be a site of pleasure and experimentation and a relief from the "manly" demands of Bible work. Rosemary Guillebaud, who "converted" *The Pilgrim's Progress* into Rundi, recalls that she did it as a form of relaxation from the more arduous New Testament translation that she was doing at the same time.[21]

The Zulu version of *The Pilgrim's Progress* commences with a short foreword by the translator, John William Colenso, the Bishop of Natal. The book appeared in 1868 at a time when Colenso found himself embroiled in an international dispute about his theological scholarship, which had questioned the literal truth of the Bible. Colenso had been excommunicated by the southern African branch of the Anglican Church and had had to fight legal battles both at home and in England.[22] Against this background, the opening sentences of the foreword unsurprisingly apologized for the delay in the text's appearance:

> Christians, I have written this book about Christian that I would like you to read and get to know. But I beseech you my people, do not be dissatisfied that it has taken me this long to write this book. . . . I was preoccupied with something very big that I had not foreseen. . . . I have written this book so that you may read it and acquire the power to see [get its powers/wisdom], and know how to page [investigate] it like the white people. Here it is, then, the book of Christian. You have heard others talk of his existence, and that he has his own book that talks about the suffering of a person who wants to know our Father, the Lord, and to have faith in Jesus Christ our King.[23]

Colenso was no ordinary mission translator. A Bishop and an international figure, he is probably the most prominent of all Bunyan translators. Nonetheless, as a mission translator in Africa, he faced similar problems to his colleagues. The first and most obvious of these was a lack of time. As the extract makes clear, the translation stretched over a much longer period than he had anticipated. The second point worth noting is that the book is already known to its intended readers. Christian, the protagonist, and his story already live among Zulu believers. Bits of the book have migrated in and around the Zulu mission world. Pieces of the text have been "peeled" off and been immersed in the new language community. The "book" has cleared a space for itself and settled down before its printed incarnation arrives. Like any translated text, then, the Zulu *Pilgrim's Progress* has a "biography," more complex than one might initially anticipate.

Unfortunately, the records for Colenso's translation are patchy and do not permit us to put together a detailed picture of the text's "biography."[24] Instead, let us turn to another translation of *The Pilgrim's*

Progress (this time into Kele, a language of the Upper Congo) where evidence is more plentiful. If we consult bibliographies or published mission accounts,[25] we will see that the translation appeared in 1916. Such entries create the impression that the translation was one neat and finite "event," but it was, of course, only the tip of an iceberg. Below this just-visible apex lay a deep and byzantine story.

The Kele translation of *The Pilgrim's Progress*, part 1, took shape in and around the mission station, Yakusu, established in 1895 as part of the BMS advance up the Congo River. The station operated in a complex linguistic environment that by some accounts included fourteen different languages and dialects. The initial decision was to work in Lingala, the trade language of the river, and Swahili. These were, however, second-languages for the target population and, furthermore, some missionaries judged them to be "mongrel" tongues. The station consequently changed strategies and decided to work in Kele, the first-language of its desired convert group.[26]

One of the earliest staff members at Yakusu was W. H. Stapleton, the noted Baptist linguist, who arrived in 1897. Working with his assistant, Bondoko, Stapleton undertook several translations including Matthew, Luke, John, Acts, and one-fifth of *The Pilgrim's Progress* into Kele. This fragment was completed in 1902 and then sent back to London for printing. It finally appeared about three years later as a freestanding thirty-two-page book in 1905, a year before Stapleton's death.[27]

The baton then passed to H. Sutton Smith, like Stapleton from the Rye Lane Baptist Chapel in Peckham, London. He arrived at Yakusu in 1899 and soon established a close working relationship with a young convert, Itindi. Together, this pair tackled Hebrews and Colossians. In 1909 Sutton Smith and Itindi undertook the next chunk of Bunyan, but managed only a half-dozen more pages before Sutton Smith became ill and relocated to China.[28] In the same year, the energetic Charles Pugh arrived and found that pupils on the station were familiar with the story and could recite parts of it from the Stapleton translation.[29] Possibly spurred by this enthusiasm, Pugh took up where Sutton Smith had left off and quickly added another twenty pages.[30]

By early 1910, the sections translated by Sutton Smith/Itindi and Pugh began to be serialized in the Yakusu periodical *Mboli ya Tengai*. The first episode appeared in April 1910 and the serial ran for two years.[31] This curtailed form of the story proved popular among readers ("more acceptable to the native mind," in Pugh's words) and no doubt because of this popularity, Pugh was requested by the station committee to compile a "complete" abridgement of the story.[32] Performing six hours of translation a week, he abridged the entire part 1 by revising earlier translations and by undertaking a summarized translation of the remainder of the text.[33] His version finally appeared in a 64-page edition in 1916. Pugh's version proved to be so popular that it was again serialized in 1925, in extracts that were sometimes less than one hundred words.[34] Subsequent editions in book form of Pugh's abridged translation appeared regularly until at least 1958 and are quite probably still in print amongst Kele-speaking Protestants.[35]

As this story of one translation demonstrates, any Bunyan edition was made in a tangled web that stretched across continents. Within this web lay a number of interacting sites linked by filaments of cooperation and conflict. The first of these, in our Kele story, concerns the complex linguistic environment in which translation proceeded. In a multilingual situation, the decision to work in Kele registered a variety of political interests. Those missionaries favoring the large-scale languages, Lingala and Swahili, were in all likelihood modernists (or aggressive evangelicals, or both). For them, the reach of such languages offered the economies of scale they sought.[36] Those favoring small languages were generally antimodernist in outlook and wanted to protect the "purity" of African societies from social change. For some Kele-speakers (a small group today numbering only 160,000), the chance to get their language promoted by the mission must have held considerable political attraction. However, at the same time, other Kele-speakers probably regarded the opportunity as a double-edged sword given that mission transcription often produced a language not entirely recognizable to its speakers. Part of this problem had to do with "mission station jargon." Eugene Nida of the American Bible Society explains:

> Earlier missionaries have in some instances decided to 'improve' on the language of the natives by introducing some of their own ideas about how its grammar should be changed, or perhaps they have just not learned the language well and the natives . . . have actually come to copy the mistakes of the missionaries. . . . On the other hand, some natives employ a 'reduced' form of the language around the mission station just because they discover that the missionary is not competent to understand fully the more elaborate and intricate grammatical forms.[37]

At Yakusu, this general mission problem was compounded by the fact that mission converts and hence translators were slaves, runaways, and young boys, as was the case with Stapleton's and Sutton Smith's assistants,

Bondoko and Itindi. The mission station jargon and its written manifestation inevitably reflected the sociolects of these groups.

Also contested, if not to the same degree as the question of target
language, was the issue of whether and when to translate Bunyan. Most
Nonconformists, of course, considered *The Pilgrim's Progress* an evangelical priority. One might consequently anticipate little mission disagreement about devoting resources for translating Bunyan as soon as possible. Stapleton did indeed put Bunyan very high up on his list. By the time
his fragment of *The Pilgrim's Progress* appeared in 1905, the "Bible" comprised only a handful of books: Matthew, Mark, Luke, John, Acts, Epis-
tles, and Nehemiah.[38] Judged alongside this huddle of booklets, *The Pilgrim's Progress* must have seemed nearly as weighty as the "Bible."
Stapleton was, however, a Baptist and Bunyan would have been especially
significant to him.

However, even Baptists sometimes argued about Bunyan's useful-
ness. The fractious Whitehead, for example, felt that the text was "obscure" and "awkward" but did concede that it may "be alright later on."[39]
Beyond the Baptist fold, arguments about Bunyan became more acute.
Many of these disagreements were staged in the Congo Mission Conference, an organization that attempted to institute cooperative production
of literature between Protestant mission societies in the Catholic-domi-
nated Belgian Congo. Herbert Smith of the U.S.-based Disciples of Christ
Congo Mission commented: "It is surprising to some of us to find Pilgrim's Progress in nine different tongues."[40] J. A. Clark commented:

> Then there is the Pilgrim's Progress which ought to be very
> useful in spite of many difficulties. I would however cut out
> with unsparing hand the greater part of the long theological
> discussions. . . . And the book should be translated literally, but
> very freely. It strikes me too that the second part is likely to be
> more popular than the first, as it contains more humour and
> the larger number of pilgrims, some of them children, makes
> for more human interest for the readers.[41]

E. Guyton of the Congo Balolo Mission, a small British-based nondenominational organization, somewhat surprisingly, felt that Bunyan was
not the best choice: "We must consider the mind of the native so as not
to give him ideas which are distinctly European. In the Pilgrim's Progress
there is much that is incomprehensible on that account."[42] G. Thomas, a
Baptist, stoutly defended the book: "the Pilgrim's Progress will become a
large factor in the imagination of the native."[43]

However, when it came to funders (another crucial link in the translation chain), such local differences of opinion evaporated. In reporting back to their funding structures, missionaries presented translations of *The Pilgrim's Progress* in an unrelentingly favorable light. The text was well known to home audiences and around this point of familiarity, mission publicity wove a story of the miraculous book that could compel spectacular changes in "heathens." Pugh, for example, told a mission breakfast at the Cannon Street Hotel in London about the Kele translation. Part of his story reads:

> when I reached the station [Yakusu] . . . many boys and girls were able, not only to read the book, but also to recite passages from it. And not only so, but there were many who had read the book to such good purpose that they had set out from the City of Destruction with their faces steadfastly set towards the glorious City, and as they had journeyed along the pilgrim way had come to that place, somewhat ascending, on the summit of which stood the Cross, and there, near the Cross, the burden had rolled off from their shoulders, and rolled and rolled until it fell into the grave there and was seen no more.[44]

Pugh, a superb publicist, was speaking to an English evangelical audience who knew Bunyan intimately. He invokes what many regard as the core segment of the text, namely the scene at the cross where Christian loses his burden. For many readers, it was an electric moment in the narrative and was quoted and requoted in evangelical circles.[45] Hearing Pugh's story, which employs phrases from the original, the guests at the breakfast must have felt that African converts understood the text exactly as they did.

But what did converts make of the text? This question is often difficult to answer, since in this case we have to work only with pronouncements from missionaries. Yet, with careful reading, there are some deductions we can make. With the Kele translation, as we have seen, Yakusu readers had the choice of Stapleton's version or the abridged nuggets in the periodical. They voted for the latter. One possible explanation for this popularity (apart from ease of reading) is that the serial version gave readers only the narrative highlights and cut out the theological discussion. Much of this theological discussion exemplified core evangelical Protestant belief. Yet, as research on African Christianity reveals,[46] converts were discriminating in which parts of the Protestant package they accepted. One cornerstone of Protestant belief that never took any hold in the continent was the idea of original sin.[47] Yet, the central image in the text, namely the burden on Christian's back, stands precisely for his original sin, which is then elaborated upon in the theological discussions elsewhere in the text. By sloughing off the text's theology, African readers could bypass those sections of Protestant thought that made no sense to them. As we shall see in the chapters that follow, by adopting this strategy, African converts could also redeem certain images in the story—like the burden on Christian's back—and put these to work to explain the new and burdensome colonial circumstances they had to face. Through these strategies, the popular taste of converts registered itself in how Bunyan was translated and helped to dictate the final form of the book as a series of abridged episodes.

In looking at the Kele translation saga, one "event" turns out to be underpinned by an extensive network of relationships along which ideas and images of the texts traveled. Different players in this field (Baptist missionary, Kele convert, cross-mission council, funders, and so on) supported divergent understandings of the text rooted in their various local worlds. But, at the same time, missionaries worked to promote the idea of a "universal" story, read in the same way by all participants. In the zone created by this publicity, "images" of Bunyan could start to confront each other and produce a chemistry that, as we shall see in chapter 10, was to affect his standing in England profoundly.

Striking, too, in this Kele saga, is the fragmentary nature of the translation. The text did not evolve smoothly from English to Kele in one complete unit: bits and pieces were translated, earlier versions were revised and abridged, and fragments were "trialed" in periodicals then reformulated in an abridged edition. This "magpie" method, as others have shown,[48] was central to mission endeavor, which, of necessity, had to experiment with shreds and patches to see what would appeal to their new audiences. In their attempt to create a shared field of metaphor and image, missions had to be permanent experimenters, trying out new strategies and media at every turn. In keeping with these practices, *The Pilgrim's Progress* (even once it was translated) was broadcast from many sites. These included the classroom, Sunday school (figure 8), pulpit, choir, debating society, and school play.[49] It was also disseminated via different media: magic lantern slide, poster, postcard (figure 7), book illustration, periodical, school reader, drama, sermon, and hymn.[50]

In all these various sites and via these different media, versions of *The Pilgrim's Progress* were crafted and recrafted, fashioned and refashioned—a process that stretched out over decades. It is consequently impossible to locate any translation as one finite spot in time. It is likewise impossible to locate it as one neat dot in space. When I first commenced this research, I kept a map showing each Bunyan translation in Africa as a dot. Every time I located a new one, I proudly added it to my collection until I had a "measled" map of the continent showing eighty translations. However, as the research progressed, I came to understand that such a representation was misleading. Each dot implied that a translation is a bounded and local event, cut off from the international threads that run into and from it. Particularly if we wish to understand how cultural history is made transnationally, then it is crucial that we trace these threads both through time and space. Having looked at one translation through time, let us turn to another in space. This story concerns Joseph Jackson Fuller and Bunyan in the black Atlantic.

The first chapter of W.E.B. Du Bois's *The Souls of Black Folk* sketches out his famous notion of double consciousness as "this sense of always looking at one's self through the eyes of others, of measuring one's soul by the tape of a world that looks on in amused contempt and pity."[51] His first chapter also outlines an African American history of attempts to overcome this doubleness "to merge [a] double self into a better and truer self," of attempts to be "both a Negro and an American, without being cursed and spit upon by his fellows, without having the doors of Opportunity closed roughly in his face."[52] In this struggle, there have been what Du Bois terms many "false gods" of utopian expectation. Emancipation, black male enfranchisement, and then educational advancement—all these promised redemption and each in turn was blocked by continuing violence and racism—"the holocaust of war, the terrors of the Ku-Klux Klan, the lies of carpet-baggers, the disorganization of industry."[53] In describing the grim journey along this careworn path, Du Bois introduces a number of images from Bunyan. He speaks of the "highway of Emancipation and law, steep and rugged, but straight, leading to heights high enough to overlook life." He continues:

> Up the new path the advance guard toiled, slowly, heavily, doggedly. . . . It was weary work. The cold statistician wrote down the inches of progress here and there, noted also where here and there a foot had slipped or some one had fallen. To the tired climbers, the horizon was ever dark, the mists were often cold. . . . Canaan was always dim and far away. If, however, the vistas disclosed yet no goal, no resting-place, little but flattery and criticism, the journey at least gave leisure for

reflection and self-examination; it changed the child of emancipation to the youth with dawning self-consciousness, self-realization, self-respect.[54]

A few lines later, the submerged Bunyan references become explicit: "For the first time [the Negro] sought to analyze the burden he bore upon his back, that dead-weight of social degradation partially masked behind a half-named Negro problem."[55]

Du Bois's politicized interpretation of Bunyan's allegory, in certain respects, resembles the Kele reading strategies outlined above. Both retain key Bunyan symbols, empty them of their prior meaning, and then fill them with new political content. Both, importantly, construe the central figure of the story as a black character. This "translation" of the story was one of the consequences of its journeys—across the Atlantic and into Africa—and raises fascinating questions about Bunyan in the diaspora and African American uses of *The Pilgrim's Progress*.

Curiously, this is a story that, to my knowledge, has never been told. When it is, a key figure in the saga will be Joseph Jackson Fuller, born a slave in Jamaica and for much of his life a missionary in the Cameroon in West Africa. During his mission tenure, he was to complete two Bunyan translations, one into Isubu and the other into Duala, the trading language associated with the city of the same name. As this section seeks to show, Fuller, in undertaking these translations, was able to draw on a multiple Jamaican Bunyan inheritance that was shaped by three major streams. One part of this bequest came to him from a black Baptist tradition forged first in the American South and then brought by African American missionaries to Jamaica. A second part of it was bequeathed to him by British Baptists who began working in Jamaica in 1814. A third part of it was formulated in the terrain of slave religion, where bits of Bunyan were reshaped to fit into a world of African creole spiritual experience. Inheriting these streams in which Bunyan characters could be black, white, American, Jamaican, British, slave, or free, Fuller could only have been "doubly conscious" of the text as a prism revealing the fluidity of racial identities, even where such identities had been violently created, imposed, and upheld. It was an insight that he would draw on as he walked the tightrope of being a black West Indian missionary among predominantly white British colleagues.

Our story proceeds in three sections. We first trace the spread of the text from Bedford (Bunyan's hometown) to Jamaica. We then examine how, in Jamaica, different Bunyan traditions arose around black Baptist preachers, slaves, and British Baptists. Finally, we examine Fuller's mission experience in West Africa and how he used his Jamaican Bunyan inheritance, not so much among converts (a subject on which there is little information) but among his colleagues.

The Pilgrim's Progress was written in the wake of the collapse of the English Revolution. In a climate of renewed persecution against Dissenters, Bunyan was jailed for illegal preaching and most of the text was produced in prison. The first part of the book appeared in 1678 (the second in 1684) and immediately found favor among the poor and religiously persecuted. Many of these Dissenters fled (or were transported) to New England and the popular Bunyan text went with them. As a Puritan classic, it was strongly woven into the secular and spiritual lives of the early settlers.[56]

In the three decades after the American War of Independence, the text widened its reach, courtesy of popular evangelized versions of Christianity. From these demotic religious sites, evangelical ideas (and Bunyan as part of them) seeped into slave Christianities. Baptists and Methodists spearheaded this process. Their enthusiastic evangelical style was accessible, and its raptures and spectacles approximated the religious heritage of Africans. One text they often imparted was *The Pilgrim's Progress*, which left an imprint on some of the central metaphors of slave Christianity.[57] Abolitionists, too, took up the text. A book entitled *Pilgrim's Progress in the Last Days* turns Bunyan's story into an abolitionist tract in which Christian is of "dark hue" and is accompanied by a fugitive slave, White-heart.[58]

One feature of early African American Christianity was the figure of the preacher. These men not only played a decisive role in shaping African American Christianity but also established independent congregations and churches.[59] Some of these preachers turned themselves into missionaries and took on the task of spreading a distinctively black Christianity. One such person was George Liele, a slave who capitalized on the disruptions of the Revolutionary War to establish a separate black Baptist church in Silver Bluff, South Carolina.[60] During the War, Liele, like many other slaves, fought for the British. After the war, Liele was freed by his owner Henry Sharp but then reenslaved by Sharp's family. He managed to free himself again and made his way to Jamaica in 1782 with his wife and four children. In Kingston, he started preaching and soon attracted hundreds of converts.[61] Liele was joined by two other African American ex-slaves, Moses Baker and George Gibbs, who subsequently set up their own churches.[62] At the request of Liele and other church leaders, an invitation was issued in 1803 to the BMS to send envoys to assist the church. BMS representatives finally arrived in 1814 to find a black-initiated religious movement, eight thousand strong.[63]

Liele was a reader of Bunyan.[64] It also seems that he may have used Bunyan as a source for instructing his congregants.[65] His interest in Bunyan is hardly surprising for a Baptist, but the parallels in their lives may also have sparked Liele's curiosity. Both were Dissenters laboring under Established Church rule; both fell foul of a ban on unauthorized preaching; and both were imprisoned. Contemporary descriptions of Liele's incarceration in 1794 could have come directly from Bunyan's trial. Liele was arraigned for "uttering dangerous and seditious words." One extant report observed: "He was charged with preaching sedition, and was cast into prison and put in irons."[66]

However, Liele was not only a Dissenter but also black, and so suffered compounded oppressions. In addition to being arraigned for illegal preaching, he was imprisoned for preaching to slaves. He was also persecuted as a black intellectual in a white slave-holding society. His colleague, George Gibb, was likewise imprisoned. "He was once thrown into Spanish Town jail, and confined there for four days, for having been caught teaching the slaves. He was many times found on estates at night, and cast into the dungeon, and his feet placed in the bilboes, for having dared to enter into a negro house to teach those by night to whom he could not have access by day."[67]

In this black Baptist context, Bunyan's story offered preachers a model of maintaining faith under conditions of persecution. The narrative could easily be "doubled" so that it encompassed both a religious and a political message. As Christopher Hill has frequently pointed out, the text can be read not only as an evangelical drama of redemption from sin but also as a story about redemption from feudal slavery.[68] Christian, we learn, is subject to a tyrannical lord, Apollyon, who ruthlessly exploits his laborers. Christian has fled his service and pledges himself as a follower of a new humane master, Jesus. Apollyon, figured as a fearful monster, confronts Christian, who refuses to return to his oppressive service. A fight ensues, with Christian finally putting Apollyon to flight. In a Jamaican context, where Christian was probably read as a black character, such scenes would have allowed readers to interpret *The Pilgrim's Progress* as an allegory on the burdens of religious persecution of black Dissenters in the Caribbean, as well as an allegory about the burdens of slavery.

The British Baptists who arrived from 1814 were ardent Bunyan fans. Bunyan had long been scripted into their denominational traditions and, of all Nonconformists, they were the most active propagators of *The Pilgrim's Progress*. The British Baptists who traveled to Jamaica were also abolitionists, and so would have been sympathetic to the interpretations of Bunyan evolved by Liele and other preachers. A black Baptist reading of Bunyan, which stressed a double salvation from the bondage of both sin and slavery, would have made sense to them.[69] However, at the same time, the British Baptists differed in theological orientation from their black Baptist colleagues. Both groups were nominally evangelical but came out of very different traditions. The black Baptists laid great stress on spiritual experience and charismatic gifts. The British Baptists emphasized conversion and pastoral guidance.[70] These were also the themes they liked to extract from Bunyan. Bunyan's autobiography and *The Pilgrim's Progress* offered a model of what an evangelical conversion should be. Its ingredients were a great awareness of sin, and an emotional conversion followed by close contact with a pastor. In Bunyan's own life, this figure was the preacher John Gifford and, in *The Pilgrim's Progress*, the character Evangelist takes on this role. The autobiographical writings of James Mursell Phillipo, an important British Baptist figure in Jamaica and a teacher of Fuller, exemplify this British Baptist understanding of Bunyan. Phillipo's life story commences with an account of his conversion that is prefigured by a terrible sense of sin. He decides to join the Baptist church and then experiences a profound moment of conversion, which he describes through language drawn from *The Pilgrim's Progress*.[71] For black Baptists, conversion did not have to take this form. Instead, dreams, visions, or spiritual visitations could all betoken conversion that, furthermore, did not have to be mediated through a trained minister.[72] For British Baptists, however, Bunyan offered the "recipe" for guided evangelical conversion, and they propagated these views systematically from their churches and schools.

Such debates about Bunyan were, of course, open only to those who could read the text in considerable and careful detail. Slaves were seldom permitted to acquire any literacy and so would not have read the text. But, from both British and Jamaican Baptist preachers, they would have heard fragments of the story, and a few of these made their way into popular slave religious practice. The contours of this religion, as others have shown, were strongly gnostic, and religious experience was primarily about spiritual encounters and mystical revelation.[73] Dreams and visions were highly prized and came direct to the believer rather than being mediated via a minister or a written text. As Edward Brathwaite and others have shown, this creole Christianity was indebted to African notions of spiritual life that stressed spirit-contact and possession rather than "worship" in the European Christian sense.[74]

In the records of Jamaican slave Christianity, the Bunyan remnants are noticeable. Some of these are, no doubt, random phenomena. Take, for example, the case of a dream reported by a slave from the north of the island. In this dream, he found himself sitting under a tree with a heavy basket at his feet. A white man approached him and bade him pick up the load and follow. They proceeded until they came to a large hole and the guide told the dreamer to cast the basket into the hole.[75] This dream fragment is reminiscent of *The Pilgrim's Progress*. Christian carries a load, he meets a stranger who directs him on his way and eventually his burden rolls into a large hole when he confronts the cross. In evangelical terms, this episode makes up the core of the story. The dreamer can hardly have been aware of this but he may have encountered versions of this key piece of Bunyan via the black Baptist network (or "Black Family," as it was sometimes known).[76]

Other uses of fragments from *The Pilgrim's Progress* appear to be more purposive. Most notable in this regard is the idea of the "passport to heaven."[77] In this practice, tickets were given out by local Baptist leaders to their group members to vouch that they were suitably prepared for important church rituals. These pieces of paper were known as "passports to heaven" and, in some cases, slaves were buried clasping their tickets.[78] The origins of this practice have been located in two spheres. First, as Philip Curtin has indicated, the piece of paper is subject to African creole religious beliefs and is treated as a sacred object or "fetish" that can compel spiritual events: in this case, causing the gates of heaven to open.[79] Second, documents in slave societies were a key part of the apparatus of ruling and were used to control the movement of slaves who had, for example, to carry a permissory letter to travel. Consequently, the idea of entry to a venue of power being conditional on a piece of paper would have accorded with slaves' everyday experiences. To these two explanations, we can add a third that concerns the final scenes of *The Pilgrim's Progress*, part 1. Here Christian and Hopeful arrive at the gates of heaven and are asked for their "certificates." After these are scrutinized, the two characters are admitted to paradise. Those without certificates, like the character Ignorance, go straight to hell.

Slave ideas of "passports to heaven" share parallels with this scene, which must have been one tributary for the notion, either via oral retellings of the story or possibly through illustrations.[80] The scene further provides "proof" of the idea, particularly as it comes from a text that

carried almost as much authority as the Bible. The episode also dramatizes a creolized view of literacy and of documents that draws together
"African" and "European" understandings. In "African" terms, the documents in the scene function as magical and protective tokens and so
embody "African" notions of spiritual power. But, at the same time, the
documents also appear to be part of a bureaucratic apparatus of slave-
owner rule and so encapsulate the power of the slave-owning state. The
piece of paper, then, represents a portfolio of power in which its holder
might share. As we shall see in chapter 6, African readers, too, often
singled out this scene and for broadly similar reasons. Both communities
of interpreters were, in effect, formulating a diasporic mode of reading
Bunyan. In this hermeneutic practice, parts of the text were extracted and
then used as a template to analyze situations of great inequality with a
view to understanding the nature of power at work in these contexts.

In Jamaica, then, *The Pilgrim's Progress* arrived from the Baptist
American South already shaped as a book about black experience. In its
new context, the text was further "baptized" in the currents of Caribbean
intellectual traditions. Among slaves, usable bits of Bunyan were resitu-
ated in the landscapes of popular spiritual religion and redemption.
Preachers, drawing on experiences in the American South and Jamaica,
elaborated a reading of the text in which notions of redemption carried
both a political and evangelical meaning. British Baptists expounded a
similar reading, but, because of their denominational history, strongly
underlined Bunyan's evangelicalism.

These particular traditions of Bunyan that swirled together in
Jamaica were to take yet a further journey, this time as part of the post-
emancipation West Indian missionary contingent to West Africa.[81] This
movement was inspired by the belief that "Africa must be civilized by
Africans" and that those who had African ancestors would be less prone
to the diseases and fevers of the continent. One of the first Jamaicans to
join the venture was Alexander McCloud Fuller and, at his express be-
hest, his son, Joseph Jackson, also joined the mission in 1844.

The mission was destined for failure. Recruited in evangelical
haste, poorly trained, demeaningly supervised by white missionaries, re-
sented by coastal chiefs seeking white British agents, and ravaged by ma-
laria, the Jamaicans mostly left the continent after only a few years. Fuller
persevered, working initially under the mentorship of another Jamaican,
Richard Merrick, who died in 1849, only five years after Fuller's arrival.[82]
Like many missionaries, Fuller passed through trials—he lost a wife and
two children, his house was attacked, he suffered from all manner of

illness. Yet, as a black missionary, he experienced additional burdens. Unlike his white colleagues, he had only restricted rights to furlough and in forty-five years had just two such breaks. He had to live the life of an "example" to Africans—a black man living with one wife. He had to occupy the ambiguous terrain of the black Jamaican missionary in Africa. As one missionary observed, "The natives . . . are natives, and the Europeans are Europeans; but those from Jamaica are neither."[83] These conditions notwithstanding, Fuller was one of the very few to remain behind. He built up a successful mission and worked there until 1888, when the Germans seized the Cameroon and his station was handed over to the Basel Mission. He left the Cameroon privately heart-broken ("the pain of leaving a life's work I can scarcely d[e]scribe") but publicly conciliatory ("He who ruleth on high knows that which is best for his children").[84]

Part of Fuller's work included translation, and he "converted" Bunyan into two languages, Isubu and Duala. We know little about these translations or how they were received. Available evidence does suggest, that in some respects, Fuller presented his translation in an orthodox evangelical vein. The introduction to the Duala translation (1885) expresses the hope that the text "will tend to expand [converts'] knowledge of the Christian religion so different from their former superstition."[85] At the time of doing the Duala translation, the only book available in the language was the "Holy Scriptures," and so, in selecting Bunyan, Fuller was again making a standard evangelical choice.

Because evidence on Fuller's translations is limited, it does not allow us detailed insight into whether he carried forward any "Jamaican" inflections of the text. We do know, however, that Fuller defined his mission vocation from a West Indian perspective and felt that he had a particular calling to return to Africa: "God intends that Africa, which has long had to bear the burdens of oppressions of all nations, shall take her place among the children of men."[86] He saw himself as an agent carrying "messages of love and salvation to those . . . in our fatherland who had been so long held in bondage of sin."[87]

As an evangelical Jamaican Baptist, Fuller would almost certainly have seen Bunyan as one of the "messages" that he was carrying to Africa, and he was indeed very proud of his translations, which feature in his autobiography and his obituary.[88] As a Jamaican, he had inherited traditions of the text in which characters changed race and nationality, transmuting from seventeenth-century English folk to African American and then Caribbean slaves. His Cameroonian translations of Bunyan may have aimed for a similar outcome in which his Duala Baptist converts could read the text as a story about themselves and their struggles. Such a translation strategy would, of course, unmoor traditional conceptions of Bunyan as a "white" writer telling a "white" story. Freed of its moorings, the text could become a zone of experimentation in which identities ("Jamaican," "Cameroonian," "slave," "free," "black," "white," "African," "European," and so on) could be "tried out" and shifted around.

Seen in this way, *The Pilgrim's Progress* could become a surprisingly useful resource for negotiating the contradictions of being a black missionary in a white world. In a situation where missionaries were generally white and converts black, the position of the black missionary was ambiguous. One BMS strategy for managing this topsy-turvy environment was a particular politics of the public and the private. In terms of this tactic, black missionaries were treated as "white" in public and "black" in private. In an obituary of S. C. Gordon, a Jamaican missionary in the Congo, one of his colleagues said: "[Those who dealt with him] forgot his colour, and indeed, in the best and highest sense of the word, he was to his colleagues, as well as to officials and others, a 'white man.'"[8] [9] In private, white missionaries at times expressed different opinions, railing against their colleagues, who became redefined as "black." G. K. Prince, a leader of the Jamaican mission to the Cameroon, referred in private correspondence to the West Indians as "spots and canker worms to the Society."[90]

Another type of response was for white missionaries to position themselves as "black." Fuller, in fact, witnessed such an episode at close range, when in 1859 a dispute arose between a hotheaded new recruit, Alexander Innis, and Alfred Saker, the senior missionary in the Cameroon. Seeking to position himself as the "quasi-black" "friend of the native," the working-class Innis accused Saker of violently assaulting African converts. In order to try and gain support, Innis wanted Fuller to come out publicly as a black missionary supporting a white colleague (Innis) against another white colleague (Saker), all on behalf of "helpless" African converts crying out for Innis's protection. Fuller demurred. In his reading of matters, the home committee would brush the event aside, saying, "'Oh, it's only th[at] black fellow again.'" Innis was dismissed from the BMS and made something of a minor career retailing the Saker saga in public forums. In later years, he attacked Fuller by playing the "class card," dubbing him "the black doll of the society . . . acting the gentleman in London and other places."[91]

In this world of perilously rotating identities, Fuller mostly held his tongue. In public, he remained intensely loyal to the BMS and generally only raised criticism in private. He did, however, evolve some techniques for expressing dissent publicly and these drew on the "Jamaican-Bunyan" method of inverting identities and shifting roles. An opportunity arose for Fuller to employ this strategy at an international Protestant mission conference in 1888. Here he made an intervention from the floor concerning current soap advertising:

> It is said that Fuller's soap whitens, but I believe you have tried to compete with Fuller's soap in adopting Pear's soap. I have seen it put up at places that Pear's soap can make the dark skinned African white, but if they try it on me it would be labour in vain, for they would not make me a bit whiter than I am.[92]

Fuller was referring, of course, to a style of imperial soap advertisements in which black characters wash off their "color" to reveal a white skin underneath. This set of images in turn drew on a long-established tradition of European iconography of "washing the blackamoor white." The idea itself comes originally from Jeremiah 13:23 ("Can the Ethiopian change his skin, or the leopard his spots? Then may ye also do good that are accustomed to do evil?") and betokens any vain or impossible labor.[93]

Those in the audience who knew their Bunyan well would also have recognized a reference to *The Pilgrim's Progress*, part 2. Here, in a brief scene, we see two characters, Fool and Want-wit, washing an Ethiopian in an attempt to make him white. The more they wash, the blacker he becomes. Whereas much scholarship on *The Pilgrim's Progress* pays close attention to seventeenth-century contextual detail, relating many aspects of the book to the world from which Bunyan came, this episode has not been read to see what it can tell us about contemporary attitudes to race. Where there has been comment, it has restricted itself to allegorical interpretations, and the episode has been glossed as representing a vain attempt to give a bad person a good name (and hence any hypocritical endeavor).[94] As a nineteenth-century abridged version of the story puts it, "Thus shall it be with all who pretend to be what they are not."[95]

It is, of course, difficult to assign one meaning to what Fuller intended with his comments. He may in part have been playing "the black doll" of the mission world, by making what the audience would see as a humorous intervention. Yet, at the same time, the piece is riven with ambiguity as Fuller experiments with racial identities like counters on a board. If, for example, Fuller in fact is "white," then his "white" colleagues must be "black." They consequently need "whitening" by means of Fuller's soap, that is, by Fuller himself. Fuller, then, becomes the "whitening" agent of the Protestant mission world. Why its "whites" may need "whitening" was made explicit by Fuller in a subsequent intervention that he made at the conference. "Brethren," he said, "the oppression and cruelties that Africa has suffered call for your sympathies; and as you have helped in her ruin in bygone days, now is the time to try and lift her from the depths to which she has been brought."[96] To continue in Fuller's terms, "whites" have a "black" history that needs "whitening" by an "Ethiopian." The roles of "washer" and "washed," "clean" and "dirty" need to be reassigned if Africa is to be redeemed.

To translate this back into *The Pilgrim's Progress*, the "Ethiopian" in the text should become "white" and the "white" characters "black." This shift is what translations like Fuller's precipitated. In these texts, characters generally acquired African names and at times appeared in Africanized illustrations. In pageants, performances, and illustrations, the book's "white" characters could be played (or represented) by black performers and so become "black." Such possibilities sharpened questions around one of the central contradictions of the mission enterprise, namely claims of belonging based on conversion as opposed to those based on race. In theory, evangelical Protestantism promised equality to all who converted, irrespective of background (or, in Paul's words, "There is neither Greek nor Jew, there is neither bond nor free, there is neither male nor female." Galatians 3:28). In practice, as aggressive forms of social Darwinism "bit" into mission thinking, boundaries of privilege were increasingly racialized. Once translated, *The Pilgrim's Progress* dramatized these concerns in vivid ways. Was this a story only about white British Protestants or could it become a story about all Protestants? If characters became African (in illustration, dramatic performance, and translated language) was Bunyan still "white"? These questions came to matter a great deal, particularly in the latter quarter of the nineteenth century when the emerging English literature lobby set out to claim Bunyan as a symbol of white Englishness, both at home and abroad. Having crossed the boundary of race, *The Pilgrim's Progress* raised profound questions about where to draw boundaries in the mission imperial domain. Bunyan was not only a story about white Britons. It was a story for all Protestants.

Through his translations, Fuller played a role in this democratizing process. His Jamaican background had prepared him for the task, equipping him with a version of Bunyan that had already been broadened in the black Atlantic.[97] As we shall see in chapter 10, it was a boundary that those associated with the emergence of English literature sought to roll back. For these intellectuals, one of the major tasks of English literature was to provide a marker of racial and cultural distinctiveness for those in the empire. "Having" or "owning" English literature consequently became a sign of whiteness. Bunyan, who had been democratized in the black Atlantic, unsettled this picture considerably and so had to be "reeled in" and brought "home" where he could once again become unequivocally "white."

4

Mata's Hermeneutic
Internationally Made Ways of Reading Bunyan

In the days leading up to her death in 1923, Emily Lewis (third wife of Thomas Lewis) spoke often of *The Pilgrim's Progress*. Her funeral was held at the Camden Road Chapel and, in the oration, Rev. George Hawker told the congregation how, on her deathbed, Emily alluded to her favorite portion of the story—Christiana in the Land of Beulah. She spoke of "how the allegory . . . accorded with her own experience."[1]

This section invoked by Emily comes toward the end of the second part of the book. Beulah Land borders on heaven and acts as a celestial waiting room. Here faithful pilgrims at the end of their journeys recuperate before being summoned by a heavenly postal service to cross the River of Death. We receive detailed reports of how eight pilgrims in turn are called, we hear their last words and wishes, and then we witness each person crossing the River in their own trademark style: some pause midstream to issue last instructions, some cross over in a flash, some wade through singing, some require a helping hand, and some discover stepping stones that see them to the other side.

In invoking Beulah Land on her deathbed, Emily Lewis was practicing the well-developed art of Nonconformist dying. As the moment around which Protestant belief is arranged, Nonconformists not only invested time preparing themselves for death but also choreographed the details of their own departure. Believers were urged to think about which books they would have by their deathbed and which people they would summon.[2] *The Pilgrim's Progress* was recommended as "a book to live and die upon."[3] One nineteenth-century commentary observed: "the descriptions of the pilgrims' crossing the river are full of instruction and comfort for dying believers, and have been helpful to many in looking forward to a dying day."[4] The language of the final scene—"receiving a summons from Beulah Land"—had also entrenched itself as a euphemistic discourse for dying.[5]

Like many Nonconformist women, Emily chose to invoke the second half of the book and so to compare herself and her life to the pilgrimage of Christiana. There has, of course, been much debate on the gender meaning of Bunyan's text.[6] Much contemporary opinion maintains that the story of Christiana offers women only circumscribed forms of spiritual authority. The first half of the story concerns Christian and narrates his epic struggle for religious truth and interpretive authority, defined as men's business. The second half tells a story of community and church within which women must take their obedient places. This view is quite possibly one that Emily Lewis (a good Baptist woman) endorsed. But she might simultaneously have entertained other readings of the story as well. Perhaps Christiana's travels became a way of summarizing Emily's time as a missionary along with husband Thomas in northern Angola. Perhaps, like other Nonconformist women, she also identified strongly with Christiana's companion, the knight Great-heart, who defends the party against dragons, giants, and hobgoblins. Like some of her later Nonconformist female colleagues, she may have dreamed of herself becoming "Woman Greatheart" (the name of a Methodist pageant).[7] Similarly, she might have admired Great-heart and Christiana for their platonic yet intimate relationship and, like others, construed it as a model of marriage in which women commanded chivalrous respect.

Whatever Emily Lewis thought of these matters, it is clear that the story—both in life and death—offered her a way of talking about the delicate and unspoken dimensions of her life. Many other Protestants applied the text to their lives in similar ways, and throughout the nineteenth century, as we have seen, Nonconformists used the book's allegorical dimension to put their personal spiritual feelings into words. A Scottish pastor reported that his congregants conscripted the language of Bunyan to "give expression to their personal Christian experience." One man, suffering from doubt and despair declared, "*I* am the man in the iron cage." He refers to the well-known tableau that Christian observes in the Interpreter's House. Here Christian sees a sighing figure, eyes downcast, sitting in an iron cage. Christian engages the man in conversation and learns that he is a "man of despair," unable to flee his cage. He once had faith and was a devout believer. However, he turned to a licentious life and was then rejected by God. In comparing himself to this image, the Scottish congregant taps into an accessible field of reference and finds a way of talking about his depression and doubt, while possibly hinting at some unsavory episodes in his past life. Another of the Scottish minister's flock underwent a dangerous operation that might have robbed her of her speech. After the operation, the pastor visited her in hospital. Turning to him, she whispered, "The jewels are all safe!" Her phrase refers to a scene in which the character Little Faith is robbed. The assailants make off with his spending money but fail to find his jewels—his belief in Christ. The woman in hospital uses the image to signal that both her voice and her faith have survived the operation.[8]

Like this woman, many readers wove the text into the inner recesses of their lives. They were able to do this by summoning up a widely shared and deep knowledge of the text. This implicit understanding hung like a backdrop to much Nonconformist discourse and could easily be activated through a phrase or name from the text. Such words could in turn ignite a moment of becoming a Bunyan character like Christiana in Beulah Land, or the Man in the Iron Cage.

This method of reading in which one likened oneself to a character was not only found on Camden Road. The case of Mata, a Kongo-speaker and head porter for the BMS at San Salvador provides an instructive example. His association with the mission society dated back to the earliest arrival of the BMS in the Kongo Kingdom in the 1870s and Mata accompanied Baptist notables on their initial itinerations. He also led many of the "pioneering" BMS explorations into the interior, including the dash to "discover" the Stanley Pools in 1881, where they earned second prize (the French explorer, de Brazza came in first; the BMS, second; and the much ballyhooed Stanley—ultimately the eponymous winner—traipsed in third).[9] In July 1899, Thomas Lewis asked Mata to act as head porter for an expedition to Zombo, a highland region seventy miles east of the Kongo Kingdom. During the journey, the party encountered difficult terrain. Thomas Lewis explains:

> Our troubles increased considerably when we got into a swamp
> . . . all of us made many slips and disappeared over our heads
> in the muddy water. There were plenty of papyrus to cling to,
> so we were all able to draw ourselves in eel-like fashion to a
> place of safety. At one point, just as I was reappearing after a
> slip into the mud, I saw Mata, who was supposed to help me,
> standing on a tuft of papyrus laughing as if it were great fun.
> He wanted to know from me if this was Christian's 'Slough of

Despond'! He had only just emerged from a dip himself, and his face was all slime, and he named himself 'Pliable,' which was far from being true. After about two and a half hours we got out of the mire 'on that side which was farther from our own house,' and looked in vain for the man who carried our dry clothes.[10]

In this passage, Mata interprets Bunyan's text by comparing himself to one of its characters, Pliable, a neighbor of Christian. With his associate Obstinate, Pliable initially tries to dissuade Christian from setting out on his journey. Pliable, is however, won over by Christian's determination and, along with Obstinate, accompanies the protagonist briefly on his journey until they both stumble into the Slough of Despond. A disgusted Pliable berates Christian for misleading him, scrambles out of the bog, and heads for home leaving Christian to press on to the bank "on that side of the Slough that was still farther from his own house."[11]

Emily and Mata, then, both employ similar textual strategies that involve likening themselves to characters in the story. How might we figure the relationship between their two reading methods? Are they the same thing in that Emily's is the "original" practice and Mata's the "belated" copy (despite being chronologically prior)? Or, to put it in more contemporary terms, does Mata "subvert" or "rewrite" Emily's original? Indeed, are these terms even useful? Might the relationship between these two reading strategies not be more interesting than these tired scenarios suggest? Might these two intellectual strategies not be more unpredictably wrought in the tangled web of the Congo and Camden Road?

One may argue that the Baptist missionaries were the most powerful players, and it is consequently their methods of reading that prevail. This sense of mission prerogative, for example, is apparent in Lewis's extract about Mata as Pliable, an anecdote that exemplifies a set of standard mission conceits for portraying the "gauche" convert. The reader back home is provided with a familiar point of reference—*The Pilgrim's Progress*—and shown a naive but sincere convert striving to use the text. Thomas Lewis—as knowing missionary—winks at his metropolitan audience who chuckle indulgently at Mata's childish comparisons while admiring Lewis's level-headedness. The clownish convert plays foil to the missionary's sturdy good sense.

One response to such episodes is to dismiss them as so much mission ballyhoo. Indeed, how do we even know that Mata in fact said what Lewis claimed? Lewis, it seems, scripts the scene on his own terms. He has "voice" and Mata has none. Lewis writes the story. Mata, the head porter, carries the burden. There is little more to say on the matter.

Yet, if we look beyond this immediate extract, the picture becomes more intricate. Comparing oneself to Bunyan characters was something of a pastime among porters on such trips. Elsewhere in this text, Lewis tells us of a guide who led the party miles out of the way.[12] The porters on the expedition named him Mr. Talkative, no doubt because like his counterpart in *The Pilgrim's Progress*, he too misled people. The porters and Mata, then, were not averse to entertaining themselves by "trying on" different characters.

It was a game of deceptive simplicity. Take, for instance, Mata's self-comparison with the character Pliable. On one level, the comment could be quite straightforward. Pliable is the character who, along with Christian, sinks into the Slough of Despond. Likewise, Lewis and Mata stumble into a swamp and Mata may simply have been trying to make light of a tense moment. Yet, the original episode in *The Pilgrim's Progress* presents a number of complications. Pliable, as we mentioned earlier, is someone who has been persuaded against his better judgment to undertake a difficult journey. The expedition to Zombo—to establish a new mission—was exceedingly dangerous. Zombo had for centuries been a slave-raiding zone for the Kongo Kingdom. A party coming from that kingdom would not be well received. If it included men in trousers, who would be taken as Portuguese or Arab, fears of slave-raiding would only increase and the party would be unlikely to survive. Indeed, the first time Lewis set off for Zombo in June 1898, Mata flatly refused to go. Only after Lewis threatened to replace him as head porter did he reluctantly agree. As matters turned out, everyone survived the first expedition. A second was undertaken in July 1899 and it is from this journey that Lewis's swamp episode comes.[13] Both journeys were exploratory trips with a view to establishing a new mission at Quibocolo that Lewis ultimately headed. The mission proved to be less than a success and by 1912 had enrolled only ten converts.[14]

Mata's comparison can be read, then, on various levels. Most obviously, it diffuses a number of tensions by acknowledging everyone's folly—beginning with his own. Like Pliable in the text, he tries to persuade the protagonist not to undertake an apparently suicidal mission. However, as matters turn out in *The Pilgrim's Progress*, Christian is, of course, right and achieves his goal. Like Pliable, Mata thought Lewis would not succeed in his expedition and, like Pliable, he was wrong. But at the same time, by taking on the role of someone who warned against over-hasty ventures, Mata comments on Lewis's pigheadedness in pursuing a mission venture that could never work. Anticipating many twentieth-century critics, Mata's comparisons raise questions around who the hero of the text really is. Christian is nominally the "hero" in so far as he is the main character. But as critics have suggested, he is a "wobbly" protagonist.[15] Right up until the very end, he is prone to being led astray and could backslide at any moment. He needs constant guidance and propping up from stronger and more experienced characters like Evangelist and Interpreter. Like other African Christians, Mata uses *The Pilgrim's Progress* to question the distribution of spiritual authority in mission stations. Is Lewis really the hero? Does he really know where he is going? Also, if Lewis is Christian, then who is Evangelist? Who, in the mission venture, is guiding whom? This question became ever more pressing on the Zombo expedition, where, from existing accounts, it is clear that Mata did much of the negotiating and proselytizing.[16]

So far, of course, Mata's reading strategy is indistinguishable from Emily's or Fuller's, which we examined in the previous chapter. In all instances, the text becomes a kind of checker-board. On it, one could "try on" different characters and take up different positions. This method of teaching Bunyan—and indeed other texts—was widely used in Protestant mission stations. Although not set in Africa, this description of using Bunyan slides in Palestine/Lebanon in 1899 gives an insight into how converts or would-be converts were encouraged to think of themselves as characters in Bunyan's story:

> the schoolroom was packed full of people, men, women and children. . . . Our catechist . . . explained the pictures and brought out the story of redemption very well. A few days later we went to Zaneb [a Druze girl of twelve] and she was full of the pictures. Those of Christian seem specially to have struck her. His burden, the losing of it at the cross and his crossing the river were her chief favourites. . . . It was now quite easy to tell her to put herself in Christian's place and her burden would fall off too, and so on. [After a second showing] the impress of the first night was deepened and in subsequent visits she often alluded to Christian's experience.[17]

Closely allied to illustration was the role of pageant, tableau, and performance, a form routinely used on missions. Productions of *The Pilgrim's Progress* were common and, in these, students acted out the story and thus briefly became the characters.[18] These tableau-like forms often functioned like living illustrations and possibly furnished a forum where participants began to think of creating Africanized illustrations for the text. As we shall see in chapter 8, in two cases these illustrations took the form of photographs in which prominent members of the mission took the parts of the characters in the text. To a local audience, these individuals had quite literally "become" the characters in the text. As chapter 8 discusses, such conjunctures opened up new possibilities for reading the text as a "biography" of those appearing in its illustration.

A further factor promoting this method of reading was the ways in which the text was fractally reproduced, as we have seen, in media like magic lantern slides, wallcharts (figure 8), postcards (figure 7), and pageants,[19] a method in turn made possible by the episodic and hence friable nature of the text. Like many allegories, the relationship between scenes in *The Pilgrim's Progress* is not strongly causal or driven by "normal" rules of plausibility.[20] There is, of course, the overarching framework of the journey, but this simply acts as a backdrop to a series of episodes, many of which could be extracted, as mission forms of teaching the text showed, and disseminated as freestanding items. Part of the missionaries' strategy was no doubt to reassemble these units at some later point, and they were clear on how the scenes related to each other. For them, the "string" on which these various "beads" could be threaded was the stages of Christian spiritual experience and growth. This point is illustrated by an account from an LMS missionary, David Carnegie, who describes how he taught the text to a class of Ndebele enquirers in present-day Zimbabwe:

> Some fourteen anxious inquirers came forward of their own accord asking me to explain to them the way of salvation. I formed them into a class, which, with one or two exceptions, has been going on ever since. . . . *The Pilgrim's Progress* has been my text book, and a more suitable one I think could not be found for giving these people a clear conception of what the Christian life really means. The whole outline of the book, with its simple illustrations, has been more or less explained to my class, and we hope the words of wisdom and power have touched some of their hearts. We have had over four months at this work weekly, and it does my heart good to see how one or two of them appreciate and understand my explanations of the various stages of progress in the Christian life.[21]

From this description, it is clear that Carnegie taught the book in weekly "rehearsals" using illustrations to "summarize" the various episodes in the story. (These classes were done in Ndebele at the time Carnegie was completing a translation of the text with his wife and assistant. These class discussions no doubt helped to suggest at least some phrases and forms of discourse for the final version.) Carnegie is very clear on how these various episodes hang together: they are to be collated as "the various stages of progress in the Christian life." However, there is no guarantee that this is how the enquirers saw them. They could have extracted individual episodes that interested them, particularly since the story was related orally. In local oral narrative traditions, episodes can be shifted from one story to another or added and subtracted (rather, in fact, as Bunyan himself did in his various versions of the text).[22] Given that, in this case, The Pilgrim's Progress appears to be the very first Christian text they encounter in the mission, they might have regarded it as important enough to preserve the original sequence that Carnegie set out. Yet, whatever the case, Carnegie's method of teaching encouraged his inquirers to see themselves as characters, either in the whole story or in its parts.

This mode of "being someone else" was an interpretive technique that characterized much teaching on evangelical mission stations. That Mata derived his reading techniques from such mission teaching is beyond doubt. Mata had had contact with missionaries since the late 1870s and, although the Kongo Pilgrim's Progress only appeared in print in April 1897 (two years before the expedition), parts of the book were disseminated verbally and "rehearsed" by means of magic lantern slides, sermons, Sunday school classes, choir services, and the like.[23] The Kongo Protestant community was small and close knit, so Mata would undoubtedly have encountered the story.

Yet, at the same time, there were other sources of interpretation on which Mata drew. His primary interpretive community would have been other Kongo Protestants, who, as the scholar Mpiku has shown, evolved their own reading strategies.[24] These, as Mpiku argues, entailed formulating novel ways of reading on the back of traditional literary techniques. One strategy was to "embezzle" (détourner) the oral story or "folktale" (nsamu or kimpa) by "extorting" or "extracting" (tirer) a new Christian message or meaning from the tale.[25] Mpiku cites the following story as an example of this method. A father sends his four sons to hunt and demands that they bring back many birds. The first two sons construct their traps badly and return empty handed to the village. The third son works diligently and shrewdly and catches many birds while the fourth son whistles away his time. The father rewards the third son and punishes the rest. Traditionally, the story was taken to underline the need for filial obedience and reward for personal attainment. Pauli Dikoko, a member of the Swedish Mission (on the north bank of the Congo River and about sixty miles from San Salvador), reworked this story for the mission station periodical *Minsamu Miayenga* by attaching new meanings to the anecdote. In his view, the father stands for God; the forest where the sons hunt represents the assembly of nations that have already been evangelized; the third son is the evangelist who accomplishes his task by following God's commandments; the other brothers are those who reject their pastoral calling.[26]

Another Protestant convert, Davidi Malangidila similarly "embezzled" a story, "The Slaves who Became Apes." In this tale, a group of slaves, seeking to escape their perpetual suffering transpose themselves from a human to an animal species and become apes. In terms of the story's traditional moral economy, this switch is seen to be cowardly since the slaves run away from, rather than face up to, their difficulties. For Malangidila, however, the story carries a different meaning. In his view, the slaves represent Christians who have fled Satan's world in order to seek shelter in God's kingdom.[27]

Mission periodicals printed such traditional stories but with their new Christian exegeses appended. A well-known proverb separated the story from its explanation: "If you use a proverb, you must be able to explain it."[28] With this proverb, the Kongo Protestants proclaim the superiority of their new Christian analogical method. The interpretation that follows after the proverb is a demonstration that those who have "spoken" or written the story can explain it properly. The proverb, relying on indirection, can also politely imply that non-Protestant practitioners tell stories but cannot explain them properly or systematically.

In using such methods of "the Congo parable" (as such stories became known in English mission discourse),[29] these early evangelists weave together the "folktale" and the proverb and redirect their value and power toward a new enterprise. They also did much the same with the dream. Dreams had always been popular and were interpreted as predictions of future events. Kongo catechists began collecting, writing down, and publishing records of dreams in mission periodicals. These were then explicated as Christian allegorical visions in which each element in the dream was linked analogically to some aspect of Christian belief.[30]

The new Kongo Protestant interpretive matrix is made from grafting together the "folktale," the parable, the dream, and the proverb.

In so doing, several intellectual fields are aligned in new ways and generic boundaries are redrawn. The "folktale" and the Bible, for example, become intellectual neighbors, both sources of hidden meaning that can be revealed by using the same method of interpretation in which stories are extrapolated in a parable-like fashion. Both sets of texts ("folktale" and Bible) are applied in the same way and their shared methods of interpretation confer on them a kinship. This idea of approaching the Bible through "folktale" is, of course, very Bunyanesque. As much criticism has shown, Bunyan, prior to his conversion, was an ardent consumer of ballad, popular narrative, and folktale. *The Pilgrim's Progress* is consequently a mixture of romance and biblical form in which the latter "disciplines" the former. Harold Golder has demonstrated this point in relation to the episode of Giant Despair in which Christian and Hopeful trespass on the Giant's land and are imprisoned.[31] In this episode, Bunyan takes several folktale elements (namely the outline of the well-known story, Jack the Giant Killer, and the folktale formula of the two brothers) and freights these with doctrinal "ballast." This doctrine is introduced by means of a series of metaphors associated with religious melancholy. For example, the by-way that leads Christian and Hopeful from the narrow way and into Giant Despair's land betokens a turning aside from the true road into a side road of indulgence. Christian and Hopeful are prevented from returning to the true road by driving rain that mounts into a small flood, a symbol of doubt and despair that at times threaten to overwhelm believers.[32] Through this doctrinal "ballast," Bunyan is able to contain the worldliness of the folktale and turn it toward more spiritually edifying ends.

However, at times, the attempt to import doctrinal issues is not so subtle and, in many instances, Bunyan inserts his "theology" insistently and "raw" into the text. For example, in his discussion with Mr. Talkative, Faithful delivers himself of an extensive lecture on the relationship of faith and works and the conviction of sin as a necessary precondition to salvation.[33] As we have seen in the previous chapter, Kele readers circumvented these dollops of theology and foregrounded the narrative "skeleton" of the story. Under such treatment, the story loses its ideological padding and the narrative bones of the story stand out.

In seeking to expunge the theology, African readers were not necessarily attempting to make Bunyan less religious. Indeed, they could have been doing the opposite. By taking out the theology, they could in fact have been making the book more amenable to religious exegesis. As we have seen for Kongo Protestants, a precondition for religious analysis was a "clean" story with the interpretation happening outside the boundary of the narrative. Attempts, then, to "abridge" the theology, could in fact have originated in this form of exegesis that presupposed an uncluttered story as a necessary prerequisite for hermeneutic investigation. This strategy of interpretation also serves to make the story more allegorical. As Kaufmann has pointed out, *The Pilgrim's Progress* is not consistently allegorical and often breaks out in lengthy "literal-didactic" excursions.[34] It was precisely these sections that the Kele and Kongo Protestants weeded out.

Such interpretive techniques proved to be enduringly and tenaciously popular among Kongo and Kele Protestants. William Millman, who worked at the mission station Yakusu, reported in the early 1900s that he had translated forty of Aesop's fables, but burnt the lot after being questioned by a young man if they were God's word.[35] Millman interpreted the comment as ignorance on the questioner's part, which it could well have been. But it might also have been an interesting generic classification at work in which a fable and the Bible belong together because they both use similar literary and explanatory techniques.

By burning his translations, Millman attempted to withstand popular opinion and taste. Many missionaries of necessity gave in and attempted their own forms of "embezzlement" by colonizing existing African forms. Particularly from the post–First World War period when ideas of "de-Westernizing" Christianity became more widespread, mission thinking and practice produced a rich stream of "mimicry." Jesus, for example, became an "African storyteller."[36] Missionaries became "Christ's medicine men," while Charles Wesley found himself described as an "ancestor in the tribe of Christ."[37] Missionaries received advice on how to make their forms look "old and familiar," or, as another mission commentator said, "There are other ways in which we can be NATIVE. We can learn their proverbs and love their ancient history and bring it into our talks with them."[38] This mimicry came full circle when in the 1950s, BMS missionaries indicated that there was an urgent need for a book of "African Fables with Christian Applications."[39] What they were requesting was "the Congo parable," a genre originally pioneered by Kongo catechists in the nineteenth century. It was a form that Mata had clearly mastered. Just prior to the departure of the second Zombo trip in July 1899, the new church at San Salvador was inaugurated. There were extensive celebrations with many sermons, speeches, eulogies, and prayers. Mata was one of the speakers. After telling a travel story of a previous expedition, he concluded with a number of "Congo parables," which Gwen Lewis found "entirely incomprehensible to Europeans."[40]

Mata, then, practiced different Kongo Protestant reading strategies. One of these involves the "Congo parable" technique in which a folk story is taken (or extracted from other texts) and then subject to Christian exegesis. It is, of course, very similar to the exegesis applied to parables, but its distinctiveness is to subject non-Christian material to this form of interpretation. British Baptists at San Salvador likewise brought with them a range of reading strategies. With regard to *The Pilgrim's Progress*, one of these was an inherently dramatic technique of reading in which one imagines oneself as a character. From the report of the Zombo trip, we know that Mata added this method to his hermeneutic repertoire. We also know that British Baptists were aware of the "Congo parable." Gwen Lewis might initially have found them incomprehensible, but from the early 1900s, the form was being reflected in the *Missionary Herald* and in BMS publications.[41] It was presumably one of the Congo forms that Camden Roaders likewise followed with interest. The Baptist call in the 1950s for a book of "African Fables with Christian Applications" was a belated recognition of the importance and durability of the form. Baptists had finally adopted Mata's hermeneutic as their own.

PART TWO

Bunyan, the Public Sphere, and Africa

5

John Bunyan Luthuli
African Mission Elites and *The Pilgrim's Progress*

In the introduction to his Xhosa translation of *The Pilgrim's Progress*, *Uhambo lo Mhambi* (1868), Tiyo Soga, a missionary of the United Presbyterian Church in the Eastern Cape, in present-day South Africa, begins by welcoming the reader and provides some advice on how to approach the text.

> Folks! Here is a book for you to examine. The book tells the story of a traveler who walks the road which many of you would like to travel. Accompany the traveler whilst slowly trying to make acquaintance with each other—stopping to take rest whilst listening to things the traveler tells and reports to you; move along with the traveler to his destination, the end of his journey.[1]

The advice is fairly specific: take things slowly, do not rush, read carefully and thoughtfully. Stop and think about what you have read. Read all the way through to the end and do not skip anything along the way. Take time to know the main character and become his friend. The advice is recognizably evangelical and instructs the readers on how to place themselves in the text.

Giving advice on how to read was something that Soga did quite often. In 1862 in the editorial of a new newspaper, *Indaba*, he gave specific instructions on how to read the publication.

> Those who have no pocket money should go to the forest and bring home dry wood which will be good as fuel so that the head of the family on newspaper day when the fire-wood is

burning well will lie on his back on the upper side of the hut and place one leg over the other and proceed to open the newspaper saying, 'My family, will you please listen to the news.'[2]

Elsewhere in the editorial he provides further—but more implicit—advice on how to read. He likens the newspaper to a visitor and outstanding conversationalist. He also compares it to a corn-pit that provides nourishment, or a container where treasures and valuable things are kept. Both of these metaphors supply readers with suggestions of how to approach this new medium of communication.

The advice to readers in Soga's introduction to *The Pilgrim's Progress* is likewise multifaceted. Readers are invited to situate themselves in multiple audiences. On the one hand, they are urged to see themselves as part of an international evangelical community while, on the other, being reminded of the text's local application. In terms of the first prerogative, Soga's introduction shares many of the standard features of evangelical editions of Bunyan. We hear, for example, that this book comes second only to the Bible. Like all evangelical editions, this one includes a minibiography of Bunyan ("an artisan who specialized in making buckets") that condenses his experiences as set out in *Grace Abounding to the Chief of Sinners* and traces the arc of his conversion from reprobate sinner ("he sinned as if he wanted to get to the root of all sin") to firm believer. We hear how he becomes a preacher and how he was imprisoned. The reader is informed that "there are many nations that have read this book in their language although these were not known during the lifetime of the author." The reader joins an international community marked by their belief in the word of God and their friendship with John Bunyan: "In all the nations through which the word of God has found its way, there is no place where John Bunyan is without friends, friend who would be grateful to him if he were to rise from the grave." Through Bunyan, readers may be converted and, in so doing, join a worldwide public and insert themselves in a global history.[3]

But Soga does not only address his readers as members of a world religion. He also speaks to them as Xhosa Christians having to navigate a tangled world of local politics. This imperative has left a number of traces in the introduction. For example, in discussing Bunyan's delinquent youth, Soga writes: "As a boy, he was an incurable idler—a master of dirty games like cursing people with property, use of obscenities, lying and criticizing all that is good." As his autobiography makes clear, Bunyan did indeed commit all manner of wickedness.[4] Cursing those with property was not one. In the Eastern Cape, however, this "sin," which called attention to those who were not redistributing their wealth as tradition required, was well known: to curse the wealthy was to show evidence of envy and possibly even of practicing witchcraft against the propertied. Such murmurings were often directed at "hoarders" who "stingily" refused to redistribute their property as social custom demanded.[5] Soga's father had been one such person. "Old Soga," as he was known, had been among the earliest converts to Christianity. He maintained very strong ties to the chieftaincy and had eight wives, but, at the same time, he gathered around him a small band of likeminded men who took advantage of the new religion in order to accumulate property, unimpeded by older constraints.[6] On occasion, Old Soga—and possibly his sons—must have borne the brunt of such "envious" cursing.

In alerting his readers against sin, Soga sets out both evangelically defined "universal" transgression and then more locally defined variants: in this case, the "sin" of the idle intimidating the industrious. To Xhosa Protestants, such threats (which combined forms of "heathen" witchcraft with criticism of their aspirant lifestyle) were especially repellent and fully deserving of being defined as "sin-worthy." Having read Soga's introduction, a Xhosa Christian, who initially formed part of a tiny minority, might be strengthened to stand firm against such "bullying."

The introduction offers readers several other such routes into local affairs. For new converts living in a para-literate environment, aspects of Bunyan's life would have provided points of identification. Such readers might have noted that in Bunyan's household "books were not many because both [his and his wife's] family were poor." Similarly, converts in a situation where the spoken word carried great weight would have understood how the words of a sermon "pierced through his heart and . . . overwhelmed [him] with fear." The notion that Bunyan had been upbraided by a "female witch" may also have had local resonances, as did the fact that "he gave up friendship with all heathens" after he heard God's call. Satan also tempts Bunyan in a locally recognizable form: "he tried all the proverbs in his power to confuse, stop and distract this servant of God."[7]

In his introduction, Soga suggests that people can be united not only by what they read but, crucially, how they read it. Not only might the content of the text assist believers and create new ones but common methods of interpreting the text could also weave people together. Soga could have had little idea of how successful this strategy was to be, since he died a few short years after the translation appeared. However, as the critic A. C. Jordan has noted, Soga's translation was to exercise an influence on written Xhosa literature comparable to that of the Authorized Version on English literary history.[8] His translation, as well as its English original, was to form a powerful theme in the lives of the African elite in the Eastern Cape.

One of the major problems confronting this elite was the routes it was to forge into a modernity from which many wished to exclude it. On the one hand, members of the mission elite had to distinguish themselves against a chiefly class and to invent new forms of authority for themselves. On the other, they chafed under white-dominated mission institutions, subject to the mixed message of nineteenth-century Protestantism, which preached equality of the spirit but seldom of the body. Beyond the mission and chiefly world, the African elite faced the acrid racism of the settler world, ever ready to condemn the "educated native" for wishing to rise above his feudally ordained station. One pressing need in such circumstances was to fashion a public sphere through which an emerging elite might rehearse and refine a self-definitional repertoire of ideas, images, and discourses.[9]

These issues were the sources of endless discussion around the themes of betterment, progress, improvement, "civilization," and so on. The landscape of *The Pilgrim's Progress* was to provide one site in which these debates were pursued. Dominated by the spine of the journey, the story became an alembic that could distill these broader debates and provide an image fluid enough to accommodate very different ideas of where one may be headed. The mnemonic landscape of the book, experienced again and again by numerous audiences in a plethora of media, could in Jürgen Habermas's words, "condense [flows of communication] into public opinion."[10] The image of a familiar landscape dominated by a burdened man on a journey could collate a dispersed audience into a purposive public united by a sense of going forward, even if the destination imagined varied considerably.

This chapter examines how the Eastern Cape elite in South Africa came to use the text in this way. We begin by tracing the story of the Xhosa text's translation. We then attempt to construct a history of how it was read by examining the reading methods that were forged by both pupils and teachers at Lovedale, the alma mater of most of the Eastern

Cape elite. Finally, we examine how the African elite used *The Pilgrim's Progress* as a political resource between the 1880s and 1940s, the heyday of the text's influence.

On 21 November 1866, Tiyo Soga noted in his journal: "Quarter past nine o-clock, night.—Finished, through the goodness of Almighty God, the translation of the first part of Pilgrim's Progress, my fingers aching with writing." To a colleague, he wrote:

> You will be glad to hear that I have got the length of
> having finished the translation of the Pilgrim's Progress in
> Kafir [nineteenth-century term for Xhosa]. It is being printed
> at Lovedale. We applied to the Religious Tract Society for
> their woodcuts, so as to have it illustrated, and they cheer-
> fully granted our request. I long to see the reception of this
> noble work by our native Christians, as well as by our
> people who can read. We publish only the first part of it, and
> it is all that is finished, until we see how it takes among the
> people. The reception will indicate whether or not I should
> complete it. It will be something new for our people. I
> translated a large portion of it when a student in Scotland;
> but, as then translated, the Kafir of it would have spoiled the
> work.[11]

Characteristically for a mission translation, Soga's Xhosa version was done between several points in an international evangelical arena. The first of these was Glasgow, the fiercely evangelical "Gospel City" where Soga trained as a minister in the United Presbyterian Church in the mid-1850s. The second site was the Tyumie Valley in the Eastern Cape, Soga's birthplace and, since 1799, the focus of the earliest mission en-deavors in the African interior and the most heavily missionized spot in the inland subcontinent.

These two points anchored a Xhosa-Scottish evangelical world in which Soga grew up and into which his translated text would subse-quently flow. Soga himself was born in 1831 against a background of bloody frontier colonial dispossession as the British-controlled Cape Col-ony sought to conquer the adjoining and independent territory of the Xhosa. His father, Old Soga, as we have seen, was a modernizing tradi-tionalist. He enthusiastically adopted new agricultural methods and cast off customary forms of redistribution. Yet, at the same time, he had eight wives, acted as a councilor to the Xhosa paramount, Sandile, and on at least one occasion took up arms against the encroaching British colonial regime. His children were funneled toward a more narrowly modern future, and he packed them off for secondary schooling to the nearby Lovedale Missionary Institution, which had been opened by the Glasgow Missionary Society in 1841. Tiyo entered Lovedale in 1844, at the age of twelve, but only two years later, in 1846, he and the staff had to flee as the Tyumie Valley was once again engulfed in war. Soga was taken by the Lovedale principal, William Govan to Edinburgh to complete his schooling. He returned in 1848 and taught for a few precarious years before again fleeing another frontier war. This time he went to Glasgow where he was ordained in 1856. He returned in 1857 with his Scottish wife, Janet Burnside, and took up his position on the Gwali station in the Tyumie Valley where he and his family stayed until 1868. They then moved further into the interior to the station, Tutura, where Soga died in 1871.[12]

According to contemporary reports, Soga's translation was "everywhere welcomed."[13] The quality of the translation was praised: "he has adapted the shades of meaning peculiar to the Caffre [Xhosa] language to the niceties of English ideas." The same reviewer also noted that "the meaning of the text has been most forcibly and strikingly given in expressive native idiomatic form." Another reviewer pointed out that the language is "simple . . . and terse" and characterized the translation as "chaste and classical."[14] Unusually for a mission translation, the book was not abridged and the entire first part was translated (the second part being done by Soga's son, John Henderson, in 1929). The doctrinal parts were precisely rendered, no easy task for a translator working with a recently minted Christian terminology and an unsteady orthography.

The text soon become a great success and went through countless editions. It is still in press today. Its popularity is, of course, largely attributable to the quality of Soga's translation and his own stature as a revered intellectual, preacher, and the first Xhosa ordained minister. However, at the same time, part of its appeal may also be due to the fact that, like the Zulu translation, the book had already cleared a space for itself by the time Soga's translation arrived (although Soga does note that the book would be "something new").[15] The text itself probably first entered the region in 1799 with the Hollander, Johannes Van der Kemp, the first missionary to proselytize in Xhosa country. Van der Kemp was a Bunyan fan and may have disseminated bits of the story and its illustrations via his own broken Xhosa or that of his Khoi (Bushmen) assistants who had long lived on the fringes of Xhosa society.[16] In addition to Van der Kemp's assistants, there were also independent Khoi evangelists sent by the LMS from Cape Town, who entered the region from the very early 1800s.[17] They proselytized in Dutch and, in all likelihood, would have been familiar with Dutch versions of *The Pilgrim's Progress*, either in its full or abridged tract form.[18]

Evidence of some Bunyan presence in Xhosa society prior to Soga's translation comes from the figure of Sifuba-Sibanzi (Broad-chest). Van der Kemp was a retired military captain and favored the military metaphor. He may consequently have popularized the figure of Great-heart.[19] (In all likelihood, he also drew on Bunyan's *The Holy War*, a text of an epic battle between the forces of Diabolus/Satan and the city, Mansoul. The story is crowded with armed soldiers like Captain Resistance and Captain Conviction.) One person who heard Van der Kemp and/or his assistants preach was Ntsikana, subsequently to become the great Xhosa prophet and saint. In some of his visions, Sifuba-Sibanzi appears as a Christ-like figure and the term today is a common praise name for Jesus.[20] The provenance of the figure could equally be drawn from Xhosa oral narrative tradition where Sifuba-Sibanzi appears as a young chief with a wide chest made of "glittering metal that shone in the sun."[21] These two sets of images, namely that of Great-heart and those from Xhosa oral tradition, may have mapped themselves onto each other.

In the millenarian predictions of Nongqawuse, Sifuba-Sibanzi also appeared. In 1856 this teenage girl prophesied that the dead ancestors would arise. In preparation, all Xhosa were to kill their cattle and destroy their grain in expectation of the day when two suns would rise and the cattle and grain would be reinstated in abundant quantities. These instructions had been brought to her by two spirits who presented themselves as the messengers of Sifuba-Sibanzi and Napakade (the Eternal One).

Significant numbers of Xhosa-speakers heeded the injunction. The resulting devastation and famine accelerated colonial dispossession. Jeff Peires, the major historian of this episode, indicates that Sifuba-Sibanzi draws on both Xhosa and Christian traditions. The form of the name is "typical of the sort of heroic apostrophe which fits in as well with Xhosa praise poetry as with Christian moral tales in the vein of *Pilgrim's Progress*."[22] John Knox Bokwe, like Soga, a Lovedale alumnus and an early documenter of Ntsikana's life, also likens Sifuba-Sibanzi to Bunyan's Great-heart.[23]

When it appeared then in 1868, Soga's translation could enter a landscape that had already been prepared for it. Through the circulation of bits of the story in Xhosa and Dutch by Van der Kemp and the Khoi evangelists, motifs of the story opened up spaces of recognition into which Soga's text could subsequently flow.

Lovedale Missionary Institution was one of the subcontinent's Bunyan epicenters. The institution was run by Scottish Presbyterians for whom Bunyan was a revered and theologically significant figure. *The Pilgrim's Progress* had had a long history in Scottish Presbyterianism and had been present since the seventeenth century, when it was strongly woven into the Calvinist traditions of covenanting.[24] Bunyan's theology had also played a decisive part in the Scottish evangelical revival, which conferred a distinctive identity on the middle classes (or would-be middle classes) and positioned them vis-à-vis the older landed classes "above" and the working classes "below."[25] The book's emphasis on perseverance, dedication, and spiritual discipline could adumbrate the value system of middle-class evangelicals by casting a critical shadow on the indiscipline of the poor and the laxity of the landed classes. It was also this evangelicalism that had fueled the Disruption of 1843, which split the Established Church of Scotland, the evangelicals breaking away to form the Free Church of Scotland.[26] It was under their mission wing that Lovedale fell after 1843.

Students entering Lovedale were consequently to encounter an environment that was Bunyan saturated and they were to meet him in both Xhosa and English in an array of forums. These included primary school readers, secondary school English literature classes, examination papers and essays, sermons, the events and activities of the Students' Christian Association (SCA), school plays, debating contests, and newspapers.[27] What kinds of reading strategies did students acquire in these various forums and how did these interact with the techniques of interpretation they brought with them from home?

With regard to the reading strategies students brought with them from home, two related techniques are worth singling out. The first of these derived from Protestant religious instruction that most students, particularly by the late 1800s, would have encountered in some form prior to entering Lovedale. The second arose from the world of oral literature. In relation to the first, religious education relies heavily on teaching concepts allegorically. Take, for example, the following instance of how Tiyo Soga conveyed the ideas of Christianity to two

Xhosa enquirers. Soga recorded his interaction with the two men in his diary:

> the ideas of the narrow way and the narrow gate and of the broad gate, impressed their minds and lead to a continuation of some interest. They said they liked the narrow way and they never knew that they were in any other—in fact they were in the narrow way—they asked what does a person do who is in the broad way and what does a person do, who is in the narrow way.[28]

In this evangelically derived technique, the inquirers are encouraged to insert themselves in a landscape, that of the Broad and Narrow Way, an image extensively disseminated in the Protestant mission world.[29] They are also asked to perform certain allegorical translations whereby both the broad and the narrow way are interpreted as particular lifestyles.

This ready adoption of an allegorical method by both Soga and his interlocutors could also have its roots in literary methodologies nurtured in riddle and "folktale." Many riddle forms, for example, are mini-allegories in which the listener unknots an enigma by proposing a one-to-one correspondence between the text and the world. Take, for example, this riddle: "I have a sack full of corn. The corn is thrown away and the sack is cooked and eaten." The answer is the stomach of a ruminating animal cooked as tripe. The interlocutor must identify the stomach as the sack and its contents as the corn.[30] Likewise, some riddles require their performers to draw a parallel between a person and the qualities of a bird. Jordan gives the following example:

CH(ALLENGER): Do you know the birds?

PRO(POSER): I do know the birds.

CH: What bird do you know?

PRO: I know the wagtail.

CH: What about him?

PRO: That he is a shepherd.

CH: Why so?

PRO: Because he is often to be seen amongst the flock.[31]

Similarly, the owl is like a sorcerer "because he always comes out in the depths of the night to kill other animals." The female dove is a jealous wife "because she never allows her husband to go out without her." The white-necked raven is likened to a missionary because "he wears a white collar and a black cassock, and is always looking for dead bodies to bury."[32]

Likewise, in "folktales," characters can have certain abstract qualities attached to them. Take, for example, the story of the frog that wants to become like the cows, grazing on the riverbank. The frog bloats itself up to such a point that it bursts. The frog and its behavior betoken stupidity, vanity, or inappropriate and self-defeating ambition. However, the idea of explicitly drawing such links was not generally practiced until the advent of mission rewriting of folktales. Drawing on Aesop's fables or La Fontaine's, the template of the folktale with which they were familiar, many missionaries wrote down stories and attached a moral that made the allegorical weave of the story explicit. For example, in the case of the story of the overreaching frog, a Lutheran mission reader concluded: "What does this folktale teach us? It says that a person should not be vain. When you exalt yourself, others will laugh at you. He who is boastful often ruins the beauty that is within him. Moreover, a person with vanity is never aware of this himself. He will never reach the greatness that he yearns for; he will ultimately die with a bad reputation. He who exalts himself will be laid low."[33]

These techniques would, of course, train anyone to deal with Bunyan, and students who encountered him at Lovedale (or indeed even before entering) must have felt themselves to be on familiar ground. On entering Lovedale, however, students' existing reading techniques would have been supplemented with others as they encountered *The Pilgrim's Progress* in different settings in and around the school. The first of these was the classroom. Here students in the higher levels of primary school would have read Bunyan in their Xhosa and possibly their English readers. The Standard Five Xhosa reader, for example, included several illustrated extracts from the early part of the story. As students entered secondary school, they would have encountered the full text in the English and the Xhosa classes, where it was a setwork from at least 1883.[34]

It is difficult to know exactly how the text was taught. Examinations do give some insight into this topic, and judging from the examination papers, a repertoire of teaching approaches was employed. In many cases, there was a strong emphasis on knowing and recalling content through questions like "Give a description of Vanity Fair, and its history to the arrival of Christian and Faithful"; "Where was the country of Beulah?"; "Who were its inhabitants?"; "To whom did the gardens and the vineyards belong?"[35] Drilling and memorization were also important. S.E.K. Mqhayi, the great Xhosa writer and dramatist, attended Lovedale and, by the time he was thirteen, could recite the first chapter of the book.[36] In the upper reaches of secondary school, students learned the historical background to the text and had to be able to relate the two. The 1876 Cape matriculation examination, which some Lovedale pupils wrote, asked candidates to "Give some of the virtues and some of the faults of the Puritan literature."[37] Students also had to give an outline and characterize the style of *The Pilgrim's Progress*. In some cases, students were required to demonstrate some grasp of allegory: "Give in Xosa a brief account of any *four* of the scenes which were shown to Christian by the Interpreter (*u-Mtyileli*), and explain the lesson taught by *one* of them."[38] In addition, they also had to translate portions of the text from Xhosa into English and write a general essay on Bunyan: "Write a Xhosa essay . . . on . . . Bunyan's knowledge of human nature, as shown in *Uhambo*."[39]

In studying Bunyan in the classroom, students were familiarized with a number of reading and interpretive techniques. Significantly, many of these taught the text in a secular way and exposed students to the idea of literature as a field of study in its own right. More strictly religious interpretations of the text occurred outside the classroom, where students would have encountered Bunyan in their extramural activities. Those who joined the popular SCA studied the English text in detail for several months. We do not know how it was taught, but these lessons probably laid great stress on the religious and spiritual import of the text. Students also saw the story represented in magic lantern slides and enacted dramatized excerpts in both Xhosa and English. They might also have heard talks and, at times, sermons that drew material from Bunyan. As Lovedale had a significant number of Sotho- and Tswana-speaking students drawn from the more northerly regions of South Africa, these learners from time to time held their own SCA meetings in these languages. Quite possibly, they made use of the Sotho and Tswana versions of Bunyan. At times, there was a school-wide Bunyan play, notably a Xhosa translation (*Iziganeko zomKristu*) of E. U. Ouless, *Scenes Dramatised from Bunyan's Pilgrim's Progress*, which was performed on several occasions.[40]

The text also traveled into the immediate environs of Lovedale. A student organization, the Missionary Band, evangelized in the neighborhood, as did the candidates from the Bible School. This institution had been started in the 1920s and trained lower-level evangelists and Bible women. *The Pilgrim's Progress* was used for reading exercises in English, Xhosa, and Afrikaans, used by "coloured" candidates as a first-language. Bible School students also dramatized bits of the play as part of their training.[41] Both groups, the Missionary Band and the Bible School, quite possibly used excerpts or pictures from the text in their itinerations. Students returning home took their books with them, while the Lovedale Book Depot supplied trading stores in the region with copies of *The Pilgrim's Progress* in Xhosa.[42]

Students were provided with a repertoire of reading techniques: detailed content recall; memorization; recitation and quotation; reading in historical context; allegorical interpretation; sustained textual study; dramatic reenactment; analysis of illustrations and magic lantern slides; evangelical interpretation; allegorical reading and the like. Some of these methods, such as allegorical interpretation, memorization, techniques of quotation, and certain modes of performance, most students already possessed. Others they encountered for the first time at school. How did these various styles and layers of interpretation interact?

The Lovedale Literary Society provides a forum in which we can see some of this complex chemistry at work. The society was a staff/student organization for lectures, talks, debates, and musical items. It met every Friday evening during term time. A detailed set of minutes from 1936 to 1948 survives and allows us insight into its workings. From these minutes, it is clear that the aims and objectives of the society were often fiercely contested, with staff generally seeing it as a vehicle for edifying talks on literature, while students wanted to redefine it as a debating society. The resulting disagreements give us some insight into how students attempted to articulate and implement an alternative set of interpretive procedures that reconfigured the hermeneutic repertoires of both home and school.

Some critics have seen this forum as yet further evidence of the alienated black Englishness of the Lovedale elite.[43] By these accounts, senior Lovedale students "mimicked" the dominant forms of European culture in discussing topics like "The Crusades"; "Wordsworth"; "What Position Does Cromwell Deserve in English History?"; "Whether the Battle of Marathon, or the Battle of Waterloo Has Had More Influence on the World"; "Is Queen Elizabeth Worthy of Admiration?"; "Oliver Goldsmith"; "Life of Sir Philip Sydney"; "Life of Sir Walter Raleigh," and so on.[44]

However, such accounts rely on a partial view of proceedings. These "European" topics made up only a portion of the annual programs. The remainder was taken up with discussion of local issues of burning concern to an emerging African elite. These local topics ranged widely and included debates on progressive farming methods ("Whether is Stock or Agricultural Farming Best for the Natives of this Country?"; "Is it Justifiable to Kill All Cattle on a Farm Where There is Rinderpest?"); changing gender roles (bride price; monogamy vs. polygamy; should women enter the ministry); the nature of education (should it be academic or technical; in which language; compulsory or not; free or not; could it erase "superstition"); forms of government (chief /monarchy vs. republic); how to shape public opinion (pulpit or press). Questions of what constituted "progress" and "civilization" were also common and appeared in topics like "Though the Bantu are Progressing, They Are Not Progressing Fast Enough"; "Has the Time Come for Heathen Custom to be Put Down by Act of Parliament?"; and "Does Education Remove Superstition?"[45]

The Literary Society thus functioned as one forum for defining the interests of this new African (and largely male) elite. This group occupied a complex social position pinioned between traditional chiefs, white missionaries, and rabidly racist settlers. In relation to chiefs, the elite stressed their modernity; in relation to missionaries, their knowledge of African tradition; and in relation to settlers, their superior claims to "civilization." These issues were often hammered out in the events of the Literary Society, which functioned less as a series of literary discussions and more as a debating forum where the new elite could prepare themselves for leadership and public office. Indeed "debating" came to acquire a wide ambit of meaning that meant more than just standing up to defend an opinion. It was also a shorthand term for a training in the performances of a new elite leadership. Such leadership comprised many levels and skills. Most obviously it was about learning eloquence and self-discipline, or as one Lovedale alumnus told the society, "develop[ing] powers of speech to know how to oppose a person without offending him or her, self-control in speech, politeness and respect."[46] "Debating" prepared students for this leadership: "Many a leader had been fashioned and modeled by this society."[47] The society also forged networks for the future: "The Literary Society is the foundation of our future careers."[48] (Indeed, it was not uncommon for some students to join the society for "CV purposes" without becoming actively involved.) One teacher, Mr. Mdledle (a Lovedale alumnus) informed his audience that the society prepared students for life after school and taught them how to be "cultured." "A cultured man is often distinguished not by his dress but by what he does and says, a man who faces the situation objectively with coolness, and he that gets into the truth first and gets heated afterwards."[49]

This notion of leadership was also explored in the discussion and performances of Xhosa literature and drama that featured from time to time on the society program. These performances, which invariably drew the largest crowds, returned again and again to themes of dispute resolution and the political leadership skills it required. The minutes of one production of *Ityala lamawele* (*The Case of the Twins*) by the great Xhosa writer S.E.K. Mqhayi notes that the function of the play "was two fold . . . it was for amusement as well as it brought to light, to those who did not know anything about pure African life, how complicated cases . . . used to be successfully and easily settled by consulting the old sages."[50] The reference to those "who did not know anything about pure African life" was perhaps a dig at white teachers and missionaries. By contrast to this "ignorant" group, the new male elite apparently possessed such knowledge and could, on occasion, borrow the robes of chiefly power in order to position themselves critically vis-à-vis the white mission authorities.[51]

For the school authorities who ran the Literary Society, its primary and proper function was literary. For these literature proponents, the term "literature" carried a particular meaning compounded from evangelical views of reading overlaid with notions derived from the emerging discipline of English literature. In this amalgam, literature was heavily moralized: on the one hand, it could "improve" its readers and "save" them from corrupting pastimes; on the other, it could show them an instance of an elevated national product to which "their" people could aspire. Students at the society consequently heard comments like the "Bantu are not a leading people because they do not read," or the "Bantu must read more great literature whether in Latin, English or mother tongue . . . such men as Lincoln rose to the rank of great orators only by reading great literature."[52]

For the debaters, literature had a role to play but more as a subordinate category that could provide fuel, themes, ideas, and quotations for debate and hence for the preparation of leaders. The distance between the two positions—literature or debating—is usefully captured in some comments from an irritated teacher: "In recent years the whole character of the Literary Society had changed. Formerly one of the great educative influences on the life of the students, it has become merely a debating society entirely dissociated from direction or guidance by members of staff. These are fatal defects and cannot be allowed to continue."[53]

The disagreement over these terms (which mostly but not always ran along lines of staff/student) was fueled by other factors: increasing censorship; a ban on discussing "political topics"; greater surveillance of students; cut-backs in resources; militancy among students; racialized conflict between staff and students and within the staff body; and so on.[54] At the same time, however, the disagreement was equally driven by opposing literary "moral economies." In terms of these competing frameworks, literature came to betoken very different things. For the literature lobby, the category was primary; a resource whose power could, almost single handedly, improve, moralize, and mould the students. For the debaters, literature was a secondary category: a source of quotation, a compendium of messages, subordinate to the larger design of training male leaders. In forging this definition of "literature," the male students in the society reconfigured their sets of interpretation inherited from school and home. On the one hand, they "borrowed" the authority of literature as a category of value, but, on the other, they wedded it to ideas of performance, eloquence, use of apt quotation, and memorization. This amalgam of techniques in turn functioned as a social "apprenticeship" for positioning oneself vis-à-vis the missionaries, the chiefly authorities, and settler society. It was in short a tailor-made preparation for the local exigencies of African leadership in the Eastern Cape.

Bunyan, who featured from time to time in Literary Society talks, was likewise subject to this mode of localizing analysis. Talks on him (in both his English and Xhosa incarnations) were surrounded by discussion on a suite of local themes close to the heart of the Lovedale African elite. These included local agriculture ("Rotation of Crops"); technology ("Which Does the Country Need Most—Irrigation or Railways?"), "progress" and "civilization"("Is Westernization of the Bantu Undesirable?"); chiefly and monarchial tradition ("Tshaka [the famed Zulu military leader] and his Successors"; "Was the Execution of Charles I Justified?"); changing gender politics ("Girls Should Not be Educated to the Same Level as Boys"; "Women are Cleverer than Men"); and colonial history and policy ("Was the Dutch Period Beneficial to the Natives of South Africa?"; "Were the Missions Justified to Impose Christianity by Means of Warfare?").[55] Once pulled into these fields of debate, the meaning of Bunyan's text could, of course, shift, and his book could provide a source of insight, illustration, and quotation to underline the arguments of an emerging African elite. Such reading strategies become apparent if we examine the political re-allegorizations of Bunyan that emerged on a sustained basis in the press in and around Lovedale.

Perhaps the best example of this local Lovedale reading strategy comes from the Xhosa newspaper, *Isigidimi samaXhosa*. The date of the passage is uncertain, but probably comes from the 1880s when the African elite yet again had to decide how to cast their vote for the Cape Legislative Assembly. Since 1853 franchise in the Cape Colony was determined by gender, age, property, and literacy, and a fair proportion of the African elite qualified for the vote. At each election, there was considerable debate in the Cape African press on which candidates (who were almost invariably white) to support.[56] Jordan provides a translation of one such instance where a columnist uses an episode from Bunyan to explore the options facing enfranchised Africans.

> Readers of *Uhambo lo Mhambi* will remember the story of Christian and Hopeful, the day they were found by Giant Despair. It is said that the giant put them into his castle, into a very dark dungeon, nasty and stinking to the spirits of these two men. Here, then, they lay from Wednesday morning till Saturday night without one bit of bread or drop of drink, or light, or any to ask them how they did.
>   Now Giant Despair had a wife, and her name was Diffidence: who, when she heard about the prisoners, told her husband 'to beat them without mercy.' True enough, on the following morning they were beaten fearfully. The next night she, understanding that they were still alive, '*did advise him to counsel them to make away with themselves.*' Truly then, the giant did give them this advice, and again he beat them. But they, though tempted by his counsel, finally resolved not to accept it. *If they must die, it must not be by their own hands.*

The columnist then goes on to draw out the lessons of this episode:

> We are reminded of this story by a number of men who are at present scattered amongst us, black folk, counseling us how to get out of this slough, this dungeon of suffering into which our community has been cast these past years. We have complained of laws that oppress the black man alone: the branding of

cattle, pass laws, disarmament without even adequate compensation for our guns. We have complained of the imprisonment of our ministers of religion, their being arrested by the police while carrying out their duties to the Word of the Lord. We have been pushed around by so-called location regulations. These and other things have been heavy on our necks, and many of them still remain so, and we do not know what to do about them. And now the time has come to elect men to go to parliament. Among the men who are going to parliament there are those who are going there to add to the burdens we already have. These men make no secret of the fact that they still regard the black man as an enemy, a thing to be treated as an enemy, a thing to be deprived of education grants.

Today, it is those same men who have come to our people and expect that it must be we ourselves who send them to parliament. Hence, we say that they have come to counsel us to do away with our own selves. Giant Despair said, 'I bring you counsel that will help you when I say that you had better kill yourselves.' In like manner these men come smiling up to us and say, 'It is our ardent love for you that makes us say that you had better elect us, the people who will truly destroy you.' Diffidence was enthusiastic about her counsel. In like manner these men are enthusiastic about the counsel they bring to us.

It will be well for us to confer on this matter. The two men we have used as an example conferred before they resolved what to do. The day is very near when we must resolve what to do, hence our suggestion that there must be unanimity among those who have the right to vote. For our part, we say we must not accept the counsel to do away with our own selves. If we must die, it must not be by our own hands.[57]

The columnist addresses a situation of straitened choice and raises question of how to pursue political objectives in an oppressive context. He employs two techniques in this task. First, he shifts the allegorical field of the book. In this account, the text loses its "original" meaning and is de-allegorized. It becomes instead a story about colonial rule in the Cape Colony—the burdens and trials represented in the plot become the burdens and trials of life under colonial oppression. Within this framework, the writer introduces his second technique, that of re-allegorizing the text by reconfiguring the "data" of the story to render it amenable to a local interpretation. In this account, the story of Giant Despair and his insidious wife is refocused so that it pivots around her attempts to get the two prisoners to kill themselves. From this narrative node, the writer can then leverage the political points he requires. These concern the hypocrisy of colonial rule, where those who oppress and "imprison" black citizens also parade as their benefactors.

The writer can carry out his techniques of de- and re-allegorization because the story is so well known. As such, it becomes an orientation point around which political discourse can revolve. Take, for instance, another re-allegorization that cropped up in a rather different set of circumstances in the 1920s. During these years, a Bunga (or council of chiefs) was set up by the colonial Native Affairs Department (NAD) as a forum of indirect rule. There was considerable disagreement as to whether the institution should be supported or not. A proponent of the scheme, Tennyson Makiwane, progressive farmer and Bunga councilor, wrote in the Lovedale newspaper, *Christian Express*, in 1925. In his letter, he tries to persuade urban Africans that, despite its colonial sponsorship via the NAD, the Bunga is worth supporting:

> Our Native people . . . who are afraid to join the Council
> system on the ground of its control by the Magistrates may well
> be likened to Christian in 'The Pilgrim's Progress' who at a
> certain place seeing two lions on either side of the road was
> afraid to go on his way. But on approaching these he found
> they were fastened by chains to the ground and could do him
> no harm. I suggest that much that to outsiders appears
> embarrassing in the Council system could on closer view be
> found to be both harmless and innocent.[58]

In both of these examples, the writers assume that readers are intimately familiar with Bunyan's story. The text consequently becomes something of a public sphere in which political debates of the African elite can be pursued. The text becomes a shared set of references and a taken-for-granted landscape onto which positions can be plotted.

This use of Bunyan as a positioning device among African Protestant elites in the Cape Colony emerges as well in a travelogue from John Knox Bokwe, another Lovedale graduate and public intellectual. On his first trip to Cape Town in 1884, Bokwe, then postmaster at Lovedale, decided to visit the Theatre Royal. Expecting to enjoy an agreeable evening of culture and upliftment, he found instead a distasteful place full of "rowdies," probably lower-class white and "coloured" spectators. The two barrooms further offended Bokwe's teetotaler sensibilities. He longed back to the Lovedale Literary Society: "on Friday night, 3 Oct., while you in the Literary Society were profitably discussing the lives of John Bunyan and John Milton, I was among the rowdies and low characters of Cape Town, who had gone to pass their time in the gallery of the Theatre Royal."[59] Having bought a cheap ticket in the gallery (the theatre being segregated by money rather than race), Bokwe had to rub shoulders with the working class. Imaginatively, he distances himself from those around him by positioning himself as part of the audience of the Lovedale Literary Society, whose discussions of Bunyan can confer on him a spiritual, moral, and class distinctiveness that proves his superiority to his supposed racial betters. Here again Bunyan is constructed as an orienting point on a political and social landscape.

The journey and landscape in *The Pilgrim's Progress* likewise provided shorthand points of reference to facilitate political debate. In 1865 one of Soga's colleagues writing in the press launched an attack on African communities by predicting their extinction since their "indolent habits" would prevent their progress.[60] Using a pseudonym, "Defensor," Soga responded. At one point, he described the converts of his station as "staunch men, who for consistency of character, considering the 'Slough of Despond' out of which Christianity had lifted them, will compare with the multitudes of their white brethren, who can boast of greater advantages."[61] At first glance, it would seem as though Soga invokes the story as a predictable metaphor for a journey from "heathenism," "tradition," and "backwardness" to "Christianity," "modernity," and "progress." The rest of the sentence, however, makes it clear that while Soga calls up a familiar landscape of *The Pilgrim's Progress*, the projected destination lies in the direction of a distinctly African Christianized modernity defined in Soga's thinking by the idea (current in much mission writing by Africans) that African converts make better Christians than Europeans.

For writers like Soga, the landscape of Bunyan provides the "latitude" for exploring different political destinations. In this case, the "spine" of the journey provided a site of experimentation in which various subjunctive futures could be imaginatively trialed. This image of the purposive journey became a metaphor and flexible shorthand for broader debates on progress, betterment, advancement, "civilization," and modernity in a hostile world. In 1942 a serial entitled "The Pilgrim's

Progress" by "Gaoler" appeared in a South African newspaper, *Inkundla ya Bantu*. The series announced itself as being "for the amusement of students . . . but also about the grim realism of the African pilgrim's progress in a hostile world."[62] Indeed the image of the burdened traveler was to become something of a staple genre in southern African literature as a way of criticizing racial oppression.[63]

The political home for most members of the Eastern Cape elite was the South African Native National Congress (after 1919, the African National Congress or ANC). The nature and objectives of this organization formed an ongoing strand in public debate, and *The Pilgrim's Progress* was at times invoked as part of this discussion. The following poem by a woman, Nontsizi, appeared in the newspaper *Umteteli wa Bantu* in 1924. The translation is by Jeff Opland.

The Hill Difficulty the Black Man Scales

Look! Today I want you to understand
the essence of our distress.
Compatriot, wrestle with what I say,
let's engage in debate.

The Hill can't be scaled! It's slippery.
I won't mince words, I'll bare my heart:
to this point in time,
just what have blacks achieved?

Take the African National Congress:
we once praised it till our ribs burst.
Now we go round seeking it:
"Has anyone seen where's it gone?" . . .

Vying for status is lethal poison
that weakens Congress from within.
Hamstrung by people riddled with envy,
the black man's actions lose all worth.

This Hill Difficulty's got us beat,
we've tried and tried to scale it:
it can't be scaled by blacks
strapped with the millstone of custom.

Envy's an obstacle up this hill,
money's another obstacle:

so we battle to scale it.
Old Greyhair, am I wrong?

Unity's an obstacle up this hill,
so, burdened, we no longer praise it,
like plains cattle lost in the mist,
black as crows in our ways. That's us!

Why, my good man, are we slumped at the foot
of this Hill Difficulty the black man scales?
You've set your hand to many things
but which of them still work?

The way you despise and goad traditionalists
are obstacles up this hill—
yet how you covet their cash!
Sweat all you like, you won't reach the top. . . .

This Hill frustrates attempts to scale it,
lions and leopards ring it;
the Hill stands firm, our people slip
on slopes with carpets of cash. . . .

This Hill the black man scales is steep,
so steep it nearly daunted Christian;
his mouth frothed with a sloven's foam,
his ears rang as he scaled this Hill.

And so it is for blacks today:
we sit on the fence, we won't take a stand.
We don't even know why we squabble,
but we bolt our fruit before it's ripe. . . .

Sweat blood, you won't make the top
of this Hill Difficulty the black man scales;
you don't love the Nation, only bargains.
That's the truth. Have I got it wrong?

Our customs abandoned, we're left empty-handed,
in this generation apostasy's rampant.
I've said it before: scratched and bleeding,
we won't make the top of this Hill.
    We agree![64]

In this poem, Nontsizi addresses the political context of the 1920s, when the ANC, a largely elite organization, was riddled with internal problems. The poem lays these out: disunity, lack of delivery, internecine political rivalry, corruption, venality, greed, contempt for the less-educated followers of "tradition," and so on. The poem is addressed to a "Compatriot" and, as such, is intended to jolt discussion within an African elite public sphere. This debate is facilitated by means of a Bunyan landmark, Hill Difficulty, which Christian must scale on his journey. In Nontsizi's poem, she explores the Hill as a symbol both of the colonial obstacles that Africans must overcome and of how these obstacles are exacerbated by political disunity within the ANC. In this poem, the landscape of *The Pilgrim's Progress* provides a backdrop against which to enter a debate about political strategy and direction.[65] At the heart of such discussions, lies the idea of the journey as an analogue for political activity.

This notion of the political journey was to become a powerful metaphor later in the twentieth century, as the ANC led the antiapartheid struggle in and outside South Africa. Bunyan's influence itself started to wane after the 1940s, as the ANC acquired a mass-based following whose rank-and-file members had seldom encountered *The Pilgrim's Progress*. Yet, the secularized idea of the struggle as a purposive and teleological journey remained strongly imprinted on ANC discourse. At times, its Bunyan dimensions reappear. The work of "Rebecca Matlou," *nomme de guerre* of Sankie Nkondo, now Sankie Mthembi-Mahanyele, at the time of writing, Minister of Housing in the ANC-led government, furnishes an apt example. In her poetry, Nkondo often invokes a Bunyan-like landscape. Prison is referred to as a "grim den" and "the dungeon den of grim death."[66] The poem "Swim Comrade" is arranged around the idea of crossing a river to the heaven of freedom. The poem "Bent Back" features a hunch-backed figure going along a path.[67] In "The Bivouac," a composite "freedom fighter" says: "I am the wanderer warrior / who walks on a road / laden with hot charcoal / I tread on hot rock / that always cuts and bleeds my toes."[68] This idea of the struggle/path and its link to Bunyan emerges explicitly in a poem entitled "This Path":

> Child of the soil
> Child of own destiny
> cross this path
> cross the sword
> ride the lion's back and hold the mane
> bound on with shoulders high

sky in heavens light the path
echoes from this thorny bush guide the way
Luthuli, Kotane, Mandela, Sisulu trod this path
Pull hard, hack the prickly shrubs
burden beads on your brow
pilgrim yoke on your back
will balm the people's tortured heart
and bid the sod to seed freedom.[69]

In this poem, the history of the ANC is played out against a biblical and Bunyanesque landscape of a difficult path along which a series of ANC notables make a burdened journey. The poem urges a new generation to pick up the burden and follow the same route. By inserting the ANC into such a landscape, Nkondo reworks a trope whose history goes back to the reading and intellectual formations that had crystallized around *The Pilgrim's Progress*. By the 1970s, of course, such invocations of Bunyan were rare and, as indicated earlier, the book's favored position in the public sphere of the African elite did not last beyond the massification of the ANC in the 1940s. The book did appear occasionally as a reference in some worker-based newspapers but such invocations came via the British trade union movement upon whom Bunyan and Nonconformity generally left a strong secular imprint.[70] The text's wane around this period is usefully illustrated by the case of Albert Luthuli, head of the ANC between 1952 and his death in 1967 and, after Mandela, one of South Africa's most noted political leaders. Luthuli's father was christened John Bunyan Luthuli.[71] Luthuli's own biography *Let My People Go* (1962), however, shows no evidence of or interest in Bunyan and in the text he uses only his father's first name.

The fact that the apartheid government which came to power in 1948, ruled out the use of translations in African language classrooms in pursuit of ethnic purity, only hastened the demise of the text. Under this new ruling, texts in translation could no longer be recommended for African language school syllabuses. Unsurprisingly, in 1964, Lovedale dispatched 4,902 copies of *Uhambo lo Mhambi* for pulping, just a few years before the book's centenary.[72]

In retrospect, the "reign" of the text from the 1870s to the 1940s appears short. Its role during this period in the formation of an African elite was, however, considerable. As we have seen, it informed the political discourse of the elite and provided a set of metaphors for debating questions of how to fashion an African modernity. In this task, Bunyan was applied to political circumstances by means of a set of locally forged interpretive procedures. Through this intellectual grid, the text was filtered and refiltered in homes, schools, and public forums. The motifs that remained behind had sufficient consensual currency to act as points around which public opinion could be shaped.

6

Dreams, Documents, and Passports to Heaven
African Christian Interpretations of *The Pilgrim's Progress*

In a recent discussion of *The Pilgrim's Progress* in the *New York Times*, a columnist referred to the book as an ancestor of the B movie.[1] Anyone chancing upon the Ndebele translation of the story would have to agree. Turning to the final pages, one encounters a lurid illustration entitled "Ugulahlwa gu ka Naziyo" ("The casting aside of Ignorance") (figure 15).[2] In the foreground, two white angels have pitched the black body of Ignorance head first into the flames of hell. An owl (the bird of witchcraft) hovers above the smoke as a snake rears its head through the flames, ready to strike the unfortunate Ignorance. In the background, the protagonist, Christian, and his companion, Hopeful, arrive at the gates of heaven, after their arduous pilgrimage from the City of Destruction. In the illustration, they hand over their documents for inspection to two sentry angels.

This edition was the work of David and Mary Carnegie (and possibly their colleague, Moholo) of the LMS, based at Hope Fountain in Matabeleland in present-day Zimbabwe. The illustrations were executed by C. J. Montague and were probably the earliest instance in which Africans were used to depict characters in Bunyan's story.

At first glance, the picture may appear unremarkable—just another example of predictable mission iconography. In this colonially conceived drama of sin and salvation, the "saved" wear Western-style clothing, while the feminized body of Ignorance has only a loincloth as covering. Spiritual authority is racialized with the angels depicted as white. Yet, when judged against most traditions of Bunyan illustration, the picture becomes more interesting. There are, of course, thousands of renditions of Christian and Hopeful entering heaven. The scene represents the triumphant climax of the first part of the story and in various editions, we see Christian and Hopeful making their way into paradise in every conceivable way—they fly, they walk, they fall on their knees, they are lifted up by angels.[3] Yet, whatever their mode of transport, nowhere do we see them holding any documents. The text, by contrast, is very specific on this point. At the gate, the two pilgrims, Christian and Hopeful, are asked for their "certificates," which had been issued to them earlier in their journey. They produce their papers, which are first taken to the King of Heaven for checking. Thereafter, the pilgrims are ushered into the glistening streets of paradise. Ignorance, who arrives shortly afterward, is not so lucky. He has no certificate and when asked for one, he feebly "fumble[s] in his bosom . . . and found none." The two Shining Ones direct him to a side exit plummeting straight into Hell. The narrator comments, "Then I saw that there was a way to Hell, even from the Gates of Heaven, as well as from the City of Destruction."[4]

Evidently, to nineteenth-century European and American readers the idea of gaining entry to heaven by a piece of paper seemed far-fetched, despite the fact that this is exactly what the story shows. Yet, for some African converts, this scene was of considerable importance and it recurred in a number of different contexts. The first of these is the dream. Take, for example, the case of a man whom we know only as Bayolo. A resident of the Loma region of the Upper Congo, he fell ill in his middle years and "died." As the funeral was about to commence, some mourners noticed that Bayolo seemed to be twitching. These movements quickened and soon Bayolo had returned to life. He reported his experiences to an amazed audience. In his trance, he had traveled to the gates of heaven. There, two men stood and asked him for his "road book." He did not have one. "Return and get your road book," they said, "confess your sins, remove your camwood powder and make yourself clean."[5]

After narrating his dream, Bayolo asked to be taken to the mission church, which he had never entered before. There he expressed his desire to become a Christian and retold his story to a curious crowd. He also predicted that within two to three days he would die, an event that indeed came to pass. Many hundreds—or so the mission report said—decided to join the church in the wake of these happenings.

A cognate set of concerns emerges from an early Sotho novel, *Monono ke moholi ke mouoane* or *Wealth is a Haze, a Mist* (1926), by Everitt Segoete, a member of the PEMS in present-day Lesotho.[6] Toward the end of the narrative, the protagonist, Khitsane, like Christiana in the second part of Bunyan's story, receives a perfumed epistle written in gold lettering inviting him to heaven. He is instructed to present the document on arrival at the gates of heaven. The letter is a source of great anxiety to him and he shakes and sweats at the prospect of the journey before him.[7] A similar idea occurs in a popular Sotho song genre sung by migrant workers who, before the collapse of the gold-mining industry, earned a precarious living working several miles down in South Africa's deep mines.

> If it were possible to write to heaven,
> I would send the old folks there,
> So that [if] they find Jordan flooded,
> [It] is crossed by books,
> . . . and by certificates.[8]

The river Jordan, this poem maintains, is crossed only by books and certificates. The poet wishes he could write to heaven to pave the way for his old relatives who, lacking the necessary education, will find Jordan flooded and thus difficult to cross.

In other contexts, we encounter variations on this theme of conditional entry to heaven. In 1938 an agent of the Africa Inland Mission (probably in western Kenya) reported that Ukok, an erstwhile "soldier of Satan" had—like Bayolo—miraculously arisen from the dead. He testified that he had traveled to heaven's gate, but had been refused entry. He was instructed to return to earth and to destroy the little huts he had built for sacrifices. Once he had completed this task, he could retrace his steps to heaven and gain access.[9] Bengt Sundkler, who has examined African-initiated churches in southern Africa, reports several cognate prophecies concerning heaven and its stringent entry qualifications. In some of these prophecies, the injustices of apartheid South Africa are reproduced in heaven: a black messiah, for example, opens the gates for black Christian, while Jesus admits whites. In another version, twelve gates of heaven are reserved for whites and only one is open to blacks.[10] By contrast, Isaiah Shembe, founder of the Church of the Nazarites (one of South Africa's major African-initiated churches), reversed preexisting inequity. In the view of his followers, Shembe, after his death, became a keeper of the gates of heaven, where he turned whites away "because they, as the rich men, have already in their lifetime received their good things, and [Shembe] opens the gate only to his faithful followers." Nazarite theology places great emphasis on the idea of the keys to heaven. In some cases, the idea is used metaphorically: the Nazarite church itself is likened to a key that will provide access to heaven. In other cases, the key is more literal. Sundkler reports that Nazarite adherents "who have returned from heaven" (that is, had visions and dreams) have seen Shembe with a key. Shembe is also known as the Zulu Holder of the Keys at the Gates of Heaven.[11]

These dreams and visions all point to a complex understanding of literacy and spiritual authority. Many of them bear some "family resemblance" to the final scene of *The Pilgrim's Progress*, part 1. What might Bunyan's book tell us about literacy and heaven?

In keeping with the para-literate world that Bunyan inhabited, *The Pilgrim's Progress* depicts a social order in which documents are not an everyday occurrence.[12] Documents appear infrequently in the text and, when they do, they are foregrounded, often becoming a center of theatricalized or proscenium-like attention. Images of books, for example, appear framed or in visions and dreams.[13] God sits on a cloud with the book of judgment open on his lap.[14] Every now and then, the pilgrim protagonists encounter some public signage, often associated with a monument or statue of some kind.[15] They stop and observe these "billboards" as if they were observing some kind of pageant. Elsewhere in the story, literate objects become the fulcrum of important episodes. Christian, in the famous opening scene, carries a Bible. He also receives a parchment roll from Evangelist bearing the inscription "Fly from the Wrath to Come."[16] These two documents serve to "kick start" the plot. At the cross—another fulcrum in the story—Christian loses his burden. Three Shining Ones appear to him and hand him a "roll," which he must keep in order to gain entrance to heaven.[17] As we have already seen, Christiana, in the opening scenes of part 2, is summoned to heaven by a letter from God, perfumed with the best scent and written in gold.[18] When she reaches Beulah Land, the heavenly waiting room, she and her co-pilgrims each receive a letter from the heavenly mailman calling them to their rest.[19]

Yet, despite the rapt attention that they merit, documents are regarded with some skepticism in this para-literate environment. Written messages by themselves are slightly suspect and are always "reinforced" by some additional and more trustworthy form of communication.[20] Christiana, for example, receives the message to join her husband in heaven both through a dream and through a letter.[21] When she and her co-pilgrims receive their summons to cross the River of Death, each letter is accompanied by a "sure token"[22] that vouches for the messenger's—and presumably the message's—veracity. When Christian is presented with his roll, it is paralleled by a mark on his forehead as the sign of his election.[23] These instances all point to the fact that written documents by themselves are not entirely reliable for conveying information. To have authority, they must still be embedded in older and more trusted forms of communication.

In *The Pilgrim's Progress*, then, letters and documents are ambiguous—they are held in awe, yet are not entirely trusted. Another ambiguity is that they can entertain and please, but can equally cause considerable anxiety. In terms of pleasure, they are not only physically alluring with their scent and golden letters but they also portend great heavenly bliss. Equally, they are tokens of spiritual power. In some cases, letters come directly from God and are potent messages from him. Documents also protect their bearers and literally cause heavenly doors to open for them. Those without documents enjoy no such protection or power. Indeed, at least one illiterate character, Hopeful, carries a book with him,[24] not because he can read its content but because he believes it to be a talisman of authority. The book also allows him to participate indirectly in a documentary culture and to utilize its props in his performances of piety. Elsewhere in the text, documents provide other forms of pleasure. Christian, for example, carries a roll with him and at times reads from it, an activity that consoles and comforts him. For some of the male characters, books are a necessary precondition for spiritual authority and confer interpretive power on those who can use them.[25]

But pieces of paper can also cause worry and anxiety. Christian, for example, at the opening of the story is reading a book, but it brings him little succor and makes the burden on his back seem heavier than before. Evangelist provides him with a parchment containing onerous advice: "Fly from the wrath come." The advice scares and confuses Christian. "Whither shall I fly?" he asks anxiously. At another point in the journey, Christian, exhausted from struggling up Hill Difficulty, takes a short nap in an arbor and loses his roll. Unaware of his oversight, he proceeds on his journey. When he realizes he has mislaid the precious piece of paper, he is overcome with "great distress." He feels he has lost his "pass into the Celestial City." He turns back, weeping, sighing, and chiding himself for his foolishness: "O wretched man that I am, that I should sleep in the day time!"[26]

Another site of trauma is Vanity Fair. Here in the bawdy hubbub of the market place, documents such as titles to houses, lands, places, and preferments change hands.[27] Christian and his companion, Faithful, boycott the merchants who abuse and torment them. They are tried for disturbing the peace and for holding seditious opinions. Faithful is found guilty and burned at the stake. Part of the legal process entails documentary paraphernalia, such as the indictment sheet and presumably the parchment from which the sentence is read.[28] These become ominous props in the drama of the court. This power-laden use of documents is echoed at other points, as we have seen, in the images of God as a judge perusing the great book of life in which the saved and the damned are recorded.[29] Elsewhere in the text, volumes of bureaucratic records likewise chronicle the names of sinners and saved.[30] Such images equate the grim inevitability of judgment with the relentless record-keeping that bureaucracy enables. Part of God's power evidently resides in his efficient paperwork and administration. Through these images, documents are implicated in the mechanics of ruling, and having to carry them can betoken powerlessness. In keeping with Elizabethan vagrancy laws, Christian, a masterless man, has to carry a "pass"[31] to indicate that he has permission to be traveling.

Another source of anxiety is illiteracy and at least one character, Hopeful, cannot read.[32] In some views,[33] Christian is also of uncertain literacy, although in comparison to Hopeful, he is described as "learned."[34] At the opening of the story, he cannot fully understand the Bible. Reading, too, is by no means straightforward. At one point, Christian and Hopeful encounter "an old monument" resembling a woman transformed into the shape of a pillar. Hopeful spots an inscription "in an unusual hand" above the statue and he asks Christian to read it for him. Christian does a "little laying of letters together" and determines that the inscription reads "Remember Lot's Wife." The process of first noticing and then decoding these three words takes some time. Reading is by no means effortless and requires intense and cumbersome effort, rather as Bunyan and his class must have found it—"a physical pilgrimage in print" or "a slow and persistent toiling towards meaning," as one Bunyan critic describes it.[35]

Documents can also bring trouble. Christian and Hopeful, for example, land themselves in difficulty over a note that is given to them by the shepherds in the Delectable Mountains. The note furnishes directions for their journey, but they, fatefully, forget to read it. As a result, they are waylaid by Flatterer and enticed into a net where they become ensnared. A Shining One releases them and whips them for their forgetfulness.[36]

Documents are paradoxes: on the one hand, they are props in the theatre of ruling, policing, and dragooning; on the other, they betoken enchantment and spiritual authority. These multiple functions are usefully distilled in the changing nature of Christian's roll. He receives the roll when he encounters the cross and his burden falls from his shoulders. Three Shining Ones appear to him and outfit him with a new set of clothes and a sealed roll for him to "look on."[37] Along with his new clothes and name—he was first called Graceless[38]—it betokens a new identity. The roll also provides entertainment and enlightenment since, on his journey, the roll becomes a book/Bible from which he reads, an activity that refreshes and delights him. In this guise, as Margaret Soenser Breen has pointed out,[39] the roll confers spiritual authority on Christian as he sharpens his interpretive abilities. (By contrast, Christiana, as Breen indicates, appears seldom to read and is relegated to the oral/aural sphere.) But, at the same time, the roll carries ominous overtones. When Christian loses the roll, he refers to it as a "pass."[40] He also speaks of it as his "evidence" (both of election and also of his right to be on the road).[41] By the end of the book, the roll has become a "certificate," which is taken to the King of Heaven, who reads it first before admitting its owner. In this guise, the piece of paper becomes a power-laden object with magical properties. This function is prefigured when Christian identifies the roll as an object that can "vanquish" his "carnal cogitations."[42] One of Christian's traveling companions, Little Faith, also carries a certificate, but at times it becomes a set of jewels.[43] In both these instances, the roll functions like a charm that protects its bearer.

Characters in the story, then, are not always in control of their documents. Pieces of paper can prove troublesome. They change shape and form; they disappear and reappear. They demand different types of attention, behavior, and deportment. At times, they must be contemplated as objects. At times, their content must be read attentively. At times, they must be carefully carried. Documents, in other words, are dangerous and unpredictable. But, they are also priceless and precious— they are, after all, passports to heaven.

In 1898 Andrew Cindi sent a pleading letter to his former principal, James Stewart. Cindi had graduated from Lovedale, but because he had been caught smoking marijuana ("I never knew it was sin . . . I found out afterwards that you don't reckon it as tobacco."), Stewart refused to release his "religious certification."[44] Cindi found himself nearly a thousand miles away in Mafeking and wished to join an LMS congregation. They, however, required the certification before Cindi could be admitted as a member of the church. Cindi begged:

> I ask only my Daily soul's bread from you, which is the blood of Christ and Body.
>
> I ask my religious certification to be received in the congregation I am at now. . . .
>
> Sir I am in great trouble of doubting my forgiveness from God the Omnipotent.[45]

The letter ended with a postscript that invoked Bunyan.

> I can't live without Christ. You have the Celestial City's key. And please give it to me or let me in you don't know the day I'll be summoned at.
>
> Let me in let me in let me in.[46]

The use of Bunyan in this context is not unexpected. Lovedale, as we saw in the previous chapter, was a veritable Bunyan epicenter and, as a Lovedale pupil, Cindi would have known the text well. In his letter, he relies in part on the story to underline his plight and to add weight to his appeal. Like Christian, Cindi has lost his documents and is desperate to reclaim them since they will open the gates of heaven. Without them, he, like Ignorance, is doomed. For Cindi, documents are absolutely essential for access to spiritual authority, but they also make him demeaningly dependent on mission authority. Pieces of paper become a zone of contradiction between power and powerlessness.

This paradoxical pattern of documents was common in the lives of many nineteenth-century African Protestants who faced a para-literate world not dissimilar to that inhabited by Bunyan. As in Bunyan's sphere, documents in a colonial context played a prominent role in the exercise of authority and so could provoke considerable trepidation. In the religious domain, by contrast, they became potential ciphers of spiritual authority and pleasure.

Like many other kinds of social contradiction, this one was to become a site of painful creativity, as those caught in it attempted to understand, control, or imaginatively resolve its strictures. In many instances, this creativity took the form of call-dreams and visions. One characteristic motif in these "dream-geographies of heaven"[47] is that of miraculous literacy. In these stories and dreams, believers instantaneously learn to read. The famous Xhosa prophet, Ntsikana, discovered hymns fully formed on the hem of his cloak or on the tailbrush of his cow.[48] Likewise, Simon Kimbangu, the prophet who led a breakaway church from the Baptists in the Lower Congo in the 1920s, could "fetch" hymns from the "other side."[49] Walter Matita, a prophet from Lesotho who founded the Church of Moshoeshoe, learned to read from an angel in heaven.[50] In 1925 Abiodun Akinsowon, a Nigerian, had a vision in which she was "transported into a celestial realm and instructed in various heavenly mysteries." Here, she passed a "rigid spiritual examination."[51]

One could adduce further examples. They reiterate a shared cluster of themes: a protagonist demonstrates his or her power through "fetching" literacy and its products from a sacred realm. Literacy is defined as a type of sacred energy that is retrieved "whole." In such transactions, literacy resembles electricity. It comes on-stream magically, as though through a switch. The prophet's creativity lies neither in laboriously mastering the component skills of the technology nor in the slow craft of composition. Rather it resides in the gift and ability to "fetch" the power of literacy from another realm where it seems platonically already to exist.

In this inspired theory of creation, authorship does not reside with the person but comes from some higher power. *The Pilgrim's Progress* itself conforms to this idea. As the foreword to a 1956 Zulu translation says, "Bunyan wrote/'fetched' [the story] as if he was 'fetching' a dream.'"[52] In this formulation, deriving in part from the Zulu verb "to tell" (*ukulanda*, literally "to fetch"), Bunyan does not "author" or compose the story. Rather it comes to him whole, as a picture/vision. His creativity resides in his ability to "cross over" and redeem the story from the dream world. *The Pilgrim's Progress* elsewhere provides support for this view of literacy. In the text, many documents come straight from God and dreams remain a respected form of prophecy.

These narratives of miraculous literacy subordinate technologies of writing to "traditional" conceptions of the sacred. In so doing, they address some of the contradictions attendant upon the documentary culture of the colonial world. Instead of being a force controlled by colonial bureaucracies and mission schools, literacy becomes a source of divine energy accessed and controlled by those with prophetic talents. The tedious and laborious necessity of learning a set of mechanical skills also disappears in these visions, where literacy is "fetched" or "switched on." As a type of revelation, literacy comes directly from God and not via the compromised agency of missionaries. This "direct" route bypasses the demeaning tutelage that missions often demanded from converts wishing to rise up the mission hierarchy. At times, these apprenticeships were absurdly lengthy. As one desperate group of would-be Presbyterian ministers in Nyasaland said in a famous phrase: "Let us be ordained before we die!"[53] As in the case of Andrew Cindi, certificates—whether for confirmation or ordination—appeared as hurdles, put in the way of those wishing to progress up the church hierarchy (or even move sideways within it).

When it came to colonial bureaucracies, of course, documents were even more of a hurdle and were often used literally to hold people back. Documents like passes were used to control, harass, and persecute. Official papers like tax receipts, birth certificates, and exemptions of various kinds formed part of a colonial network of control.[54] Documents were also used as ritualized instruments of ruling and as a way of drawing boundaries between Africans and Europeans. At times, pieces of paper were surrogates for settler authority. Simeon Mwase, for example, reported from colonial Nyasaland that European planters used letters as their proxies in bringing charges against workers. The planter would send the "accused" with a letter containing allegations against its bearer to a local magistrate. "The whiteman was not to appear in Court at all, but only by his letter. A native was to be punished by the letter's evidence, which evidence, he could not cross-examine it."[55]

Mwase, a clerk in the colonial service, narrates this episode in a book that he produced while imprisoned for embezzling taxes. It was originally entitled *A Dialogue of Nyasaland Record of Past Events, Environments and the Present Outlook within the Protectorate*, and its major burden was to provide a biography of John Chilembwe, leader of a brief but famous revolt against harsh plantation conditions in the Shire Highlands of Nyasaland. In addition, Mwase also includes chapters on colonial "race relations," colonial law, and penology. In setting out to tell his story, Mwase draws heavily on Bunyan, and the opening and closing paragraphs of the text are taken almost word for word from *The Pilgrim's Progress*, part 1. In addition, sections in the body of the text are also reproduced from Bunyan.[56] Like Cindi, Mwase was in all likelihood schooled by Free Church missionaries, this time at the famous Overtoun Training Institute in the north of Nyasaland, where Bunyan was taught intensively in at least two languages. So thoroughly was he instructed that, while in prison, Mwase could recall substantial chunks of the text by heart. As a writer in prison and as an admirer of radicals in the English Revolution, it made sense to raid Bunyan, a fellow prisoner and dissident (if not a tax embezzler).[57] Bunyan likewise provided an authorizing framework through which he could "speak." By beginning and ending the book with Bunyan to signify "bookness," Mwase also opens an experimental space for himself in which he can narrate and explore a whole suite of issues: Chilembwe, penology, colonial jurisprudence, and so on.

In Mwase's account of how settlers abused literacy, documents appear as "heavy"—they almost literally oppress and punish people. In the dream-geographies of literacy encoded in so many visions, documents by contrast become "light." They often exercise an "open sesame" effect through which problems disappear and forbidding doors open. They function rather like talismans or "fetishes."[58] By manipulating the physical object of the document in the world, practitioners aimed to bring about transformations in other realms. As we saw in chapter 2, Mpambu followed just these techniques. This "African" hermeneutic had previously traveled to other parts of the world with slaves in the diaspora who likewise saw documents as magical objects or passports to heaven.

Such "fetishistic" regimes around paper objects were also practiced by evangelical Protestants who imbued documents with extraordinary power and force. In evangelical thinking, printed documents have an astonishing capacity to "seize" and "capture" readers and bring about radical transformations and conversions in them.[59] Little wonder, then, that the Bible—and sometimes books more generally—were referred to as the "white man's fetish."[60] Not only does this phrase elucidate the ritual and magical ways in which missionaries deployed documents but it also carries a suggestion of how the practices of missionaries and converts converge and come to resemble each other.

In its depiction of documents, the extraordinary autobiography of Legson Kayira[61] provides an instructive instance of how these two theories of textuality—namely the evangelical and the talismanically traditional—combine. The story itself narrates Kayira's decision to walk to America to gain a tertiary education. He sets off from his hometown Karonga in the north of Nyasaland, Central Africa, in October 1958. He walks, hitchhikes, and sails 2,500 miles northwards through Tanzania, Lake Victoria, Uganda, and Sudan to end up in Khartoum early in 1960. Here the U.S. embassy intervenes on his behalf and he enrolls at Skagit Valley College in Mount Vernon, north of Seattle, where he had already applied for a position.

The book's title itself *I Will Try* comes from the school motto of Livingstonia, the Scottish Presbyterian mission where Kayira completed his secondary schooling. The motto is embroidered on the left pocket of the school shirt that he wears on his journey. Throughout the trek, the motto functions as a textual talisman, so that, when discouraged, he recalls the embroidered phrase that "speaks" to him. "I WILL TRY, my shirt said, and I repeated the words to myself as I had done several times."[62] This is much as Bunyan himself does, by entering a dialogue with his text in the prefatory poem to part 2, where he personifies his text as a traveler and then enters into a conversation with it, urging it to forge fearlessly into the world, and allaying any anxieties that the "talking book," in its turn, raises.[63]

Kayira's "talking motto" becomes a model for how texts are deployed both before and during his journey. At school, he collects narratives of self-improvement about figures like Booker T. Washington and Abraham Lincoln. Fortified by these stories, he realizes that he, too, can overcome his poverty and reach America: "I saw the land of Lincoln as the place where one literally went to get the freedom and independence that one thought and knew was due to him."[64]

As he sets off on his epic journey, he takes a white bag containing some flour, an extra khaki shirt, a blanket, and two books: the English Bible and *The Pilgrim's Progress*. Like the motto on his shirt, *The Pilgrim's Progress* propels both the protagonist and his story forward. The journey to America is carefully figured as another "Pilgrim's Progress" with the U.S. being the "heaven" toward which Kayira is journeying. The chapter titles also invoke Bunyan: "I Have a Dream"; "'I Have Laid My Hand to the Plough'" (a quote from *The Pilgrim's Progress*); and "Legson's Progress." At critical junctures in the story, he also stops to read the text from which he extracts further "mottos."

> Then I turned to my *Pilgrim's Progress*.
>
> OBSTINATE: What are the things that you seek, since you leave all the world to find them?
>
> CHRISTIAN: I seek an Inheritance, incorruptible, undefiled, and that fadeth not away, and it is laid up in Heaven, and fast there, to be bestowed, at the time appointed, on them that diligently seek it. Read it so, if you will, in my Book.
>
> OBSTINATE: Tush . . . away with your Book: will you back with us or no?
>
> CHRISTIAN: No not I . . . because I have laid my hand to the Plough.
>
> I had already started my journey and had already gone so far, and there was no reason to turn back. I would go forward. There where I was going I would get an education,

incorruptible and undefiled, and one that would not fade away. I was leaving my family, I was leaving all my friends, and I was leaving all that I had at home in order to find that education.[65]

This scene with Obstinate and Pliable, which the narrative returns to insistently,[66] becomes a source of mottos or maxims that Kayira deploys to strengthen his resolve.

> I sat in front of the fire and pulled out my *Pilgrim's Progress* again. 'And if you will go along with me,' says Christian to Obstinate, 'and hold it, you shall fare as I myself, for there, where I go, is enough and to spare.' I am going to America, I said to myself, and there too, where I go, is 'enough and to spare.'[67]

In this story, documents become a force that compels one forward. In Kampala, Uganda, Kayira goes to the U.S. Information Service Library. He chances upon an open copy of *The Enduring Lincoln* and starts reading it until he encounters a word he cannot understand. He goes to find a dictionary and his eyes light on a volume entitled *American Junior Colleges*. The book falls open on Skagit Valley Junior College and Kayira posts off an application. Two weeks later the reply arrives. The magical moment is figured almost as if he has received a letter from heaven.

> I read it, and read it again, and still read it again. . . . I had heard of America, I had read of America, I had dreamed of America, but was this letter really coming from America, the America I had heard and read and dreamed of? Was I only dreaming? . . . Here is that magic letter for those who wish to read it and share with me the joy that I had when I read it.[68]

This magic letter, which subsequently persuades the U.S. embassy in Khartoum of Kayira's seriousness, helps to open his way to America and functions as a type of provisional passport of heaven. It stands in contrast to the "pass" or "passport" that a relative at the start of his journey warns he will need.

> 'Do you have a pass?'
>
> 'What for?' I asked.
>
> 'You can't go to Jubeki (Johannesburg) without a pass. . . .
>
> You can't go to America with one, either. You need a passport.'[69]

Kayira makes his journey without these oppressive documents and instead turns his own textual mottos into his "passes" and "passports."

They become the talismanic texts that can open doors and cause the portals of paradise (in this case the U.S. embassy in Khartoum) to admit him to heaven.

While Kayira's text is broadly secular in its orientation, it nonetheless provides a further instantiation of the "magical" properties attached to documents in general and *The Pilgrim's Progress* in particular. This theory derives both from evangelical views of texts as things that can seize readers and transform them utterly and "African" understanding of documents as "fetishes" that can compel events in the world. In setting out on his journey, driven by his "talking mottos," Kayira demonstrates a theory of textuality in which these two notions combine.

As Kayira's text demonstrates, part of the appeal of *The Pilgrim's Progress* is the multidimensional portrayal of documents that it offers, a model that accorded closely with the experience of many African Christians. Part of Bunyan's depiction of documents captures their magical dimensions as charms, talismans, "fetishes," and passports to heaven. The form of the book itself as a vision "fetched" from a dream has reproduced, in some respects, ideas about miraculous literacy. As a site that exemplified both evangelical and "African" talismanic views of the text and its powers, *The Pilgrim's Progress* offered a profitable "archive" from which to derive models of texts and reading. Bunyan's book also held advice for those in the mission world seeking to understand the vexed links between literacy and religious power. With regard to the realms of colonial authority, *The Pilgrim's Progress* describes a familiar world where documents become instruments of ruling, policing, controlling, and punishing. Importantly, Bunyan maps these ideas of documents as agents of oppression onto a Calvinist doctrine of election. Just as this doctrine includes some and excludes others, so too can documents enable access or prohibit it. Christian's roll embodies this doubled idea—it is simultaneously a "pass" and a "passport to heaven."

7

African Protestant Masculinities in the Empire
Ethel M. Dell, Thomas Mofolo, and Mr. Great-heart

Thomas Mofolo's first novel, *Moeti oa Bochabela* (*The Traveller to the East*),[1] began life as a mission periodical serial in *Leselinyana la Lesotho* (*The Little Light of Lesotho*), a publication of the PEMS. The first episode appeared in January 1907, and on the same page was a picture of the members of the Bible School that Mofolo had himself attended in 1894.[2] It is a standard mission photograph with rows of immaculately besuited, serious male students (plus a few teachers) standing in front of a building.

The positioning of Mofolo's story below this solemn group is emblematic of how critics have generally seen his story. For most, it is a pious piece of missionalia, an earnest first attempt from a novelist who would go on to produce substantially better work, most notably the novel *Chaka*, which was translated from Sotho into several languages.[3] The influence of *The Pilgrim's Progress* on Mofolo's first novel has often been noted.[4] Mission commentary on the book liked to stress the novel's link to Bunyan and more recent scholarship has likewise identified *The Pilgrim's Progress* as one of the novel's intertexts.[5] In such discussions, it is generally assumed that the version of Bunyan that influenced Mofolo was the 1868 Sotho translation undertaken by Adolphe Mabille and Filemone Rapetloane.[6] This, however, was not the only edition of which Mofolo was aware. He almost certainly read both parts of the book in English, and at least one scene in his novel derives from an illustration that appeared first in the Ndebele and then in the Zulu translation.[7] (Mofolo probably encountered both editions in his travels to Zululand.)[8] In so far as Mofolo used Bunyan, then, he was interested in multiple versions of the text and also in the routes and journeys that it had taken into and around the continent. His concern with Bunyan was consequently not only as an evangelical presence but also as a writer who had already been filtered through other African societies.

One of these societies was the Ndebele polity in present-day Zimbabwe. For converts in this society, *The Pilgrim's Progress*, like the Bible, had become a resource for dealing with one of the most urgent issues that they faced: the pressure to reshape older martial forms of masculinity. In part, this insistence had been brutally forced upon Ndebele society, which was defeated by Cecil Rhodes's mercenaries in 1893 and then mercilessly crushed after an uprising in 1896/7. The Ndebele state was a somewhat significant military power in the subcontinent, and an increasing British imperial presence, sparked by the discovery of gold and diamonds in the 1870s and 1880s, attempted to destroy the power of such societies so that they could render up laborers and converts rather than warriors. The settler-dominated state that took shape subsequent to the uprising focused considerable attention on demobilizing Ndebele society and instituting more servile forms of masculinity.[9] The desire to rescript ideals of masculinity was, however, not only driven by the settler state. Converts themselves had an interest in new models of manliness. As commoners and marginal men, often intensely persecuted for their beliefs, they stood outside the ambit of chiefly patronage and so were not entirely invested in its militarized structures and martial masculine ideals.[10] In 1897 an Ndebele convert, Mazwi, commented on these shifts: "What has been left to us these days? . . . Shields? They have been eaten by rats. Assegais? We cut grass with them. You see that book [the New Testament] that is our shield."[11] For Mazwi, the older ideals of military manhood have been rendered redundant and new forms of masculinity need to be formulated around the discourses of Protestantism.

This idea of rescripting martial ideals is strongly written into the illustrations of the Ndebele edition of *The Pilgrim's Progress*. Their creator, C. J. Montague, made this point explicitly: "The strenuous career of the [protagonist, Christian] will no doubt be appreciated by the men of the great fighting race for whom the book has been prepared."[12] The pictures carefully plot and develop this point. In the first illustration, Christian, dressed in Western clothing, leaves his village. In the foreground, a group of "unclothed" "heathen" men sit around a cooking pot, attending to their worldly appetites. In front of the cooking pot lie two fighting sticks, while a third is shaken menacingly in Christian's direction by one of the men (figure 11). The picture's message is clear. Christian not only flees the "sin" and "heathendom" of his village but he also seeks to escape its militarized norms.

In this opening image, Christian appears to be unarmed. In the next image, he acquires that great Protestant weapon, the Bible, which he clasps as he makes his way out of the Slough of Despond (figure 12). A few images down the line, we encounter him standing before the cross while his burden falls from his back. Lying close by is a Bible and a fighting stick (figure 13). For the remainder of the story, these two will act as equivalents for each other—sometimes we see Christian armed with shield, spear, or fighting stick, sometimes we see him armed with the Bible. In these images, then, the Bible can stand as a new counterpart of the old fighting stick. The Bible consequently opens up the potential to formulate alternative ideals of manliness.

This concern with masculinity may on the face of it appear to be mission-driven, particularly in the Ndebele-British conflict, in which missionaries fully supported colonial military intervention. Missionaries also sought to supplant many of the central institutions of African society, such as initiation, ancestor worship, divination, polygamy, and chieftaincy. These were all deeply bound up with definitions of gender in African society, and the project of scripting new masculinities was consequently important to missionaries. Yet, as we shall see, this was a theme that interested Mofolo and other converts who had their own reasons for wanting to reform ideals of masculinity. Like Mazwi, they were often "refugees" from gerontocratic chiefly and lineage rule, whose demands of tribute and whose control over when the young could marry sat heavily on the shoulders of ambitious men. Missionaries and converts consequently shared an interest in the moral economies of masculinity, even if they viewed the issue from differing perspectives.

As with all such social debate, this issue was pursued through existing fields of discourse that connected mission and convert. One such field was *The Pilgrim's Progress*, which was to be conscripted in this long dialogue around the meanings of Protestant masculinities. One figure in the text recruited for this purpose was the chivalric knight, Great-heart, who in the second part of the story offers Christiana and her party safe conduct to heaven. Great-heart had long been used as a template for discussing and negotiating questions of masculinity in the Nonconformist mission world, both "at home" and abroad. These debates around Great-heart were in turn conscripted by converts as they sought to fashion new forms of male African Protestant identity. This chapter traces this story. I begin by examining Great-heart in the imperial arena before

Figure 11. Christian leaves the City of Destruction. Illustration
by C. J. Montague from the Ndebele edition, 1902. Source:
Bunyan, *Ugwalo*, opp. 8. For permission details on figures 11–
16, see figure 2.

Figure 12. The Slough of Despond. Illustration by C. J. Montague from the Ndebele edition, 1902. Source: Bunyan, *Ugwalo*, opp. 16.

Figure 13. Christian loses his burden. Illustration by C. J. Montague from the Ndebele edition, 1902. Source: Bunyan, *Ugwalo,* opp. 50.

Figure 14. Hill Difficulty. Illustration by C. J. Montague from
the Ndebele edition, 1902. Source: Bunyan, *Ugwalo*, opp. 58.

Figure 15. The casting aside of Ignorance. Illustration by C. J. Montague from the Ndebele edition, 1902. Source: Bunyan, *Ugwalo*, opp. 184.

Figure 16. Evangelist points the way. Illustration by C. J. Montague from the Ndebele edition, 1902. Source: Bunyan, *Ugwalo*, opp. 20.

turning to see how Mofolo's *Moeti oa Bochabela* (*The Traveller to the East*) can be read as part of this dialogue.

> PHYLLIS: You say "Woman Greatheart"—well, that doesn't sound quite right to me—it's too masculine.
>
> CLIO: Why?
>
> PHYLLIS: It's too muscular a way of speaking about woman.
>
> CLIO: I suppose you mean the term is not very ladylike?
>
> PHYLLIS: Yes.
>
> CLIO: Bunyan, of course, you remember, mentions "Greatheart" in his "Pilgrim's Progress."
>
> PHYLLIS: Yes—and it is the picture of "Greatheart" I remember which makes it difficult to think of a woman "Greatheart." He is portrayed as a very big and heavily armoured soldier.
>
> CLIO: The armour is only a symbol of inward strength and resolution—that's all. The "Greatheart" spirit can use either sex, and equally well both.[13]

This excerpt comes from a play, *The Pageant of Woman Greatheart*, specially written in the 1930s for Protestant women's unions and guilds. By using the figure of Great-heart, the playwright builds on a long-standing tradition in the Nonconformist world—both at home and in the mission empire. In terms of this convention, those who were deemed to have given faithful service were likened to the chivalric knight. One long-standing member of the Camden Road Chapel, for example, was referred to as Mr. Greatheart of Camden.[14] The name was also a common honorific applied to missionaries who had given long and devoted service. A. E. Scrivener, who worked as a BMS agent for nearly thirty years, was known as Greatheart of the Congo.[15] Mission biographies with titles (or subtitles) like *Greatheart of Maoriland*, *Greatheart of Papua*, *Greatheart of China*, *Great Heart of New Guinea*, *A Greatheart of the South*, and *The Story of a Missionary Greatheart in India* provide similar evidence of this trend.[16] The term was also applied in mission literature to African Christians who had rendered significant service. *A Greatheart of Africa* tells the story of the legendary and saint-like Rev. Canon Apolo Kivebulaya, who worked with the CMS in Uganda for most of his adult life.[17] The story of another African Christian notable, Cornelius Sejosing, this time from southern Africa, is narrated in *African Greatheart*.[18] At Inyati Teachers' College in Southern Rhodesia, the name appeared in praise poems: Hugh

Rowland, a teacher at the institution was addressed in his praises as "Greatheart that accommodateth high and low."[19]

At some levels, this Protestant fascination with Great-heart is easily explained. Great-heart is the gallant gentleman who protects the women and children who make up Christiana's party. As a knight, he embodies ideals of chivalry, service, and "British fairplay,"[20] while also representing the glamor of medieval gallantry and valor. As Mark Girouard has shown, such chivalric principles ran as a thread through much imperial and mission thinking.[21] Colonial officials and, at times, missionaries saw themselves as chivalric knights serving their nation, their queen, their god, and (however improbably) their imperial subjects. Yet, the higher up the colonial hierarchy one went, the less these images applied. Those at the apex of colonial authority were so lofty in their power "that it was easier to see them as rulers ruling, than knights protecting, the peoples of the countries in which they served."[22] The best chivalric causes were often slightly unpopular and, as Girouard reminds us, applied more comfortably to those who "tilted against the Empire rather than for it."[23] For some missionaries at least, such circumstances applied. Those working in areas with large settler populations at times found themselves at loggerheads both with the white community and with the colonial state, ever solicitous of settler interests. In circumstances like these, the idea of representing oneself as a noble knight protecting one's weak wards against the might of settler and state made sense.

Within the mission world, there were additional reasons why Great-heart found favor. The first of these concerned changing ideals of Protestant manliness, which, from the mid-nineteenth century, began to emphasize a more pronounced masculinity. This shift came partly as an attempt to "muscularize" "effeminate" and over-aestheticized High Church practices, but also to try and attract more male working-class members (the most unchurched section of society) into congregations. Ideals of sport, physical fitness, character-building, patriotism, and militarism permeated many levels of both the Established and Nonconformist churches. Uniformed organizations like the Boys' Brigade recruited working-class boys by appealing to a quasi-militarized manliness. As Girouard shows, some of these organizations elaborated a working-class code of chivalry, derived in part from the successful Boy Scout movement and its use of knightly discourses and iconography. Mission heroes also provided exciting models of manliness, undertaking acts of valor and Christian service in exotic locations.[24] These mission versions of manliness stressed self-sacrifice and self-discipline, ideas that could be mapped onto the template of Great-heart, as the number of mission biographies bearing his name show. Some of these became extremely popular, most notably *Greatheart of Papua*, the story of James Chalmers, the LMS missionary whose spectacular death by "cannibals" gripped the popular imagination. This book was recycled into other media, most notably a musical performance for use in Sunday schools, entitled *Great Heart of New Guinea: A Missionary Cantata for Boys and Girls.*

This shift toward a hypermasculinity also registered itself in Nonconformist discussions around Bunyan. In these forums, commentators began to express fears that both the author of *The Pilgrim's Progress* and his protagonist were not sufficiently manly. In 1928, for example, a biographer of Bunyan, Gwilym O. Griffiths, spelled out these concerns regarding Bunyan's feeble manliness while also trying to dispel them:

> We all remember the early woodcuts which represent him as a sedentary and languid figure and which might have borne the title 'Portrait of a man with a sick headache.' Even the title, 'dreamer' is misleading. We have to remind ourselves that that term, with its suggestion of visionary aloofness, was not one that sat easily upon him in the eyes of his contemporaries. . . . Bunyan was no pacifist.[25]

Another Bunyan commentator, Robert Stevenson, likewise voices concerns that Christian, the protagonist, is unmanly. As Stevenson points out, when the story opens, we find Christian confused and weeping. Shortly afterward, in an act of apparent unmanliness, he abandons his family. Stevenson continues:

> We admit at once the utter unlikeness of this burdened man to the ordinary 'hero' of Romance. A reader may well be disappointed in his first introduction to Christian. He may object that tears and sighs are not heroic. He may incline to think that we would have preferred a manlier hero—one setting out on his adventure in the conventional way, with a firm step and a dauntless brow.[26]

Against this background, where the manliness of both Bunyan and Christian was called into question, Great-heart came to the fore as the ideal manly representative in *The Pilgrim's Progress*. In one publication entitled *Greatheart: Some Talks with Him*,[27] Great-heart is shifted from the second to the first part of the story, where he takes the place of the character

Evangelist, a key figure in directing and guiding Christian. In this re-arrangement, Great-heart is instated as the "hero" of the text. Through such moves, the uneasy taints of "effeminacy" that clung to Bunyan and Christian are sidestepped, and Great-heart is ensconced as a flexible and heroic model of masculinity that could speak to different groups of men from varying class constituencies.

Yet, as the quotation from the women's pageant shows, Great-heart could also speak to Protestant women in the mission movement both at home and abroad. As Susan Thorne has shown, from the mid-nineteenth century, women gained more and more authority in mission organizations. Whereas women initially filled adjunct and subordinate roles, they increasingly used the opportunity of mission philanthropic work to gain a public presence and to place themselves in positions of authority. When presented with the prospect of being recruited as paid professional missionaries, numbers of Protestant women seized the chance. Thorne describes this involvement in mission activity at home and abroad as the "largest mass movement of women in nineteenth-century Britain."[28]

This involvement had several consequences for gender relations. Much mission discourse, of course, stressed the virtues of the Victorian family and its separate gender spheres, and mission workers both locally and globally sought to propagate it as the ideal family form. Yet, at the same time, as Thorne illustrates, mission work took women outside the household and shifted key assumptions about the correct distribution of power between men and women. The presence of significant numbers of single women missionaries questioned the necessity of marriage. Paid employment for women threw the idea of separate spheres into some doubt as male and female missionaries now operated in a shared and salaried professional realm. In such situations, women required new im-ages to embody their authority and, at least for some women, Great-heart, who combined ideals of leadership and service, fitted the bill.[29]

There was also another characteristic of Great-heart that could serve the purpose of women in this position, namely his singleness and celibacy. Through Great-heart, unmarried women working at home or in the foreign field could see themselves as heroic figures, aided rather than hampered by their singleness. Likewise, his celibacy could be put to good symbolic use. Not only could it denote purity and single-minded dedica-tion to a cause, but it could also elevate women above the sphere of the physical body, ever a zone of potential contamination. Women in the mission and philanthropic field worked closely and often intimately with the working class at home and "heathens" abroad. They were consequently susceptible to allegations of being "contaminatable" by their close proximity to the poor and the "savage." These discourses were often cast in sexualized language, making mission and philanthropic women vulnerable to imputations that they were weakening boundaries of race and class. By occupying the celibate "space" of Great-heart, women could elevate themselves above this zone of "contamination" while still presenting themselves as guides and caregivers.[30]

Yet, as at least one commentator has noted, while Great-heart is single and celibate, there is a strangely intimate relationship between himself and Christiana, and in some ways they behave rather like a family.[31] Christiana's husband has already made his way to heaven and Great-heart stands in as a substitute. Put another way, he "husbands" and "fathers" Christiana and her party.

This model of the celibate family is similar in outline to the paradox of the imperial "family" that Anne McClintock has outlined. Imperial thinking pivoted around constructing lineages of white men and white male myths of origins, ownership, and succession. As women and black subjects were generally written out of this schema (except as negative points of reference), the problem of how to represent continuities was by no means self-evident. How could a lineage from which women were absent "reproduce" itself? One figure for dealing with this contradiction was the idea of the "Imperial Family of Man" in which time is represented as an evolutionary series of male bodies culminating in the figure of the European. By relying on the metaphor of the family, such images implied a continuity and succession, but one without women.[32]

Considered against this background, the figure of a celibate white knight sexlessly reproducing families had its uses and could be put to work in thinking through questions of authority and subordination in the "imperial family." If this should sound far-fetched, we need only turn to the popular English novelist, Ethel M. Dell (1881–1939)[33] and her "imperial family saga," the bestselling novel, *Greatheart*.

The novel's central character is a young woman, Dinah Bathurst, daughter of Lydia, a cruel and violent circus woman of gypsy origins who, on discovering that she is pregnant by another man, entraps into marriage Guy Bathurst, an indolent member of the lesser Bedfordshire gentry. Through her father's connections, Dinah is invited on a Swiss holiday. Here she encounters two brothers, Scott and Eustace Studley—adult, but orphaned, siblings. Scott has been disinherited by his father both because Scott's birth precipitated the death of his mother and because he is slightly disabled.[34] Sir Eustace, the favored son, has inherited the family estate, title, and fortune.

In the enchanted atmosphere of Switzerland, Dinah is swept off her feet by Eustace, the novel's alpha male. Eustace and Dinah become engaged and return to England to prepare for the wedding. At the last minute, however, Dinah breaks off the engagement. She realizes she does not love Eustace and has instead come to revere Scott. Dinah also learns from her mother that Guy Bathurst is not her biological father and that she is a "child of shame."[35] In despair, Dinah attempts to kill herself. Scott comes to the rescue and eventually they marry.

The central plot, then, revolves around Dinah, referred to throughout as being "brown": she has a "brown face"; she is a "brown little thing"; "little brown girl"; "brown elf"; "brown witch"; "brown-faced monkey"; and an "urchin" who has inherited her mother's "gipsy darkness."[36] Dinah is the text's colonial subject and the novel juxtaposes different philosophies for how to deal with her, or in other words, how best to rule such subjects. The first model is provided by Dinah's mother, who abuses her daughter physically and emotionally. As a member of the lower orders, she is unfit for proper colonial rule and, if given the chance, would resort to violent and crude forms of governing. Contrasted with the violence of the mother's rule is the benign neglect of the father who ignores the abuse going on in his own household. Bathurst's indolence and irresponsibility unfit him for imperial rule and, if left to administer the empire, would let it run to wrack and ruin while he went off pursuing his only love—foxhunting. Sir Eustace, also a member of the landed classes, shows more capacity for ruling, but is equally judged wanting. His model of rule is based on arrogance and is untempered with mercy.

Scott, of course, offers the ideal of what a responsible "gentleman" colonial ruler should be. He is chivalrous, courteous, moral, just, firm, and always cheerful. He has the best traits of the landed classes, but, as he is disinherited, he is not corrupted by their wealth. He protects Dinah, who initially cannot make her own decisions, and gradually through a process of "indirect rule" encourages her toward a limited form of independence. He shows patience and firmness, understanding that she is a "mere child."[37] She in turn christens him Great-heart "because you help everybody."[38]

The novel can be read as a way of trying to figure out relationships in the imperial family. As with many other themes of colonial fiction, the story involves re-parenting. Because of the lower class brutality of her mother and the upper class neglect of her father, Dinah has not been properly mothered or fathered. To Scott/Great-heart falls the burden of "mothering," "fathering," and "husbanding" his colonial subject, Dinah. However, for such a cluster of ideas to hold together, the marriage of Scott/Great-heart, the ideal figure of imperial authority, to Dinah, the erstwhile colonial subject, has to be cast in celibate terms. And this is indeed how events transpire.

After the wedding ceremony, Eustace, who no longer bears Dinah any ill feeling for breaking off the engagement, kisses her. Scott, however, refuses. "He had not attempted to make love to her, and she had not felt the need of it. Grave and practical, he had laid his plans before her, and with the supreme confidence that he had always inspired in her she had acquiesced to all."[39] Only after they have set up house together does he attempt to kiss her—apparently attracted by the "voluminous apron"[40] in which she is engulfed. The apron belongs to the Irish nurse, Biddy Malone, and in donning it, Dinah becomes part-nurse maid, part-servant, part-colonial subject, part-wife, and part-child.

The story thus becomes one of how the relationships of parent/ruler to child/subject obtaining between Scott and Dinah are transformed into that of husband to wife. Such a situation demonstrates that the subject may "advance" in status from that of child/subject to wife. However, the conditions for realizing such an advance are impossible since the racial boundaries of the imperial family demand that a colonial ruler cannot have sexual relations with a colonial subject, just as a "parent" cannot commit incest with a "child." The only way through which this impossibility can be achieved is if the imperial family reproduces itself celibately. Great-heart—long-established as the celibate "father" and "husband" of the weak in the Empire—was the man for the job.

Existing critical opinion on Thomas Mofolo's first novel has, thus far, not been uniformly enthusiastic.[41] In part, this situation can be attributed to the book being a first novel. Technically less accomplished than his later work, it has attracted commensurately less attention. Yet, this factor alone cannot explain the "arm's length" attitude to the novel that one detects in much of the scholarship. Gérard, for example, describes the book as "insincere," a quality emerging from Mofolo's uncritical use of mission and imperial symbols.[42] Other critics, too, see the book as an act of bad faith arising out of Mofolo's assimilation of "foreign" ideas and religious beliefs. For these critics, Mofolo is a victim of false consciousness, uneasily pinioned between "two cultures": "Africa" and "the West."[43]

Yet, the social relationships from which Mofolo emanated cannot be exhausted by terms like African/European or Western/indigenous. As we shall see, he sought to author a cluster of identities centered on being a commoner, a Sotho, a male, an African, and a Protestant. Against this background, his first novel can be read as an attempt to script a new form of masculinity appropriate to this grouping.

In undertaking such a reading, we understand Mofolo's Christian belief as a knowledge-producing activity (rather than as a "foreign" imposition). Via this route, we can also avoid the assumption implicit in much Mofolo scholarship that his Christianity was a regrettable act of assimilation and submission to new dominant ideas. As Gauri Viswanathan has argued, conversion is much more than assimilation. Rather, it is an unsettling and radical act of "cultural criticism," a process of entangling and disentangling numerous strands "and cast[ing] upon each strand the estranged light of unfamiliarity."[44] By casting a Protestant eye at the "feudal" institutions of Sotho society, Mofolo critiques the inequalities of age, gender, and unwarranted chiefly power. He likewise casts an estranging gaze at the central character of Christianity, namely Christ, and thus provides an early and interesting instance of an African Christology.

The project that Mofolo attempted was one of scripting a layered identity—commoner, Protestant, male, and Sotho. His novel experiments with this task, by collating different templates of masculinity, derived from a range of sources: Protestant mission discourse, Sotho historical trope, travelogue, colonial adventure novel. In our analysis, we single out two strands from this thicker thread, namely *The Pilgrim's Progress* and the literary genres around cattle keeping, a powerful source of image and discourse regarding "traditional" masculinity. We examine how Mofolo sets these two templates of masculinity alongside each other in order for them to show each other's weaknesses and enable a new space of spiritualized manliness to emerge.

The story itself (set in a precolonial period) is straightforward enough. The protagonist Fekisi is a dedicated cattle herder. He is a model of diligence, fair mindedness, and integrity and is disgusted by the forms of "feudal" despotism and conspicuous consumption that he sees around him. He is particularly galled by the gerontocratic and patriarchally driven oppression that characterizes Sotho society. Fekisi is also a seeker after truth who constantly wonders at the mysteries of life and their origins. He consults with the elders of the society who inform him that the Sotho have a notion of God but that, in disappointment at human vice and failure, he has removed himself from society. God may, however, be reached by prayer and supplication. One day, in the midst of an eclipse, Fekisi calls out to God and he hears a still small voice reply. This religious experience is followed with a series of visions and Fekisi is ultimately convinced that he has to abandon his society and go in search of God. After bidding his beloved cows farewell, he heads east, because Sotho belief holds that the source of all life lies in that direction. He crosses present-day Lesotho (in southern Africa) and descends the escarpment. Here he traverses a symbolic wilderness before reaching the Indian Ocean. Weak with hunger and exhaustion, he is rescued by three elephant hunters who take him on board their ship. They sail eastward until they arrive in an unnamed city, where Fekisi learns more about Christianity. The novel ends in a church with Fekisi seeing a vision of Jesus who takes him up to heaven.

Even from this plot outline, it will be clear that the book invokes Bunyan. Fekisi, like Christian, is overwhelmed by the "sin" of his society and deserts it in order to get to heaven. In addition to this broad similarity of plot, smaller Bunyan "modules" are sprinkled throughout the text. The Slough of Despond, for example, features in the story. Shortly after Fekisi flees his village, he encounters a marsh. "He crossed the marsh to the east of the village, and found it cool, even cold there, but he just passed on."[45] Unlike his counterpart, Fekisi, at this stage of the narrative, has few hesitations and so does not fall into self-doubt and depression as Christian does in the Slough of Despond. At one point, Fekisi passes through a Vanity Fair-like "wicked village." Afterward, he encounters a man and converses with him in a question-and-answer style that closely resembles sections of Bunyan.[46] The river that Fekisi crosses has echoes of Bunyan's River of Death. Fekisi, we are told, "picked up his belongings and went into the water. He went on, he went on, he went on, and when he was in midstream, he stumbled and the water came up to his neck. He recovered and rose."[47] In Bunyan, the equivalent passage reads: "They then addressed themselves to the water; and entering Christian began to sink, and crying out to his good friend, Hopeful, he said, 'I sink in deep waters, the billows go over my head, all his waves go over me.'"[48]

While Fekisi is crossing the river, he sees a crocodile, "its mouth open," coming toward him. He scrambles desperately toward the bank, only to be confronted by a snake, "a spotted thing, of many colours." He is trapped: "A crocodile behind, a snake in front!"[49] He stands frozen but then remembers that the snake is not poisonous, thus he can escape his entrapment. Like Christian, who is imprisoned in the castle of Giant Despair, Fekisi is paralyzed by his own doubt. Christian, in his own desolation, allows the Giant to imprison him. Only when he rises above his despondency does he remember that he in fact holds the key to his prison cell. In much the same way, Fekisi overcomes his self-doubt and realizes that the snake is harmless.

These Bunyan "signposts" in the text suggest that we are intended to see a parallel between Christian and Fekisi who both single-mindedly undertake a difficult journey from earth to heaven. This parallel, however, inevitably raises concerns about the protagonist's "manliness," particularly in the context of an African society where Fekisi's defection would be seen as eccentric if not crazy. By taking the Protestant journey to salvation as the basic template of the story, Mofolo certainly signals an affinity with Bunyan. However, he, like many other commentators on Bunyan, flags a critical absence with regard to Christian's masculinity. Mofolo would in all likelihood have agreed with the Ghanaian journalist Mabel Dove Danquah, who noted in her own rewriting of *The Pilgrim's Progress*: "I thought at first it was a very wrong thing for a man, a great Christian, to desert his wife and family and try only to save himself."[50] Like Danquah, Mofolo indicates the need to supplement Christian's character with other templates of masculinity, which, in Mofolo's case, are derived from the world of cattle keeping.

The world of cattle herding is deeply imprinted in the text. Much of the first part of the novel is devoted to recreating this domain in considerable detail. The passing of time in the story, for example, is marked by the animal husbandry season. Many of the discourses of cattle keeping are reproduced in the text: praises to cattle, riddles, and mnemonics used among herd boys. The depictions of landscape are also seen through the eye of a cattle herder. Unsurprisingly, the protagonist Fekisi is a "model herdboy," "a real herd, a true herd, one herding by love."[51] In depicting Fekisi in these terms, Mofolo draws together two models of herding. The first of these invokes a traditional moral economy in which cattle herding and the herd boy are an analogue for diligence, steadfastness, husbandry, and leadership. Herders are guardians and sentinels and herding is the activity through which boys become men. Chiefship is often compared to images of herding.[52] However, herding and shepherding are also a powerful organizing metaphor of Christianity, and, like many other Sotho Christians, Mofolo uses this as a point of entry to inhabit Protestantism.[53]

The text compares and contrasts the idea of the Sotho cattle herder and the Christian shepherd as templates of masculinity. The cattle herder in certain respects embodies valuable qualities, namely leadership, husbandry, and diligence. However, in its ultimate form, chieftaincy, where the chief "herds" and "husbands" his people, the idea is marred by the gerontocratic and patriarchal authority underlying the institution of chiefship. These strengths and shortcomings are set out in Fekisi's relationship to the other herd boys with whom he works and to whom he demonstrates qualities of leadership, guidance, and concern. The herd boys in turn respect him, not because of tradition or convention but because of his performance and achievement. Fekisi refuses to make use of the chiefly forms of authority writ small that older herd boys traditionally exercise over younger. Instead, Fekisi inspires their respect through example and evenhandedness. Fekisi also offers a new model of manliness that does not depend on violence or "feudal" authority for its power. Instead, it is a manliness based on love for one's followers as well as a disinterested and nonascriptive exercise of power. It is, in short, a model of manliness based on meritocracy rather than inherited position and authority. A similar point emerges from the Sotho translation of *The Pilgrim's Progress*. Here one of the characters called Presumption is translated as Chief Herd Boy (*mpodi*), a word that denotes dictatorialness but, in this use, indicates that the "feudal" right and privilege traditionally bestowed on the chief herd boy is, from a mission perspective, an unmerited presumption.

This theme of a new style of manly meritocracy is developed further in a subplot where one of Fekisi's friends, Sebati, is killed by the chief's agents for refusing to give in to chiefly demand for tribute. Sebati sees these demands as excessive and unreasonable. He is "proud of his wealth," which he feels he has worked for and with which he will not part.[54] It is this meritocratic hubris that ensures his death.

This cluster of concerns is powerfully expressed in a series of praises that Fekisi sings to his favorite cow, Tsemeli, just prior to his departure. These praises include the lines:

> Tsemeli, you imitate whom
> With your lowing so loud and so long?
> What say the men of the chief
> At the court when they hear?
> They will say: 'Tis not fitting, Tsemeli,
> For a cow so to low in a village'[55]

Tsemeli's lowing is not "fitting" since the cow belongs to a commoner and not the chief. For a commoner to have too many cattle or for their lowing to upstage the cattle of the chief is inappropriate. Like his beloved cow Tsemeli, Fekisi is also out of kilter with the "feudal" demands of chieftaincy and stands in danger of upstaging the chief.[56]

Fekisi's flight is hence not only from the sin of his society but also from the excesses of chiefly masculinity with which he finds himself in increasing conflict. The model of masculinity that Fekisi embodies is one composed of Sotho ideals of leadership and guardianship, tempered with a narrative of Protestantism, all embedded in a matrix of meritocracy.

If Protestantism moderates the forms of patriarchy inherent in chiefly masculinity, then this latter template likewise reflects back on Protestantism.[57] Not only does Mofolo implicitly comment on the manic single-mindedness of Christian but he also supplements this with the "chivalric" ideals of custodianship that Fekisi demonstrates and that Mofolo sees as the essence of true "herdmanship." Fekisi, like Christian, abandons his society, but he does this out of a higher sense of social responsibility and with a view to saving the entire society in the long run. Christian seems motivated only by the destiny of his own soul.

Cast in terms of *The Pilgrim's Progress*, we could say that Mofolo's ideal of manliness is one that combines the single-mindedness of Christian with the noblesse oblige of Great-heart, the cattle herder. Seen in this way, Fekisi, who importantly is celibate and unmarried, could be read as a Sotho Great-heart, protecting the weak, challenging the corrupt and powerful, and, like all knights, tilting bravely at the excesses of power. Such an interpretation is, of course, somewhat fanciful, even if, as seems likely, Mofolo was familiar with the second part of the book. (In later years, he may even have come across Dell's *Greatheart*. Dell was extremely popular in Africa,[58] as was her counterpart, the bestselling novelist Marie Corelli, whom Mofolo admired. The final scene of *Moeti* derives from a Corelli novel, *The Master Christian*.)[59]

Yet, however speculative the idea, it would in all probability have appealed to Mofolo. His book is very much a "parliament" of texts and a book of conspicuous quotation. Even a brief glance through the text reveals poems, songs, passages, and oral narratives dropped as direct quotation into the text. In addition, the book relies on a number of second order quotations. Here genres and discourses from the mission world and beyond are incorporated. These include the literary forms of Protestantism like prayer, liturgy, and the "minidrama" of the catechism. Sotho historical tropes and discourses appear alongside the convert's biography and the mission travelogue. Writers like the colonial adventure novelist Henry Rider Haggard and the bestselling author Marie Corelli are also invoked.[60]

In this gallery of genre and quotation, forms are consciously juxtaposed and contrasted: prayers are set alongside praise poems; Protestant and Sotho myths of origin are superimposed on each other. Sotho narratives are grafted onto Protestant topographies like the Broad and Narrow Way that is invoked in the text.[61] In such a landscape, the idea of "Sothoizing" Great-heart appears quite normal. He is, after all, one of the Protestant templates for imagining masculinity. In formulating a new masculinity, Mofolo shifts around and experiments with a repertoire of such templates, looking for optimal placements where such texts estrangingly reflect each other. A cattle-keeping metaphor—this time of transhumance—seems appropriate in conclusion. Like cows that are moved around seasonally to obtain optimal grazing and conditions, so Mofolo practices a type of intellectual transhumance. Here a repertoire of texts is likewise shifted around a landscape to find their most optimal placement. In the process, the meaning of figures like Great-heart is extended and pulled into new fields of religious being.

8

Illustrating Bunyan

In a brief memoir, "Named for Victoria, Queen of England," the Nigerian novelist, Chinua Achebe, recalls some of his early childhood reading. The selection of books he encountered at home comprised a random assortment of readers, primers, an abridged version of *A Midsummer Night's Dream*, a biology textbook, and a selection of Anglican pamphlets and tracts. Included in this collection was the Igbo translation of *The Pilgrim's Progress*.

> I remember also my mother's *Ije Onye Kraist* which must have
> been an Igbo adaptation of *Pilgrim's Progress*. It could not have
> been the whole book; it was too thin. But it had some
> frightening pictures. I recall in particular a most vivid
> impression of *the valley of the shadow of death*. I thought a lot
> about death in those days.[1]

In Achebe's recollection, two aspects of the text stand out: firstly, it was abridged and, secondly, it was illustrated. These two features in turn succinctly summarize how *The Pilgrim's Progress* altered as it traveled into Africa. As we have seen in previous chapters, the book generally changed its physical form, breaking up into smaller units as it was disseminated in bits and pieces by mission organizations. In the case of the Igbo translation, the book "loses weight" as it travels and, like many other African editions, ends up in an abridged form. The physical manifestation of the book thus tells us something of its history. A second material feature of the text that betrays the changes it undergoes is the illustration. In Achebe's edition, these pictures were, in all likelihood, photographs showing African characters acting out scenes from the story. The presence of illustrations in *The Pilgrim's Progress* was, of course, not unusual. Editions of the book had, since the fifth printing of *The Pilgrim's Progress*, part 1, in 1681, routinely been illustrated.[2] These images represented European characters in every imaginable pictorial medium, such as line-drawing, engraving, woodcuts, or painting. Photographs, however, were never used.

The Igbo edition with its illustrations points back to earlier European editions of Bunyan. Yet, at the same time, these illustrations— with their African characters and their photographic medium—demonstrate that the text had also changed. By examining a variety of illustrations in African editions of Bunyan, this chapter probes exactly what these changes are and asks what this evidence might tell us about how the text was remade under pressure from the local intellectual formations it encountered. As with the process of translation, the final pictorial forms that emerged in African editions were likewise made across time and space and were the result of diverse intellectual interests in the international mission domain. We begin by examining the different traditions of Bunyan illustration that made their way to Africa, and then turn to some examples of how and why these illustrations were reformulated to accommodate different audiences and constituencies in the mission arena.

The use of Bunyan illustrations has to be understood as part of the field of "visual evangelism." As practitioners sensitive to the capacity of different media, missionaries were quick to appreciate the proselytizing potential of visual material. Pictures could create a spectacle and draw a crowd. In the minds of some, illustrations were a "universal language"[3] that could promote the illusion of shared understanding. As one missionary working in India commented in 1897, "I felt there were two short and sure ways to Biblical knowledge. To doctrine, there was the Catechism; and to New Testament history there were pictures. How these young preachers have mastered the life and teaching of Jesus by those pictures! and how readily and easily they preach by their aid."[4] Images were at times favored as appropriate for "literal-minded" converts or, as one missionary said, "a native always talks in pictures."[5] Missionaries increasingly identified pictures as seminal to the success of any printed publication.[6] Herbert Griffiths, writing from Angola in 1956, observed: "Africans as you know are keen on pictures and a few in a book . . . will make all the difference."[7] One report from Nigeria stated that pictures were so popular that they were torn out of books and sold separately.[8] Such images also became a major form of spreading publicity and propaganda about the mission to its supporters at home. Mission stations were, in short, picture-laden environments.

As a key instrument of proselytization, *The Pilgrim's Progress* came to Africa orbited by its own galaxy of visual confetti. For the nineteenth and part of the twentieth centuries, these illustrations were the European set of images to which their originating mission societies had access. These pictures were overwhelmingly evangelical in provenance. Most of these illustrations had originated with the RTS, which had funded the majority of African editions. The RTS (founded in 1799) had first started to produce its own illustrations from the 1820s, when the organization had adopted *The Pilgrim's Progress* as one of its tracts (not without some opposition, as some did not agree with the use of nonscriptural material for evangelical purposes).[9] Its earliest illustrations feature characters in extant dress often in interior settings. This style derived in part from eighteenth-century traditions of Bunyan illustration that favored naturalistic polite "genre" conventions dominated by domestic family settings.[10] This convention in turn had arisen in response to the crude woodcuts characteristic of many seventeenth-century editions (a style to which Blake returned in his illustration of Bunyan). These early RTS series were superseded by others. One commonly used RTS sequence, for example, drew on biblical conventions of illustration and showed Palestinian characters in a "Holy Land" setting. Yet another strand within the RTS repertoire were the late nineteenth-century paintings by Harold Copping of seventeenth-century characters in Puritan dress. These images in turn reflected a turn-of-the-century tendency to interpret Bunyan as "English" that, in pictorial terms, registered itself in a move to reinsert Bunyan into the seventeenth century and the southern English shires.[11]

From early on in the twentieth century, these European Bunyan illustrations began to be supplanted by images reflecting African characters. These Africanized images generally originated as locally inspired initiatives in particular mission stations. The range, style, and competence of these renditions varied enormously and ranged, on the one hand, from rather amateurish sketches and stick-figure characters to accomplished renditions by professional artists, on the other.[12] These drawings were all by Europeans and it is generally only in postindependence mission and commercially produced school editions that the work of African artists is reflected (although in the 1930s the RTS did commission the South African artist George Pemba to undertake a sequence of illustrations, but these were never used).[13] Alongside these various traditions of drawn illustration were also photographs. Two sets of photographic illustration were undertaken: the first in 1919/20 in northern Angola at the Baptist mission at San Salvador, and the second in 1927 at Muhono College in Uganda.[14]

The spread and reach of these various sets of illustrations varied considerably. In some cases, illustrations were limited to one edition that circulated within a single language zone and, at times, only among the stations of the same mission society in that zone. Other sets of illustrations traveled more widely and appeared in several different language editions across the continent. This reach was enabled by a series of international Protestant literature organizations that actively sought to promote cooperation and rationalization among those mission societies working in the field of "Christian literature."[15] The major player in this regard was the International Committee on Christian Literature for Africa (ICCLA). The impetus for this committee and others like it lay in a perception that rates of literacy had risen without a commensurate increase in "suitable" reading material. Newly literate readers required appropriate publications to counter the "threat" of secular and increasingly communist-inspired texts. Toward this end, the ICCLA energetically pursued different strategies: they audited what was available, made recommendations to missions, coordinated and strengthened regional cross-mission literature committees where these existed, shared resources and ideas, and produced a journal *Books for Africa*. Older organizations in the field, like the RTS (renamed the United Society for Christian Literature, or USCL, in 1936), the American Tract Society, and the Society for Promoting Christian Knowledge (SPCK), an Anglican organization, continued to undertake similar work, but not without some irritation at the new and more aggressive methods of the ICCLA.[16]

As with all other Protestant organizations, the ICCLA continued to earmark *The Pilgrim's Progress* as an important text. The pages of their publications recommended it for evangelical and educational purposes.[17] They urged school libraries to acquire copies, and they reviewed new editions.[18] They also recommended it as a prize book.[19] Books that resembled Bunyan or carried a similar message were favorably reviewed. Thomas Mofolo's *Moeti oa Bochabela* (*The Traveller to the East*) was discussed as "an African Pilgrim's Progress."[20] Elsewhere, the ICCLA shared information on *Pilgrim's Progress* coloring books for Sunday schools.[21] ICCLA publications provided advice on how to obtain or generate illustrations for *The Pilgrim's Progress*.[22]

Through the work of organizations like the ICCLA and the RTS, four sets of "canonical" Africanized illustrations came to predominate

Figure 17. Photographic illustration from the Kongo edition, 1920s. The character playing Evangelist is Miguel Nekaka. Source: BMS Archives. Reproduced with the permission of the BMS.

(figures 2, 3, 17 to 19). For ease of reference, and in roughly chronological order, we can label them as (1) the Montague/Burton drawings; (2) the Austin photographs; (3) the Burton Lingala sketches; (4) the Kamba illustrations. The Montague/Burton illustrations began in 1902 as a set of sketches by C. J. Montague for the Ndebele edition, which we encountered in chapters 6 and 7 (figures 11 to 16). These drawings, however, reflected a lot of specific southern African detail in terms of clothing, headdress, and—to a lesser extent—landscape, and because of this they

THE HILL DIFFICULTY FAITHFUL AND CHRISTIAN MEET TALKATIVE BYE-PATH MEADOW

Figure 18. Section of collage of photographic illustrations from Kongo edition, 1920s. Source: P. H. Austin, "*The Pilgrim's Progress* in a Congo Setting," *Missionary Herald*, July 1923, 151. Reproduced with the permission of the BMS.

had limited portability. In order to give them a wider purchase, W.F.P. Burton of the Congo Evangelistic Mission redrew them, probably in the 1930s. Burton generalized the background landscape and changed the clothing, turning the central character into a schoolboy figure in short khaki pants and shirt, an addition meant no doubt to appeal to a school audience (figure 3). The Austin photographs (figures 17 and 18) (which Achebe probably looked at) were originally done in 1919/20 for the Kongo edition and were then widely disseminated, ending up in at least eight editions. The third set of pictures was also executed by Burton, probably in the 1940s, initially for the Lingala edition, a trade language of the Congo region (figure 19). These migrated into at least two other versions. The final set, which also gained a modest distribution (mainly courtesy of the RTS/USCL), was done by the Heart of Africa mission for the Kamba edition in Kenya (figure 20). The defining feature of these images was that the characters' faces and bodies are completely one-dimensional and monotone without any distinguishing physiognomical features.

These sets of illustrations were not the only ones available but they gained popularity by being recommended by the ICCLA and the RTS/USCL. This recommendation in turn probably arose from the close links between these latter organizations and certain Nonconformist mission societies. The CMS (an Anglican group) and their publishing arm,

Figure 19. Illustration for the Lingala edition by W.F.P. Burton,
1930s. Source: John Bunyan, *Njela na Mokristu* (*The Pilgrim's
Progress*, part 1) (Ibambi: Heart of Africa Mission, n.d.), 21.
Reproduced with the permission of the trustees of the CAM,
U.K. charity no. 1049246.

the SPCK, sponsored a lavish and unprecedented sequence of sixty-four
photographic illustrations for both the first and second part of the book
in Ganda. These, however, were (to my knowledge) never reproduced in
any other language editions, although line drawings of the photographs
do appear in some editions.

In choosing which illustrations to adopt, there was, of course,
considerable debate. One missionary, Ralph Wilson from Angola, wrote
to the ICCLA in 1956 seeking help with illustrations for a new Umbundu
version of Bunyan. The illustrations of the existing edition were not popular, as the faces of characters were blank and without any features (these
images had been derived from the Kamba illustrations, the fourth set of
canonical illustrations listed above). Wilson wrote: "Almost all object to
the black smudgy faces. They are quite sensitive and say 'We don't look

Figure 20. Illustration from the Kamba edition. Source: John Bunyan, *Kuendeea kwa Muendi wa kyalo* (*The Pilgrim's Progress*, part 1) (London: Lutterworth Press, n.d.), 116. Reproduced with the permission of the USCL.

like that.'" Wilson had two other sets of illustrations on hand. The first was by Burton (from the Lingala version) and offered more physiognomical details.[23] The second was a Portuguese edition printed in Brazil that contained British linecuts representing characters in a seventeenth-century setting. The respondents to Wilson's survey rated Burton's pictures first, the Portuguese/British pictures second and the existing "black smudgy"/Kamba pictures third.[24] As matters turned out, and unbeknown to Wilson, this "black smudgy" set had already been ordered and so this is what was printed.[25]

Underlying Wilson's comments, and indeed much of the venture of Africanizing Bunyan's illustrations, was a mission preoccupation with making things appear "African." This movement, as Dana Robert has demonstrated, stemmed from mission involvement in post–First World War internationalism. A concomitant of this "one-world" vision was a concern with local particularity that could help define internationalism. As Robert indicates, in the mission domain these ideas expressed themselves in projects like the indigenization of Christian literature and attempts to "de-westernize" Christ.[26]

Such debates were inevitably permeated with contradictions. Any attempts to define what was "African" immediately threw up contesting claims and definitions. Take, for example, the "black smudgy" featureless images that Wilson's interlocutors rejected. For the RTS/USCL, these were imminently "African" and thus, in their estimation, could be used in any part of the continent. By contrast, pictures with too much specific detail could betray the characters' ethnic background and so have limited circulation potential. Such images portraying "one particular tribe [were] therefore lacking in universal appeal among the many tribes." The RTS solution was to recommend the blank, featureless faces "whose tribal markings are undecipherable."[27] How RTS/USCL officials in London detected "tribal markings" is not clear, particularly since the pictures they were discussing comprised rather rough line drawings of a photograph of a character dressed up pageant-style. Their perception of "tribalness" was hence largely chimerical. Nevertheless, it played a role in providing the negative definition underlying their understanding of "African," namely a "universal" continent-wide African Christianity, standing in opposition to any local and troublesome social categories like ethnicity.

The decision, then, about which illustrations to print was by no means straightforward and was wrought in different locales and institutions. The web of debate shaping the choice of any illustration extended across a wide zone reaching, on the one hand, from local preferences among converts to the recommendations of international agencies, on the other. In between lay the inclinations of individual missionaries, the traditions of particular mission stations, the capacities of printing presses, the perceived tastes of particular markets (for example, school readers), and so on. Very often, this transnational debate registered itself not only in the choice of illustration but, in some instances, in the pictorial conventions of certain images themselves. A brief consideration of two of the "canonical" sets of illustrations listed above, namely the Austin photographs and the Montague drawings, will throw further light on this assertion.

The first set of photographic illustration for The Pilgrim's Progress was made under the direction of a Baptist missionary, P. H. Austin at San Salvador in northern Angola (figures 17 and 18). Austin felt that the existing illustrations with "white men in early Victorian costume" were not appropriate and were "scarcely likely to convey a helpful impression to the natives." In order to remedy the situation, he decided to "take pictures in a native setting, with natives representing the characters." (These explanations were provided in an article that he did on the pictures for the Baptist *Missionary Herald* of 1923.)[28] The photographs were used both in the Kongo edition and for magic lantern slides.

The people chosen to play the parts of the various characters were prominent mission personalities: Miguel Nekaka (figure 17), a leading convert and translator, played Evangelist; Ambrose Luyanzi, secretary of the church, took the role of Interpreter; and Kitomene, another prominent personality and the leader of the mission porters, was chosen to play Christian. The photographs were taken on the mission precinct and feature some of its landmarks such as the church, the ruins of the Roman Catholic cathedral on the boundary of the station, and Ambrose Luyanzi's house.

The photographs evidently proved to be popular and attracted crowds at magic lantern showings.[29] This popularity is hardly surprising. The book had been intensively propagated since the mission station's inception in 1878 and had been broadcast via every available medium— sermon, pageant, choir service, magic lantern slide, mission periodical, and schoolbook—and in every available forum—pulpit, classroom, sewing circle, choir vestry, and Sunday school.[30] From the 1920s, the Kongo version could no longer be used in the classroom, since the Portuguese colonial state, seeking to enforce a policy of assimilation, forbade the use of vernacular in schools in favor of Portuguese. This prohibition notwithstanding, Bunyan continued to be broadcast from church-related sites and continued to play an important part in the life of Kongo Protestants.

Part of the book's success, however, must be attributed to the photographs, which helped to stitch the text even more firmly into the history and traditions of the Kongo Protestants. The photographs, after all, showed characters who were known to local readers. Such a conjuncture opened up the possibility that Bunyan's story could be conflated with the biographies of the "characters" in the illustration. It is evidently an interpretive strategy that readers exploited. As João Matwawana, who lived in San Salvador in the 1940s and 50s, is reported as recalling: "The people identified with the characters in the stories and because of their own history and folk memories of the rebellion of 1913–1[5] (The Buta War), read political significance into the struggles of the Christians in the book."[31]

The Buta War was a rebellion that erupted around San Salvador in response to Portuguese forced labor policies.[32] Antipathy was directed both toward Portuguese colonial officials and the Kongo King who recruited workers for plantations on the island, San Tome, and the coastal enclave, Cabinda. The uprising was led by an erstwhile recruiter, Chief Tulante Alvaro Buta. Miguel Nekaka was to play a major role in the event: firstly, through his attempts to negotiate a settlement, and then as a target of the Portuguese authorities, as he, along with three others from the mission, was imprisoned for several months. His imprisonment in turn formed part of a Portuguese attempt to implicate the Protestant mission as instigators of the uprising.

The Bunyan photographs in which Nekaka featured were taken some four to five years after the end of the Buta War in 1915, at a time when the memory of the event still persisted. Nekaka and others in the photographs were prominent personalities and, as Matwawana's comments suggest, their presence in the book's illustrations invited readers to see them as the text's protagonists. The story consequently became a kind of biography in which events in the story are made to fit the experiences of the people in the photographs. Nekaka had been a central character in the Buta War and thus the book could be interpreted as a story about that event.

In the case of the Kongo edition of Bunyan, then, the illustrations played a key part in how the story was read. Yet, what did these pictures mean to an audience far away? In probing this question, it is perhaps useful to pause and ask why photography as a medium was chosen. At first glance, the decision may seem unremarkable. Missionaries used photography widely and its inclusion in one of their favorite texts would seem inevitable.[33] However, if considered against European traditions of illustration, the presence of photographs in a fictional text becomes noteworthy: no European edition of Bunyan ever used photographic illustrations.[34] Indeed, such a convention would be unthinkable for a European edition. Photography has, after all, always been associated with evidence and scientific verisimilitude. As a form of illustration, it accompanies works of nonfiction. Fiction, by contrast, has always been illustrated by means of drawing, painting, or engraving. Photography and fictional writing were hence deemed mutually exclusive: if brought together, the presence of the one would automatically throw doubt on the status of the other. *The Pilgrim's Progress*, a work of fiction, and the photograph, a source of evidence, inhabited incommensurate domains. In its centuries-long existence in Europe, the book was to be adorned by every type and convention of drawing, painting, woodcut and engraving, but never by a photograph.

Yet, when the text traveled to Africa, photographic illustration became possible. The boundary between fiction and photograph is breached and the two cohabit quite happily. How does one explain this conundrum? What is it about the history of photography in Africa and the history of Bunyan translation that enables this shift? One way to answer this question is to examine the repertoire of visual conventions that missions evolved to communicate with a home audience, for it is in part from this enabling matrix that the "fictional" photograph emerged.

In examining the photographs and Austin's description of their making, it is clear that they encompass several mission genres. The first of these is the ethnographic photograph, which is, as many others have indicated, a form widely practiced by missionaries.[35] They identified themselves with the "scientific" endeavor of documenting and creating racial difference and many missionaries worked in conjunction with academic and scientific institutions. W.F.P. Burton, for example, created an entire ethnographic photographic archive for the University of the Witwatersrand in Johannesburg. Several of these images make their way into his Lingala line-drawing illustrations of *The Pilgrim's Progress*. In some cases, it is simply a matter of borrowing background. In others, the "quotation" is more pointed. In the case of his depiction of Vanity Fair, we see Christian and Faithful dressed in "Western" clothing against a background of "heathen" figures in extravagant ritual dress (figure 19). The codes Burton invokes for this "heathen" costume derive from his photographs (and ongoing study) of the Bamdudye Dancing Society, the major form of ideological and spiritual opposition to Christianity in the Luba area in southeastern Congo where Burton worked.[36]

While Austin's images are less obviously ethnographic, he does at times give them an ethnographic gloss, evident in comments like: "This illustration gives a good idea of the various types of dress adopted by the natives," and the "photograph [of Vanity Fair] . . . gives a fairly good idea of a native market." In this regard, the illustrations provide a certain kind of "evidence" of "native" habit and dress. Austin likewise undertook the whole project because "it was thought a good idea to take pictures in a native setting, with natives representing the characters."[37] The genre that suggested itself for depicting "natives" was the photograph.

A second genre invoked in the photographs is that of the mission station landmark. This photographic form was well developed and constituted one of the major vehicles through which mission periodicals acquainted supporters back home with mission progress. An almost standard opening for a mission periodical article on any station was "I enclose a few photographs."[38] Thereafter followed text that directed the reader's attention to details of the adjacent photographs. Through this method, readers built up a knowledge of schools, churches, the general layout of the station, the "ethnographic" character of the surrounding people, and so on. In Austin's photographs, readers' attention is likewise directed to mission station features. "In the next illustration we see Christian knocking at the 'wicket gate' which is the door of the San Salvador Church; and in the fifth picture he arrives at the house of 'Interpreter.' This character was taken by Ambrose Luyanzi. . . . In the picture he is standing at the door of his house, which he constructed himself." Another feature of the mission station was the ruin of the Roman Catholic cathedral on its boundary. This landmark, too, cropped up in the photographs, and readers have their attention directed to this feature in the photograph. "Doubting Castle, the residence of Giant Despair, which is clearly seen in the background, is the ruin of the ancient Roman Catholic Cathedral, which was built during the first Portuguese occupation of San Salvador."[39]

As many discussions of mission photography have shown, the form was largely devoted to establishing boundaries between Christian and heathen. One strategy in this bigger framework was to personalize the convert in opposition to the anonymous heathen. The biography of the convert was one genre that undertook this work of personalization. The photographs, which nearly always accompanied such texts, assisted in the process of individualizing the convert. The Austin pictures invoke this convention, which takes the form of a short biographical write-up about some of the actors: "The making of the pictures was most interesting. It was important to secure a good 'pilgrim' who was at once intelligent and familiar with the story; and such a man was found in Kitomene, one of our teachers. He is a fine Christian man, and being the head man on our caravan journeys, is well acquainted with 'sloughs of despond,' 'hills of difficulty' and other hardships of the way." Nekaka, taking the part of Evangelist, also merited a brief biography. "This character [Evangelist] was taken by Nekaka, and it would be hard to find in all Congo a man more worthy of the name Evangelist, for he has shown many of his countrymen the way to the 'wicket gate' and has helped them in their difficult journey to the 'Celestial City.'" The Interpreter, Ambrose Luyanzi, is described thus: "This character [Interpreter] was taken by Ambrose Luyanzi, secretary of the native church. His knowledge of the English language is a constant source of wonder to the missionaries, and he is a master in the art of interpretation. In the picture he is standing at the door of his house, which he constructed himself, and in his hand he holds the interpreter's lamp."[40]

The final form invoked by the photographic illustrations is that of the religious tableau or pageant. As we have seen, this genre was routinely employed by missionaries at San Salvador and, indeed, elsewhere in the mission world where drama was a favored method of education and evangelism.[41] Austin's pictures were not part of a pageant, although they were clearly posed for the occasion. However, so pageant-like did they appear that at least one viewer assumed that they had been "taken from an African Christian performance of the story."[42] This anticipation of theatricality in turn relates to the high degree of spectacle and performance that viewers came to expect of colonial and mission encounters.

This genre of the "fictional" photograph emerges at the crossroads of these forms: ethnographic photography, the mission station photograph, the image and biography of the convert, and the religious pageant. As mission station photography, the images can be seen as "evidence" of mission success and the universality of Protestant belief. This idea is underlined by the collage presentation in the *Missionary Herald* that accompanied Austin's article (figure 18). The pictures are presented as a gallery of photographs with English captions, an arrangement underlining the impression that this is a universal story that is read in the same way throughout the world. Some of Austin's observations reinforce this point:

> In the eighth picture Christian is seen standing before the Cross. As he gazes fixedly upon it, the burden falls from his back into the sepulcher. This is surely a parable of what is happening in Congo to-day. Men and women are discovering that at the foot of the Cross of the Redeemer they are losing their burden of superstition and of bondage, and all kinds of sin.[43]

Similarly—and even possibly at the same time—the photographic medium can cut across this universalistic belief and instead betoken an imaginative segregation. "We" (namely home viewers) have "our" story in painting, drawing, or linecuts. "They" have their story that unfolds in the ethnographic space of mission photography. This tension between identifying with and disavowing the actors in the photographs is evident as well in the mixture of the convert biography and the ethnographic photograph. As converts, the actors are personalized and furthermore, like their home audience, they are Baptist. Yet, as ethnographic "objects," they are anonymous African Christian "types" and hence different from audiences "at home." As performers in a pageant, the actors again proclaim their similarity to home viewers, most of whom had probably taken part in such events. However, as figures in an ethnographic space, they dramatize the "belatedness" of Africa. For viewers in 1923, accustomed to English illustration, which showed Bunyan in a seventeenth-century setting, the English version of the story unfolds in the distant past. Because of their photographic medium, Austin's illustrations, by contrast, suggest that, for Africans, the story unfolds in the present. Africa, in other words, is still in Europe's past. However, for many Baptists, Bunyan's story did not necessarily exist in seventeenth-century Bedford but rather in an evangelical present. For such viewers, the presentness of the photographs may have heightened rather than weakened a sense of identification with the actors in the illustrations. Indeed, this attempt to shift the story, via its illustrations, into the present may have come from Austin himself, who in Africa could, through photographs, make Bunyan live in the present, a pictorial option not open to him back in England.

The form of Austin's illustrations was determined, then, by the generic competencies of the various audiences to which it was directed, namely Kongo Protestants, a home audience, and missionaries themselves. Via his illustrations, these audiences could sustain different interpretations of the story and its significance. For Kongo Protestants, the illustrations converted the book into an allegory on the Buta War. For Baptists in Britain, the illustrations could be read to demonstrate the universality of Bunyan's story and the Protestantism that underlay it. However, because the illustrations were photographs, they could equally be read in a racialized way to demonstrate the ethnographic difference of African Christians. For missionaries themselves, the photographs could open up ways of dramatizing and realizing the complexities of evangelical time in which Bunyan's—and hence God's—story is always in the present.

While Austin's photographs were shot in Angola, other sets of "African" illustration were in all probability made back in England. One such set of pictures was that done by C. J. Montague in 1902 for the southern African Ndebele version (figures 11 to 16).[44] In constructing his images, he must have taken advice from missionaries and used photographs, books, and documents on the region he was depicting. He consequently undertook a peculiarly mission-inspired form of art, produced in one place about another thousands of miles away and addressed simultaneously to at least three audiences, namely mission, convert, and home supporter. The set of images he produced bears traces of his attempts to manage the contradictory demands of this task.

The first of these traces comes in the frontispiece, which, like thousands of other editions, carries an image of Bunyan. This tradition goes back to the seventeenth century and, in its classic form, shows Bunyan asleep and dreaming. His head rests in the palm of his hand. Below him is a cave-like den that Bunyan aficionados would recognize as his prison. Above his head, in the top half of the image, the dream/story unfolds and we see Christian setting out on his journey (figure 1).

In selecting this image to launch the text, Montague orients the book for British readers and provides a framework of familiarity within which they can "read" the non-English object in their hands. Yet, the image, while broadly similar to its original counterpart, also has some significant differences (figure 2). In the Montague edition, Bunyan lies in his characteristic posture, head in hand. However, rather than sleeping, he is awake and is writing with a quill in a book. The character in the "dream space" above his head has also changed and we now have an African rather than a European Christian. The reasons for these alterations are not hard to fathom—having a white man sleeping in "public" in a colonial context would hardly provide a propitious beginning for a mission text. Likewise, the image of Bunyan writing embodies the idea of this seminal Protestant text "authoring" the experiences of African converts. Europe writes and Africa reads.

British readers who knew their Bunyan well would have had no difficulty in recognizing the fifteen images that follow. They represent well-known scenes in the story and some, like Evangelist pointing the way to the Shining Light (figure 16), bear a resemblance in their composition to earlier British versions of this picture, like Copping's. Yet, there is much local detail that such a reader might have missed. Montague, however, assisted English viewers, and the *Chronicle of the LMS* in 1902 ran an explanatory article on his illustrations. Rather like Austin, he invites viewers to regard parts of his images ethnographically. In relation to the first picture of the hero setting out, Montague says: "Christian starts from a kraal, where the careless of his race are typified by a group around a cooking pot eating 'skoff'" (figure 11). In the picture of Hill Difficulty, readers are invited to observe Mistrust, "who wears charms around his neck to counteract the baleful influences of witches, night animals mostly, who are supposed to be in league with the resentful dead" (figure 14).[45]

Very attentive LMS readers with a particular interest in Carnegie's station at Hope Fountain may also have recognized a section of one illustration that comes from Carnegie's book, *Among the Matabele*, published in 1894.[46] The text includes an illustration entitled "A Matabele

Village,"[47] and Montague uses this as the background to his rendition of the Slough of Despond. Carnegie's book, published in the lead-up to the Ndebele uprising of 1896/7, forms part of standard mission/white settler historiography on the "warlike" Ndebele, whom both groups had a shared interest in conquering.[48] The book is a fairly typical piece of mission ethnography that seeks to typify the "savage" and "heathen" customs of the Ndebele. Through his illustration, Montague links the two texts, namely Carnegie's treatise on the Ndebele and the translation of *The Pilgrim's Progress*. In the first, the reader experiences life among the "heathen" Ndebele. In the second, through the images, the reader lives briefly among the "convert" Ndebele.

There is a further link between these two texts, which again only close followers of events in Matabeleland would have noticed. The figure of Evangelist bears a more than passing resemblance to Carnegie himself. To equate the two was not Montague's intention. For him, Evangelist "is a sturdy missionary in traveller's outfit, instead of the seventeenth century divine that two centuries of illustrators have made us familiar with."[49] Nonetheless, the question of whether Evangelist was David Carnegie must surely have arisen, particularly for readers in Matabeleland. If Carnegie is Evangelist, then who is Christian, who is Faithful, who is Hopeful, and so on? Might they not also be real people and hence African Christians at Carnegie's station, Hope Fountain? As with Austin's photographs, the possibility of this book as a biography of notable African Christians opens up.

A further imprint of convert interpretation on Montague's illustrations is, of course, the final scene in which Christian and Hopeful hand over their documents at the gates of heaven (figure 15). As chapter 6 argued, this focus on the pieces of paper was peculiar to African Christianity and never featured in European illustrations of the text. Left to his own devices, Montague would probably never have thought to include such a scene. However, possibly via Carnegie, African interest in this scene might have been conveyed to the artist and has left its impress on the illustrations. That this imprint was reasonably strong can be seen from the fact that Montague's illustrations made their way into the Zulu edition. Harriet Colenso (daughter of Bishop Colenso), who had good links to Zulu Christians, wrote to Montague requesting permission to use the pictures, which in her assessment had "delighted" people.[50]

Montague's pictures thus have their being in the multiple audiences for which he produced his images. While he modeled his work on existing British traditions of Bunyan illustration, the nature of the audiences to which he "spoke" determined a number of key shifts in these images. Bunyan, for example, wakes up. An African Christian interest in the presentation of documents at the gates of heaven, never before chosen for illustration, made its way into Montague's line drawings. Like the translation alongside, these images could only have been made in the international space of mission evangelicalism.

9

Bunyan in the African Novel

A few years back, the musician Talvin Singh, a leader of British-Asian fusion and the "Asian underground" sound, was asked about his views on international influences in music. Weary of endless media categorizations, Singh put forward his opinion. "Music's like . . . a potato. . . . You go to different parts of the world, and there are loads of dishes containing potato. But nobody asks where a potato's from, it's just; 'Yeah, this tastes good.'"[1]

Glib as the formulation is, it confronts us with crucial questions. Do cultural products that meander through an ever-integrated international economy retain marks of their place of origin? Are they indelibly stamped with labels of provenance? On being opened, do they exude a continental flavor or aroma? Judged from the standpoint of much poststructural thinking, such an imprimatur would be impossible—texts are but strings of language with no essential meaning. Turn to postcolonial scholarship, however, and—its dalliances with poststructuralism notwithstanding—texts traveling from the center generally carry an a priori imperial meaning.

Homi Bhabha, for example, speaks of "the English book." He does admittedly use the term as a symbolic catchall, an emblem or insignia of colonial authority and presence. Nonetheless, the looseness of the term obscures any historical specificities regarding different types of books. Whether one is talking of the Bible translated into Hindi, Conrad's *Heart of Darkness*, or V. S. Naipaul's novels (as Bhabha does), they all recapitulate the "originary myth" of "the English book."[2] In any encounter involving this "book," all parties apparently recognize its "Englishness" and hence where it comes from.

Another example, more pertinent to our purposes, comes from a recent discussion of the Nigerian novelist, Amos Tutuola. It notes that while Tutuola's corpus draws on Yoruba orature, it also makes use of "Western sources," one of which is *The Pilgrim's Progress*.[3] We are told that Tutuola "borrows . . . from the cultures of the colonizer and colonized alike" (Bunyan being identified as belonging to the former category). Yet, by the time Tutuola began writing in the late 1940s, *The Pilgrim's Progress* had been present in Nigeria in a printed Yoruba version since 1868. In its English form, the book had been available since at least that date, if not before. Seen from this perspective, is Bunyan—after nearly a century of residence in Nigeria—still "Western"? Can one simply talk of him as "belonging" to the colonized? Does his text still bear the marks of the place from which it comes, or has it become "naturalized"? Has the text not in effect become deterritorialized, its original "Western" provenance, no longer of any moment? Conversely, is there in effect not an "indigenized" Bunyan tradition on which writers draw, rather than each writer interacting de novo with a "Western" Bunyan?

By tracing how Bunyan is treated by four African novelists, this chapter explores these propositions. The novelists are two Nigerians, D. O. Fagunwa (who wrote in Yoruba) and Amos Tutuola (who wrote in English), the Kenyan, Ngũgĩ wa Thiong'o, who wrote first in English and then Kikuyu, and finally the Zimbabwean, Tsitsi Dangarembga, writing in English. It examines not only how these writers use Bunyan but also how they draw on African interpretations of the text as well as each other's readings of Bunyan.

The Pilgrim's Progress was a text that interested Fagunwa. To him, Bunyan was useful because he could throw light on life after death, or what Fagunwa called "the mysterious." In an article in the *Teacher's Monthly*, Fagunwa argued:

> The mysterious interests us in one way or another. What for instance happens to us after death? Is it true that if we behave well on earth, we go to paradise and otherwise to hell? Are there ghosts? Do spirits inhabit trees, rocks, rivers, streams etc.? What a novelist does is to present one or more of these aspects of life and weave a long story around whichever he takes.[4]

Fagunwa goes on to note that writing a "mysterious" novel is one of the hardest genres to execute. Romance is perhaps the easiest: "A novel based on love is not very difficult to write because even if all the true stories of love we hear are written and joined, they easily look like fiction." He continues: "Equally a novel based on money is not very difficult to write since stories connected with misappropriation of money are common in real life."[5] By contrast, "A novel which involves the mysterious is perhaps the most difficult to write. In such a case the writer goes really into the world of imagination and therefore it is necessary for him to have had an inborn gift of imagination. In literary history, only few brains had produced this type of writing and the products have lived long." Fagunwa identifies Bunyan ("the father of English novels") as such a mysterious writer. "His *Pilgrim's Progress* describes no other thing than the journey from this world to the world to come." He adds, "So is Spenser's *Faerie Queene* a novel in verse."[6] Fagunwa notes that a preponderance of novels written in western Nigeria concern themselves with the "mysterious." He calls these "phantasia novels." Not only are they concerned with questions of the "mysterious" but they also favor an allegorical technique. Fagunwa explains:

> I usually term these [phantasia novels] Spenserian because they so much resemble the works of an English writer, whose works were published in the late sixteenth and early seventeenth century A.D., called Edmund Spenser. The fact about them is that if well handled they have a peculiarly forceful way of driving an idea home. They interest Nigerian readers a good deal and I have always encouraged rather than discouraged them. Compare this personification in Book I of Spenser's *Faerie Queene*. In Spenser's view, the reformed Church was full of misdeeds. He does not as a result describe these acts of omission and commission in mere words, but instead, he personifies Error as a horrible monster half-serpent half-woman living in a dark, filthy cave, to be fought by a knight who himself was the son of a fairy. Here, when everything of the misdeeds of the Church could have been forgotten, the picture of this monster would remain in the mind.[7]

This passage makes several points on allegory. Fagunwa indicates that allegory is an effective technique that somehow outstrips the capacity of "mere words." Instead, it is a form of visual spectacle that is consequently highly memorable. Partly because of this visualness, allegory is an "exportable" form that can travel. The vehicle of the allegory may carry an "original" meaning: in this case, the corruption of the Established Church. However, this meaning may be lost and the text or passage then becomes de-allegorized. The vehicle nonetheless continues unencumbered by its old meaning and finds a new life. In Nigeria, a writer like Spenser—or indeed Bunyan—undergoes just such a process. The surface of their stories, often concerned with the supernatural, or what Fagunwa terms "phantasia," falls on the fertile ground of popular taste in Nigeria, where most people, in Fagunwa's words, are interested in "juju, spirits, ghosts etc."[8] The "original" meaning of the allegory may be lost, but the story, through its memorable images, lives on.

Fagunwa found a writer like Bunyan useful for two reasons: firstly, Bunyan could tell his readers something about heaven and, secondly, his allegorical technique, like Spenser's, offered strategies in the field of didactic narrative. By examining two of Fagunwa's novels that have been translated into English, we can see how he put these two ideas into action. The novels in question are *Ògbójú Ọdẹ Nínú Igbó Irúnmalẹ* (*The Forest of a Thousand Daemons*) (1938) and *Irìnkerindo Nínú Igbó Elégbèje* (*Expedition to the Mount of Thought*) (1954).[9]

In order to understand how Fagunwa employs *The Pilgrim's Progress*, it is useful to grasp the type of fictive world he establishes and hence the environment into which elements of Bunyan are inducted. Fagunwa's novels unfold in a layered world of "morphed" or extended folktale into which elements of realism are spliced.[10] Onto the patchwork cosmology of the text—comprising (in Wole Soyinka's translation)[11] spirit forests, countries, kingdoms, abodes, and villages—ordinary measures of time and space—miles, minutes, and calendar years—are superimposed. These worlds are crowded with a panoply of beings—in Soyinka's translations represented as ghommids, trolls, bog-trolls, dewilds, spirits, kobolds, gnoms, and the dead. We also have birds and animals with human capabilities, as well as giants, monsters, witches, and mythical figures, like the Smith of Heaven. Even the odd Old Testament character, like King Solomon, appears. The protagonists are always humans: brave hunters who proceed part-picaresquely and part-epically through these topsy-turvy worlds. Humans and spirits generally occupy different ontological spheres, but they do interact: they trade, exchange gifts, maintain diplomatic relations, and, in some instances, marry.

Unsurprisingly, the religious world of these novels is plural. In *The Forest of a Thousand Daemons*, at a moment of danger, we hear that "the Christians called to their Saviour, the Moslems called Anobi, the masqueraders called on their ancestors, Sango followers called on Sango, Oloya called on Oya."[12] This fictive world can consequently be typified as an expansible portfolio of spiritual and supernatural possibilities. In such a world, further religious options can easily be added without upsetting the principles of the text's fictive space. In both novels, a Christian-style heaven and hell are tacked on to Fagunwa's fictive geography. These domains, however, simply melt into the background, so to speak, becoming yet two further spiritual alternatives among many. Heaven and hell are consequently localized in scope and influence. Hell may indeed punish sinners, but its reach does not appear to be universal. Heaven only fascinates some: the majority of the party of hero-hunters traveling in the vicinity of heaven choose a side road that bypasses paradise. One hunter, however, is overcome by the beauty of the hymns that sound from Heaven, so he heads off in that direction, never to be seen again. The book's narrator at times invokes a concept of God that appears to be largely Christian, although this is contradicted elsewhere in the text. In the first novel, God himself, for example, proves to be irascible and bad-tempered, while, in the second, the Devil, at times, emerges as a thoughtful and contemplative being, appalled by humanity's capacity for avarice and violence.[13]

In this expansible portfolio, elements of Bunyan can easily be accommodated. Three of these are pertinent for our purposes. The first, which as we shall see is taken up by subsequent writers, is the presence in both novels of a female "evangelist." Her name is translated as Help or Helpmeet and, like the figure Evangelist in *The Pilgrim's Progress*, who appears at critical moments to give advice and assistance, she, too, materializes at decisive junctures to help the party of hunters. Unsurprisingly, the second Bunyan element in *The Forest of a Thousand Daemons* concerns the depiction of documents, in this case "a letter written in a mixture of liquid silver and gold" that is sent by the immortal figure Iragbeje to the king of the hunters. This letter recalls the one, also written in gold, received by Christiana at the beginning of the second part of the story summoning her to join her husband in heaven.

A third Bunyan feature relates to the depictions of heaven and hell. Heaven, as we have seen, is one subregion of his first novel. Its physical appearance is derived from *The Pilgrim's Progress*. The approach to heaven, for example, is on a straight paved road similar to sections of Bunyan's narrow way. On the road are "two good-looking youths dressed in shining white," rather like the Shining Ones who welcome new arrivals to heaven. Yet, heaven is also constructed from Yoruba motifs. One of its most important residents is Ogodogo, the potter "who moulds the unborn children whom the Creator assigns to humanity every year."[14]

In *Expedition to the Mount of Thought*, aspects of hell resemble the House of the Interpreter in which Christian is shown various emblematic pictures and spectacles whose allegorical import is then expounded to him. Roger Sharrock has aptly described the Interpreter's House as an "emblem theatre."[15] In Fagunwa's novel, the Devil conducts the character Endurance and the hero-hunters (who have made themselves invisible) around the sights of hell. These include a series of Bunyan-like tableaux that fall into three categories: the first exemplifies temptation; the second the enactment of evil; and the third the punishment that follows.

The first category of tableau (of which there is only one instance) involves an emblematic object called "Lucifer's Trap." This "installation" takes the form of a bird's cage filled with gold coins behind which a cobra rears up. The object has a twofold purpose. It is Satan's own mnemonic and reminds him to perform evil at all times "lest forgetfulness should overtake [him]." The object also tempts humans on earth: "'[W]hen I come into Earth and egg a man to pick his neighbour's money, that which does not belong to him, he will little realize that he is plunging his finger into a cobra's mouth."[16] This tableau is very similar to those in the Interpreter's House, where a verbal message is attached to each aspect of the scene.

The second category of tableau is slightly different and takes the form of a mimed scene. Satan, who appears to be choreographer and producer, initiates each interlude with an instruction to the "actors" who evidently repeat the same sequence of action whenever commanded to do so. When directed by Satan to "proceed," a man clubs his wife's head. Satan then enunciates the moral of the tableau: "[O]bserve how the man broke the head of the woman, and yet they are husband and wife." It is clear that after performing their piece, the "characters" in this tableau resume their original position and wait for their next instruction to commence. In another scene, a man, on the Devil's instruction, plucks his colleague off a ladder and takes his place, only to be eaten by a snake. Satan explains the message: "He sought blessings through a fraudulent means but waits not to enjoy its pleasures." In yet another tableau, Satan tells a beautiful woman to "perform your act for us to see." She duly lures a man to his death over a waterfall. In another scene, four men are told to "reveal [their] normal behaviours" to the audience. Three of them turn on the fourth to rob and kill him.[17]

A third category of tableau involves spectacles of punishment that unfold in the Region of Recompense. A man who in his lifetime plucked out the eyes of six people has a peg hammered into his own eye.

Another man who has committed atrocious violence on earth is boiled in a pot so that his "skin peeled off in rinds."[18] And so it goes.

As we have seen, Fagunwa was attracted to Bunyan for two reasons, namely his depiction of heaven and his allegorical technique. Fagunwa certainly draws on aspects of Bunyan's heaven to construct his own. Yet, particularly in his second novel, it is clear that hell exercised a far greater attraction. Not only does it provide a more compelling site for moral instruction but Fagunwa also turns it into an "emblem theater" of allegorical spectacle. In this scenario, the Devil becomes the new Interpreter, and Hell becomes a site of public education via the use of mini-allegorical performances.

Debates about the House of the Interpreter had long formed a strand in African Christian and mission discussions of the text. The interlude itself comes near the beginning of the text, when Christian is still a neophyte. He has just entered the Wicket Gate and has yet to face any momentous challenges. The House is his first place of instruction (the other two are Palace Beautiful and the Delectable Mountains). Here he is shown a "curriculum"[19] of seven scenes for interpretation. These comprise a picture hanging on the wall and then various enacted tableaux. Throughout, he is led by the Interpreter, who explains, expounds, and poses questions.

Within the mission domain, questions often arose as to who took on the role of the Interpreter. Missionaries with strong Bunyan traditions liked to compare themselves to Bunyan's Interpreter,[20] and, as we have seen, in one Baptist missionary exhibition, the Interpreter's House featured as a symbol of the mission effort. Missionaries spent a lot of time explaining religious pictures that were widely and consistently used in evangelization and hence must at times have resembled the Interpreter. The role, however, was one that converts could equally claim. They were often literally interpreters and translators for missionaries. They also took on the task of religious interpretation and, in their itinerations, catechists would have spent time showing people pictures and interpreting the hidden truths of the Scriptures. In the Sotho translation (1872), the Interpreter appears as *Mosenoli,* the one who reveals (*ho senola*), in turn the verb underlying the Book of Revelation—*Tshenolo*. Here an Interpreter takes on a work of revelation very different from that of a literal interpreter (*toloko* derived from the Afrikaans *tolk*).

Seen superficially, it may appear as if Fagunwa is entering this domain of debate. By equating the Interpreter with the Devil, the text may seem to be casting aspersions at mission pretensions to be the sole interpreters. Fagunwa, however, was never in an adversarial dialogue with Christianity, which in his novels is but one of several options. Rather, what interests Fagunwa, a writer with a strong didactic agenda, is the idea of hell as a compelling theater of instruction. Borrowing from Bunyan's House of the Interpreter, Fagunwa establishes hell as a site of moral teaching, achieved via visual and allegorical spectacle. It is almost as if hell becomes a space of public educational theater, where a series of didactic lessons is "broadcast" to an audience. This metaphor of broadcasting becomes even more apt when we remember that the audience of hunters is invisible. Through these techniques, Fagunwa opens up the possibility of imagining hell as a place of public performance in which audiences are convened to observe spectacles of various kinds.

In this regard, it is also noteworthy that some of these spectacles repeat themselves whenever the Devil-director instructs them to commence. This is also a characteristic of the House of the Interpreter (and indeed of much of *The Pilgrim's Progress*). When Christiana and her party visit the House of the Interpreter, some of the scenes that Christian saw repeat themselves. Likewise, Christiana and company on their route reencounter many of the characters seen by Christian. As Kaufmann points out, these characters appear to wait like props at the side of the road, ready to reenact their part for any pilgrim who passes. Kaufmann comments perceptively that the book as a whole reminds one of "those funhouses, in amusement parks where, regardless of the number of trips one had made through their circuitous passages, the same little dramas and surprises will be staged at certain junctures: piled boxes begin to fall, creatures start from hiding, or doors open and shut ominously." In relation to the Interpreter's House, Kaufmann reads this "tripwire" repetition as an allegory on Puritan reading. The scenes exemplify different Puritan technique for interpreting the Scriptures and their repetition captures the nature of reading: "the didactic events redramatized as many times as one cared to return to the page."[21]

It is clear from Fagunwa's depiction of hell that he also understood the House of the Interpreter, if not as an allegory on Puritan reading, then certainly as a theater with endlessly repeating acts. He may also have seen the entire text of *The Pilgrim's Progress*, as Kaufmann does, namely as a rambling stage-set with clusters of "prop characters" repeatedly being sparked into mechanical action. This way of grasping the story may in turn be linked to what Karin Barber has identified as one of Fagunwa's major projects, namely to create "a new kind of writing and a new kind of reading public."[22] Much of his fiction is consequently aimed at "convening" both a pan-Yoruba audience, calling them together as modern, and Yoruba subjects, in much the same way as the Devil's "broadcasts" convene an audience. Fagunwa's insight that such an enterprise of convening new modern publics involves repeated and often tawdry performances by the "theater state" is prescient and has become a theme of interest to theorists of the state in Africa who are paying increasing attention to the role of spectacle in modern power.[23]

These possibilities that Fagunwa inaugurates were to prove suggestive. At least two other novelists, Tutuola and Ngũgĩ, were to adopt and develop this idea of hell as a site of public education in their novels.

As critics have frequently noted, Tutuola's work draws heavily on that of Fagunwa.[24] The fictive geography of both writers is broadly similar; the plot outlines resemble each other; the range and conceptualization of characters is analogous. Even Tutuola's use of Bunyan is seen as derivative. Lindfors, for example, notes that Tutuola "follows Fagunwa's example in Africanizing Bunyan."[25]

In certain respects, this claim is true. In his first novel, *The Wild Hunter in the Bush of Ghosts*,[26] which we consider here, Tutuola introduces many Fagunwa-Bunyanesque features. These include a female evangelist, a missionary named Victoria Juliana who teaches and guides the hunter-hero Joseph Adday in his travels. Tutuola's depiction of heaven also comes straight out of *The Forest of a Thousand Daemons*. In Fagunwa, the route to heaven (like Bunyan's narrow way) is "a paved road which spread straight towards the road of heaven."[27] In Tutuola, the path to paradise is similar: "a road, four feet wide and twenty feet deep, it was as straight as railway lines."[28] Like Fagunwa, Tutuola introduces a Yoruba potter into his heaven.

Yet, in his use of Bunyan, Tutuola does not simply copy Fagunwa's model. Instead, his first novel actively extends Fagunwa's symbolic apparatus of hell as a space of public spectacle. The novel also picks up on broader African readings of documents as both passes and passports to heaven. In his novel, Tutuola combines these two concerns. The result, as I attempt to demonstrate, is a Weberian comedy of hell as a colonial bureaucracy.

The world in which the story unfolds is the Bush of Ghosts. It comprises five towns, but the space appears potentially expansible—one would not be surprised to learn that there were many more towns beyond the horizon. However, unlike Fagunwa's world, the spaces in this novel are not all equal. Heaven and hell loom large and everyone in the novel is fated for one of these two destinations. Again unlike Fagunwa, Tutuola's heaven has strict entry criteria. In *The Forest of a Thousand Daemons*, the only requirement was that one be dead and on occasion even this condition is waived. In Tutuola's novel, as in Bunyan, entry to heaven is governed by documents. These are issued when a person is first molded from clay by the angels of heaven. The documents are then sent to earth, where, depending on one's moral conduct, a decision to send the person to heaven or hell is taken. These documents are then forwarded to heaven or hell depending on the individual case. Both heaven and hell maintain extensive bureaucracies to manage these records.

This bureaucratic vision is most extensively developed in relation to hell, which, on closer examination, resembles a comic minicolonial state. It is headed by the Devil, who oversees a complex bureaucratic hierarchy with ambassadors, labor commissioners, exchange managers, and clerks. Hell also boasts various government divisions like an engineering section, a fire department, and a standing army. Its space is subject to urban planning principles: it has street names and numbered addresses, as well as public squares with monuments. Its time is governed by industrial rhythms with work ending at 4.30 sharp in the afternoon.

Unsurprisingly for someone who himself worked in a colonial government department, Tutuola's distinctive emphasis concerns an analysis of bureaucratic documentation as a modality of power. As others have argued, bureaucracies through written documentation play a key role in creating, regulating, and policing identities such as voter, tax payer, marriage partner, criminal, and so on.[29] Likewise, in Tutuola's novel, the chief business of the Devil's office is to receive and preserve the records of those identified as sinners. Once such an identity has been written into one's records, there is no escaping one's fate.

In this question of one's long-term destiny, Tutuola sees document- and record-keeping as a decisive factor in determining social outcomes. Yet, at the heart of this system is a mystery because in the novel, no one knows exactly where or how the verdict is made on whether one is to be saved or damned. One also does not know how this information comes to be entered on the documents, or how the documents arrive at their destination. One hears that the documents are issued in heaven when a person is created.[30] The Devil tells us that one's conduct does play some role in the verdict that is entered on one's records.[31] But over and above this information, one knows nothing about the heart of a system that determines everyone's fate. At its center, then, is a mystery that, as much political theory has taught us, lies at the heart of state power and bureaucracy. This mystery masks the core extractive functions of state apparatuses. In Marx's words, "The general spirit of the bureaucracy is the secret, the mystery, preserved within itself by the hierarchy and against the outside world."[32]

Such an insight regarding the exploitative nature of bureaucracy was, of course, not difficult for an African colonial subject, like Tutuola, to arrive at. More interesting, perhaps, are the terms in which Tutuola chooses to portray and hence implicitly theorize the manifestations of that abstract and half-obscured power. If modern power can no longer be embodied in a person, but is rather a "thing" like money, or an apparatus,[33] then the question of how to portray it becomes of more than passing interest. Tutuola's choice is an idiosyncratic but instructive one: for him, the "secret" workings of the colonial bureaucracy are best figured by means of the postal service, since it is the postal system that carries out the mysterious function of transporting everyone's records from heaven to earth and then back again, either to heaven or hell.

The novel is consequently dominated by the postal system. Heaven, hell, the various ghost-villages through which the protagonists pass, and even author and reader are linked by a gargantuan postal network. Indeed, Tutuola urges readers to send letters, both to himself and the Devil. The instructions for sending letters to hell—to inquire if one's name appears in their records—are elaborate.

> The Devil suggested that the person should use two envelopes.
> He or she should write his or her name on the back of one of
> the two envelopes, and the correct postage stamp should be
> affixed to it. After that, the second envelope should be
> addressed as follows:

> To His Majesty the King of Hell
> 17896 Woe Lane
> 5th Town of the Ghosts
> Bush of the Ghosts
> HELL

> After addressing the second envelope, the person should put his
> or her letter inside it, gum it well, and post it to hell. But the
> person should bear in mind that his or her original record
> would not be sent but only a copy of it. To make things easy

and fast, a postal order or money order for five shillings should be sent with the letter to the "Wild Hunter" who would help the person.[34]

Letters and telegrams travel back and forth in the novel, traversing both "real" and mythical spaces, but wherever they go, they are subordinated to the workings of a sprawling but relentless postal system. Also traveling back and forth in this space of administrative rationality are all the records of humankind. These pieces of paper are perfect ciphers for the abstracted individuality of the modern subject. In this modular version of citizenship, each person becomes an identical template upon which modern power may be written. Like minibillboards, these modern subjects are inscribed with information that makes them legible to the bureaucracy.

Tutuola, however, is no Orwell and one must stress that the novel is essentially comic. This comedy resides in part in the defamiliarization of the colonial state bureaucracy that Tutuola achieves by relocating its workings to hell. The result, as Lindfors says, is "comically Kafkaesque."[35] However, part of Tutuola's comic impulse resides as well in the admiration that he expresses for hell's infrastructure. Like their counterparts in Fagunwa, the hunters are shown around the sights of hell by the Devil and they are clearly impressed by the spectacles of technology and bureaucracy that they see: the engineering department, the complex machinery for making fire, serried ranks of clerks filling out forms in red ink, and so on. Being condemned to hell may in fact not be such a bad thing after all. Heaven, by contrast, is anodyne and, furthermore, filled to the brim with worthy but boring missionaries. In this comedy of inversion, the doctrine of the elect is humorously reworked: being saved and going to heaven may be less desirable than being damned and going to hell with its infrastructure and bureaucracy.

In this inversion, Tutuola adds yet a further reading to the idea of election inherent in Bunyan. As we have seen, in the case of the Eastern Cape elite, the idea of election, where few are chosen and many excluded, was used to comment on the inequities of colonial state power. For the persecuted Christians in Madagascar, the idea of election functioned as a counter to their social marginality and as a way of claiming moral superiority over their royal betters. In both of these instances, the idea of election is used to critique forms of power. In Tutuola's case, the comic treatment of the doctrine of election becomes a way not of resisting or critiquing state power but rather of embracing it, of choosing it as the desired future. Tutuola clearly favors more, not less state infrastructure. In this enthusiasm for state structures and apparatuses, Tutuola's book, although written in the 1940s under colonial rule, contains the early outlines of the comedy of the bloated postcolonial state. This literary form is now common and is best exemplified in writers like Sony Labou Tansi, whose work burlesques the excesses of postcolonial governmentality.[36] One tributary leading to this stream is Tutuola's work, which, in turn, is indebted to Fagunwa's initial move to establish hell as a zone where public power might be imaginatively experimented with. It was an experiment that Ngũgĩ wa Thiong'o was to take forward—via Tutuola—in his novel *Devil on the Cross*.

In his collection of essays, *Decolonising the Mind: The Politics of Language in African Literature*, Ngũgĩ wa Thiong'o makes passing reference to the role of *The Pilgrim's Progress* in the history of the African novel. In Ngũgĩ's view, Bunyan's text forms part of the mission enterprise, which through its control of printing, publishing, and education has exercised an adverse influence on the history of literature on the continent. "The early practitioners of the African novel, particularly in South Africa, were products of missionary educational institutions and they were more likely to have been exposed to Bunyan's *Pilgrim's Progress* and the King James or Authorized version of the bible than to Tolstoy, Balzac or Dickens."[37] In this formulation, Bunyan is part of a mission evangelical tradition that is defined in opposition to that of the secular novel. The first, according to Ngũgĩ, exercises a deleterious effect on traditions of African writing. The second bequeaths a better but nonetheless ambivalent legacy, in that it promotes the use of europhone rather than African languages as the vehicle of African literary expression.

As is well known, Ngũgĩ, after writing for many years in English, switched in the early 1980s to using Kikuyu. His first novel *Caitaani Mũthabaranĩ* (*Devil on the Cross*) perhaps somewhat surprisingly revisits Bunyan and invokes *The Pilgrim's Progress* in sustained and systematic ways. Given his pronouncements on Bunyan, this move is curious. What might be his intentions and motives in revisiting a text that he had identified as being a negative influence on African writing?

At first glance, it may appear that he is "subverting" an "imperial" text by offering a secular and Marxist reading of a mission evangelical story. In some senses, such a reading is valid. The book does indeed invert the evangelical aspects of Bunyan in a Marxist framework. The Broad and the Narrow Way, for example, become the true and the false roads: the one leading to workers' revolution, the other to capitalist perdition.

However, if we consider that one of the book's intentions is to root itself in popular narrative forms, then further—and more interesting—possibilities present themselves. One genre to which the novel indeed addresses itself is the popular religious narrative. As Gareth Griffiths has noted, the references to Bunyan form part of this domain.[38] Seen in this way, Ngũgĩ's novel becomes an engagement with prior and popular African readings of Bunyan rather than simply a subversion of Bunyan as an "imperial" target.

In broad outline, the novel tells the story of five people traveling in a taxi from Nairobi to Ilmorog to attend the Devil's Feast—a competition to select the leading experts in "Modern Theft and Robbery." The central section of the novel narrates the testimonies given at the Feast as various capitalist contestants vie with each other to prove their achievements in the field of exploitation, graft, and profiteering. The final part of the story traces a partly successful workers' attempt to close down the Feast, while we also follow the careers of the five who attended the Feast and the impact that it had on their lives.

References to *The Pilgrim's Progress* are woven carefully into the text. The protagonist Warĩĩnga, daughter of a peasant family, is faced by a series of overwhelming burdens that derive from the class, race, and gender oppression she suffers. These issues are repeatedly figured in terms of a "load" or "burden," whether it be the burden of unwanted pregnancy, unemployment, sexual harassment, or gender discrimination.[39] Her companion and subsequently her lover, Gatuĩria, likewise experiences a sense of carrying a burden—in this case a lighter one, that of the African male petty bourgeoisie.[40] When the novel opens, Warĩĩnga feels so overwhelmed by her burdens that she tries to kill herself by throwing herself in front of a bus. She is saved by a man who calms her down and then gives her a piece of paper, which turns out to be an invitation to the Devil's Feast. The man is a student activist. This element of the plot invokes the figure of Evangelist, who at the opening of *The Pilgrim's Progress* discovers Christian in a confused and agitated state. Evangelist gives Christian advice and then gives him a parchment roll that sets him off on his journey. This is his odyssey from the way of error to the way of truth. Warĩĩnga likewise is given a piece of paper that precipitates a similar journey from "false" to "true" consciousness. Along the way, she meets various "evangelists" who assist in the process of her conscientization. The student leader who gives her the invitation is the first. He knows that at the Devil's Feast (a cross between Vanity Fair, the House of the Interpreter, and Plato's Cave) she will gain "true" insight into the nature of class and capitalist exploitation. The other two "evangelists" are the worker, Mūturi, and the peasant Mau Mau fighter, Wangari, both of whom accompany Warīnga in the taxi. Together this "Holy Trinity" of peasant, worker, and student comprise the vanguard of enlightenment and set Warīnga on the path to "true" consciousness.

After being "enlightened," Warīnga, like Christian, is armed—in her case, with a small gun. This gives her a great sense of empowerment and her burdens of doubt and fear disappear. Armed in this way, she proceeds on the road of higher gender and class consciousness and trains as an engineer. She becomes engaged to Gatuīria, a fellow traveler in the taxi and a university academic. She seems destined for a happy marriage and a date is set for the wedding. Gatuīria's wealthy parents are to host the engagement party at their estate, Ngorika's Heavenly Orchard (a satire of the Land of Beulah). On the way to the party, Warīnga and Gatuīria stop off at a point called Golden Heights to look at the view, rather as Christian and Hopeful stop at the Delectable Mountains. At the party itself, Warīnga (who has never yet met her future in-laws) is horrified to discover that Gatuīria's father is the old man who seduced her as a teenager, made her pregnant, and then dumped her. He begs her to give up his son and to once again become his mistress. He then attempts to rape her. She pulls out her gun, shoots him, and then leaves. The book ends with her fiancé standing undecided—he didn't know what to do "to deal with his father's body, to comfort his mother or to follow Warīnga."[41] Like all members of the petty bourgeoisie, he has to choose and, for Ngũgĩ, there are only two options: the road of the worker (which Warīnga has chosen) or the road of the capitalist.

This notion of having to make a choice between these options is frequently figured through images of the Broad and Narrow Way, a picture powerfully woven into African Christianity and closely related to Bunyan's landscape. At one point in the taxi journey, Mūturi berates the driver Mwaūra (whom we gather is on the side of evil), "Driver! There are two ways: the one that leads people to death, and the one that leads people to life."[42] When Warīnga first gets involved with the older, corrupt man in her teenage years, she feels that the gifts that he showers on her illuminate "a road that was broad and very beautiful."[43] When he abandons her, and so inadvertently forces her on to the road of "true" consciousness, she "saw the road that she had previously thought of as wide and very beautiful now suddenly become narrow, covered with thorns."⁴⁴ When she has gained "true" consciousness, she looks back on this period of her life as "a broad highway carpeted with the flowers of self-seeking individualism."⁴⁵ The text's message is evangelically clear: "nobody c[an] walk along two roads at the same time." Each character in turn must make their decision.

Throughout the novel, the question of documents and pieces of paper as passports to heaven or hell features prominently. In the opening pages, Wariinga, who is being evicted from her lodgings receives a piece of paper from the thugs who have come to throw her out. They present her with their "visiting card" that, à la Tutuola, is reproduced in the text:

> We Are the Devil's Angels: Private Businessmen.
>
> Make the slightest move to take this matter to the authorities, and we shall issue you with a single ticket to God's kingdom or Satan's—a one-way ticket to Heaven or Hell.⁴⁶

A second set of documents are the invitation cards that Wariinga and Gatuiria receive to the Devil's Feast. As with the parchment that Christian receives in the first scene of *The Pilgrim's Progress*, these documents propel these two characters into the narrative. They also function as their "passports" to conscientization so that they can come to understand the nature of class exploitation. However, documents also stand as reminders of state and capitalist oppression. In her narrative in the taxi, Wangari, the erstwhile Mau Mau fighter, talks about her experiences in Kenya and how postindependence vagrancy laws compel her to carry permits and pass books. However, Ngũgĩ also adds a revolutionary spin to these representations of documents as passes and passports. Documents are indeed a crucial tool for mobilizing and awakening political consciousness, either by alerting people to new sets of ideas or by provoking their anger at forms of unwarranted state control. Documents can then function as instruments of conscientization and hence liberation. They do, however, have limitations and in the novel are superseded by what Ngũgĩ sees as the ultimate weapon of liberation—the gun. When Mũturi, the worker leader, gives a small revolver to Wariinga, he says: "This gun is an invitation to the workers' feast to be held some time in the future."⁴⁷ The message is plain: to enter the "heaven" of a workers' state, one will have to travel the narrow way of revolutionary armed struggle.

Like both Fagunwa and Tutuola, Ngũgĩ develops the idea of hell as the House of the Interpreter, a place of public "broadcast" where characters will be conscientized. To this, he adds also the image of Vanity Fair, where the worst dimensions of greedy commerce are apparent. Here, at the Devil's Feast, we are offered a series of excessive spectacles in which the workings of international capitalism are laid bare. Some delegates' suits are tailored from their national currencies. Others are adorned with flashing neon badges with bloated slogans like "Money-Swallowing Insurance Schemes and Industrial Gobblers of Raw Material." One of these badges contains a Bunyan reminder: "Arms for Murder and Motor Vehicle Assembly Plants for Vanity Fair at Home and Bigger Profits Abroad."[48] The task of the speakers is to dramatize their exploits of extortion and greed. One delegate, Gītutu wa Gataangūrū, son of a family that made money collaborating with the colonial regime, brags of his exploits as a postindependence land shark. His next scheme is to commodify air and sell it in tins. Another contestant, Kīhaahu wa Gatheeca, specializes in pandering to the eurocentric tastes of the Kenyan bourgeoisie: he runs a nursery school with motorized white mannequins in order to attract customers keen to send their children to "white" schools. Nditika wa Ngūūnji wants to start a factory for manufacturing human parts so that the wealthy might have multiple organs to feed their excessive appetites.

This spectacle of the Devil's Feast, rather as in Fagunwa's hell, instructs its audience by dramatizing the excesses of evil or, in this case, the system of international capitalism and its ready ally, the Kenyan bourgeoisie. The stories told at the Devil's Feast deal with the repetitive performances of power through which capitalist ideological control is maintained and, as such, can be read as a gloss on Fagunwa's insight into the stage-managed nature of public culture. In Ngūgī's text, the point of the story is that characters should see through its façades and detect its tripwires. The excesses of the spectacle likewise invoke Tutuola, and *Devil on the Cross* can be seen as the savage comedy on the bloated postcolonial state that Tutuola's novel hinted at, albeit in a less harsh register.

Overall, Ngūgī's intention appears to be to colonize the evangelical message of *The Pilgrim's Progress* and to fill it with revolutionary socialist content. In arriving at this goal, his route leads not directly from *The Pilgrim's Progress* but rather via Fagunwa and Tutuola and their reshaping of Bunyan. In so doing, he suggests a way of thinking about the African circuits of Bunyan and what this might mean for the trajectory of the African novel.

Another writer concerned with this issue is Tsitsi Dangarembga. Her novel, *Nervous Conditions*, has been noted for its attempts to reshape the terrain of the African novel from a perspective of gender. Perhaps unsurprisingly, a subpart of this project involves an engagement with *The Pilgrim's Progress* and its gendered meaning for the African novel.

Nervous Conditions unfolds in the 1960s in late colonial Rhodesia (presently Zimbabwe). It traces the stories of two young girls and captures a few decisive years in their teens. The first girl, Tambudzai, comes from the grinding poverty of a rural peasant household. The second, Nyasha, is the daughter of a middle-class mission school teacher. She has spent much of her childhood in Britain, where her father gained his doctorate. The girls are cousins: Nyasha's father, Mr. Sigauke, is the older and grimly disciplined brother of Tambudzai's feckless father, Joshua. Sigauke (known throughout by the honorific Babamukuru or "Great Father") is determined to try and uplift his brother, whose lack of respectability offends him. Toward this end, he takes in Joshua's only son, Nhamo, to educate him. Nhamo dies suddenly and Tambudzai takes his place in the Sigauke household. Initially, she is deeply obedient to her patriarchal uncle and is slightly disapproving of her cousin Nyasha's rebellious and open-minded ways. The two girls, however, soon grow close and Tambudzai is won over by Nyasha's exuberance. Under Nyasha's influence, Tambudzai becomes more assertive and stands up to her uncle. Tambudzai does well at school and proceeds to a mostly "white" convent in the capital, Salisbury. At the same time, however, she becomes more and more aware of the patriarchal and racist order of the society around her. While she is away, Nyasha's rebellion turns inward: she becomes increasingly anorexic and has a nervous breakdown. The novel ends with Nyasha being taken off to a psychiatrist, while Tambudzai's mother reflects upon the effects of "too much Englishness" upon people.

Much criticism of the novel has highlighted Dangarembga's role in rewriting the nationalist (and masculinist) narrative that has dominated much African fiction.[49] The book covers the opening years of the Zimbabwe war of liberation, but avoids virtually any mention of the conflict. The terrain of the anticolonial armed struggle has been a favored locus of much male-dominated African fiction. Indeed, by the time Dangarembga came to write (1988), much Zimbabwean autobiography and fiction almost routinely paralleled the career of the male protagonist with the trajectory of the anticolonial war, both culminating triumphantly in independence.[50] Dangarembga consciously chooses a different path. By focusing on two female protagonists (and the women around them), it provides a female-driven narrative and critically considers what templates are available for narrating these experiences.

The novel's engagement with Bunyan is tied up with just these concerns. This investigation into *The Pilgrim's Progress* comes in the fourth chapter of the book. The brother Nhamo has died and Tambudzai is to move across to the Sigauke household, where her uncle will sponsor her education. Her uncle arrives to pick her up and drives her from her rural homestead to the Sigauke's house in the mission school precinct. Tambudzai is elated to abandon the poverty, dirt, squalor, and endless labor of peasant life. She feels that she is leaving a great burden behind and is heading for a place of "palace[s] . . . mansion[s] and castle[s]."[51] In her terms, she is moving from the City of Destruction to the Celestial City. Babamukuru has rescued her and she regards him reverentially as her savior. In relation to him, however, she feels unworthy and thus, at one point on the trip, Tambudzai descends briefly into her own Slough of Despond, a "swamp of self-pity."[52] On arrival at the house itself, she is confronted by two fierce dogs, one black and one white. Like the lions that Christian encounters at the entrance to Palace Beautiful, they are chained, something that Tambudzai does not initially notice. "To me they were loose, ferocious guardians of the gates to this kingdom, this kingdom that I should not have been entering."[53] By making these comparisons, the text asks us to compare the Sigauke's house to Palace Beautiful, one of the sites of Christian's instruction. Christian encounters the Palace after he has climbed Hill Difficulty. He is admitted to the Palace by Watchful, the Porter who tells him that the lions are chained. A woman, Discretion, receives him into the Palace where he narrates his experiences to Piety, Prudence, and Charity. After sleeping the night, he is outfitted with a suit of armor and sent on his way to do battle with Apollyon.

In the novel's scenario, Anna, the domestic worker, would be the Porter Watchful and Nyasha, who runs out to meet Tambudzai, the character Discretion. Piety, Prudence, and Charity could apply variously to the women in the Sigauke household, namely Anna, Tambudzai, Nyasha, and her mother, Maiguru. In the house, which to Tambudzai appears as a "palace," she likewise acquires her "armor," namely her new school uniform. In Bunyan, the Palace belongs to the "Lord of the Hill" (namely God) and, in the novel, the uncle occupies a similar position of authority: "Babamukuru was God, therefore I had arrived in Heaven. I was in danger of becoming an angel, or at the very least a saint, and forgetting how ordinary humans existed—from minute to minute and from hand to mouth."[54]

In the comparison that the novel asks us to make, Tambudzai's narrative is plotted on a story of linear progress, often adopted as we have seen in chapter 5, by a male African mission elite as a template to envision their own advance against the burdensome conditions of colonial rule. One route for this advancement was formal education, and *The Pilgrim's Progress* was invoked by both missionary and convert as a parable of African advancement through formal education.[55] In such scenarios, some of which we examined in chapter 5, the story becomes a model for the difficult path of male African elite upward mobility in a colonial context. By invoking this template, Dangarembga dramatizes the choices that Tambudzai and the other women in the house have to make about how to fit or not fit into this preordained story. They can, as Tambudzai initially does, attempt to take up the masculinist position of Christian, by abandoning her rural peasant family without a second glance. However, as the story unfolds, Tambudzai realizes that she cannot simply wish away her class provenance. Her narrative becomes one of coming to terms with her background and finding a way of acknowledging that experience. In terms of gender and race, the narrative of progress also breaks down. As she advances, she bumps headlong into the structures of a patriarchal and racist society. She consequently finds the promised road of linear progress much less straightforward than she had initially contemplated.

An alternative to trying to take up the male role of Christian is to occupy the spaces of the female characters like Prudence, Piety, and Charity. However, these positions, with their absurd demands of female self-denial, are impossible to fill. Nyasha's mother, Maiguru, for example, attempts to play the part of the ideal mother, wife, and long-suffering relative to her own family and her husband's extended family. She attempts in effect to play out simultaneously the roles of Prudence, Piety, and Charity. She might also be seen as a female Christiana patiently following the path blazed by her husband. The toll of occupying any of these self-sacrificing positions is, however, extreme and toward the end of the novel, Maiguru has a nervous breakdown. Unlike her mother, Nyasha fiercely resists any imposed role. From the moment we meet her, it is clear she will never play the part of Discretion and will instead indiscreetly challenge any form of authority she encounters. However, the toll for her, too, is heavy: she ends up with an eating disorder and a nervous breakdown. The character Anna is the only one to live up to her name, Watchful. In discussing the fierce lion/dogs with Tambudzai, she says: "'But sometimes they aren't tied—just think!—because they go off and we can't find them. When that happens, ha-a!, you don't catch me out-side, not even to hang the laundry.'"⁵⁶ Like the other women domestic workers in the story, she has to adopt a watchfully pragmatic attitude in order to survive in a social order where she occupies virtually the lowest rung.

In this analysis of *The Pilgrim's Progress*, Dangarembga rejects it as a possible narrative template for capturing the experience of her fe-male protagonists. She suggests firstly that it as an outdated story, appro-priate at best for the mission-educated generation of Mr. Sigauke, but no longer relevant to a younger generation. She also lays bare the use of Bunyan as a model for upward male mobility. By demonstrating how her female protagonists struggle to fit into this mould, she rejects it as a narrative possibility. Her decision to focus her engagement with Bunyan around Palace Beautiful is also significant. This episode has generally been read as an allegory on church fellowship in which a new convert joins a congregation and gives an account of his religious experience and conversion.⁵⁷ In the text, Christian consequently retails his exploits at some length. Palace Beautiful is, then, the place of self-narration. How-ever, the forms of such narration are implicitly male and do not provide the female characters with the conventions to tell their stories. Indeed, in the second part of the story, when Christiana and her party arrive at Palace Beautiful, they do not recount their adventures at all. Instead, Christiana and her companion, Mercy, share confidences with each other; Christiana's children (all male) are catechized by Prudence; Mercy has a near-offer of marriage from Mr. Brisk who then takes fright because she is a bad economic proposition (she charges nothing for the handiwork she does and instead gives it away to the poor); Christiana's son, Mat-thew, falls ill and when recovered, engages in a riddling session with Prudence. In short, Christiana and Mercy involve themselves in private matters, while in public it is the men who continue to talk. Prudence, Piety, and Charity do, of course, speak and lead catechism, but their function, particularly in the first part of the story, is largely that of audi-ence and, in the second, that of teachers carrying out a prepared "curric-ulum." The role of "original" narrator accrues to Christian, who is the only one to recount his personal experiences.

In considering Dangarembga's depiction of Palace Beautiful— one of the sites of Christian's enlightenment—we can use the novel to reflect back on Fagunwa, Tutuola, and Ngũgĩ and their reworkings of the House of the Interpreter, another of the sites of Christian's education. In the first three novels, this site becomes hell and is furthermore a zone of predominantly male theatricality with almost no female performers. They may, like Warĩĩnga, form part of the audience, but they seldom appear on stage. The performances, in all three novels, are concerned with issues of state, economy, nation, and public culture. These places of public education are consequently given a masculinist and statist bias. Dangarembga's engagement, then, with Bunyan as a presence in the African novel, helps to throw into feminist relief two of the major features of African fiction, namely its masculinist emphasis and its insistent engagement with questions of nationalism.[58]

Dangarembga's attempt to debate the text in relation to a female protagonist was not the first. Fagunwa gestured in this direction by having a female Evangelist, Help (or Helpmeet). Ngũgĩ, too, has a female "Christian" in the figure of Warĩĩnga. However, before both Fagunwa and Ngũgĩ, the Ghanaian journalist, Mabel Dove Danquah, writing in 1934 under the pseudonym Marjorie Mensah in the *Times of West Africa*, had carried out her own experiments in this regard. As Stephanie Newell, who unearthed these stories, shows, her starting point was George Bernard Shaw's parody of Bunyan, *The Adventures of a Black Girl in Search of her God*, written in 1932 on a visit to South Africa. In this story, a young black girl, having been inducted into Christianity by an obtuse missionary, sets off to find God. Along the way, she encounters differing conceptions of God and destroys each in turn. Finally, she marries a red-haired socialist Irishman who, as Newell notes, "bears more than a passing resemblance to Shaw in his youth," and she accepts his secularized idea of God as "an eternal but as yet unfulfilled purpose."[59] In 1934 Dove Danquah, in her column, began a serial entitled *The Adventures of the Black Girl in her Search for Mr. Shaw*. In her rewriting, she updates Shaw's protagonist, in her view not sufficiently modern: "The object of my present attempt is to give a picture of a *modern* black girl—as she is *today*, the product of a missionary school with some considerable English polish, who after having read Bunyan's Pilgrim's Progress, and to be more *up-to-date*, Mr. Shaw's 'Black Girl in Her Search for God,' considers also undertaking a similar search for Mr. Shaw."[60] Instead of the small stick or knobkerrie that Shaw's heroine carries, Danquah's brandishes a tennis racquet. She also replaces the Bible that Christian clutches throughout his journey: the "black girl" instead carries Shaw's *Adventures*. The journey of the character takes her to London to seek out Shaw. However, as Newell indicates, the final episode is missing and so we never hear what she had to say to him.

Danquah's revision of Shaw's reworking provides an apt conclu-

sion for this chapter. In her engagement with Bunyan, she was not interacting with a text that had come directly from the metropolis. Instead,
she was dealing first with Bunyan's "original" text that had a long presence in the region in several languages, and then with Shaw's retelling,
which with its parody of racist mission Christianity soon attracted a local
following. Writing in her own literary column that, as Newell shows, was
a local laboratory for trying out and applying texts in different ways,
Danquah can then enter a conversation with Shaw and Bunyan that pre-
supposes this layered history of reading and reception. As this chapter
has demonstrated, other African novelists who used *The Pilgrim's Progress*
followed much the same route. They engaged with Bunyan not as a product of the "colonizer" (as the critic on Tutuola suggested) but instead
they go to work on the already existing meanings that the text has generated in its varied encounters with African intellectual formations.

As the previous chapters have demonstrated, these meanings
were diverse and had arisen in a variety of locales where *The Pilgrim's
Progress* was taken up in African intellectual and spiritual traditions. Yet,
what did all this mean for Bunyan's standing back in Britain? In earlier
sections of the book, I traced how nineteenth-century Nonconformists
"at home" popularized Bunyan's successes as a means of adding luster to
their cause. In the next chapter, I pursue that story into the twentieth-
century to examine a different interpretation that emerged via the field of
English literature as a discipline, namely that of Bunyan as a canonical
figure and as "father" of the English novel. From being a transnational
writer of the world, Bunyan became a national writer of England. How
did this transformation come about?

PART THREE

Post-Bunyan

10

How Bunyan Became English

The Bunyan tercentenary celebrations of 1928, organized by the World Evangelical Alliance, were international in their reach. Throughout the year, there were events in various parts of Britain as well as celebrations in Australia and the United States. Commemorative publications, biographies, and memorabilia flooded the market. At one gathering outside Bedford, the speaker mused: "if the people of Bunyan's time could return to earth, which would amaze them most—the fame of the young tinker or the R33?"[1]

Predictably enough for such an internationally driven event, the idea of Bunyan as a writer of the world cropped up frequently as a motif in speeches and sermons. By 1928, after nearly a century of Nonconformist publicity around Bunyan's universal successes, such ideas had become common sense and thus were invoked by speakers including the Archbishop-elect of Canterbury and the Home Secretary, Stanley Baldwin, who noted that "all pilgrims of earth find points of contact in the story."[2] Woven into this talk of Bunyan—"the marvel of other lands"— there was another theme. This stressed Bunyan's Englishness and his status as "father" of the English novel.[3] In some speeches, these ideas were linked. The Bishop of Durham (Handley Carr Glyn Moule), for example, spoke of Bunyan as "English but universal."[4] This idea of Bunyan as father of the English novel had been current since the 1830s,[5] but was first systematized and popularized in the public domain by those working in the discipline of what we now call English literature.

What was the relationship between this idea of Bunyan's Englishness and the older Nonconformist notion of Bunyan as "universal"? These two ideas—Englishness and universality—are, on the face of it, contradictory. How then did the Bishop of Durham come to invoke them in the same breath, almost as equivalents? This chapter traces out these relationships by outlining how Bunyan was taken up in the last quarter of the nineteenth century by the emerging discipline of English literature.

The discipline of English literature, as others have shown,[6] took shape in the second half of the nineteenth century and emerged as much "from above" as "from below." From below, the initial interest in the systematic study of vernacular literature took shape among those excluded from the ancient universities and their most prestigious subject, Classics, with its onerous barrier of language requirements. For workers, women, and Nonconformists, the ancient universities were inaccessible, and it was among these groupings that the study of English literature—or "poor man's Classics"—was to take root. The earliest studies of literary texts emerged in English Dissenting academies, workers' extension colleges, colleges for women, and new universities.[7]

From above, the upstart subject of English literature initially attracted disdain, particularly from Oxford and Cambridge. However, if the idea of being familiar with one's national literature found little enthusiasm "at home," elsewhere in the empire, as scholars like Gauri Viswanathan have shown,[8] there were others quick to grasp its benefits. Those in positions of colonial authority recognized the importance of being familiar with the intellectual and literary traditions of the nation one represented. As Terry Eagleton has argued, "armed with [a] conveniently packaged version of their own cultural treasures, the servants of British imperialism could sally forth overseas secure in a sense of their national identity, able to display their cultural superiority to their envying colonial peoples."[9] The first official recognition for English literature as a discrete subject came in 1855. In that year, the Civil Service of East India Company Report recommended that the competitive entrance examinations for the prestigious India Civil Service include a paper in English literature so that candidates could "show the extent of their knowledge of our poets, wits and philosophers."[10] Sections of the Civil Service in Britain followed suit and also introduced English literature as one of the subjects in their own raft of entrance examinations.

This growing set of public examinations created a market for textbooks dealing with English literary history. In these texts, which functioned in Chris Baldick's words like "museums of national genius,"[11] writers were lined up chronologically and divided into epochs, centuries, and periods. Bunyan routinely featured in these collections, generally as an early exponent of modern prose and the English novel.[12] These literary histories gained a wide readership: Henry Morley's *First Sketch of English Literature* (1873) sold between thirty to forty thousand copies, while *Cassell's History of English Literature* (1875) attracted some twenty thousand buyers.[13] Partly as a result of the popularity of these examinations and partly because of public pressure and the need to control this burgeoning field, Oxford and Cambridge, from the mid-1890s, slowly and rather grudgingly moved to recognize the study of English literature officially.[14]

The nationalist frame in which English literature took shape continued to gain ground during and after the First World War. Making use of the hypernationalism of the war, scholars in the field of English literature were able to cast off an old foe—philology. This discipline had long claimed a right to dominate the study of English, boasting that its rigorous and "scientific" methodologies were superior to the "distressingly dilettante" procedures of studying literary texts then in existence.[15] Philology had strong continental, particularly German, roots and in the context of the war, English academics successfully called for the removal of the "alien yoke of Teutonic philology," allowing English literature to emerge as the major claimant to the field of English studies.[16]

This nationalist climate around English literature was further boosted by the influential Newbolt report of 1921. Commissioned originally in 1919 to investigate the state of teaching in the field of English, the report (entitled *The Teaching of English in England*) argued for English literature as a cornerstone of national education. To literature fell the role of promoting national consciousness and building on the postwar sense of national pride. The report laid great stress on literature's ability to promote harmony between adversarial sectors of society and to "link together the mental life of all classes."[17]

As a writer with a wide social reach, Bunyan assumed a prominent place in discussions of English literature. Newbolt, for example, was a particular fan of Bunyan—in his estimation, "one of the greatest Englishmen."[18] On these grounds, Newbolt devoted a generous amount of space to him in his *English Anthology of Prose and Poetry Shewing the Main Streams of English Literature through Six Centuries* (1921). Another important player in the field was the English Association, whose leadership had provided nine of the fourteen members making up the Newbolt report committee. Established in 1906, it performed a crucial role in encouraging the teaching of English literature in schools and adult education forums. In its material aimed at educators, the Association frequently recommended Bunyan.[19] In the last quarter of the century, Bunyan also began to attract attention from the major literary critics, both serious and popular.[20] A recurring emphasis in these works was to define the essence of Bunyan's Englishness. This project was pursued on different levels.

The first of these involved language. Despised in the eighteenth century as vulgar and un-English, Bunyan's language gradually became the desired model of Anglo-Saxon purity. This shift is apparent in changing editorial practices. Some eighteenth-century editions, for example, edited Bunyan's language to make it more polite. Hence, in one instance the phrase "O, they say, hang him, he is a turn coat" had been deemed too robust and was changed to "They tauntingly say, that he was not true to his profession." Nineteenth-century editions reversed these circumlocutions and reinstated Bunyan's original phrasing.[21] Critics also lauded the language of *The Pilgrim's Progress* as pure and accessible, "a well of English undefiled" in Southey's famous phrase that echoes through subsequent commentary.[22] This view of *The Pilgrim's Progress* as a book whose language was accessible to all classes ("It is one of the few books which has struck a chord which vibrates alike amongst the humblest peasants and amongst the most fastidious critics")[23] matched well with nationalist interpretations of English literature as a unifying factor and promoter of national consciousness. By the early twentieth century, these views had become commonsensical. Bunyan was a "master craftsman of the English speech who took the common clay of the language and shaped it into a thing of joy and beauty forever," who used "virile and lucid English" and an "essentially English" style.[24]

A second level related to characters in the text. In general, these are allegorical figures and are not precisely located in time and space. Yet, in the literary scholarship, they increasingly became construed as typical seventeenth-century English folk. According to Charles Kingsley, an early lecturer in English literature and a great friend of F. D. Maurice, one of the pioneers of the field, "Bunyan's men are not merely life-portraits, but English portraits; men of the solid, practical, unimpassioned midland race."[25] Charles Firth, an influential academic and Bunyan scholar, described the characters of *The Pilgrim's Progress* as follows: "the actors are ordinary men and women of the time, and the fact that their names have a moral significance makes no difference to the story. We are passing, in fact, from allegory to the novel."[26]

Another site for elaborating Englishness concerned the setting of the book, on the face of it an unpromising proposition since descriptions of landscape in *The Pilgrim's Progress* are sparse. In style, they are biblically based and highly conventional. This difficulty notwithstanding, tremendous energy went into identifying sites in the Bedfordshire area as models for the original, and some of these today appear authoritatively in tourist brochures. A major site for this work was Bedford, where generations of intellectuals—drawing in part on popular oral knowledge about Bunyan banked in the landscape—systematized the belief that *The Pilgrim's Progress* was rooted in Bedford and was hence essentially English, since Bedfordshire enjoyed the status of being among the magic southern shires that provided the templates for "typical" English landscape and topography.[27] This emphasis was also apparent in illustrations, which increasingly came to reflect the landscapes of the southern counties with their hedgerows, stiles, and characteristic church architecture.[28]

What such interpretations did was to narrow the focus of the story dramatically. Instead of being an international story about evangelicalism, it became a story of southern England at its broadest and Bedford at its narrowest. Yet, despite this narrowing, the fact of Bunyan's universality (based on the fact of his wide translation) continued to be invoked. In 1898 Firth observed that *The Pilgrim's Progress* was "the prose epic of English Puritanism; it contains much that is only temporary and local in its application, but unlike Milton's epic it can be understood everywhere, and has been translated into most tongues."[29] Similarly, Arthur Mee, an influential popular intellectual, remarked that *The Pilgrim's Progress* was "printed in 120 languages, and in whatever language it is read the reader feels that it is true. It is passing strange that a prisoner in Bedford Gaol should write a book for his own delight and touch the hearts of men in every land and in every age." Elsewhere, he added: "He is our immortal tinker. He is one forever with the fame of our great Island story. But he is more than one of us, for he belongs to mankind, and after all these crowded years he stands for all the nations, for every kindly serious man, among the Shining Ones."[30] What such passages, and others like them,[31] do is shift the meaning of Bunyan's universality. Increasingly, it is his Englishness rather than his evangelicalism that is seen as the key to his success.

While Nonconformists continued to promote Bunyan's evangelical message, some of them also grasped the chance to add this new level of luster to their treasured writer. As firm supporters of the Liberal Party and as persons who still experienced forms of civil and religious disability, they had long been reluctant nationalists and imperialists (their support for missions notwithstanding).[32] However, as the last vestiges of discrimination were removed and as sections of the Liberal Party moved to support imperial rule,[33] then as the New Imperialism of the 1880s to the 1920s made Englishness appear universal, Nonconformists more readily adopted ideas of Englishness. Bernard Cockett, for example, an Australian by birth and later pastor of Bunyan's church in Bedford (1925–1931), played a central role in the production of Bunyan tercentenary material in Bedford. With the Homeland Association, he produced a guidebook, *John Bunyan's England*. Part of it reads:

> England is a garden, and the wild flower in Bunyan's genius is blossoming into strange beauty in 1928, his Tercentenary, for the whole world honours his memory. Visitors from the Dominions coming 'Home', Americans of British ancestry and pilgrims of all nationalities long to drink at the ancient springs of life and literature in these sea girt isles. John Bunyan . . . is one of the great names of our race. [He] found in Jesus Christ, a Saviour . . . [he] became a passionate preacher and his determination to proclaim the Gospel cost him twelve years in prison.[34]

In these comments, Cockett combines muted ideas of Bunyan's evangelicalism together with his white Protestantism and his appeal to a range of constituencies in the empire.

The racialization of Bunyan apparent in Cockett's discussion was hardly remarkable in a situation where aggressive racial ideas of the New Imperialism had been in circulation since the 1880s. As Frank Court has shown, these ideas also affected English literature, which acquired a strongly racial veneer under the influence of Social Darwinist thinking. In Court's words, "Rising nationalism combined with increased evolutionary speculation promoted the idea that English language and literature expressed the indigenous spirit of the English racial inheritance." In his interpretation, "racial history, social evolution and the inherent nobility of the English spirit provide the philosophical grounds for the primacy of English literary study."[35]

Seen in this way, English literature plays a role in creating racial categories. Such boundary-defining work becomes particularly visible when seen outside Britain in an imperial context. For example, Froude noted in his 1880 biography that Bunyan is a man "whose writings have for two centuries affected the spiritual opinions of the English race in every part of the world more powerfully than any book or books, except the Bible."[36] Here Bunyan confers a racialized Englishness on settler-emigrants scattered through the empire. Several decades later, another commentator, Alice Law, noted a particular affinity between Britons in the empire and Bunyan:

> [I]t is particularly because we are a nation of pilgrims that Bunyan's great work should especially appeal to us and help us. Travelling as members of our great Empire often must, upon seas and continents on which the banner of Britain flies, from the English home-centre to the outermost circumference and back, one cannot conceive any comparison more suitable or helpful . . . than this tinker's masterpiece.

She continued: "Nor need anything be feared for that Empire, so long as she cherishes and practices the teaching of the immortal spiritual allegory which stands eternal witness to the truth that it is righteousness alone that exalteth nations."[37]

In passages like these, Bunyan becomes a hallmark and guarantor of white Britishness. Such claims are, of course, at odds with older evangelical ideas in a number of respects and hence raise a range of questions. Is the boundary of Bunyan's reach ultimately to be determined by conversion or is it to be determined by race? If the universality-by-conversion idea prevails, what becomes of universality-by-race and its notions of Englishness? Will this core idea not be "tainted" and so have to be protected from "contamination" by the "wrong" Bunyan?

These questions began to play themselves out in public debate and emerged clearly around discussions on the racial character of illustrations in foreign editions of *The Pilgrim's Progress*. C. J. Montague, for example, commenting on his sequence of illustrations for the Ndebele version, says: "It is a shock at first to have all one's associations with the book disregarded, but the universalism of 'Pilgrim's Progress' as heart history is certainly emphasized. Time and place does not affect essentials in that great allegory, and there is no reason against an interpretation according to local environment to suit any race in the world."[38] Elsewhere in the article, Montague discusses the need for new conventions of mission art. In this context, he mentions a picture that he saw at an exhibition. The image depicted the following scene: "a bronzed and emaciated friar, accompanied by a negro convert, had returned unexpectedly after years of wandering to the convent from which he had been sent . . . the artist has chosen the moment of shock when the ascetic enthusiast, seeking partners in spiritual rejoicing, looked blankly into the bloated and unrecognizable faces of men demoralised by home comforts. The shame of the scene was heightened by the look on the face of the gaping negro."[39]

The exhibition picture captures the ambiguities of mission work. On the one hand, the home community and the missionary are bound by ties of race, marked off in this image by the "gaping negro." But, at the same time, the missionary has more in common with the convert than with his former compatriots. Conversion in this instance opens up unpredictable lines, and in effect sets up a cleavage between an effete Christian community "at home" and a more rigorous Christian grouping in the colony. By discussing Bunyan in the context of this picture, Montague makes the important point that *The Pilgrim's Progress* can create new and unexpected communities that challenge and cross over predictable lines of belonging.

A similar idea emerges from other discussions of African illustrations. In 1947 the RTS responded to criticisms of the "Kamba" illustrations that we discussed in chapter 8. In these pictures, the characters had monotone faces that lacked any physiognomical features. For the RTS, the illustrations showed that the protagonist, Christian, was not simply "a *mere* Briton" but was rather "a New Man in Christ."[40] These two phrases throw into stark relief the contending claims for Bunyan's success. The first holds that his story is primarily about and for white Britons. The second insists that it is for anyone (or at least all men) who converts to Protestantism.

Alongside these discussions, misgivings started to register themselves around the idea of how Bunyan's Englishness could be universal. Initially, the doubts expressed themselves as puzzlement that Bunyan's Englishness should have such wide appeal. Speaking at the tercentenary celebrations, the Bishop of Durham said: "In view of the intensely English tone and temper of the work, it is particularly surprising that it should have commended itself so extensively to foreigners."[41] A decade earlier, another commentator had noted the same problem:

> *The Pilgrim's Progress* is a book of paradox. It is at once universal and insular. Wide as humanity, it is nevertheless narrow in its social outlook. It is so truly catholic in spirit that it may be described as a book for all men, and yet its author was a man of little education and meager knowledge of the great world. Written in the homely phraseology of an English village, it has been translated into seventy or eighty foreign

languages, including those of Asia and Africa, as well as the majority of European tongues.[42]

Here Bunyan's Englishness and his universality make uneasy bedfellows. The tension between the terms at times becomes patent. Writing in 1923, Christina Knox notes the books universality, and that it is read in "Asia . . . Africa and even in the Islands of the Pacific." She then comments, almost with relief, "For us the life and charm of the story need not be blurred by a translation."[43] Knox implicitly ranks Bunyan's Englishness above his universality with the latter being seen as an unfortunate drag on the clarity of his true local meaning.

This anxiety about Bunyan's universality damaging his Englishness became most apparent in 1928 with Alfred Noyes's now-famous attack on Bunyan in *The Bookman*.[44] Writing against a backdrop of effusive tercentenary praise for Bunyan, Noyes slated him as an overrated, theologically outdated, and "piously repulsive" writer driven by a punitively narrow set of Calvinist ideas.[45] His article attracted an avalanche of accusatory responses.[46] Noyes defended himself by explaining that he was "writing secular literary criticism" and contrasted his endeavors to the existing work on Bunyan, "an author whose reputation has largely been built up, and is now being defended, by ministers of religion."[47] Assessments of Noyes's intervention (while criticizing its polemical character) have located its importance in this secular emphasis, in turn seen as anticipating modern contemporary critical practice.[48] One aspect of the article, however, that has attracted less attention is its strongly Social Darwinist emphasis (which has been excised from anthologized versions of the piece). In attacking Bunyan as fanatical, crude, and superstitious, Noyes likens his work to "the lowest and most squalid levels of the primitive races of Africa." Elsewhere in the article, he characterizes *The Pilgrim's Progress* as "a revelation of something dreadful and primitive and insane, something that has only half emerged from the squalor of the sub-human. Caliban crying for the Celestial City may be a subject for literature, but he is not a maker of it." He continues to stigmatize the author of *The Pilgrim's Progess* as "poor Caliban-Bunyan," and in a subsequent piece describes his language as "Hottentotish."[49]

In some senses, the evolutionist analogies used by Noyes are unremarkable for the period and are no doubt chosen as one available register of abuse. However, given that Noyes was an arch-traditionalist and writer of intensely patriotic "English" verse, the article merits further attention.[50] Ordinarily, one might have expected someone like Noyes to embrace Bunyan enthusiastically for his Englishness. Yet, for Noyes, as we have seen in chapter 2, Bunyan is a menacing presence: he is lower class, inadequately modern, and insufficiently "white." He consequently needs to be relegated to the outer reaches of empire, there to dwell among the "savages" with whom Protestant missionaries had so long associated him. In this tainted Caliban-position, Bunyan has lost any claims to belonging to an implicitly "white" tradition. Like Caliban, he may be the subject of literature, but his literature is no longer worthy of the English tradition. It is as though Noyes wishes to erase the memory of a contaminated Bunyan from his version of "white" Englishness.

In some respects, Noyes's outburst was atypical and his attack notwithstanding, Bunyan easily secured a place in the Leavisite tradition of English literature. As Eagleton has shown,[51] this tradition was to become decisively influential from the 1930s onwards, partly no doubt because of the waning impact of Nonconformist intellectual circles, precipitated in turn by the late-nineteenth-century middle-class defection from the chapels and public forums of Nonconformity.[52] Within this literary field of debate, Bunyan was to be included in the "Great Tradition" and was unsurprisingly canonized as narrowly white and English. Q. D. Leavis, for example, saw Bunyan's enduring popularity as lying in the biblical English he used. For her, this language was also implicitly "white": "the characteristic effect of reading a passage of Bunyan is a stirring of the blood—the Biblical phrases and cadences evoke overtones, and the peculiarly thrilling quality of the prose is due to this technique which enables a precise particular occasion to draw on the accumulated associations of a race. Bunyan's work could no more than Shakespeare's have been done in any other language."[53]

This stress on an intense Englishness continued to be accompanied by the idea of Bunyan as universal. The meaning of this universality, however, takes on a slightly different guise, best captured in F. R. Leavis's comments on Bunyan. He phrased the issue thus: "For what makes *The Pilgrim's Progress* a great book, one of the great classics, is its humanity—its rich, poised and mature humanity."[54] In this formulation, the status of Bunyan's universality has modulated. Instead of connoting the concrete circulation of his texts to numerous societies, the term "universality" denotes something much more vague and abstract. This configuration within the Leavisite tradition of a narrow Englishness alongside an abstract and universal "human nature" offered possibilities for muffling the contradictions that had arisen around Bunyan. On the one hand, a stress on white Englishness rooted the writer in England, while maintaining Bunyan as a literary icon who could confer racial distinctive-ness on Britons. An ethereal universality, on the other hand, could elevate Bunyan above the black colonized societies with whom mission discourse had so long connected him. Such societies had initially provided the pre-condition for nineteenth-century ideas on Bunyan's universality. Their erasure from the critical record became one precondition for twentieth-century Bunyan scholarship to take shape and for *The Pilgrim's Progress* to become unequivocally a book of England.

Lifting the Tollgates

Despite the fact that Bunyan's influence beyond England has been excised from the critical record, the question of his "universality" has continued to exercise a lingering fascination for mainstream critics. Roger Sharrock, for example, has pointed to the paradoxical contrast between Bunyan's "universal appeal . . . and the uncompromising dogmatism of the author's religious belief." He continues: "Bunyan wrote a book to express the views on God, man, and salvation of an English seventeenth-century Particular Baptist and created a work for the world which has appealed even to those of other religions than Christianity."[1]

This study has concerned itself with the history of how this question regarding Bunyan's universality comes to be posed in this form, namely as the paradox of a narrow parochial writer who appeals to a worldwide audience. I have suggested that the question itself arises from the legacy of evangelicalism and the history of English literature as a discipline, and that furthermore the consequences of these phenomena for Bunyan have been read in the wrong order. Evangelicalism made Bunyan international, English literature made him national. To ask, as the critics quoted above do, how a parochial Bunyan comes to appeal to the whole world is to assume that he is first a "national" writer and that he is then broadcast to the world and becomes "international." This book has suggested that it is more profitable to think about these processes the other way around. Bunyan as a "national" writer is an interpretation of relatively recent provenance arising out of the intellectual formation that we now call English literature. This way of seeing him is shaped in opposition to older evangelical traditions in which Bunyan's reach is seen as "universal/international." This conclusion asks what the broader implications of posing the issues in this order might be and is a very preliminary contribution to attempting to chart what a "post-Bunyan" landscape might look like. What if, this conclusion asks, we were to dismantle the categories "national"/"international" by which Bunyan has been "disciplined?"

The first step in such a dismantling is to reassess the meanings of "universality" and to recognize that the way the term is generally invoked in much Bunyan scholarship derives in effect from the lingering evangelical interpretations of the word. A core element in such propositions was the idea that everyone read the same text, a notion in turn driven by the imperatives of Nonconformist publicity back "home." In these representations, *The Pilgrim's Progress,* rather like the Bible, appeared to travel unchanged through the ether of language and culture. Evangelical views of texts as having the capacity to "seize" their readers have equally contributed to such thinking. Questions of exactly how the text was disseminated and in what form did not present themselves as matters of any moment. Instead, texts were seen as spirits moving invisibly through time and space.

Contemporary speculations about the "universality" of Bunyan still operate implicitly from these assumptions. Christopher Hill's discussion of why Bunyan is "universal" provides an instructive example. For Hill, the book's attraction lies in its political message regarding the divisions between rich and poor. The story is about a man in rags who stands up to giants who oppress him.[2] However, over and above this general message of poor versus rich, the book, in Hill's analysis, also offers readers the concept of a self-conscious ideology. Christian is not "just a brave individual fighting his way through enemies and a hostile environment." He possesses "an ideology of resistance."[3]

For Hill, it is this self-conscious ideology that gives the book its universal purchase.

> So—curiously—it is the Puritanism, the sense of dedicated and
> *principled* effort, that universalizes the story of fights with
> dragons and giants: and gives it a potential appeal to Chinese
> or African peasants which was something very different from
> what was intended by the pious missionaries who translated
> *The Pilgrim's Progress.*[4]

Hill does, of course, recognize that readers transform texts. However, the animating assumption of his discussion is that readers read the whole text. They may reinterpret it, but their activity is based on much the same text that he reads. Hill can consequently maintain that oppressed readers in colonial contexts will grasp the text's "true" meaning, which is about class struggle.

However, as much of this book has attempted to show, texts change shape and form as they travel. In relatively rare instances was the entire book reconstituted in translation. The book was generally abridged and often shed, as we have seen, precisely the theological sections to which Hill ascribes its universal appeal.

There are also other unstated assumptions that occasion prophecies of what will happen when Bunyan travels. One of these is that we can predict beforehand the outcomes of the book's travels in Africa because the continent is exclusively divided into colonizer/colonized. With this as one's starting point, the need for detailed investigation falls away since we know already what we will find. In this regard, Hill's discussion of Bunyan's international circulation is again instructive, although entirely understandable given the lack of data on this topic. As indicated above, Hill locates the book's appeal in its ideology of resistance. He consequently suggests a scenario in which "pious missionaries" foist simple evangelical readings on "politicized peasants."[5] These smart peasants, needless to say, outwit the naive agents of an oppressive Christianity by evolving a resistant, anticolonial reading of the text. Where there was such a resistant reading of the kind Hill seeks, it came not from peasants but entirely predictably (as it did in England) from the lower-to-middling sort—in a colonial context, the African elite. It was they who used *The Pilgrim's Progress* to articulate national anticolonial ideologies of the type Hill posits. Such systematic ideologies seldom came from "the peasants," who were never ardent nationalists at the best of times and were generally more interested in other intellectual agendas. However, because Hill and others read the colonial universe only in terms of colonizer/colonized, these questions of class—oddly enough for a Marxist reading—disappear.

In the face of such assumptions, this book has striven, through detailed tracking of the text as a material object, to highlight the superfluity of textual practices, the diversity of audiences and reading strategies, and the unexpected outcomes that arise when texts travel from and into complex and crowded worlds. In tracing out the journeys of Bunyan in Africa, I have, for example, examined Kongo Protestants interacting with British Baptists to produce a form of the text that becomes photographic political biography. Kele-speakers help shape an abridged version that both circumvents the doctrinal dollops of the text and "cleans" up

the remaining sections, thereby rendering them more amenable to interpretation and, indeed, more allegorical. Middle-class African mission
elites de-allegorize and re-allegorize sections of the text to articulate anticolonial ideologies. Popular versions of African Christianity elaborate on
the role of documents in the text, showing these to be both passes and
passports, thereby formulating an "African" hermeneutic that also appears in Jamaica. A writer like Thomas Mofolo engages with the story to
rescript ideas of masculinity and, in so doing, enters a broader debate on
Protestantism, gender, and empire. His interest in Bunyan also arose
from the text's travels within the continent and this study has attempted
to illuminate some of the intra-African routes that the text took and the
ways in which *The Pilgrim's Progress* is enfolded and "archived" in African intellectual formations. This archive is one to which African novelists
return when they engage with Bunyan, not as a product of metropolitan
Britain but as a long-standing presence in the continent itself.

In examining these diverse reading and interpretive strategies, we
have conceptualized Bunyan's text as operating in the Protestant Atlantic,
a zone brought into being by a vast cast of players. In this study, I have
understood this zone as a type of transnational "echo chamber." Certain
categories of reader may apply the text in local ways, as the Eastern Cape
elite did, but they are cognizant of the text as an international field or
public sphere in and through which claims may be made. When John
Knox Bokwe, for example, invoked Bunyan to lift himself imaginatively
above the "rowdies" around him in the gallery of the Theatre Royal, he
was not only identifying himself with a Lovedale audience but also with
an international Protestant one, who likewise deployed Bunyan to position themselves as the moral betters of those around them. When Bokwe
discusses the link between Great-heart and Sifuba-Sibanzi, he does so in a
tract commissioned by the International Bible Reading Association and
aimed at a transnational audience. Such layering of inflection is well illustrated in the case of Joseph Jackson Fuller and his consciousness of the
multiple versions of Bunyan that he carried with him. Equally, readers in
England who bought an African RTS edition of *The Pilgrim's Progress* to
see how the text "appealed to African readers" entered such a reading
zone.[6] In such reading practices, the text becomes a "web" stretched
across the Protestant Atlantic, which registers and reverberates with the
inflections of its different audiences. Through these constant uses of
The Pilgrim's Progress in the "echo chamber" of the Protestant Atlantic,
readers across the entire zone became accustomed to see it as a text with
an inbuilt form of international address made possible by the accumula-

tion of local inflections garnered in the transnational networks of the text. Indeed, this international addressivity is embedded in the text itself. When part 2 appeared in 1684, the text was prefaced by a poem entitled "The Author's Way of Sending Forth His Second Part of the Pilgrim." This lists the places to which part 1 had already traveled (France, Flanders, Holland, the Highlands, "wild" Ireland, and New England)[7] and readers are invited to approach part 2 bearing this enlarged audience in mind.

This type of "echo chamber" could promote surprising forms of convergence in which different textual practices came to "discover" and resemble each other. One theme that this study has pursued is the magical practices around documents common to both evangelicalism and African religious traditions. In this "zone," English Nonconformists and African Christians could support notions of texts as objects that could compel extraordinary changes in the world. In mission discourses, these understandings were phrased as the opposites of each other—the fetish and the antifetish. Yet, this distinction notwithstanding, these practices reinforced each other and opened up a domain of "magical" reading and literacy practices in which readers took it for granted that *The Pilgrim's Progress*, as a textual object, could precipitate miracles.

Today, such practices have largely disappeared from view. Evangelicalism itself has fallen into disrepute and approaches to Bunyan— post-Noyes—have become secular. The fact that in popular thinking, secularized understandings of *The Pilgrim's Progress* have become a byword for historicist progress has also helped to obscure these earlier "magical" perceptions. Such reading practices are, however, worth recuperating, particularly in terms of the complicating sidelight they can throw on ideas of historicism. As Chakrabarty indicates, one way around the implicitly evolutionist assumption in much historicism is to think instead in terms of "hetero-temporality" and "time-knots."[8] By excavating such "magical" reading practices of *The Pilgrim's Progress* (itself a combination of both pre- and post-Cartesian views of time and space),[9] one can see the text as a "theater of hetero-temporality" in which different temporal orders are billeted. For some Nonconformists, the text, particularly in the Madagascan case, became a time machine via which to contemplate the early history of Dissent and hence the beginnings of their denominational history. This experience was one of the "pleasures" of chronology that colonialism enabled as one was given the illusion of visiting (in Africa, for example) prior versions of one's own society. However, at the same time, these experiences were overlaid with others, most notably evangelical temporal notions that seek to collapse time. The method of becoming a character in the text was one such practice. In taking up this position, one was not seeking to become a seventeenth-century character in Bedford. Instead, one sought to enter the spiritual present. These readings were supplemented with others that "baptized" the text in a number of domains: the Buta War, Jamaican slavery, the struggles of the Eastern Cape elite, the dream-geographies of heaven. These temporalities are "archived" in the international "landscape" of the text, which becomes further layered and inflected with these various readings. Put another way, the text can be seen as an expansible stage into which new "textual communities" are incorporated. The "mechanics" of the text, as Kaufmann has pointed out, make themselves amenable to such a possibility. As he notes, the text accommodates different times and spaces. Old Testament characters wander among the apparently seventeenth-century "personnel" of the text. It is as if these Old Testament figures "have escaped time and live immortally as part of the landscape of Christian's pilgrimage."[10] Just as the "stage sets" of the text could be moved to encompass Old Testament representatives, so too could other constituencies be lodged in the text's capacious spaces.

Another question that arises from raising the "tollgate" between an "international" and a "national" Bunyan is: what consequences might this have for Bunyan scholarship more generally? The first, and most obvious, implication is to reinsert Bunyan back into the Protestant Atlantic. Such a possibility has already been mooted by Nancy Armstrong and Leonard Tennenhouse in *The Imaginary Puritan*. In this text, they note that the first edition of *The Pilgrim's Progress* (1681) in colonial North America, carried an advertisement for the forthcoming captivity narrative of Mrs. Mary Rowlandson.[11] This story, which told of her abduction by "Indians," proved to be immensely popular on both sides of the Atlantic. As the analysis presented by Armstrong and Tennenhouse suggests, such captivity narratives by women can be read as a catalyst in the formation of the English novel. As narratives that make apparent the very edges of "Englishness," they dramatize those features of female virtue under attack that novelists like Richardson were to encode. Indeed, the authors of *The Imaginary Puritan* argue that Richardson's *Pamela* can profitably be read as a text that imports many features of the captivity narrative and reproduces them in an English setting.

Through this argument (which I set out here very superficially), Armstrong and Tennenhouse contend that the English novel has to be seen as a colonial formation. The English novel cannot be "explained by events occurring strictly within English culture if we restrict our definition of England to modern England alone."[12] In understanding the novel, we need to grasp a transatlantic field in which cultural possibilities move back and forth rather than just radiating out from Europe in an endless one-way stream.

Such moves to embed "English" texts into colonial formations are now standard. However, in relation to Bunyan, and with the exception of Spargo's work, this possibility has yet to be explored. The first move in such a direction would be to dismantle the "national" versions of Bunyan and reinsert him in a transnational field. What, for example, did the very early export and translation of his most famous text to the seventeenth-century Protestant world mean for its reception in England? The text's circulation to these areas has often been noted.[13] The implications of this for how Bunyan is seen back in England are more rarely investigated. What might it mean to think of *The Pilgrim's Progress* in a much larger seventeenth-century world than has hitherto been the case? What if we imagine the boundaries of Bunyan's world as wider than just England, and instead see them as stretching to the boundaries of Christendom and the beginnings of the Islamic world[14] (something that Bunyan clearly did—he donated (or had donated on his behalf) part of the tiny amount of money he made in prison from capping shoelaces to support Christians under Islamic imprisonment)?[15]

Another consequence of lifting the "tollgate" would be to focus more closely on the story of how Bunyan was made "national." One major plank in this latter formation has been the idea that *The Pilgrim's Progress* is set in seventeenth-century Bedfordshire. This claim has been used to support the idea that the book is "realistic" and is hence a proto-novel. Much mainstream scholarship operates from the explicit or implicit assumption that the story takes place in Bedfordshire or southern England. Articulating a widely held assumption, Hill comments: "the countryside through which [Christian] passes is clearly England."[16] If, however, one reads the story outside England, or if one encounters it in another language, the first thing that strikes one is the oddness of this claim. As already indicated, the topography of the text is schematic. Description of landscape is invariably vague and biblical in orientation. The landscape does, of course, have certain features like stiles and by-paths, which would support a reading of the locale as Bedfordshire,[17] but these are few and far between. Also, because they are regionally specific, these features do not travel well. Nathaniel Hawthorne, for example, commented: "an American would never understand the passage in Bunyan regarding Christian and Hopeful going astray along a bypath into the grounds of Giant Despair—from there being no stiles and bypaths in our country."[18] In the Sotho and Afrikaans versions, any specific geographical and topographical features disappear as they are subsumed into regional equivalents. In the Sotho, for example, the arbor in which Christian takes his nap and loses his scroll is *mokhoro o pholileng*, an outhouse or hut where fire is made. By-path Meadow becomes *Thota ea Kheloho*, Plateau of Erring.[19] In the Afrikaans translation, geographical features are also indigenized: the wilderness becomes *woestyn* (desert); the Slough of Despond becomes *moeras van Kleinmoedigheid* (Marsh of Faintheartedness).[20] In his travels, Christian routinely strides across the *veld*. The Wicket Gate is the *enge poort*, the biblical term for "the narrow gate."[21] However, for those unfamiliar with the Bible, the term would denote a local topographical feature, namely a steep-sided passageway through mountains. Reading the text in translation creates a feeling of encountering a topographically schematic or abstracted version of one's known world.

What makes the text relatively easily translatable is, of course, the fact that references to a very local Bedfordshire landscape are relatively rare. Against a generalized background, these few particular references can be elided into local topographical and landscape idioms and thus can be relatively easily "smeared" into the translation as a whole. Seeing the "original" from the perspective of translation consequently forces one to ask the question: how could so many readers come to see the landscape as typically English and rooted in Bedfordshire? As we have seen in the previous chapter, the idea that the story unfolds in Bedford is a product of the local Bedfordshire attempts to stitch Bunyan to this environment. This local work was in turn taken up by intellectuals involved in the development of English literature, ever alert for evidence to support claims for Bunyan as national.

Looking at the attempts to "Bedfordize" Bunyan, one is immediately struck both by the extraordinary creativity of these ventures, but also how strained they are around the edges. Albert Foster, a major mover in the "Bedfordizing" process, notes the following passage in *The Pilgrim's Progress* in which Christian is shown the vista from Palace Beautiful. "When the morning was up they led him to the top of the house, and bid him look south, so he did. And, behold, at a great distance he saw a most pleasant mountainous country, beautified with woods, vineyards, fruits of all sorts, flowers also, with springs and fountains, very delectable to behold." This passage is then linked to Bedfordshire on the rather tenuous evidence that Bunyan loved "Bedfordshire streams, and Bedfordshire roads and lanes and footpaths, Bedfordshire mansions and gardens, and Bedfordshire hills were to him places pleasant to look upon."[22] The fact that Bedford has few hills and no vineyards underlines the strained nature of the comparison. So, too, does another of Foster's observations on Palace Beautiful.[23] As with other Bunyan sites, various contenders have, over the years, been identified as the model of this house. Today, the weight of opinion favors Houghton House near Ampthill, and one can visit its ruin where a National Trust plaque lends its gravitas to the claim. Turning from this heritage-speak, it is somewhat sobering to go back to the text. All we are told is that "there stood a very stately palace before him, the name whereof was Beautiful, and it stood just by the highway side."[24]

This prodigious effort at "Bedfordizing" Bunyan did, of course, attract its critics. One commented, somewhat irritably: "Bunyan was . . . writing an allegory of Christian life and not a guide book of Bedford . . . and even the members of his church were very unlikely . . . their thoughts . . . burdened with religious and temporal concerns, to trouble about the scenes of 'The Pilgrim's Progress.'"[25] Such comments, however, did little to staunch the numerous endeavors to plot out scenes from the story in and around Bedford. Indeed, so excessive did these guidebooks and tours become that even one of their organizers was forced to comment: "I want frankly to say that I am not prepared to plan out step by step the pilgrim journey on a map of Bedfordshire. It was a spiritual journey, and therefore of necessity, it is not incumbent to make a pilgrim go straight from place to place as we now have it in Bedfordshire."[26] These criticisms, however, constituted a minority opinion and, in the long run, these various endeavors, which were taken up by mainstream critics,[27] produced the commonsense wisdom that Bunyan was "realistic." As Arthur Mee said, The Pilgrim's Progress is "astonishingly real . . . as natural as life."[28] As we have seen, the characters were also packaged as English and hence as "real," so familiar that they could be in "every morning paper," so commonplace they could be "the faces on the Brighton peer."[29]

This geographical realism lent itself well to claims of Englishness and became one of the planks on which the book was seen as an early novel. Arthur Ransome, for example, wrote: "A fact is . . . very like an Englishman. . . .There is no vanity in a fact, and as a people we hate showing off. I can think of no other nation as hungry for facts as ours, none with a book of spiritual adventure so actual as the Pilgrim's Prog-

ress."[30] This idea of Bunyan's topographical "realism" has become, and continues to be, one of its major claims to "novelhood." As Homer Obed Brown's recent study on the institutions of the novel indicates, many texts were formalized as "novels" only in the nineteenth century.[31] It would be interesting to subject Bunyan to a similar type of analysis. The work of those in Bedford who stitched the text so firmly and effectively onto the landscape will be central in this account.

A third and final question arising from a lifting of the "tollgate" would be whether an investigation of Bunyan via Africa and the post-colonial world might throw any new light on the society from which he came and, hence, the texts he produced. Hill has posed the question, asking whether a consideration of Bunyan's reception in other parts of the world might teach us more "about the culture from which the book originated."[32] Leaving aside the historicist difficulties of the question, in which Africa is presumed to live a version of Europe's past, there are obvious comparative areas of investigation that could profitably be pursued. As parts of this study have demonstrated, one such theme would be that of orality and literacy, particularly the para-literate zone in-between where these two technologies mingle: a sphere that Bunyan and many African converts inhabited. These questions have been central to African literary scholarship, and Bunyan critics have also devoted attention to this theme.[33] A dialogue between these two areas, as suggested in chapter 6, could consequently be profitably pursued.

An equally useful dialogue could crystallize around the vexed question of the relationship between romance/"folktale" and realism, which has fueled much discussion around the status of *The Pilgrim's Progress* as a protonovel. Some of these claims to novelhood have been pinned to Bunyan's realism. Yet, in order for such claims of realism to hold, some critics (most notably Arnold Kettle and Michael McKeon) have minimized signs of romance and maximized signs of realism.[34]

If one were to attempt an analytical reconfiguration of these two stylistic domains, then the field of African literature, where these issues have been exhaustively debated, could alert one to the difficulties and dangers inherent in such an exercise. As critic Eileen Julien has shown, the use of oral literary forms in written texts is often assumed to be effortless and almost without craft.[35] Oral forms (often taken to be simple and "artless") are believed to migrate by apparent osmosis into writing, where they are generally read as betokening "tradition," "authenticity," and the like. This problem in turn is linked to the valorization of the terms "orality" and "literacy," themselves only technologies of communication, but currently burdened with other sets of meaning like premodern/modern; rural/industrial; undeveloped/developed; and so on.[36] The idea of "the oral" is consequently often invoked not because a serious engagement with oral literary form is intended but because sentimental notions of preindustrial pastness are required. Sharrock's comment on "story" is apposite: "[*The Pilgrim's Progress*] has the features of that very ancient but long-lasting form the story, something growing out of oral narrative like the fairy- or folk-tale."[37] This rather vague evocation of orality is in turn linked to a broader ideological statement, namely that "in our post-industrial and technological age," Bunyan, through his use of story, can still offer "us" an understanding of "the permanent outlines of our culture."[38] Not all investigations of "folktale" are this vague. Michael Davis, for example, has examined Bunyan's attempt to "discipline" the "folktale" form.[39] Such analyses might equally be brought to bear on works of African literature, where such a conjuncture has seldom been considered, the use of "oral forms" often being read the other way around, namely as an attempt to "discipline" realism.

Seen from this perspective, Bunyan's "realism" appears more flimsy than some accounts (like Kettle's, for example) would have us believe. Realistic representations of time and space, as James Turner has argued, appear almost as coincidental epiphenomena on the landscape in *The Pilgrim's Progress*. As Turner indicates, in her tour of House Beautiful, Christiana is taken successively "to a closet, to the place where Jacob's ladder goes up to heaven, to the actual mountain where Abraham offered up Isaac, and then immediately 'into the dining-room.'"[40] Turner's comments on time and space in Bunyan recall Karin Barber's analysis of Fagunwa, whose texts, in her view, stage "a kind of simulacrum of realism, ostentatiously marking out clock and calendar time in the phantasmagorical wastes of the forest of spirits."[41] Elsewhere, she comments: "Miles, minutes, and days, and writing itself, are pasted onto the radically unstable world of the forest in a way that renders them both flimsy and incongruous."[42] These comments could apply as well to *The Pilgrim's Progress*, a heteroclite fictional space, some of whose "incongruities" have been lost in the attempts to package the text as "realistic" in order to render it as a "national" space, suitable for inclusion in the English novel.

Yet, however much one unravels the ways in which Bunyan has been constructed, the question of his "universality" is unlikely to go away, particularly in a context of mounting globalization and an increased interest in mass transnational objects and texts. If this study has one "message," then it is that any understanding of these processes has to be rooted in a serious engagement with "local" intellectual formations. As the opening sections of this introduction noted, critics are quick to speculate on Bunyan's appeal. These speculations are, however, almost invariably wrong because they pay no heed to the intellectual formations into which *The Pilgrim's Progress* traveled. If the text gained a meaningful life in parts of the continent, this was not because it was imposed by missionaries but because it was popularized by Africans. As much recent research on missions has shown, Christianity in Africa took such deep root because it was spread by Africans. Missionaries, as one of their number put it, were "too few, too expensive, too European, too short-lived"[43] and most proselytizing was done by African evangelists. In most cases where *The Pilgrim's Progress* or its parts found a popular audience, this African intellectual agency was central.

Much of this study has concerned itself with the ways in which the "chemistry" of African intellectual formations can be factored meaningfully into transnational equations. With regard to Bunyan, it has suggested not only that his circulation in Africa is important to how he is seen back in Britain but, more importantly, that the nature of the African "archives" into which he is enfolded shapes, at times quite precisely, how he is understood in Britain. Intellectual production in the mission imperial domain is consequently wrought in a series of overlapping fields and circuits. This book has attempted to suggest how one might begin to understand the complex intellectual "chemistry" of these circuits. In doing so, it has sought to institute a more "symmetrical knowledge," where the intellectual complexity and depth of all the "points" in the circuit are factored in. Thus it has endeavored to "complete" the story of Bunyan's international circulation. As African readers noted, *The Pilgrim's Progress* appeared as a half-story. This study has suggested that the current academic understanding of Bunyan has been likewise only half the story. This book has proposed some initial ways in which that story might be completed.

Bunyan Translations by Language

Language	Country	Place of Publication	Publisher	Mission Society	Date	Translator
Afrikaans	South Africa	Cape Town	NGK Publishers	NGK	1920s?	?
Alur	DRC/Uganda	London	RTS	AIM	1930s?	?
Amharic	Ethiopia	St Chrischona	EV Fosterland/RTS/LSPCJ	SM	1892	Gerba Georgis Terfe
Bambara	Senegal/Mali	Kankan	CMA	CMA	1949	?
Bangala Uele	DRC	Ibambi	HAM	HAM	1944	?
Bangi	DRC	Bolobo	BMS	BMS	1923	?
Basa	Cameroon	"West Africa"	APM	ABCFM?	1933	?
Bemba	Zambia/DRC	London	RTS	LMS	1910	W Freshwater
Benga	Gabon	New York	?	BFMPUSA	1886	C de Heer
Bulu	Cameroon	Elat	Imprimerie Halsey	ABCFM?	1959	?
Chokwe	Angola/Zambia	London	USCL	CMML	1941	JJ Fuller
Duala	Cameroon	London	Alexander & Shepheard	BMS	1885	Alexander Robb
Efik	Nigeria/Cameroon	Edinburgh	Muir & Paterson	UPC	1868	?
Ewe	Togo/Ghana	?	?	Bremen MS?	1915	Jacob Benjamin
Fante	Ghana	London	RTS	WMMS	1886	?
Ga	Ghana	Accra	SMBD	?	1923	"Jacob"
Galwa	Gabon	Lambarene	PEMS	PEMS	1915	Pt 1 EC Gordon, Pt 2?
Ganda	Uganda	London	RTS	CMS	1896	?
Gbari	Nigeria	?	SIP	SIM	1960	?
Guéré	Ivory Coast	London	?	?	1958	Pt 1?, Pt 2 Ethel Miller
Hausa	Nigeria	?	RTS	CMS	1919	?
Herero	Namibia	?	FMS	FMS	1915	?

Igbo	Nigeria	London	CLS	1932	?
Ijaw	Benin/Nigeria	Oshogbo	?	1960	BHEA Nyananyo
Ika	Nigeria	Ika	Stewarts Press	1966	?
Ila	Zambia	London	USCL	1940s?	Moses Mubitana
Kalenjin	Kenya	Nairobi	OUP	1967	Commercial
Kamba	Kenya	London	USCL	1897	AIM?
Kanuri	Sudan	?	SUM	1960	?
Kele	DRC	London	RTS	1916	See chapter 3
Kongo	DRC/Angola	London	RTS	1897	Pt 1 T Lewis, Pt 2 G Lewis
Kikuyu	Kenya	Nairobi	?	1960	?
Kingwana	DRC	Yakusu	BMS	1931	?
Kongo-Fioti	Angola	?	SM	1921	Ruth Walfridsson
Kwanyama	Namibia/Angola	London	SPCK	1953	?
Lingala	DRC	London	RTS?	1894	?
Lozi	Zambia	Sefula	PEMS	1943	?
Luba-Lulua	DRC	Yakusu	BMS	1931	?
Luba-Katanga	DRC	Soni	Vuga Press	1941	?
Lunda	DRC/Angola/Zambia	London?	RTS?	1926	WS Fisher
Luo	Kenya	Nairobi	SPCK/Highway Press	1926	?
Lwena	Angola/Zambia	London	USCL	1929	?
Malagasi	Malagasy	Antananarivo	LMS	1835	?
Malinke	West Africa	?	CMA	1947	AE Loose
Mende	Sierra Leone	London	USCL	1935	?
Meru	Kenya	London	USCL	1956	?
Mongo Nkundi	DRC	London	RTS	1924	C Lemaire
Mundang	Cameroon	Lere	LFM	1959	?
Ndau	Zimbabwe/Mozambique	?	?	1929	?
Ndebele	Zimbabwe	?	LMS	1902	David and Mary Carnegie
Ndonga	Namibia	?	FMS	1926	?
Ngombe	DRC	London	BMS	1921	JH Marker
Ngonde/Nyekosa	Malawi/Tanzania	London	Thomas Nelson	1940	ABM Mwakasungula
Nkoya	Zambia	London/Redhill	USCL	1944	EM Jakeman
North Sotho	South Africa	Pretoria	Unie	1966	JM Rammala

Language	Country	Place of Publication	Publisher	Mission Society	Date	Translator
Nyanja	Malawi	London	SPCK	Ch of Scotland	1894	?
Ronga	Mozambique	London	RTS	SMR	1916	Charles Borquin
Rundi	Burundi	London	RTS	CMS	1940s?	Rosemary Guillebaud
Rwanda	Ruanda	London	RTS	CMS	1930s?	H Guillebaud
Shona	Zimbabwe	Bulawayo	Rhodesian Christian Press	Lit Bureau	1966	?
So	DRC	Yalemba	BMS	BMS	1918	WR Kirby
Somali	Somalia	Cairo	Nile Mission Press	?	1930?	?
Sotho	Lesotho/South Africa	Morija	RTS/PEMS	PEMS	1872	Adolphe Mabille, Filemone Rapetloane
Swahili	East/Central Africa	London	RTS	UMCA	1888	?
Temne	Sierra Leone	London	USCL	Lit Bureau	1959	T Warner
Teso	Uganda	London	SPCK	CMS	1956	?
Tetela	DRC	Wembo Nyamba	MECM	MECM	1941	?
Tigrinya	Eritrea	Asmara	RTS	?	1934	Teresa de Pertis
Tiv	Nigeria	London	RTS/DRCM	DRCM	1933	?
Tonga	Zambia	London	USCL	SMR?	1916	?
Tshwa	Mozambique	?	RTS	?	1921	D Maperre
Tsonga	Mozambique	Inhambane	Inhambane Mission Press	SMR?	1921	?
Tswana	Botswana/South Africa	London	RTS	LMS	1848	Robert Moffat
Tumbuka	Malawi/Zambia	London	RTS	UFS	1933	Charles Chidongo Chinula
Twi/Ashanti	Ghana	Basel	Basel MS	Basel MS	1885	?
Umbundu	Angola	New York	American Tract Society	ABFCM?	1904	WH Sanders
Venda	South Africa	?	Natal Union Bible Institute	Bib Institute	1956	BA Johanson
Xhosa	South Africa	Lovedale	Lovedale	UPC	1868	Pt 1 Tiyo Soga, Pt 2 JH Soga
Yoruba	Nigeria	London	RTS	CMS	1866	David Hinderer
Zulu	South Africa	Pietermaritzburg	P Davis/E London	CofE	1868	JW Colenso

Notes: This table represents an attempt to collate information pertaining to the earliest edition in each language of which I am aware.

Abbreviations used in table:

ABCFM = American Board for the Committee of Foreign Missions
AIM = Africa Inland Mission
APM = American Presbyterian Mission
BFMPUSA = Board of Foreign Missions of the Presbyterian Church in the USA
BMS = Baptist Missionary Society
CBM = Congo Balolo Mission
CLS = Church Literature Society
CMA = Christian and Missionary Alliance
CMML = Christian Mission in Many Lands
CMS = Church Mission Society
CofE = Church of England
DRC = Democratic Republic of the Congo
DRCM = Dutch Reformed Church Mission
ESM = Echoes of Service Mission
FMS = Finnish Mission Society
GEM = Garenganze Evangelical Mission
HAM = Heart of Africa Mission
LFM = Lutheran Fraternal Mission
LMS = London Missionary Society

LSPCJ = London Society for Promoting Christianity among the Jews
MECM = Methodist Episcopal Congo Mission
NGK = Nederduits Gereformeerde Kerk (Dutch Reformed Church)
OUP = Oxford University Press
PEMS = Paris Evangelical Mission Society
RTS = Religious Tract Society
SPCK = Society for Promoting Christian Knowledge
SAGM = South African General Mission
SIM = Sudan Interior Mission
SIP = Sudan Interior Press
SM = Swedish Mission
SMR = Swiss Mission Romande
SMBD = Scottish Mission Book Depot
SUM = Sudan United Mission
UFS = United Free Church of Scotland Foreign Mission Committee
UMC = United Methodist Church
UMCA = Universities' Mission to Central Africa
UPC = United Presbyterian Church
USCL = United Society for Christian Literature
WMMS = Wesleyan Methodist Missionary Society

A Social Profile of Bunyan Translators

The social profile of Bunyan translators is more diverse in terms of extant race, class, and gender definitions than one might initially expect. Most of the translators were, unsurprisingly, white European men. However, ten of the thirty-seven named translators were black (nine African, one Jamaican) and six were white women. In addition to Fuller, Charles Chinula, and Moses Mubitana, the black male translators included Tiyo Soga, who undertook the 1868 Xhosa translation. Other translators are more obscure and often appear as no more than a name like "Jacob," who translated sections of a 1901 Galwa edition in Gabon, or "Jacob Benjamin," who in 1886 clearly did the bulk of the Fante translation in Ghana while the nominal translator, W. M. Cannell, undertook editing and the transliteration of some names. As commercial school editions became more common in the 1960s, so too did African translators. Two examples here are J. M. Rammala, who did the North Sotho translation in South Africa, and A.B.M. Mwakasungula, who completed the translation into Ngonde/Nyekosa, a language straddling northern Malawi and Tanzania.

The number of black male translators is, however, much higher than reflected here. Any mission translation venture routinely involved more than one person and relied heavily on the work of male converts, known sometimes as "language boys."[1] Given this teamwork method, the number of white women involved was also probably higher than the visible profile indicates. African women were at times included in translation work, although I have not been able to establish whether this was the case for any Bunyan translations. With regard to the known women translators, some are obscure—a name ("C. Lemaire") on a title page and an entry or two in the minutes and correspondence book of the home organization.[2] The records of others, like the South African Eva Milton (subsequently Jakeman), were destroyed at sea, although she did write a memoir of her two decades on a mission in western Zambia.[3] Another South African-born translator was Mary Carnegie, the daughter of the Scottish LMS missionary, William Sykes. In 1885 she married the Scot, David Carnegie, also an LMS employee, and together they worked on the Ndebele translation (probably along with Moholo, a leading figure at Hope Fountain). Ethel Miller, who translated the second part of the story into Hausa, worked initially with the CMS in northern Nigeria before resigning and staying on as a self-funded, single, and poverty-stricken missionary in Kano. Here she used to sit in the marketplace, reading her translation of *The Pilgrim's Progress*, part 2, to passersby.[4] The life of Gwen Lewis (figure 5) of the BMS, who like Miller undertook one of the very few African translations of the second part of *The Pilgrim's Progress*, has been well documented.

In terms of class and social background, the classic profile of the early nineteenth-century mission recruit was that of a lower class white man drawn from an artisanal background.[5] However, as many historians of Protestant missions have indicated, the social provenance of mission recruits was in fact more variable than this popular picture suggests.[6] Mission societies themselves had long been differentiated in terms of their support bases and histories. The CMS, for example, was attached to the Church of England and, although much more low church and evangelical in orientation than its mother body, still attracted missionaries of a higher social caliber than equivalent Nonconformist bodies. Also, as the century progressed, the class background of missionaries shifted upward. The social provenance of Bunyan translators consequently varied considerably. The near-patrician E. C. Gordon of the CMS, who did part of the Ganda translation, was educated at Lincoln Grammar School and Marlborough College.[7] Bishop John Colenso, who did the Zulu version, while not as upper class as Gordon, came from a patchily privileged Cornish background.[8] Although at times precarious, Colenso's early circumstances were comfortable compared to those of that famous garden laborer, Robert Moffat, who did the Tswana version, or a figure like Thomas Lewis (figure 6), who did parts of the Kongo translation. Lewis spoke only Welsh until he was sixteen and came from a deep rural background. His father was a blacksmith, and at their church everyone sang hymns from memory, since to deem to hold a hymnbook was "an unpardonable affectation."[9]

Prologue

1. For details of mission translations other than *The Pilgrim's Progress*, see Hurry and Cirket, *Bunyan Meeting Museum Library Catalogue*, 112–15.

2. Sharrock, *The Pilgrim's Progress*, 399, note 2.

3. Wharey, introduction to *The Pilgrim's Progress*, xxxviii.

Introduction
Portable Texts: Bunyan, Translation, and Transnationality

1. Horne, *The Story of the LMS*, 223; LMS, *Fifty-Third Annual Report of the London Missionary Society*, 41.

2. Coombes, *Reinventing Africa*, 161–86; Maughan, "'Mighty England,'" 22–26.

3. Sharrock, introduction to *The Pilgrim's Progress*, 7. All further textual references to or quotations from *The Pilgrim's Progress* are from this edition.

4. The only work that systematically addresses Bunyan's international circulation in relation to his standing in England is Spargo, *Writing*.

5. Fletcher, "*The Pilgrim's Progress*"; Tibbutt, *Bunyan's Standing Today*. For evangelical approaches, see Christian History Institute, "Glimpses: Issue No. 86: John Bunyan"; "November 21, 1866: From English to Xhosa."

6. Smith, *John Bunyan in America*. See also Gérard, *African Language Literatures*, which discusses various African translations of Bunyan in passing, 18, 78, 133, 180, 190, 223, 232, 247, 249, 262, 267, 268, 273, 286; Nishimura, "John Bunyan's Reception in Japan." For perceptive comments on Bunyan in South Africa, see Chapman, "South Africa in the Global Neighbourhood," 674.

7. Hill, *A Tinker*, 375; Tibbutt, *Bunyan's Standing Today*; Fletcher, "*The Pilgrim's Progress*."

8. These figures have been compiled from a range of sources. The most comprehensive source is Hurry and Cirket, *Bunyan Meeting Museum Library Cata-

logue. The SOAS, University of London has a good collection of translated editions while the Bunyan Collection in the Bedford Library has a few translations. The papers of the RTS/USCL (housed at SOAS) have a fair amount of information while the British Museum Catalogue lists some translations. See also Tibbutt, *Bunyan's Standing Today*; Fletcher, "*The Pilgrim's Progress*"; "*The Pilgrim's Progress*," *Sunday at Home* (1907): 130–31, Box 4, Pamphlets and Newspaper Cuttings, Bunyan Collection, Bedford Library; and Nishimura, "John Bunyan's Reception." These figures must however be viewed as provisional. Records are often partial and incomplete. Also, it is at times difficult to decide what a language is, particularly in the context of nineteenth-century mission work where missionaries, desperate to evangelize, turned dialects into languages and vice versa. The question of how to represent the names of African languages is complex. All African language names have prefixes: Ki-kongo, Se-sotho, isi-Zulu, and so on. The practice for representing these languages in English has generally been to omit the prefix. This practice has been changing, however, and there are instances where the prefix is now included. However, if this prefix is included, then all others should be, too. For example, if one uses Sesotho, then one would need to talk of Basotho (plural) or Mosotho (singular) and so on. In light of this, I have decided to stick with the English convention of representing African language names without prefixes.

9. Liu, "The Question of Meaning-Value in the Political Economy of the Sign," 13.

10. Liu, introduction to *Tokens of Exchange*, 3, 5.

11. In a multilingual situation, such as exists in most of Africa, where it is standard practice for people to learn several languages at once, the terms "first-language" and "second-language" have severe limitations. However, in the early stages of mission encounter, these terms did have some meaning and so are used here.

12. For a range of such views see, Sharrock, "Life and Story," 50; Rivers, "Grace," 45; Hill, *A Tinker*, 373, 377; Greaves, "Bunyan through the Centuries."

13. Spargo, *Writing*, 105.

14. Persson, "Preparation, Production and Distribution of Literature in African Languages," 12. The mission book market was further complicated by the question of the massive subsidy for Bibles and what this meant for the profile of the market. See "Report: Christian Literature for Africa," Acc. 7548 C.168, Church of Scotland Foreign Mission Papers, Edinburgh.

15. Greaves, "Bunyan through the Centuries" for accounts of such editions and Spargo, *Writing*, 96–112, for an account that tends to elide editions aimed at white settlers and those translated in the mission domain.

16. This field is extensive. I have relied on Landau, *The Realm*; Meyer, *Translating*; Larson, "'Capacities'"; Peel, "'For Who Hath Despised'"; Rafael, *Contracting Colonialism*; Comaroffs, *Of Revelation and Revolution*, vols. 1 and 2.

17. Rafael, *Contracting Colonialism*, 110, 135, 7.

18. Pietz, "The Problem of the Fetish"; Pietz and Apter, introduction to *Fetishism as Cultural Discourse*; Spyer, *Border Fetishisms*.

19. For evidence of how Bunyan's language saturated lower-class Protestant speech, see the Candidates' Papers, LMS Papers in the CWM Papers, SOAS, University of London. These papers were filled out by aspirant missionaries and required them to write about their religious trajectories and experiences. See particularly John Mackenzie, Box 11/6, 539, 1858; R. C. Mather, Box 11/20, 299, 1833; W. Milne, Box 11/39, 133, 1812; J. H. Parker, Box 12/42, 460, 1843; W. D. Osborne, Box 12/34, 989, 1893.

20. I am grateful to Karin Barber who pointed this out to me.

21. Piggin, *Making Evangelical Missionaries*; Bebbington, *Evangelicalism in Modern Britain* and *The Nonconformist Conscience*; Thorne, *Congregational Missions*, chaps. 1 and 2; Maughan, "'Mighty England'"; Martin, *Evangelicals United*; Hilton, *The Age of Atonement*; Howse, *Saints in Politics*; Bradley, *The Call to Seriousness*.

22. Phrase from subtitle of USCL, *One-Hundred-and-Forty-Ninth Annual Report*.

23. Niranjana, *Siting Translation*, chap. 1.

24. Apter, "On Translation in a Global Market," 3.

25. Sanneh, *Translating the Message*.

26. Mugambi and Magesa, *Jesus in African Christianity*.

27. Niranjana, *Siting Translation*, 21.

28. There is a considerable body of scholarship on missions, translation, language, and the invention of ethnicity. See, for example, Ranger, "Missionaries, Migrants and Manyika"; Comaroffs, *Of Revelation*, vol. 1, 222–24.

29. Chakrabarty uses the phrases "an equality and symmetry of ignorance" and "asymmetric ignorance" in "Postcoloniality and the Artifice of History: Who Speak for 'Indian' Pasts," 2.

30. Warner, "Publics."

31. Warner, "Publics," 63.

32. Rafael, *Contracting Colonialism*, 175.

33. "Nantso-ke inncwadi yalo'muntu uMkristo, enike n'ezwa kumbe abatile beti ukona, kumbe beti ikona inncwadi yake." Colenso, "Amazwi ka-Sobantu." My thanks to Bheki Peterson for this translation. Colenso was noted as an outstanding Zulu-speaker.

34. Barber, *Readings in African Popular Culture*, "Preliminary Notes on Audiences," and "Audiences and the Book in Africa"; Hofmeyr, "Metaphorical Books"; Newell, *Ghanaian Popular Fiction*; Newell, *Literary Culture*. I am indebted to my colleagues in the "Social Histories of Reading in Africa" research group convened by Karin Barber.

35. The prophet movements generated a lot of material in Kongo, much of which has been translated into French and English: Janzen and MacGaffey, *An Anthology*; Mackay, "Simon Kimbangu"; Mackay and Ntoni-Nzinga, "Kimbangu's Interlocutor"; MacGaffey, "*The Beloved City*: Commentary on a Kimbanguist Text"; Pemberton, "The History of Simon Kimbangu." It is primarily this material that has been used as the basis for the analysis above.

36. Janzen and MacGaffey, *An Anthology*, 102–106; Struyf, *Uit den Kunstschat der Bakongos*, vol. 1, 58–64.

37. This model is proposed most famously by Scheub, *The Xhosa Ntsomi*.

38. Prakash, "Introduction: After Colonialism," 11.

39. Keeble, "'Of Him Thousands Daily Sing,'" 248–49, and Greaves, "Bunyan through the Centuries," 114–15.

40. Thorne, "'The Conversion of Englishmen and the Conversion of the World Inseparable'" and *Congregational Missions*; Maughan, "'Mighty England.'"

41. Archer, "Come, and Welcome, to Jesus Christ."

42. These figures have been compiled from the sources listed in note 8.

43. Porter, *Atlas of British Overseas Expansion*, 124–37; Pettifer and Bradley, *Missionaries*, chaps. 4, 9, 10.

44. For a back translation of sections of Mubitana's version, see "The Voice of Africa."

45. With regard to the British translations, most come from the large denominational societies (BMS, nine; CMS, seven; CMS-aligned societies, two; LMS, five; Wesleyan-aligned societies, three). Faith mission produced nine, while Scottish missions produced three.

46. Sann, *Bunyan in Deutschland*; Schutte, *Bunyan in Nederland*; Esking, *John Bunyan i Sverige under 250 år*, English Summary, 197–203. See also, Brown, *John Bunyan: His Life Times and Work*, 467–68.

47. Hewitt, *The Problems*, xiii–xiv.

48. Hewitt, *The Problems*, xiv.

49. Patton, "A World Program"; de Mestral, "Christian Literature."

50. Hewitt, *The Problems*, xvii.

51. Bernth Lindfors provided me with a copy of a page from a Nigerian photocomic, which he obtained at the University of Ibadan Library.

Chapter I
The Congo on Camden Road

1. *Camden Road Chapel*; Camden Road Baptist Church, *Sunday School Centenary*.

2. Binfield, *So Down to Prayers*, chap. 7; Brooks and Saint, introduction to *The Victorian Church*, 11.

3. See "Camden Road Baptist Chapel Sunday School Missionary Association Annual Reports and Minutes of the Sunday School Committee," Camden Road Church Papers, Camden Road Baptist Church, London (hereafter referred to as Camden Road Church Papers).

4. *Camden Road Chapel*, 8–13, 21–23; Tidmarsh, *Sale of the Century*.

5. *Missionary Herald*, August 1883, 280.

6. Tidmarsh, *Sale of the Century*.

7. Phrase from Camden Road, *Sunday School Centenary*, 10.

8. Phrase from *Camden Road Chapel*, 9.

9. Brooks and Saint, introduction to *The Victorian Church*, 11; Tucker, ser-

mon delivered on 20 July 1873, collected in a book of sermons, Camden Road Church Papers.

10. Tucker, sermon delivered 14 December 1873, Camden Road Church Papers; *Camden Road Chapel*, 8–13, 18–21; Dickens quote from Porter, *London*, 218.

11. Camden Road Baptist Church, *Sunday School Centenary*, 4–5.

12. Porter, *London*, 300–304.

13. Phrase from McLeod, *Religion and Society*, 13.

14. Tucker, sermons delivered 14 December 1873, 28 September 1873, 5 October 1873, Camden Road Church Papers.

15. *Camden Road Chapel*, 8–13, 18–21.

16. Hawker, *An Englishwoman's Twenty-Five Years*, 137.

17. Hawker, *An Englishwoman's Twenty-Five Years*, 16.

18. Thomas Comber to Mrs. Hartland, 13 May 1883, A/27-9, Hartland Papers, BMS Archives, Regent's Park College, Oxford (hereafter cited as BMS Archives).

19. Alice Hartland to John Hartland, 29 October 1879, A/27-9, Hartland Papers, BMS Archives.

20. Stanley, *The History*, 117–18; *Missionary Herald*, February 1885, 378.

21. *Missionary Herald*, February 1885, 378.

22. See note 19.

23. Thornton, *The Kingdom*, xiv, xvi; Hilton, *The Kingdom*, 6, 55–60.

24. Pigafetta, *A Representation*, 108–10; Thornton, *Africa and the Africans in the Making of the Atlantic World, 1440–1800*, 48–53.

25. Schneider, "Dressing for the Next Life."

26. Pigafetta, *A Representation*, 108–10; Broadhead, "Trade and Politics on the Congo Coast, 1770–1870," 194.

27. Miller, *Way of Death*, 143–44.

28. Hilton, *The Kingdom*, 222.

29. Lewis, *These Seventy Years*, 118.

30. Paragraph drawn from Stanley, *The History*, 116–39; Fullerton, *The Christ*, 102–15; Lewis, *These Seventy Years*, 114–70.

31. Stanley, *The History*, 106–39.

32. Fullerton, *The Christ*, 49–50.

33. Sherry, *Conrad's Western World*, 51.

34. See, for example, the following tracts [Codner], *The Missionary Farewell*; [Codner], *The Missionary Ship*; *The Missionary Ship John Williams*; *The Return to England of the Missionary Ship John Williams*; Reason, *The Ship Book*.

35. [Codner], *The Missionary Farewell*, ix.

36. Hawker, *An Englishwoman's Twenty-Five Years*, 17; *Missionary Herald*, February 1879, 36, 38–39; April 1879, 94–99; June 1884, 202, 221–23; August 1885, 290, 350; February 1889, 60–61; May 1890, 146–47.

37. *Missionary Herald*, June 1908, 188.

38. Report by Comber, *Missionary Herald*, January 1879, 17.

39. Bentley, *The Life and Labours of a Congo Pioneer*, 150.

40. "From the 'Dove' to the 'Grenfell,'" *Missionary Herald*, January 1916, 17–21.

41. *Missionary Herald*, April 1910.

42. *Missionary Herald*, January 1911, 18.

43. Samarin, "Protestant Missions and the History of Lingala."

44. BMS, *BMS Notes*, 11–12.

45. *Missionary Herald*, June 1928, 146.

46. BMS, *BMS Notes*, 4.

47. *Missionary Herald*, January 1908, 22.

48. BMS, *BMS Notes*, 7.

49. *Missionary Herald*, February 1918, 21.

50. Alice Hartland to John Hartland, [illegible] August 1879, 29 October 1879, A/27–9, Hartland Papers, BMS Archives; Hawker, *An Englishwoman's Twenty-Five Years*, 17.

51. *Missionary Herald*, January 1887, 22.

52. Hawker, *An Englishwoman's Twenty-Five Years*, 30.

53. Alice Hartland to John Hartland, 6 November 1882, A/27-9, Hartland Papers, BMS Archives.

54. Alice Hartland to John Hartland, 25 April 1879, 11 November 1881, 19 June 1881, A/27-9, Hartland Papers, BMS Archives.

55. Alice Hartland to John Hartland, 29 October 1879, A/27-9, Hartland Papers, BMS Archives.

56. *Missionary Herald*, October 1892, 400.

57. Camden Road Baptist Chapel Sunday School Missionary Association, "Twentieth Annual Report," Camden Road Church Papers.

58. Camden Road Baptist Chapel Sunday School Missionary Association, "Report Presented to Annual Meeting, 2 February 1897," Camden Road Church Papers.

59. Camden Road Baptist Chapel Sunday School Missionary Association, "Twenty-ninth Annual Report," Camden Road Church Papers.

60. Hawker, *An Englishwoman's Twenty-Five Years*, 3.

Chapter 2
Making Bunyan Familiar in the Mission Domain

1. Paragraph drawn from *Missionary Herald*, June 1928, 134, 146; November 1928, 264. For other exhibitions, see BMS, *Congo Jubilee Exhibition*.

2. Fullerton, *The Legacy* and *The Christ*.

3. Fullerton, *The Christ*, 198–200.

4. Thompson, *The Making*, 34, 37.

5. Keeble, "'Of Him Thousands Daily Sing,'" 248–51; Greaves, "Bunyan through the Centuries," 115.

6. Bebbington, *Evangelicalism in Modern Britain*, 2–4.

7. Owens, introduction to *Grace Abounding*, xxiii.

8. Quotations from Brown, introduction to *The Pilgrim's Progress*, ix–x; Birrell, "Editorial," 103; and A Pilgrim, *Some Daily Thoughts*, 10.

9. McGown, *Ten Bunyan Talks*, 209, and *The Bookman* 446, no. 75 (1928): 99.

10. Keeble, "'Of Him Thousands Daily Sing,'" 253; Mason, preface to *The Pilgrim's Progress*, vi; Stevenson, *Expositions*, ix; Cooper, *John Bunyan: The Glorious Dreamer*, 5; Birrell, "John Bunyan Today," 151.

11. Burbidge, *Half-Hours* and A Pilgrim, *Some Daily Thoughts*.

12. *Dramatic Illustrations*.

13. Blatchford, *My Favourite Books*, 191.

14. Blatchford, *My Favourite Books*, 192–93.

15. Norvig, *Dark Figures*, 119.

16. Birrell, "John Bunyan Today," 151. For another episode on the influence of pictures, see Fussell, *The Great War*, 140–41.

17. These items can be seen in the Bunyan Museum at the Bunyan Meeting House, Mill Street, Bedford, England.

18. See Borough of Bedford Public Library, *Catalogue*, Miscellaneous Section, 39.

19. The Bunyan Collection in the Bedford Library contains texts with family inscriptions over several generations.

20. Included in Welsh edition, *Taith y Pererin: Y rhyfel ysprydol*, which forms part of the Bunyan Collection in the Bedford Library.

21. This edition also forms part of the Bunyan Collection in the Bedford Library.

22. See editions in the Bunyan Collection, one with newspaper cutting (London: Routledge, Warne, and Routledge, 1861); recipe (Edinburgh: Thomas Nelson and Peter Brown, 1830).

23. "Devotion to Progress."

24. J.H.W., introductory notice to *The Pilgrim's Progress*, ix; McGown, *Ten Bunyan Talks*, 2.

25. National Sunday School Union, *Bunyan: The Dreamer*; Burbidge, preface in *Half-Hours*; Davies, *The Sunday Scholars' Service of Sacred Song*; Punshon, lectures in *John Bunyan* (these were accompanied by magic lantern slides).

26. Vincent, *Literacy*, 89; note in RTS edition, *The Pilgrim's Progress*, parts 1 and 2, in eight parts.

27. Vincent, *Literacy*, 174–75. See also Anderson, *The Printed Image*, 31.

28. Birrell, "John Bunyan Today," 152.

29. Wylie, *The Book of the Bunyan Festival*, 52.

30. Piggin, *Making Evangelical Missionaries*, 157; Peel, "'For Who Hath Despised,'" 595; Maughan, "'Mighty England,'" 20.

31. Brown quoted in Venables, *Life of John Bunyan*, 179.

32. See, for example, Rowling and Wilson, *A Bibliography of African Christian Literature*; Starr, *A Bibliography of Congo Languages*.

33. Hewitt, *Let the People Read*, 17.

34. For details of dramatic and musical arrangements of *The Pilgrim's Progress*, see Borough of Bedford Public Library, *Catalogue*, 35–36; for wallcharts and postcards, see RTS, *One-Hundred-and-Thirty-Second Annual Report*, 50, 54; for magic lantern displays, see RTS, *Seed Time and Harvest*, December 1919, 2; for talks and lectures, see Cheever, *Lectures on the "Pilgrim's Progress"*; Large, *Evenings with John Bunyan*; Overtone, *"The Pilgrim's Progress" Practically Explained*; Punshon, lectures in *John Bunyan*; Thompson, *Talks with Bunyan*; Warr, *A Course of Lectures*.

35. Landau, *The Realm*, 131–59.

36. Maughan, "'Mighty England,'" 28.

37. *Missionary Herald*, August 1888, 318.

38. Coombes, *Reinventing Africa*, 162; Maughan, "'Mighty England,'" 15; Pettifer and Bradley, *Missionaries*, 20.

39. Phrase from an article on Bunyan by Birrell, "Links of Empire," 79.

40. Lewis, *These Seventy Years*, 184–85. This section is also quoted in Hutton, *John Bunyan*, 221.

41. Sutton Smith, *Yakusu*, 242; Lewis, *These Seventy Years*, 184–85.

42. Sutton Smith, *Yakusu*, 242.

43. Holt, *Greatheart of the Border*; Obituary of A. E. Scrivener, "Greatheart of the Congo," CP/67, Scrivener's Candidate's Papers, BMS Archives; "The Interpreters on the King's High Way," *Missionary Herald*, May 1924, 107. See also chap. 7, note 16.

44. Green, *The Story*, 63; Hewitt, *Let the People Read*, 44; Fraser, *The Autobiography of an African*, see chapter headings and 80–81, 144; Callaway, *The Pilgrim Path*. This text is a composite biography of a young woman convert and most chapters start off with quotations from *The Pilgrim's Progress*.

45. Hawker, *An Englishwoman's Twenty-Five Years*, 270; Obituary of Henry Ross Phillips, *Missionary Herald*, February 1939, 31; Obituary of W. H. Stapleton, *Missionary Herald*, January 1907, A/35, Stapleton Papers, BMS Archives.

46. "Report from Old Calabar," 120; Sutton Smith, *Yakusu*, 216; *Congo Mission News*, January 1929, 19; "*The Pilgrim's Progress* in a Congo Setting," *Missionary Herald*, July 1923, 154.

47. *Regions Beyond* (journal of the Regions Beyond Mission Union) 1928 (?) [the journal is not clearly dated], 89; *Missionary Herald*, December 1931, 281.

48. See, for example, RTS, "*The Pilgrim's Progress*: List of 116 Languages and Dialects," *One-Hundred-and-Sixteenth Annual Report*, 170. These tables continued into the 1940s.

49. Green, *The Story*, 172.

50. Coombes, *Reinventing Africa*, 161–86.

51. *Seed Time and Harvest*, September 1909, 6, 44, 46; and BMS, *Congo Jubilee Exhibition*, 46.

52. "The Congo in Bristol," *Missionary Herald*, November 1928, 264.

53. *Seed Time and Harvest*, September 1909, 6.

54. Martin and Catt, *Pictures and Portraits from "The Pilgrim's Progress,"* 54; *Seed Time and Harvest*, September 1909, 6; "*The Pilgrim's Progress*," *Sunday at Home* (1907), Box 4, Pamphlets and Newspaper Cuttings, Bunyan Collection, Bedford Library.

55. Christian Literature Society for India and Africa, *Seventieth Annual Report*, back cover.

56. Larson, "'Capacities,'" 971; Gow, *Madagascar and the Protestant Impact*, 1–38.

57. Ellis, *The Martyr Church*, 107; Ellis, *Faithful unto Death*, 93; Ellis, *History of Madagascar*, vol. 2, 516; Freeman and Johns, *A Narrative*, 148.

58. Madagascar, incoming correspondence, Box 5, 1834–1840, Folder 3, 28 July 1838, CWM, LMS Papers, SOAS, University of London.

59. Freeman and Johns, *A Narrative*, 167.

60. Freeman and Johns, *A Narrative*, 166, also 167, 169.

61. Freeman and Johns, *A Narrative*, 231, 253, 256, 257, 259, 264, 273. The narrative has been constructed from letters sent by the converts interspersed with commentary and description by Freeman and Johns.

62. Freeman and Johns, *A Narrative*; Ellis, *History*; Ellis, *The Martyr Church*; Ellis, *Faithful unto Death*; *The Missionary Magazine and Chronicle, Relating Chiefly to the Missions of the LMS*, September 1840, 130; November 1840, 170; August 1836, 50.

63. Ellis, *Faithful unto Death*, 122; Budden, *The Story of Marsh Street Congregational Church Walthamstow*, 46–47.

64. See, for example, Freeman and Johns, *A Narrative*.

65. Griffiths, *The Great Adventure*; Anthony, *The Buried Bible and the Conversion of England to Christianity*; Patten and Shillito, *The Martyr Church and its Book*; Ridgwell, *Heroes in Madagascar*.

66. Ellis, *History*, 516; Ellis, *The Martyr Church*, 107; Ellis, *Faithful unto Death*, 93; Brown, *John Bunyan*, 470; Freeman and Johns, *A Narrative*, 165.

67. Green, *The Story*, 63; Hewitt, *Let the People Read*, 44.

68. Ellis, *History*, 516; Ellis, *The Martyr Church*, 107; Ellis, *Faithful unto Death*, 93; Green, *The Story*, 63; Hewitt, *Let the People Read*, 44.

69. Punshon, lectures in *John Bunyan*, 69. See also, Williams, *A Bi-Centenary Memorial*, 66.

70. Cutting with no details in Box 10, Bunyan Collection, Bedford Library.

71. See also Offor, introduction to *The Pilgrim's Progress*, cxlvi; Birrell, "Bunyan's Personal Pilgrimage," 108; RTS, *Forty-Seventh Annual Report*, 37.

72. Bunyan, *Inncwadi ka'Bunyane*; *Msafiri*; *Haj-oirku-eh (gharko)*.

73. Hutton, *John Bunyan*, 222.

74. For discussions of evangelicalism and tracts, see Cutt, *Ministering Angels*. The annual reports of the RTS also provide extensive discussions of tracts and their effects as do the various histories of the RTS: Green, *The Story* and Hewitt, *Let the People Read*.

75. Hewitt, *Let the People Read*, 19.

76. Cutt, *Ministering Angels*, 9.

77. Phrases from subtitle of USCL, *One-Hundred-and-Forty-Ninth Annual Report*; and Mair, *Books in their Hand*, 8.

78. Brown, *Bunyan's Home* (this book has no pagination); and Green, *The Story*, 172.

79. City Land Committee of the Corporation, *History of the Bunhill Fields Burial Grounds*, 36; Light, *Bunhill Fields*. For an early attempt to erect a monument on his tomb, see "Monument to John Bunyan," in *Works of the Puritan Divines: Bunyan*. Frequent wreath laying at the tomb also took place: *Daily Chronicle*, 1 September 1899, in Bunyan Scrapbook, collected and arranged by Potter, in the British Library (hereafter Bunyan Scrapbook, British Library); "John Bunyan Restoration of Tomb," unmarked cutting in Newspaper Cuttings, Bunyan Collection, Bedford Library; and *Bedfordshire Record*, 10 October 1928, Newspaper Cuttings, Bunyan Collection, Bedford Library.

80. Hargreaves and Greenshield, *Catalogue*, preface.

81. "John Bunyan: Restoration of Tomb," unmarked cutting in Newspaper Cuttings, Bunyan Collection, Bedford Library.

82. Offor, introduction to *The Pilgrim's Progress*, xi, xiv; Brown, introduction to *The Pilgrim's Progress*, xii; and Punshon, lectures in *John Bunyan*, 69, 110.

83. Punshon, lectures in *John Bunyan*; and Martin and Catt, *Pictures and Portraits*.

84. Coombes, *Reinventing Africa*, 162–65.

85. Greaves, "Bunyan through the Centuries," and Keeble, "'Of Him Thousands Daily Sing.'" Lindsay, *John Bunyan*, 249, goes against this orthodox periodization. He suggests that Bunyan's mainstream acceptance comes much later (1880s) and is forced out of the establishment by a sharpening of "the class-struggle" and a secularization of "proletarian forces." Against this background, Bunyan is seen as a writer who can "pacify" and re-Christianize the working classes.

86. Keeble, "'Of Him Thousands Daily Sing,'" 254–55.

87. Samuel, *Island Stories*, vol. 2, 281–82.

88. Froude, *Bunyan*.

89. Rutherford [William Hale White], *John Bunyan*, 234–35 and Lindsay, *John Bunyan*, 249.

90. The monument unveiling is described in Wylie, *The Book of the Bunyan Festival*. For the Westminster Abbey window, see *The Times*, 26 January 1912.

91. Williams, *A Bi-Centenary Memorial*, 96.

92. *Daily Chronicle*, 25 November 1908, in Bunyan Scrapbook, British Library.

93. *Daily Chronicle*, 25 November 1908, in Bunyan Scrapbook, British Library.

94. Bishop of Durham [Handley Carr Glyn Moule], "An Anglican's Reflection," 315.

95. Larson, "'Capacities,'" 979.

96. Larson, "'Capacities,'" 994.

97. Inscriptions in the following editions of *The Pilgrim's Progress* in the Bunyan Collection, Bedford Library: item 22621 (Plymouth: J. Bennett, 1823); item 22738 (London: W. Oliver, 1776); item 33801(London: RTS, n.d.); tear-out postcard edition, item 56699 (London: Stirling Tract Enterprise, n.d.) (these two latter numbers, marked on the books themselves, are not listed in the Borough of Bedford, *Catalogue*). On the considerable influence of Bunyan among soldiers in the First World War, see Fussell, *The Great War*, 138–44.

98. See report in *Seed Time and Harvest*, September 1924, 12, and September 1927, 8.

99. This was a common feature of reports in the *Missionary Herald*, for example, "Report of Pioneer Journey," June 1899, 311–12 (illustrations); "Religions without Scriptures," September 1907, 267–70; "Magic and the African Church," September 1910, 274–75; "Some Congo Fetishes," July 1911, 201–203. Exhibitions invariably included fetish stalls or "fetish stockades," *Missionary Herald*, September 1909, 262–63.

100. Janzen and MacGaffey, *An Anthology*, 12.

101. Offor, introductory memoir in *The Pilgrim's Progress*, 5.

102. Noyes, "Bunyan," 17.

103. Noyes, "Bunyan," 14, 17.

Chapter 3
Translating Bunyan

1. John Whitehead to Dr. Williamson, 7 June 1944, A/53, Whitehead Papers, BMS Archives.

2. Obituary of Whitehead, A/53, Whitehead Papers, BMS Archives.

3. John Whitehead to C. E. Wilson, 28 April 1924, A/53, Whitehead Papers, BMS Archives.

4. John Whitehead to C. E. Wilson, 20 December 1922, A/53, Whitehead Papers, BMS Archives.

5. John Whitehead to C. E. Wilson, 28 September 1925, A/53, Whitehead Papers, BMS Archives.

6. John Whitehead to Dr. Williamson, 7 June 1944, A/53, Whitehead Papers, BMS Archives.

7. "Bible Translation," *Congo Mission News*, October 1928, 30–32; Girdlestone, *Suggestions for Translators, Editors and Revisers of the Bible*.

8. Nida, "Congo"; Ranger, "Missionaries, Migrants and Manyika."

9. Meyer, *Translating*; Larson, "'Capacities.'"

10. Nida, "Congo."

11. Such volumes can be seen at the Morija Museum and Archive, Morija, Lesotho.

12. John Whitehead to A. H. Baynes, 7 October 1904, A/53, Whitehead Papers, BMS Archives.

13. Knott, "'Thou Must Live Upon my Word.'"

14. Kilgour, "The Order."

15. Nida, "Congo," 11.

16. Michaeli, "Bible Problems," 17.

17. *Seedtime and Harvest*, September 1923, 17.

18. See also the Bulu version, which is bound together with sections from the Psalms: *Dulu Ntone Krist.*

19. "Eye-gate: or, The Value of Native Art in the Mission Field," *Missionary Herald*, September 1897, 2.

20. Cockett, "John Bunyan—The Man," 39.

21. Guillebaud, interview by author, Cambridge, 3 December 1998.

22. Guy, *The Heretic*, 110–90.

23. "Makolwa, Ngiyikipile le'nncwadi yalo'muntu uMkristo, ngitanda ukuba niyifunde niy'azi. Kepa ngiyanincenga bantu bami, ngiti, ningasoli ngoba ngalibala kangaka anganikipela inncwadi kwaza kwakaloku, kwaza kw'eqa inkati engaka. Ai-ke! ngangilitshaziswe okunye okukulu okudhlula okunye engiti nani impela niyakufinyelela kuko, nakuba kaloku ningakuboni belu. Ehe! le'nncwadi ngiyikipe nje ng'enzela ukuba niyifunde nitole amandhla okubona, n'azi ukupenya, nifane nabelungu. Nantso-ke inncwadi yalo'muntu uMkristo, enike n'ezwa kumbe abatile beti ukona, kumbe beti ikona inncwadi yake, ikuluma ipata ukuhlupeka kwomuntu otile ofuna ukwazi uNkulunkulu uBaba wetu, atembe ku'Kristo-Jesu inkosi yetu." Colenso, "Amazwi ka-Sobantu" ("Words of Sobantu" [Colenso]).

24. I am indebted to Jeff Guy for information on this translation that was done between 1865 and 1868, probably with the assistance of William Ngidi. On Ngidi, see Guy, "Class, Imperialism and Literary Criticism."

25. Hurry and Cirket, *Bunyan Meeting Museum Library Catalogue*, 97.

26. Sutton Smith, *Yakusu*, 116, 155–56, 160.

27. Obituary of Stapleton, *Missionary Herald*, January 1907, A/35, Stapleton Papers, BMS Archives; Pugh, foreword in *Lokendo loa Bokendi* (*The Pilgrim's Progress*, part 1), trans. and comp. Pugh; Starr, *A Bibliography of Congo Languages*; Sutton Smith, *Yakusu*, 218.

28. Sutton Smith, *Yakusu*, 89–102.

29. Pugh, "Educational Work in Africa," *Seed Time and Harvest*, September 1927, 8.

30. Pugh, foreword in *Lokendo loa Bokendi.*

31. *Mboli ya Tengai*, May 1910 to February 1912, BMS Archives.

32. Pugh, foreword in *Lokendo loa Bokendi.*

33. "BMS Record of Literary Work in Preparation or Planned," 3 May 1916, CP/455, Pugh Papers, BMS Archives.

34. The serialization ran from February to July 1925. For examples of short extracts, see *Mboli ya Tengai*, September 1925 and February 1925, BMS Archives. At times, the abridgement was run in both Kele and French. The unstable and provisional nature of mission translation can be seen from the shifting title used during the serialization. It changes from "Lokendo loa Bokendi," to "Bokendi wa Kendo,"

to "Kendo ya Bokendi." The published version appeared under the title *Lokendo loa Bokendi.*

35. Hurry and Cirket, *Bunyan Meeting House Museum Catalogue,* 9–10.

36. Smith, "The Need."

37. Nida, "Some Language Problems in the Congo," 14–16. A similar point is made in the term *chizungu,* which Africans used to described mission attempts to speak Nyanja in Nyasaland. Roughly translated it would mean "white-manese." MS 3086.2, Alexander Gillon MacAlpine Papers, University of Edinburgh, Scotland. My thanks to John McCracken for putting me on to these papers.

38. Sutton Smith, *Yakusu,* 155.

39. John Whitehead to A. H. Baynes, 7 October 1904, A/53, Whitehead Papers, BMS Archives.

40. Smith, "The Need," 70.

41. Clarke, "What Literature."

42. Clarke, "What Literature," 100.

43. Clarke, "What Literature," 101.

44. Pugh, "Educational Work in Africa," *Seed Time and Harvest,* September 1927, 8.

45. Stevenson, *Expositions,* 81.

46. Mugambi, "Christological Paradigms in African Christianity," 136–64.

47. I am indebted to John Peel, who first pointed this out to me.

48. Landau, *The Realm,* 131–59.

49. For sermons, see Jennings, sermon on Bunyan, A/38, Jennings Papers, BMS Archives; for classroom and Sunday school, see "The Month's Mail: South Africa"; for debating and literary society, see Lovedale Missionary Institution (LMI), "Literary Society: Syllabus—First Session 1874," *Report for 1874;* for school plays, see LMI, *Report for 1948,* 35.

50. For magic lantern, see *Seed Time and Harvest,* December 1919, 2; Austin, "*The Pilgrim's Progress* in a Congo Setting," 151; on magic lantern slides in southern Africa, see Landau, "The Illumination of Christ in the Kalahari Desert," 26–40; for Bunyan extracts in school readers, see Stewart Xhosa Reader, Std V, Extracts in ts. version, MS 16,340 (d) (1); MS 16,343 (g); and MS 16,399 (g) (i) & (h) (ii), Lovedale Papers, Cory Library, Rhodes University, Grahamstown (hereafter Lovedale Papers); Whitehead, Report of Work undertaken by Whitehead in *Missionary Herald,* June 1916, included in A/53, Whitehead Papers, BMS Archives; for drama, see Ennals, "Last Christmas at Yakusu," *Missionary Herald,* December 1931, 281; for hymns, see Subcommittee of the Uganda Diocesan Literature Committee, 15 February 1954, S39/36—which mentions that, in keeping with the English model, a poem in *The Pilgrim's Progress* ("He who would valiant be . . .") had been a Ganda hymn for some time—ICCLA Papers, Conference of British Missionary Societies/ International Council for Mission Archives, SOAS, University of London (hereafter referred to as the ICCLA Papers).

51. Du Bois, *The Souls,* 8.

52. Du Bois, *The Souls*, 9.

53. Du Bois, *The Souls*, 11.

54. Du Bois, *The Souls*, 11–12.

55. Du Bois, *The Souls*, 12.

56. Smith, *John Bunyan*, 4–10.

57. The question of Bunyan in slave Christianity is a topic on which no research (that I am aware of) has been done. I have constructed this account by extrapolating from Hatch, *The Democratization*, 102–61; Pitts, *Old Ship of Zion*, 34. In terms of Bunyan-like images in slave Christianity, I have used Raboteau, *Slave Religion*, 251–66, which discusses the image of the journey. See also Smith, *John Bunyan*, 15–16.

58. Smith, *John Bunyan*, 25–31.

59. Du Bois, *The Souls*, 137–74; Hatch, *The Democratization*, 102–13.

60. On Liele, see Brathwaite, *The Development*, 253–65; Clarke, *Memorials*, 9–11; Curtin, *Two Jamaicas*, 32–33; Gayle, *George Liele*; Phillippo, *Jamaica: Past and Present*, 279–80; Stewart, *Religion and Society*, 127–28.

61. Gayle, *George Liele*, 6–24.

62. On Baker, see Clarke, *Memorials*, 18–30; Robb, *A Narrative*, 33–35; Waddell, *Twenty-Nine Years in the West Indies and Central Africa*, 35. On Gibb, see Clarke, *Memorials*, 15–18; Stewart, *Religion and Society*, 127–28.

63. Stewart, *Religion and Society*, 127–28.

64. In writing to the British Baptists, Liele provided an autobiography that includes an account of his conversion: Liele, in "Letters Showing the Rise and Progress of the Early Negro Churches of Georgia and the West Indies," 69–75. In these letters, he gives a classic evangelical account of his conversion, which in outline is very similar to Bunyan's autobiographical narration in *Grace Abounding*. There are as well some textual echoes. Liele explains how he became aware of himself as a sinner "condemned . . . before God; . . . at length I was brought to perceive that my life hung by a slender thread, and if it was the will of God to cut me off at that time, I was sure I should be found in hell, as sure as God was in Heaven" (70). The quotation is close to Bunyan phrases like: "Wherefore still my life hung in doubt before me . . ." (45); "so my soul did hang as in a pair of scales . . ." (54). Liele described his own library thus: "I have a few books, some good old authors and sermons, and one large Bible that was given to me by a gentleman; a good many of our members can read, and are all desirous to learn; they will be very thankful for a few books to read on Sundays and other days" (73). Some "good old authors" would almost certainly have included Bunyan.

65. Clarke, Letter [recipient unclear], 20 January 1788, in "Letters," *Journal of Negro History*, 79.

66. Brathwaite, *The Development*, 253; Clarke, *Memorials*, 10.

67. Clarke, *Memorials*, 15.

68. Hill, *A Tinker*, 212–21. See also Stewart, *Religion and Society*, 150–51, for general examples of such redemptionist discourse in Baptist preaching.

69. Stanley, *The History*, 70–89; Stewart, *Religion and Society*, 16–25.

70. Stanley, *The History*, 69.

71. Underhill, *Life of James Mursell Phillipo*, 5–6.

72. Brathwaite, *The Development*, 254.

73. Brathwaite, *The Development*, 254; Curtin, *Two Jamaicas*, 33–34; Stewart, *Religion and Society*, 133–35.

74. Brathwaite, *The Development*, 254; Curtin, *Two Jamaicas*, 33–34; Stewart, *Religion and Society*, 115.

75. Robb, *A Narrative*, 34.

76. Stewart, *Religion and Society*, 149.

77. Curtin, *Two Jamaicas*, 34–38; Stanley, *The History*, 85–87; Stewart, *Religion and Society*, 123–25.

78. Stanley, *The History*, 86.

79. Curtin, *Two Jamaicas*, 37.

80. As chapter 8 indicates, this scene was seldom illustrated in European editions. I have been unable to examine Jamaican editions to establish whether, as with some African editions, this scene was foregrounded.

81. Vassady, "The Role"; Fuller, "Autobiography," "Comments," and "Recollections," A/5, Fuller Papers, BMS Archives.

82. Clarke, *Memoir of Joseph Merrick*, 100. I am grateful to Las Newman for this point.

83. Vassady, "The Role," 290.

84. Fuller, Letter to Baynes, 7 December 1886, A/5, Fuller Papers, BMS Archives.

85. Fuller, preface to *Bedangweri ya balondo* (*The Pilgrim's Progress*, part 1).

86. Fuller, testimony in *Report*, 267.

87. Fuller, "Recollections," 1.

88. Fuller, "Autobiography"; Obituary of Fuller, *Baptist Handbook for 1910*, included in A/5, Fuller Papers, BMS Archives.

89. Phillips, "S. C. Gordon: Loyal Colleague and Brother Beloved," *Missionary Herald*, December 1932, 287.

90. Vassady, "The Role," 103, note 28.

91. Innis, *Cruelties Committed on the West Coast of Africa*, 16–17.

92. Fuller, testimony in *Report*, 265–66.

93. Massing, "From Greek Powder to Soap Advert," 181; McClintock, *Imperial Leather*, 210–31.

94. Sharrock, *The Pilgrim's Progress*, 406, note 82.

95. *The Pilgrim's Progress*, abridged by McGregor, 116.

96. Fuller, testimony in *Report*, 266.

97. Through Fuller, Bunyan has continued to have an afterlife in the Cameroon. The Basel Mission, which took over from Fuller began another translation in 1897, adding their own particularly pietist interpretation to the text (Meyer, *Translating*, 28–53). (Meyer discusses the Norddeutsche Missionsgesellschaft, very similar

in orientation to the Basel Mission.) In 1953 the book was in print and is quite probably still in use among Duala-speaking Protestants (Hurry and Cirket, *Bunyan Meeting House Museum Catalogue*, 87).

Chapter 4
Mata's Hermeneutic
Internationally Made Ways of Reading Bunyan

1. Hawker, "Funeral Address for Emily Margaret Lewis," 1923, Camden Road Church Papers.

2. White, *Bunyan Characters*, 301, 302.

3. White, *Bunyan Characters*, 299–300.

4. J.H.W., introductory notice to *The Pilgrim's Progress*, xvi.

5. Phrase from *The Free Church of Scotland Monthly*, April 1899, 88.

6. Thickstun, "From Christiana to Stand-fast"; Swaim "Mercy and the Feminine Heroic in the Second Part of *Pilgrim's Progress*"; Breen, "Christiana's Rudeness."

7. Davison, *The Pageant*.

8. Quotations from J.H.W., introductory notice to *The Pilgrim's Progress*, x, xi.

9. Information on Mata drawn from Lewis, *These Seventy Years*, 168, 174, 182–83, 185–86, 219; Hawker, *An Englishwoman's Twenty-Five Years*, 202–204, 220–21. Information on Stanley Pools from Stanley, *The History*, 122–24.

10. Lewis, *These Seventy Years*, 184–85.

11. Bunyan, *The Pilgrim's Progress*, 57.

12. Lewis, *These Seventy Years*, 184.

13. Information on the Zombo expeditions from Lewis, *These Seventy Years*, 171–82; Hawker, *An Englishwoman's Twenty-Five Years*, 198–226.

14. Hawker, *An Englishwoman's Twenty-Five Years*, 192–93; Stanley, *The History*, 134.

15. Fish, *Self-Consuming Artifacts*, 230–60.

16. Hawker, *An Englishwoman's Twenty-Five Years*, 202–204.

17. "Report," *The Female Missionary Intelligencer*, January 1899. My thanks to Terry Barringer for this reference.

18. "'Interpreter's House,'" 252 (report of a school production of the play in Mbereshi, Northern Rhodesia); Ennals, "Last Christmas at Yakusu," *Missionary Herald*, December 1931, 281 (report of pageant presentation of parts of the story at Yakusu, Upper Congo).

19. See notes 49 and 50 in chapter 3.

20. Fletcher, *Allegory*, 181–83.

21. "South Africa," *The Chronicle of the LMS* 11 (1902): 41.

22. Sharrock, "A Note on the Text," in *The Pilgrim's Progress*, 29. On a model of oral storytelling that suggests this procedure, see Scheub, *The Xhosa Ntsomi*.

23. See notes 49 and 50 in chapter 3.

24. Mpiku, "Introduction."

25. Mpiku, "Introduction," 128.

26. Mpiku, "Introduction," 128.

27. Mpiku, "Introduction," 128–29.

28. Mpiku, "Introduction," 129.

29. Pugh, "By Way of Illustration," *Missionary Herald*, March 1907, 63–64; Pugh, "In Parables," *Missionary Herald*, March 1911, 71–72; Hawker, *An Englishwoman's Twenty-Five Years*, 192–93; Carson Graham, *Under Seven Kongo Kings*, 30.

30. Mpiku, "Introduction," 129.

31. Golder, "Bunyan's Giant Despair," 361–78.

32. Golder, "Bunyan's Giant Despair," 365, 366.

33. Bunyan, *The Pilgrim's Progress*, 130–32.

34. Kaufmann, *The Pilgrim's Progress and Traditions in Puritan Meditation*, 19.

35. Section entitled "Discussion" in Smith, "The Need," 78.

36. Gwynne Daniell, *The Religion of the Hearth*, 16–17. Book included in 543/30, ICCLA Papers.

37. *Missionary Herald*, January 1929, 23; Senior, "John Wesley," 544/14, ICCLA Papers.

38. Mackenzie, "Talking Women," 543/40, ICCLA Papers; *Congo Mission News*, July 1940, 12.

39. Bangala Committee, Area Priority List for 1959, 544/14, ICCLA Papers.

40. Hawker, *An Englishwoman's Twenty-Five Years*, 192–93.

41. See note 29.

Chapter 5
John Bunyan Luthuli
African Mission Elites and *The Pilgrim's Progress*

1. "Makowethu! Naantso incwadi, kha niyihlole. Ibalisa ngomHambi ohamba indlela abanga abaninzi benu bangayihamba. Kha nimphelekelele ke, nicotho-cotho-zise ngokufundana kwenu—nihambe nisima, ninqumama; nibe niphulaphula iinto azithethayo, nanibikela zona; nide nisuke niye kumngenisa apho waya wangena khona, ekupheleni kolo luhambo lwakhe." Soga, "Intshayelelo," 7. My thanks to Monde Simelela for the translation.

2. Soga, "A National Newspaper," 153.

3. "UJohn Bunyan ebeyinchibi yokukhanda le mpahla iziibekile." "Won'e ke ngeli xesha waqongqothela, wanga isoono usibuza umlandu." "Zininzi iintlanga eziyifundileyo le ncwadi ngeentetho zazo, ezibe zingaziwa ngexesha lokuphila kom-nini-yo." "Kwizizwe eliye langena kuko iliZwi likaThixo, akukho ndawo uJohn Bun-yan angenazihlobo kuzo, izihlobo ezibe zingambulelayo, ukuba ubevukile enchwabeni lakhe ngoku wavela." Soga, "Intshayelelo," 7, 8, 11.

4. "Eyinkwenkwe, ube elinqenera laphakade—into etshatsheleyo kwiintlondi

ezinje ngokushwabulela abantu nezinto, nangokuthuka okuncholileyo, nangokuxoka, nangokunyelisa konke okulungileyo." Soga, "Intshayelelo," 7.

5. Peires, *The Dead*, 174–77. These pages offer an analysis of those who supported the Cattle Killing and those who did not, a discussion that usefully sets out the tensions between a "traditional" ethos of redistribution and a more market-oriented modernity.

6. Peires, *The Dead*, 177; Williams, *Umfundisi*, 6–10.

7. ". . . noko zibe zingezininzi, kuba nowakowayo, nowakulo-ndoda umzi—yomibini—ibe ibuswela"; "Yafika loo ntshumayelo yabinza entliziyweni—uvalo lwabetha"; "igqwirakazi"; "Wabulahla kwa ngelo langa ubulingane nobukholwane babantu ababe bengenasimilo sokulunga . . ."; "Walinga yena ngawo onke amaqhalo abenawo ukusixakanisa, ukusithintela, ukusiphazamisa, nokusididekisa." Soga, "Intshayelelo," 8, 9, 10.

8. Jordan, *Towards*, 39.

9. There is an extensive literature on the African elite. See, for example, Cobley, *Class and Consciousness*; Willan, *Sol Plaatje*; Couzens, *The New African*.

10. Quoted in Stones, *Key Sociological Thinkers*, 360.

11. Chalmers, *Tiyo Soga*, 340–41.

12. Account of Soga's life drawn from Williams, *Umfundisi*.

13. Chalmers, *Tiyo Soga*, 341.

14. Reviews of *Uhambo lo Mhambi* (*The Pilgrim's Progress*, part 1), *United Presbyterian Missionary Record*, 400–401.

15. I am indebted to Stanley Trapido for this observation.

16. Information on Van der Kemp drawn from Hodgson, *Ntsikana's Great Hymn*, 37–42, and Mostert, *Frontiers*, 287–88, 314–23.

17. Elbourne and Ross, "Combating Spiritual and Social Bondage"; Legassick, "The Northern Frontier."

18. One such version could have been Bunyan, *'s Christens reize naar de eeuwigheid* (*The Pilgrim's Progress*, part 1), trans. Stegmann.

19. Hodgson, *Ntsikana's Great Hymn*, 41–42.

20. Hodgson, *Ntsikana's Great Hymn*, 41–42; Peires, *The Dead*, 137.

21. "The Story of Mbulukazi," *The Cape Monthly Magazine* 10, no. 60 (1875), 378.

22. Peires, *The Dead*, 137.

23. Bokwe, *Ntsikana: The Story of an African Hymn*, 25.

24. Smout, *A Century of the Scottish People, 1830–1950*, 184–87; Brown, *The Social History*, 24–28.

25. Brown, *Religion and Society*, 101–109.

26. Brown, *The Social History*, 31–32 and *Religion and Society*, 107.

27. Primary school readers: see Stewart Xhosa Reader, Std V, Extracts in ts. version, MS 16,340 (d) (1); MS 16,343 (g); MS 16,399 (g) (i) and (h) (ii); Lovedale Papers; Examinations: LMI, *Report for 1876*, 29; SCA: LMI, *Report for 1940*, 36–37; LMI, *Report for 1943*, 25; LMI, *Report for 1948*, 35; Plays: LMI, *Report for 1937*, 27;

Debating: Minutes of the Lovedale Literary Society, BRN122325, 1936–1948, 21 June 1941, 3 September 1943, Lovedale Papers.

28. Soga, "The Journal," 40.

29. Meyer, *Translating*, 31–36.

30. Example taken from Jordan, *Towards*, 30.

31. Jordan, *Towards*, 31–32.

32. Jordan, *Towards*, 32–33.

33. Hofmeyr, *"We Spend Our Years as a Tale That Is Told,"* 182–83.

34. Stewart Xhosa Reader, Std V, Extracts in ts. version, MS 16,340 (d) (1); MS 16,343 (g); MS 16,399 (g) (i) and (h) (ii); Lovedale Papers.

35. Matriculation Examination, November–December 1951 and March 1953, Joint Matriculation Board of the South African Universities, University of South Africa, Pretoria (hereafter JMB Archives).

36. Jordan, *Towards*, 107.

37. LMI, *Report for 1876*, 29.

38. The use of "Xosa" as opposed to "Xhosa" represents an older orthography.

39. Matriculation Examination, February 1934 and December 1932, JMB Archives.

40. See note 27.

41. LMI, *Report for 1948*, 11; LMI, *Report for 1949*, 13; LMI, *Report for 1950*, 14.

42. Lovedale Press to A. Maggs, 22 October 1875, MS 16,289; Lovedale Press to D. Yekela, 21 June 1953, MS 16,436; both in Lovedale Papers.

43. This is the argument of de Kock, *Civilizing Barbarians*.

44. The annual program for the Lovedale Literary Society appeared each year in the LMI Annual Report. The dates for the talks mentioned are as follows and are drawn from these reports: 17 April 1874; 11 February 1881; 16 October 1896; 7 May 1875; 21 September 1877; 30 April 1875; 31 November 1876; 3 March 1876.

45. Farming: 3 September 1897, 20 May 1898; Gender: 18 November 1881, 4 June 1937; Education: 10 October 1879, 27 September 1878, 28 March 1879, 19 May 1882, 13 October 1876; Government: 28 October 1882, 24 September 1875; Public Opinion: 11 November 1899; Progress: 24 October 1941, 17 March 1876, 13 November 1897.

46. Minutes of the Lovedale Literary Society, BRN122325, 1936–1948, 4 June 1937, Lovedale Papers.

47. Minutes of the Lovedale Literary Society, 14 February 1948.

48. Minutes of the Lovedale Literary Society, 1 August 1948.

49. Minutes of the Lovedale Literary Society, 14 February 1948.

50. Minutes of the Lovedale Literary Society, 24 May 1945.

51. Minutes of the Lovedale Literary Society, 15 May 1948.

52. Minutes of the Lovedale Literary Society, 13 September 1941, 19 March 1927.

53. Minutes of the Lovedale Literary Society, 12 September 1945.

54. Hyslop, "Food, Authority and Politics," 84–115.

55. Agriculture: 16 May 1884; Technology: 8 May 1885; Progress: 24 October 1941; Monarchy: 21 August 1874, 24 October 1884; Gender: 8 August 1941, 2 August 1947; Colonial history: 21 March 1884, 24 April 1897.

56. Davenport, *South Africa: A Modern History*, 83–84.

57. Taken from Jordan, *Towards*, 92–93.

58. I am grateful to John Lonsdale for passing this extract on to me.

59. Bokwe, *Two Weeks' Trip to Cape Town*, 23.

60. Williams, *Umfundisi*, 91.

61. Soga, "What is the Destiny of the Kaffir Race?" 180.

62. My thanks to Graeme Rosenberg for passing on this reference. I have been unable to locate a full copy of the serial "*The Pilgrim's Progress*," by Gaoler, *Inkundla ya Bantu*, 26 May 1942.

63. Couzens, "Widening Horizons of African Literature, 1870–1900," 76–77.

64. I am grateful to Jeff Opland who translated this poem and passed it on to me.

65. The image of Hill Difficulty was echoed in other images. The first of these is "The Broad and Narrow Way," which shows two parallel paths: one broad and lined with bars, theatres, gambling houses, and worldly temptations, but leading to Hell; the other, narrow and spartan, but leading to heaven. The final stages of the Narrow Way are steep and mountainous and approximate images of Hill Difficulty. As Meyer indicates in *Translating*, 31–36, this image was widely used in the African Protestant world. The second image is "The Upward Path to Native Education," put out by the Anglican Community of the Resurrection, which ran another prestigious mission institution, St. Peters, this time in Johannesburg. The picture shows a mountainous landscape with a winding path leading to an illuminated peak. In the plateau of the picture is the Primary School with a path leading to Intermediate and then Secondary School. Midway stands The South African Native College and various careers "paths" that follow out of that. Victor, *The Salient*, 45.

66. Phrases from Nkondo, "Solomon Mahlangu," and "Vuyisile Mini," in *Flames*, 29, 67. My thanks to Barry Feinberg and Tom Lodge for information on Nkondo.

67. Nkondo, *Flames*, 35–36, 56–59.

68. Nkondo, "Bivouac," *Flames*, 64.

69. *Malibongwe ANC Women: Poetry Is Also Their Weapon*, 69.

70. See, for example, the poem "To Satan," in *The Worker's Herald*, 15 November 1926, in *The Return of the Amasi Bird*, 58–59. For the influence of Nonconformity on the labor movement, see Pelling, *Origins of the Labour Party, 1880–1900*, 125–44.

71. MSCE 5566/1898, Natal Archives, Pietermartizburg.

72. Statement from S.A. Pulp Rebate, 1 July 1963, MS 16,436, 1961–63, Lovedale Papers.

Chapter 6
Dreams, Documents, and Passports to Heaven
African Christian Interpretations of *The Pilgrim's Progress*

1. Cotter, "A Pilgrim's Perils in an Ancestor of B-movies," *The New York Times*, 4 April 1999.

2. Bunyan, *Ugwalo lu ka Bunyane ogutiwa uguhamba gwohambi* (*The Pilgrim's Progress*, part 1), trans. D. and M. Carnegie, opp. 184.

3. In nearly ten years of working on this project and in looking at hundreds of editions, I have yet to see a European version that features the certificates in this scene.

4. Bunyan, *The Pilgrim's Progress*, 215–17.

5. "Remarkable Story of Bayolo, Loma," *Regions Beyond* (1927–31): 26. (The dating of this journal is not clear but the year is probably 1928).

6. Segoete, *Monono*.

7. Segoete, *Monono*, 186–87.

8. Coplan, *In the Time of Cannibals*, 235.

9. Mrs. King, "The Narrow Way," 11.

10. Sundkler, *Bantu Prophets*, 289.

11. Sundkler, *Bantu Prophets*, 290.

12. Bunyan, *Grace Abounding*; Hancock, "Bunyan as Reader," 68–86; Hill, *A Tinker*; Spufford, *Small Books and Pleasant Histories*; Keeble, *The Literary Culture of Nonconformity*, 136; Knott, "'Thou Must Live Upon my Word,'" 156–57; Smith, "Bunyan and the Language of the Body in Seventeenth-Century England," 161–74.

13. Bunyan, *The Pilgrim's Progress*, 72, 80, 191.

14. Bunyan, *The Pilgrim's Progress*, 80.

15. Bunyan, *The Pilgrim's Progress*, 158, 169, 176.

16. Bunyan, *The Pilgrim's Progress*, 53.

17. Bunyan, *The Pilgrim's Progress*, 82.

18. Bunyan, *The Pilgrim's Progress*, 237.

19. Bunyan, *The Pilgrim's Progress*, 377–84.

20. This is a well-documented feature of para-literate social orders. See, for example, Clanchy, *From Memory to Written Record*; Stock, *The Implications of Literacy*.

21. Bunyan, *The Pilgrim's Progress*, 256.

22. Bunyan, *The Pilgrim's Progress*, 377.

23. Bunyan, *The Pilgrim's Progress*, 82.

24. Bunyan, *The Pilgrim's Progress*, 193.

25. Breen, "Christiana's Rudeness," 96–111.

26. Bunyan, *The Pilgrim's Progress*, 88.

27. Bunyan, *The Pilgrim's Progress*, 138–39.

28. Bunyan, *The Pilgrim's Progress*, 141.

29. Bunyan, *The Pilgrim's Progress*, 80, 191.

30. Bunyan, *The Pilgrim's Progress*, 376.

31. Bunyan, *The Pilgrim's Progress*, 88.

32. Bunyan, *The Pilgrim's Progress*, 158.

33. This view is expressed in the commentary on Bunyan in the Elstow Abbey Church in Bedford, England.

34. Bunyan, *The Pilgrim's Progress*, 158.

35. Hancock, "Bunyan as Reader," 69.

36. Bunyan, *The Pilgrim's Progress*, 185.

37. Bunyan, *The Pilgrim's Progress*, 82.

38. Bunyan, *The Pilgrim's Progress*, 91.

39. Breen, "Christiana's Rudeness."

40. Bunyan, *The Pilgrim's Progress*, 88.

41. Bunyan, *The Pilgrim's Progress*, 91.

42. Bunyan, *The Pilgrim's Progress*, 95.

43. Bunyan, *The Pilgrim's Progress*, 177.

44. Quoted in de Kock, *Civilizing*, 96, 95.

45. de Kock, *Civilizing*, 95–96.

46. de Kock, *Civilizing*, 96.

47. Sundkler, *Bantu Prophets*, 293.

48. Hodgson, *Ntsikana's Great Hymn*, 9, 11.

49. Mackay, "Simon Kimbangu," 138; Mackay and Ntoni-Nzinga, "Kimbangu's Interlocutor," 241.

50. Martin, *The Biblical Concept of Messianism*, 118.

51. Hayashida, *Dreams in the African Church*, 100.

52. ". . . uBunyan uyilanda ngokungathi ulanda iphupho." Johanson, "Amazwi esingeniso" (Introduction) to *Uhambo lwesihambi* (*The Pilgrim's Progress*, part 1), trans. Johanson, 4. Thanks to Bheki Peterson for translating this foreword.

53. Thompson, *Christianity in Northern Malawi*, 166.

54. For an illuminating study on the struggle around documents in southern Africa, see Breckenridge, "We Must Speak for Ourselves." See also the enlightening study of Opland, "The Image of the Book in Xhosa Oral Poetry."

55. Mwase, "Dialogue of Nyasaland Record of Past Events, Environments and the Present Outlook within the Protectorate," reissued as *Strike a Blow and Die* by Mwase, ed. Rotberg, 81–82.

56. Bunyan "quotations" in Mwase, *Strike*, 1, 101, 129.

57. For a biographical sketch of Mwase, see Rotberg, introduction to Mwase, *Strike*.

58. Goody, "Restricted Literacy in Northern Ghana"; Janzen and MacGaffey, *An Anthology*; Landau, *The Realm*, 144.

59. Cutt, *Ministering Angels*; Hewitt, *Let the People Read*.

60. Vassady, "The Role," 121.

61. Kayira, *I Will Try*.

62. Kayira, *I Will Try*, 89, 85.

63. Bunyan, *The Pilgrim's Progress*, 223–30.

64. Kayira, *I Will Try*, 66.

65. Kayira, *I Will Try*, 108–109.

66. Kayira, *I Will Try*, 92, 136, 155.

67. Kayira, *I Will Try*, 92.

68. Kayira, *I Will Try*, 152–53.

69. Kayira, *I Will Try*, 68.

Chapter 7
African Protestant Masculinities in the Empire
Ethel M. Dell, Thomas Mofolo, and Mr. Great-heart

1. Mofolo, *Moeti wa Botjhabela* (1906; repr. 1961) (This text uses a subsequent orthography). I have relied on Mofolo's original as well as the translation by Ashton, *The Traveller of the East*. Ashton has translated the title literally as *The Traveller of the East*. A more standard translation would be *The Traveller to the East* and, when referring to the book in the text, this is the title I have used. When Ashton's translation is referred to, the former title is used.

2. "Moeti oa Bochabela," *Leselinyana la Lesotho*, 1 Pherekong [January] 1907.

3. See Gérard, *Four African Literatures*, 109–11; Kunene, *Thomas Mofolo*, 63–86; Werner, "A Mosuto Novelist"; Molema, *The Image*, 26–44.

4. See Gérard, *Four African Literatures*, 111; Kunene, *Thomas Mofolo*, 22–23; Molema, *The Image*, 43–44; Franz, "The Literature," 173–74.

5. Werner, "A Mosuto Novelist," 430; Gollock, review of *The Traveller of the East*, 510; *The Church Assembly News*, June 1935, which notes that *The Traveller of the East* is "an African Pilgrim's Progress," 511/9, ICCLA Papers; Franz, "The Literature," 173–74. For recent commentary, see note 3.

6. I am grateful to Albert Brutsch who informed me of Rapetloane's involvement as a translator.

7. The image is that of Christian and Hopeful making their way across the River of Death, while in the background they are threatened by snakes and crocodiles. This scene is close to *Moeti*, 61.

8. See Kunene, *Thomas Mofolo*, 24.

9. Ranger, *Revolt in Southern Rhodesia, 1896–1897*. See also Jeater, *Marriage, Perversion, and Power*, which examines how ideas of sexuality—traditionally a matter subject to lineage control—are affected by settler ideas regarding sexuality as a private matter.

10. Bhebhe, *Christianity and Traditional Religion in Western Zimbabwe, 1859–1923*, 75–128.

11. Headland, *David Carnegie of Matabeleland*, 11.

12. Montague, "Bunyan for the Matabele," 252.

13. Davison, *The Pageant*, 4–5.

14. *Souvenir of the Centenary of Camden Road Baptist Church, 1854–1954*, 21.

15. Scrivener, "Scrivener of Bolobo: Greatheart of the Congo," CP/67, Scrivener Papers, BMS Archives.

16. Read, *Samuel Marsden: Great Heart of Maoriland*; Nairne, *Greatheart of Papua*; Miller, "Greatheart of China"; *Great Heart of New Guinea*; Stevenson, *Robert Henderson: The Story of a Missionary Greatheart in India*; Poteat, *A Greatheart of the South*.

17. Howard, *A Greatheart of Africa*; on Kivebulaya, see Pirouet, *Black Evangelists*, 47–49.

18. Smit, *African Greatheart*.

19. "In Praise of Hugh Rowland," 179.

20. For a satirical comment on this idea, see chap. 1, "Mr. Greatheart of Britain," in Barnes, *The New Boer War*.

21. Girouard, *The Return*, 219–30.

22. Girouard, *The Return*, 227.

23. Girouard, *The Return*, 228.

24. Paragraph drawn from McLeod, *Religion and Society*, 149–56; Girouard, *The Return*, 249–58 and illustration opp. 245; and Thorne, *Congregational Missions*, 112–15.

25. Quoted in *The Baptist Times*, 23 February 1928.

26. Stevenson, *Expositions*, 17.

27. A Pilgrim, *Greatheart: Some Talks with Him*, 3.

28. Thorne, *Congregational Missions*, 94.

29. Thorne, *Congregational Missions*, 92–104.

30. Thorne, *Congregational Missions*, 104–108.

31. Cockett, "John Bunyan—The Man," 39.

32. McClintock, *Imperial Leather*, 29.

33. Information on Dell drawn from entry in *The European Biographical Dictionary of British Women*; and Micheletti, "Tiger Skins, Sheiks and Passionate Kisses."

34. Dell, *Greatheart*, 72.

35. Dell, *Greatheart*, 478.

36. Dell, *Greatheart*, 13, 21, 83, 92, 279, 314, 246, 270.

37. Dell, *Greatheart*, 235, 389.

38. Dell, *Greatheart*, 73.

39. Dell, *Greatheart*, 500.

40. Dell, *Greatheart*, 502.

41. See notes 3 and 4 in this chapter.

42. Gérard, *Four African Literatures*, 110.

43. Molema, *The Image*, 44.

44. Viswanathan, *Outside the Fold*, xv.

45. Ashton, *The Traveller*, 67.

46. The relevant passages are Ashton, *The Traveller*, 82, and Bunyan, *The Pilgrim's Progress*, 54.

47. Ashton, *The Traveller*, 103.

48. Ashton, *The Traveller*, 210.

49. Ashton, *The Traveller*, 104.

50. Newell, *Ghanaian Popular Fiction*, 80.

51. Ashton, *The Traveller*, 22, 72.

52. I am indebted to David Coplan for his comments on this topic and for his interpretation of the praise poems in the novel.

53. Segoete, *Moya oa bolisa* [*Spirit of Herding*].

54. Ashton, *The Traveller*, 45.

55. Ashton, *The Traveller*, 65.

56. I am indebted to David Coplan for this interpretation.

57. The extent to which Mofolo departs from Protestantism is seldom recognized by critics except Beuchat, *Do the Bantu Have a Literature?* 18–19, where she notes that the text as a whole, and particularly the final scene, "little resembles anything that Mofolo might have been taught by the rather austere Protestant faith in which he was brought up."

58. For evidence of Dell's popularity in Africa, see "Is Literature Necessary in Africa?" 511/9, ICCLA Papers. For popularity of Corelli, see Mahood, "Marie Corelli in West Africa," 19–21; and Newell, *Literary Culture*, 98–115.

59. Corelli, *The Master Christian*.

60. For a fuller discussion of the points in this paragraph, see Hofmeyr, "Portable Landscapes." On the catechism in Bunyan, see Danielson, "Catechism, 'The Pilgrim's Progress,' and the pilgrim's progress."

61. The image of the Broad and the Narrow Way is invoked throughout the first half of the novel via the doubling of characters: Fekisi is contrasted with his drunken, abusive, and evil neighbor, Phakoane. The two characters are closely paralleled in order to remind us that they are on two very different paths. In his drunken stupor, Phakoane often stumbles into ditches, and Mofolo develops this feature into a symbolic topography that is associated with those who are in the wrong path. At one point, we are told that Fekisi "was . . . troubled by the sight of the whole nation travelling by this same path, the end of which they knew" (13–14). This end is the damnation awaiting those at the end of the Broad Way, where people and collapsing buildings career over precipices into the flames below.

Chapter 8
Illustrating Bunyan

1. Achebe, "Named for Victoria, Queen of England," 121. It is not entirely clear exactly which illustration he recalls. The Igbo editions I have seen carried the Austin photographs, which did not include an illustration of the Valley of the Shadow of Death. There may well have been other Igbo editions, or Achebe could have been recalling illustrations from an English edition.

2. Norvig, *Dark Figures*, 119. The 1679 edition did carry "the sleeping portrait" frontispiece, but no other illustrations: Wharey, introduction to *The Pilgrim's Progress*, xxxviii.

3. Phrase from advertisement at the back of USCL, *One-Hundred-and-Thirty-Seventh Annual Report*.

4. "Two Days in a Mugh Village," *Missionary Herald*, September 1897, 482.

5. Pugh, foreword in *Lokendo loa Bokendi*.

6. Untitled document, 5 November 1931, 501/2, ICCLA Papers.

7. Letter, 29 June 1956, 531/28 (D); ADC Religious Instruction Material, Sunday school material includes illustrations from *The Pilgrim's Progress* to color in, 527/24; both in ICCLA Papers.

8. Memo IV, 28 February–25 March 1939, 509/8, ICCLA Papers.

9. Hewitt, *Let the People Read*, 30; Green, *The Story*, 14; Anderson, *The Printed Image*, 34.

10. Norvig, *Dark Figures*, 122.

11. A good sequence of illustrations is in Harrison, "Some Illustrators of *The Pilgrim's Progress* (part 1) John Bunyan." These demonstrate the move towards using southern English landscapes as backdrops for the pictures (242, 243, opp. 244, opp. 256, opp. 260). On the southern counties as templates of Englishness, see Howkins, "The Discovery of Rural England," 62.

12. For stick figure illustrations, see *Rwendo rwo mufambi*. Such stick figures became something of an evangelical vogue and were widely used by the East African Revival, a laity-led evangelical movement that swept through much of East Africa in the 1930s and 40s (and incidentally used Bunyan widely). For one account, see Church, *Quest for the Highest*, which also includes examples of such stick figure art. Another amateur set of pictures is in the Bambara edition. For more professional illustrations, see, for example, Montague's illustrations for the Ndebele edition.

13. Huddleston, *George Pemba*, 27–28.

14. For accounts of the northern Angolan pictures, see Austin, "*The Pilgrim's Progress* in a Congo Setting," 150–53. The making of the Muhono photographs is briefly described in *Seed Time and Harvest*, March 1927, 14.

15. For information on these, see Patton, "A World Program"; Wilson, "A Survey of Christian Literature in African Languages"; de Mestral, "Christian Literature"; Wilson, "The Provision"; Ritson, "Christian Literature in the Mission Field"; de Mestral, "What is Christian Literature?" 45–46.

16. Patton, "A World Program," 575.

17. Subcommittee of the Uganda Diocesan Literature Committee, 15 February 1954, notes on Bunyan for high schools and training colleges, 532/29 (B), ICCLA Papers.

18. *Books for Africa* 2, no. 1 (1932): 9; *Books for Africa* 20, no. 2 (1950): 34; *Books for Africa* 20, no. 4 (1950): 68.

19. Minutes of CLA Subcommittee, 4 November 1927 and 27 October 1926, 500/1, ICCLA Papers.

20. *The Church Assembly News*, June 1935, which notes that *The Traveller of*

the East is "an African Pilgrim's Progress," 511/9, ICCLA Papers; *Books for Africa* 4, no. 2 (1934): 32.

21. "ADC Religious Instruction Material," 527/24, ICCLA Papers.

22. C. de Mestral to Ross Manning, 1 June 1956, 527/24; Miss Hunter to ICCLA, 25 August 1956, 529/26; ICCLA to Herbert Griffiths, 10 July 1956, 531/28; all in ICCLA Papers.

23. Jean M. Collines to ICCLA, 11 November 1955, 533/30 (E), ICCLA Papers.

24. Jean M. Collines to ICCLA, 11 November 1955, 533/30 (E), ICCLA Papers.

25. Ralph L. Wilson to ICCLA, 29 December 1953, 533/30 (E), ICCLA Papers.

26. Robert, "The First Globalization."

27. USCL, *One-Hundred-and-Forty-Eighth Annual Report*, 16–17.

28. Austin, "*The Pilgrim's Progress* in a Congo Setting," 150–53.

29. Austin, "*The Pilgrim's Progress* in a Congo Setting," 151.

30. See notes 49 and 50 in chapter 3.

31. Jim Grenfell, letter to author, relaying experiences of João Matwawana, 13 October 1998.

32. On Buta War, see Stanley, *The History*, 336–40; Marcum, *The Angolan Revolution*, 51–54; *Missionary Herald*, April 1914, 104–12.

33. For material on mission photography, see Bester, "Insecure Shadows"; Harries, "Photography and the Rise of Anthropology"; Godby, "Framing"; Becker, "The Photographs of W. F. P. Burton"; Geary, "Missionary Photography." On colonial photography more generally, see Landau, "Photography and Colonial Vision"; Morton, "'Interesting and Picturesque'"; Edwards, *Anthropology and Photography, 1860–1920.*

34. In one case that I have seen, photographs are used, but these accompany a dramatic rendition of the text and illustrate a particular performance of the published script. The text is *Dramatic Illustrations.* As Nancy Armstrong has recently argued, there is a powerful link between photography and realist fiction; however, the former is never used to illustrate the latter. Armstrong, *Fiction in the Age of Photography.* David Bunn did point out to me that there are traditions of proselytizing and moralizing narrative that were filmed or illustrated by photograph. Such evangelical material, however, was not seen as fiction as it was believed to be "true."

35. See note 33.

36. Godby, "Framing," 18; on Burton, see Nettleton, '*Of Course you Would not Want a Canoe.*' For further details of "bleeding" between his pictures and his photography, see examples of photographs of the Bamdudye Dancing Society in his collection and his drawings for the magazine, *Congo Evangelistic Mission.* Information from Burton material in the possession of the University of the Witwatersrand Art Galleries, contact sheets 1 and 2 and file marked "Personal on W. F. P. Burton."

37. Quotations from Austin, "*The Pilgrim's Progress* in a Congo Setting," 151.

38. *Missionary Herald*, January 1900, 19; March 1903, 146; January 1904, 32.

39. Quotations from Austin, "*The Pilgrim's Progress* in a Congo Setting," 151.

40. Quotations from Austin, "*The Pilgrim's Progress* in a Congo Setting," 151.

41. Peterson, *Monarchs, Missionaries and African Intellectuals.*

42. Wilson, "The Provision," 510.

43. Austin, "*The Pilgrim's Progress* in a Congo Setting," 151.

44. I am indebted to Jeff Guy who pointed out to me details in the pictures that indicate that Montague could not have been resident in South Africa. Chief of these is a representation of mealies (corn-on-the-cob) that is drawn as if the mealies were wheat.

45. Montague, "Bunyan for the Matabele," 252–54.

46. Carnegie, *Among the Matabele.*

47. Carnegie, *Among the Matabele*, 30.

48. Ranger, *Revolt*, 36–37.

49. Montague, "Bunyan for the Matabele," 251.

50. Harriet Colenso to Mr. Carnegie, 26 February 1903, Colenso Collection, A 204, vol. 74, Natal Archives, Pietermartizburg. I am indebted to Jeff Guy for giving me the location of this letter.

Chapter 9
Bunyan in the African Novel

1. Haider, "Turning the Tablas," 27.

2. Bhabha, *The Location of Culture*, chapter 6, quote from 102.

3. Tobias, "Amos Tutuola and the Colonial Carnival," 70.

4. Fagunwa, "Writing," 138–39.

5. Fagunwa, "Writing," 138.

6. Fagunwa, "Writing," 139.

7. Fagunwa, "Writing," 139.

8. Fagunwa, "Writing," 140.

9. Fagunwa, *Ògbójú Ọdẹ Nínú Igbó Irúnmalẹ* (*The Forest of a Thousand Daemons*), trans. Soyinka; *Irìnkerindo Nínú Igbó Elégbèje* (*Expedition to the Mount of Thought*), trans. Adeniyi.

10. Barber, "Time, Space, and Writing," 120–21.

11. Barber points out that the original uses only one word, "the richly significant and multi-referential word *ilu*, 'town', 'city state', 'polity', a root metaphor for any political community in a region where the city was an ancient and still dynamic entity, and most fundamental political concept." Barber, "Time, Space, and Writing," 123.

12. Soyinka, *Forest*, 107.

13. Soyinka, *Forest*, 63; Adeniyi, *Expedition*, 101.

14. Soyinka, *Forest*, 95, 98.

15. Sharrock, "Bunyan and the English Emblem Writers," 107.

16. Adeniyi, *Expedition*, 96, 98.

17. Adeniyi, *Expedition*, 98, 99.

18. Adeniyi, *Expedition*, 100.

19. Phrase from Kaufmann, *The Pilgrim's Progress*, 79.

20. "The Interpreters on the King's High Way," *Missionary Herald*, May 1924, 107.

21. Kaufmann, *The Pilgrim's Progress*, 84, 85.

22. Barber, "Time, Space, and Writing," 122.

23. Mbembe, *On the Postcolony*, 102–41.

24. For an overview, see Lindfors, "Amos Tutuola" and "Amos Tutuola and D. O. Fagunwa." See also Leslie, "*The Palm-Wine Drinkard*: A Reassessment of Amos Tutuola."

25. Lindfors, "Amos Tutuola," 336.

26. Tutuola, *The Wild Hunter in the Bush of Ghosts*, ed. Lindfors.

27. Soyinka, *Forest*, 95.

28. Tutuola, *The Wild*, 108.

29. Sayer, *Capitalism and Modernity*, 138.

30. Tutuola, *The Wild*, 121–22.

31. Tutuola, *The Wild*, 101–102.

32. Quoted in Sayer, *Capitalism*, 78–79.

33. Quoted in Sayer, *Capitalism*, 76.

34. Tutuola, *The Wild*, 106.

35. Lindfors, "Amos Tutuola," 335.

36. Bayart, *The State in Africa*; Labou Tansi, *The Seven Solitudes*, trans. Wake.

37. Ngũgĩ, *Decolonising the Mind*, 69.

38. Griffiths, *African Literature in English: East and West*, 213.

39. Ngũgĩ, *Devil*, 12, 16, 31, 46, 60, 147, 150, 182, 200, 218, 238.

40. Ngũgĩ, *Devil*, 46, 60.

41. Ngũgĩ, *Devil*, 254.

42. Ngũgĩ, *Devil*, 54.

43. Ngũgĩ, *Devil*, 143.

44. Ngũgĩ, *Devil*, 146.

45. Ngũgĩ, *Devil*, 213.

46. Ngũgĩ, *Devil*, 10.

47. Ngũgĩ, *Devil*, 211.

48. Ngũgĩ, *Devil*, 91.

49. Andrade, "Tradition, Modernity, and the Family"; Uwakheh, "Debunking Patriarchy"; Stratton, *Contemporary African Literature*, 127; McWilliams, "Tsitsi Dangarembga's *Nervous Conditions*."

50. Veit-Wild, *Teachers*, 331–38.

51. Dangarembga, *Nervous*, 62.

52. Dangarembga, *Nervous*, 65.

53. Dangarembga, *Nervous*, 66.

54. Dangarembga, *Nervous*, 70.

55. See, for example, the image of "The Upward Path to Native Education,"

Victor, *The Salient*, 45; and Callaway, *The Pilgrim Path*. With specific reference to Zimbabwe, see Veit-Wild, *Teachers*, 60–61.

56. Dangarembga, *Nervous*, 66.

57. Sharrock, *The Pilgrim's Progress*, 391, note 43.

58. For a strong statement of this view, see Stratton, *Contemporary African Literature*.

59. Newell, *Ghanaian Popular Fiction*, 71.

60. Newell, *Ghanaian Popular Fiction*, 79.

Chapter 10
How Bunyan Became English

1. *Bedford Standard*, 1 June 1928, Newspapers Cuttings, Bunyan Collection, Bedford Library. The R33 is a major arterial route. In 1928 it had probably been recently opened for motor traffic and must have attracted considerable attention.

2. *The Times*, 23 November 1928.

3. These themes recur throughout most of the speeches given at the event both in Bedford and London. See cuttings in Newspaper Cuttings, Bunyan Collection, Bedford Library. For Englishness, see particularly *Bedfordshire Standard*, 16 December 1927; 25 May, 1 June, 8 June, 29 June 1928; *Bedfordshire Record*, 25 May, 26 June 1928. For Bunyan as a worldwide writer, see Cockett, "John Bunyan—The Man," 39; and Spargo, *Writing*, 9.

4. *The Christian World Pulpit*, 2979, 1928, Box 4, Bunyan Collection, Bedford Library.

5. Keeble, "'Of Him Thousands Daily Sing,'" 257.

6. Doyle, *English and Englishness*; Court, *Institutionalizing English Literature*; Palmer, *The Rise*; Baldick, *The Social Mission*.

7. Palmer, *The Rise*, 15–28; and Baldick, *The Social Mission*, 67–70.

8. Viswanathan, *Masks of Conquest*.

9. Eagleton, *Literary Theory*, 28–29.

10. Quoted in Baldick, *The Social Mission*, 70.

11. Baldick, *The Social Mission*, 82.

12. See, for example, Saintsbury, *A Short History of English Literature*, 513–17; Dobson, *A Handbook of English Literature*, 95–96; Gosse, *English Literature: An Illustrated Record: From Milton to Johnson*, vol. 3, 133–37; Albert, *A History of English Literature: A Practical Textbook for Senior Classes*, 180–81.

13. Court, *Institutionalizing English Literature*, 144.

14. Baldick, *The Social Mission*, 112–13, 151–58.

15. Phrase from Eagleton, *Literary Theory*, 29.

16. Quoted in Baldick, *The Social Mission*, 87.

17. Baldick, *The Social Mission*, 95.

18. Letter from Newbolt to his wife, 21 February 1921, in Newbolt, *The Later Life*, 278.

19. See, for example, The English Association, *A Short List of Books on English*

Literature (Leaflet No. 3), 6; *John Bunyan* (Pamphlet 19), this pamphlet is a reissue of Firth's introduction to *The Pilgrim's Progress*; *English Literature in Schools* (Pamphlet 21), 4; *English Papers and Examinations for Pupils of School Age in England and Wales* (Pamphlet 37), 30. These pamphlets have no date or place of publication.

20. These critics include Firth, Mee, Mackail, Ransome, Lee, and Trevelyan. The work of the first two critics is cited in the text. The appropriate work of the latter is Mackail, *The Pilgrim's Progress*; Ransome, *A History*; Lee, introduction to *The Pilgrim's Progress*; and Trevelyan, "Bunyan's England."

21. Offor, introduction to *The Pilgrim's Progress*, cxl, discusses details of this particular change.

22. Southey, *The Pilgrim's Progress. With a Life of the Author*, xxxviii. For a later use of these phrases, see Stanley, "The Character," 54.

23. Stanley, "The Character," 52.

24. Phrases from "Mrs. John Brown" at a speech at Bunyan's grave, "John Bunyan: Restoration of his Tomb," unmarked cutting in Newspaper Cuttings, Bunyan Collection, Bedford Library; Bishop of Durham (Handley Carr Glyn Moule), "An Anglican's Reflection," 315; Electric and International Telegraph Company, "John Bunyan," *Our Magazine*, Item 22552, Bunyan Collection, Bedford Library.

25. Kingsley, introduction to *The Pilgrim's Progress*, ix. For further examples, see Venables, introduction to *The Pilgrim's Progress*, xxxvi; Mee, *The Children's John Bunyan*, 25.

26. Firth, introduction to *The Pilgrim's Progress*, xlvii.

27. Cockett, *John Bunyan's England*; Thompson and Robjohns, *Bunyan Home Scenes*; Foster, *Bunyan's Country*; Poynter, *Syllabus of Bunyan Lectures*.

28. See chapter 8, note 11.

29. Firth, introduction to *The Pilgrim's Progress*, xlviii.

30. Mee, *The Children's John Bunyan*, 22, 25.

31. Venables, introduction to *The Pilgrim's Progress*, xxxiv–vi; Lee, introduction to *The Pilgrim's Progress*; Barker, "The English Language—Literature and National Character," unmarked newscuttings in Newspaper Cuttings, Bunyan Collection, Bedford Library, 51; Trevelyan, "Bunyan's England"; Ransome, *A History*, 131–32; Mackail, *The Pilgrim's Progress*, 5.

32. Bebbington, *The Nonconformist Conscience*, 106–20.

33. Bebbington, *The Nonconformist Conscience*, 120–21.

34. Cockett, foreword to *John Bunyan's England*. For details on Cockett, see Tibbutt, *Bunyan's Meeting Bedford, 1650–1950*, 90–96.

35. Court, *Institutionalizing English*, 131, 137.

36. Froude, *Bunyan*, 1.

37. Law, "Some Aspects of *The Pilgrim's Progress*," 55.

38. Montague, "Bunyan for the Matabele," 252.

39. Montague, "Bunyan for the Matabele," 252.

40. USCL, *One-Hundred-and-Forty-Seventh Annual Report*, 161.

41. Report of Special Service at Westminster Abbey, 27 November 1928, unmarked newscutting in Newspaper Cuttings, Bunyan Collection, Bedford Library.

42. Fitzgerald, *The Pilgrim Road*, 11.

43. Knox, introduction to *The Pilgrim's Progress*, xii.

44. Noyes, "Bunyan."

45. Noyes, "Bunyan," 155.

46. These responses appear in *The Bookman* 446, no. 75 (1928).

47. Noyes, "Mr. Alfred Noyes' Rejoinder," 104.

48. Sharrock, *Bunyan, The Pilgrim's Progress: A Casebook*, 22.

49. Noyes, "Bunyan," 14, 16, 17, and "Mr. Alfred Noyes' Rejoinder," 106.

50. Entry on Noyes in *The Dictionary of National Biography*, eds. Williams and Palmer, 776–78.

51. Eagleton, *Literary Theory*, 30–37.

52. Thorne, *Congregational Missions*, 150–54.

53. Q. D. Leavis, *Fiction and the Reading Public*, 101.

54. F. R. Leavis, "Bunyan through Modern Eyes" (originally published in 1938 in *The Common Pursuit*, by F. R. Leavis), 206.

Conclusion
Lifting the Tollgates

1. Sharrock, "Life and Story," 50. See also Rivers, "Grace," 45; and Hill, *A Tinker*, 373, 377.

2. Hill, *A Tinker*, 377–78.

3. Hill, *A Tinker*, 380.

4. Hill, *A Tinker*, 380.

5. Point extracted from discussion of Hill, *A Tinker*, 375–76, 380.

6. Christian Literature Society for India and Africa, *Seventieth Annual Report*, back cover.

7. Bunyan, *The Pilgrim's Progress*, 225.

8. Chakrabarty, *Provincializing Europe*, 111–13, 243, 249.

9. Turner, "Bunyan's Sense," 91–110.

10. Kaufmann, *The Pilgrim's Progress*, 91.

11. Armstrong and Tennenhouse, *The Imaginary Puritan*, 210.

12. Armstrong and Tennenhouse, *The Imaginary Puritan*, 198–99.

13. See introduction, note 46; and Van 't Veld, "A New Thesis on Luyken as Illustrator of Bunyan."

14. Johnson, "Muhammad and Ideology in Medieval Christian Literature," which discusses Bunyan's views on Islam.

15. Brown, *John Bunyan*, 185–86.

16. Hill, "Bunyan's Contemporary Reputation," 9.

17. For evidence of these claims, see A Colonial Pilgrim, *Footsteps of the Pilgrim's Progress*; Foster, *Bunyan's Country*; Cockett, *Bunyan's England*; Tibbutt, "The Pilgrim's Route," 66–68; Manning, "Bedford's Historic Mile," 190–96.

18. Smith, *Bunyan in America*, 94.

19. Bunyan, *Leeto la Mokreste*, 29, 85.

20. Bunyan, *Die Christen se reis* (*The Pilgrim's Progress*, part 1), 11, 18.

21. Bunyan, *Die Christen se reis*, 14.

22. Foster, *Bunyan's Country*, 29.

23. Foster, *Bunyan's Country*, 78.

24. Bunyan, *The Pilgrim's Progress*, 90.

25. *Bedfordshire Times and Independent*, 24 June 1927, Newspaper Cuttings, Bunyan Collection, Bedford Library.

26. *Bedfordshire Standard*, 24 December 1923, Newspaper Cuttings, Bunyan Collection, Bedford Library.

27. Two major critics who popularized the Bedford angle were Kelman, *The Road*, 20; and Brown, *John Bunyan*, 298, 481.

28. Mee, introduction to *The Children's Bunyan*, 26.

29. Mee, introduction to *The Children's Bunyan*, 25; and Birrell, "John Bunyan Today," 152.

30. Ransome, *A History*, 132.

31. Brown, *The Institutions of the English Novel*.

32. Hill, *A Tinker*, 376.

33. For an excellent overview of debates on orality in the African novel, see Julien, *African Novels*. For debates on orality and literacy in Bunyan, see chapter 6, note 12.

34. Kettle, *An Introduction to the English Novel*, vol. 1, 40–43; McKeon, *The Origins of the English Novel, 1600–1740*, 295–314. For comments on McKeon's "cleansing" of romance, see Brown, *Institutions*, xii.

35. Julien, *African Novels*.

36. For a clear discussion of this, see Finnegan, *Literacy and Orality*.

37. Sharrock, "Life and Story," 56.

38. Sharrock, "Life and Story," 49.

39. Davis, "'Stout and Valiant Champions for God.'"

40. Turner, "Bunyan's Sense."

41. Barber, "Time and Space," 116.

42. Barber, "Time and Space," 121.

43. Miller, "Missionary Methods," *Congo Mission News*, January 1948, 16.

Appendix 2
A Social Profile of Bunyan Translators

1. Lewis, *These Seventy Years*, 282.

2. Information from Regions Beyond Mission Union, Congo/Zaire, 1878–1962, Correspondence and Minutes, RBMU Papers, Centre for the Study of Christianity in the Non-Western World, University of Edinburgh.

3. Jakeman, *Pioneering in Northern Rhodesia*. For destruction of her records, see letter to author from Dr. James G. Kallam of Sudan Interior Mission (SIM). The

South African General Mission of which Jakeman was a part merged with SIM; their records were shipped to North Carolina, but some were irreparably damaged by seawater.

4. Miller, *Change Here for Kano*, 20.

5. Potter, "The Social Origins," 136.

6. Thorne, *Congregational Missions*, 53–88; Piggin, *Making Evangelical Missionaries*; Potter, "The Social Origins."

7. Biographical details from *Register of Missionaries*, CMS Archive, University of Birmingham.

8. Guy, *The Heretic*, 4–5.

9. Lewis, *These Seventy Years*, 7.

BIBLIOGRAPHY

I. Archival Sources

Baptist Missionary Society, Angus Library, Regent's Park College, Oxford, U.K.
Austen, Philip Henry. Papers.
Bentley, William Holman Papers.
Fuller, Joseph Jackson. "Autobiography of the Rev. J. J. Fuller of Cameroons, West Africa"; "Comments on Early Mission in Fernando Po and Cameroons"; "Journal"; "Recollections of the West African Mission of the BMS"; and Papers.
Hartland, John S. Papers.
Jennings, R. L. Papers.
Lewis, Gwen. Candidate's Papers.
Lewis, Thomas. Candidate's Papers and Papers.
Pugh, Charles E. Candidate's Papers.
San Salvador: Church Meetings—Minutes; Logbook.
Scrivener, A. E. Candidate's Papers.
Stapleton, W. H. Papers.
Whitehead, John. Candidate's Papers and Papers.

The Bunyan Collection, Bedford Library, Bedford, U.K.
This originally comprised two distinct collections, namely The Offor Collection and The Mott Harrison Collection, although they are no longer maintained separately.

Camden Road Baptist Chapel, Hilldrop Road, Camden, London, U.K.
Camden Road Sunday School Missionary Association Annual Reports. 1890–1908.
Meeting of Sunday School Committee. 1874–1878.
Unsorted miscellaneous publications, pamphlets, sermons, commemorative volumes.

Church Mission Society, University of Birmingham, U.K.
Selections of papers relating to and correspondence of the following (all as per Precis Book):
Gordon, E. C.

Hinderer, Anna.
Hinderer, David.
Miller, Ethel P.
Oluwole, Isaac.
Pilkington, George Lawrence.

Church of Scotland Foreign Mission Papers, Edinburgh, U.K.
Christian Literature Committee.

Conference of British Missionary Societies/International Missionary Council, SOAS, University of London, U.K.
International Committee on Christian Literature for Africa. Minutes, Accounts, Correspondence, Reports, and Sets of Published Works. 1920–1957.

Council for World Mission (London Missionary Society), SOAS, University of London, U.K.
Candidates' Papers. 1796–1899.
Central African Reports. 1901–1914, 1915–1927.
Committee Minutes: Literature. 1866–1902.
Madagascar: Incoming Correspondence. 1834–1840.
South Africa: Incoming Letters. 1905–1907, 1908–1910.

Joint Matriculation Board of the South African Universities, University of South Africa, Pretoria, South Africa
Junior Certificate and Matriculation Examination Papers. 1918–1956.

Lovedale Collection, Cory Library, Rhodes University, Grahamstown, South Africa
Entertainment Committee. 1932–1938.
Lovedale Bible School: Correspondence. 1928–1936.
Lovedale Institute: Correspondence. 1932–1933.
Lovedale Press Collection.
Lovedale Publication Records. 1937–1954.
Minutes of the Lovedale Literary Society. 1936–1948.

Morija Museum and Archive, Morija, Lesotho
Handwritten notes on Thomas Mofolo in the possession of Albert Brutsch.
Miscellaneous school readers and catechisms.

Manuscripts Collection, University of Edinburgh Library, U.K.
MacAlpine, Alexander Gillon. Papers.

Natal Archives, Pietermaritzburg, South Africa
Colenso Collection.

Regions Beyond Mission Union, Centre for the Study of Christianity in the Non-Western World, School of Divinity, University of Edinburgh, U.K.
Director's Minute Book. 1908–1926.
Regions Beyond Mission Union Congo/Zaire: Minutes, Reports, Correspondence. 1878–1962; 1938–1968.

Religious Tract Society/United Society for Christian Literature, SOAS, University of London, U.K.
Miscellaneous publications and tracts.

2. Mission Periodicals and Annual Reports

Books for Africa, 1931–1963.
The Chronicle of the London Missionary Society, 1902–1939.
Church of Scotland Home and Foreign Mission Record, 1889–1899.
Congo Mission Conference, 1909–1924.
Congo Mission News, 1913–1959.
The Free Church of Scotland Monthly, 1890–1900.
Inland Africa, 1934–1958.
Leselinyana la Lesotho, 1863–1877; 1907.
Life and Work: The Record of the Church of Scotland, 1930–1935.
Lovedale Missionary Institute Annual Reports, 1873–1955.
Mboli ya Tengai, 1910–1928.
Missionary Herald, 1879–1948.
Missionary Records of the United Presbyterian Church, 1866–1868.
Ngonde ya Ngonde, 1897–1903.
Regions Beyond, 1927–1940.
Religious Tract Society/United Society for Christian Literature Annual Reports, 1820–1963.
Seed Time and Harvest, 1902–1927.
Young Africa, 1938–1958.

3. English Versions of *The Pilgrim's Progress* Cited

Part 1 of the book was originally published in 1678 and part 2 in 1684. Unless otherwise stated, all editions contain part 1 and 2. Introductions, prefaces, or forewords to *The Pilgrim's Progress* cited in the text are included in the section "Other References Cited."

Bunyan, John. *The Pilgrim's Progress*. Abridged by Mary McGregor. London: Thomas Nelson, n.d.

———. *The Pilgrim's Progress*. London: Religious Tract Society, n.d.

———. *The Pilgrim's Progress*. London: Stirling Tract Enterprise, n.d.

———. *The Pilgrim's Progress*. With an Introductory Notice by J.H.W. Edinburgh: Andrew Stevenson, n.d.

———. *The Pilgrim's Progress and Other Works of John Bunyan*. Edited by George Offor. Edinburgh: William Mackenzie, n.d.

———. *The Pilgrim's Progress*, part 1. London: W. Oliver, 1776.

———. *The Pilgrim's Progress*. With a Preface by William Mason. London: Alex Hogg and Co., 1790.

———. *The Pilgrim's Progress*. In eight parts. London: J. Tilling for the Religious Tract Society, [1810].

———. *The Pilgrim's Progress*. Three parts. Notes by William Mason. Plymouth: J. Bennett, 1823.

———. *The Pilgrim's Progress*. With a Life of the Author, by Robert Southey. Edinburgh: Thomas Nelson and Peter Brown, 1830.

———. *The Pilgrim's Progress*. Edited with an Introduction by George Offor. London: Hanserd Knollys Society, 1847.

———. *The Pilgrim's Progress*. Introduced by Charles Kingsley. London: Longman, Green, Longman, and Roberts, 1860.

———. *The Pilgrim's Progress*. With Memoir and Notes by George Offor. London: Routledge, Warne, and Routledge, 1861.

———. *The Pilgrim's Progress*. Edited with an Introduction by John Brown. London: Hodder and Stoughton, 1887.

———. *Bunyan's The Pilgrim's Progress in Modern English*. Edited by John Morrison. London: Macmillan, 1896.

———. *The Pilgrim's Progress*. Introduced by Edmund Venables. London: Oxford University Press, 1903.

———. *The Pilgrim's Progress*. Introduced by Christina Knox. London: Macmillan, 1923.

———. *The Pilgrim's Progress*. Introduced by James Blanton Wharey. Revised by Roger Sharrock. 1928. Reprint, Oxford: Clarendon Press, 1960.

———. *The Pilgrim's Progress*. Introduced by Roger Sharrock. London: Penguin, 1987.

4. Translated Versions of *The Pilgrim's Progress* Cited

For further details of all eighty translations, the reader is referred to Appendix 1.
Unless otherwise stated, all translations are of part 1 only.

Bunyan, John. *Bedangweri ya balondo o mundi ma wasi-na o mu mu mapo* (Duala). Translated by Joseph Jackson Fuller. London: Alexander and Shepheard, 1888.

———. *Die Christen se reis na die ewigheid* (Afrikaans). Cape Town: Nederduits Gereformeerde Kerk-uitgewers van Suid-Afrika, n.d.

———. *Dulu ntone Krist* (Bulu). Elat, West Afrika: Halsey, 1917.

———. *Haj-oirku-eh (gharko)* (Somali). Cairo: Nile Mission Press, n.d.

———. *Ije nke onye Kraist* (Igbo). London: Christian Literature Society, n.d.

———. *Inncwadi ka'Bunyane okutiwa ukuhamba kwesihambi* (Zulu). Translated by John William Colenso. Pietermaritzburg: Vause and Slatter, 1901.

———. *Kretie̅ ka Tama* (Bambara). N.p: Christian and Missionary Alliance, n.d.

———. *Leeto la Mokreste* (Sotho). Translated by Adolphe Mabille and Filemone Rapetloane. 1896. Reprint, Morija: Morija Sesuto Book Depot, 1988.

———. *Lokendo loa bokendi* (Kele). London: Religious Tract Society, [1916].

———. *Msafiri* (Swahili). London: Religious Tract Society/Universities' Mission, 1888.

———. *Njela na Mokristu* (Lingala). Ibambi, Wamba: Heart of Africa Mission, n.d.

———. *Omutambuze*, parts 1 and 2 (Ganda). London: The Sheldon Press, 1927.

———. *Rwendo rwo mufambi* (Shona). Bulawayo: Rhodesian Christian Press, n.d.

———. *'s Christens reize naar de eeuwigheid* (Dutch). Translated by G. W. Stegmann. Cape Town: J. H. Collard, 1842.

———. *Taith y pererin: Y rhyfel ysprydol*, parts 1 and 2 (Welsh). Edinburgh: Thomas C. Jack, n.d.

———. *Ugwalo lu ka Bunyane ogutiwa uguhamba gwohambi* (Ndebele). Translated by D. and M. Carnegie. London: South African District Committee of the London Missionary Society, 1902.

———. *Uhambo lo Mhambi*, parts 1 and 2 (Xhosa). Translated by Tiyo Soga and John Henderson Soga. Lovedale: Lovedale Press, 1937.

———. *Uhambo lwesihambi* (Zulu). Translated by B. A. Johanson. Sweetwaters: Union Bible Institute, n.d.

———. *Ulendo wa Mukristu mu chitumbuka* (Tumbuka). Translated by C. C. [Charles Chidongo] Chinula. London: Religious Tract Society, n.d.

5. Other References Cited

Achebe, Chinua. "Named for Victoria, Queen of England." In *Morning Yet on Creation Day: Essays*, by Chinua Achebe. New York: Anchor Press/Doubleday, 1975.

Adeniyi, Dapo, trans. *Expedition to the Mount of Thought (The Third Saga)*, translation of *Irìnkerindo Nínú Igbó Elégbèje*, by D. O. [Daniel Olorunfemi] Fagunwa. Ile-Ife: Obafemi Awolowo University Press, 1994.

Albert, Edward *A History of English Literature: A Practical Textbook for Senior Classes*. London: G. G. Harrap, 1923.

Anderson, Patricia J. *The Printed Image and the Transformation of Popular Culture, 1790–1860*. Oxford: Clarendon, 1991.

Andrade, Susan. "Tradition, Modernity, and the Family: Reading the Chimurenga Struggle into and out of *Nervous Conditions*." In *Emerging Perspectives on Tsitsi Dangarembga: Negotiating the Postcolonial*, edited by Ann Elizabeth Wiley and Jeanette Treiber. Trenton, N.J.: Africa World Press, 2002.

Anthony, E. A. *The Buried Bible and the Conversion of England to Christianity*. London: London Missionary Society, n.d.

Apter, Emily. "On Translation in a Global Market." *Public Culture* 13, no. 1 (2001): 1–12.

Archer, R.W.F. "Come, and Welcome, to Jesus Christ." Paper presented to a conference "The Holy War: Ideology, Culture and Dissent in Bunyan's England," University of Stirling, Scotland, August/September 1998.

Armstrong, Nancy. *Fiction in the Age of Photography: The Legacy of British Realism*. Cambridge: Harvard University Press, 1999.

Armstrong, Nancy, and Leonard Tennenhouse. *The Imaginary Puritan: Literature, Intellectual Labor, and the Origins of Personal Life*. Berkeley: University of California Press, 1992.

Ashton, H., trans. *The Traveller of the East*, translation of *Moeti oa Bochabela*, by Thomas Mofolo. London: Society for Promoting Christian Knowledge, n.d.

Baldick, Chris. *The Social Mission of English Criticism, 1848–1932*. Oxford: Clarendon, 1983.

Baptist Missionary Society. *BMS Notes for Talks with Sunday Schools: Congo*. London: Baptist Missionary Society, 1916.

———. *Congo Jubilee Exhibition: Handbook and Guide, 1878–1928*. N.p.: Baptist Missionary Society, 1928.

Barber, Karin. "Audiences and the Book in Africa." *Current Writing* 13, no. 2 (2001): 9–19.

———. "Preliminary Notes on Audiences." *Africa* 67, no. 3 (1997): 347–62.

———. "Time, Space, and Writing in Three Colonial Yoruba Novels." *The Yearbook of English Studies: The Politics of Postcolonial Criticism* 27 (1997): 120–21.

———, ed. *Readings in African Popular Culture*. Oxford: James Currey, 1996.

Barnes, Leonard. *The New Boer War*. London: Hogarth Press, 1932.

Bayart, Jean François. *The State in Africa: The Politics of the Belly*. London: Longman, 1993.

Bebbington, D. W. *Evangelicalism in Modern Britain: A History from the 1730s to the 1980s*. London: Unwin Hyman, 1989.

———. *The Nonconformist Conscience: Chapel and Politics, 1870–1912*. Boston: Allen and Unwin, 1982.

Becker, Rayda. "The Photographs of W. F. P. Burton." In *'Of Course You Would not Want a Canoe': The Collection of W. F. P. Burton*, edited by Anitra Nettleton. Johannesburg: University of the Witwatersrand, 1992.

Bentley, W. Holman. *The Life and Labours of a Congo Pioneer*. London: Religious Tract Society, 1907.

Bester, Rory McLachlan. "Insecure Shadows: Church of the Province of South Africa Mission Photographs from Southern Africa c. 1895–1945." Master's Thesis, University of the Witwatersrand, 1997.

Beuchat, P-D. *Do the Bantu Have a Literature?* Johannesburg: Institute for the Study of Man in Africa, n.d.

Bhabha, Homi. *The Location of Culture*. London: Routledge, 1994.

Bhebhe, Ngwabi. *Christianity and Traditional Religion in Western Zimbabwe, 1859–1923*. London: Longman, 1979.

Bickers, Robert A., and Rosemary Seton, eds. *Missionary Encounters: Sources and Issues*. London: Curzon, 1996.

Binfield, Clyde. *So Down to Prayers: Studies in English Nonconformity, 1780–1920*. London: J. M. Dent, 1977.

Birrell, Augustine. "Editorial." *The Bookman* 446, no. 75 (1928): 97–99.

———. "John Bunyan Today." *The Bookman* 73, no. 435 (1927): 148–49.

———. "Links of Empire—Books (IX)." *The Empire Review* 47, no. 235 (1928): 79–87.

Birrell, C. M. "Bunyan's Personal Pilgrimage." In *The Book of the Bunyan Festival: A Complete Record of the Proceedings at the Unveiling of the Statue*, edited by W. H. [William Howie] Wylie. London: James Clarke and Christian World Office, 1874.

Bishop of Durham [Handley Carr Glyn Moule]. "An Anglican's Reflection on Bunyan's Career." *The Review of the Churches* 5, no. 3 (1928): 313–19.

Blatchford, Robert. *My Favourite Books*. London: Walter Scott, 1900.

Bokwe, John Knox. *Ntsikana: The Story of an African Hymn*. Lovedale: Lovedale Press, n.d.

———. *Two Weeks' Trip to Cape Town: or, A Native's Impression of the Cape Industrial Exhibition*. Lovedale: Lovedale Press, 1884.

Borough of Bedford Public Library. *Catalogue of Bedford Public Library (Frank Mott Harrison Collection)*. Bedford: Borough of Bedford Library, 1938.

Bradley, Ian. *The Call to Seriousness: The Evangelical Impact on the Victorians*. London: Jonathan Cape, 1976.

Brathwaite, Edward. *The Development of Creole Society in Jamaica, 1770–1820*. Oxford: Clarendon Press, 1971.

Breckenridge, Keith. "We Must Speak for Ourselves: The Rise and Fall of a Public Sphere on the South African Gold Mines, 1920–1931." *Comparative Studies in Society and History* 40, no. 1 (1998): 71–108.

Breen, Margaret Soenser. "Christiana's Rudeness: Spiritual Authority in *The Pilgrim's Progress*." *Bunyan Studies* 7 (1997): 96–111.

Broadhead, Susan Herlin. "Trade and Politics on the Congo Coast, 1770–1870." Ph.D. diss., Boston University, 1971.

Brooks, Chris, and Andrew Saint, eds. *The Victorian Church: Architecture and Society*. Manchester: Manchester University Press, 1995.

Brooks, Chris, and Andrew Saint. Introduction to *The Victorian Church: Architecture and Society*, edited by Chris Brooks and Andrew Saint. Manchester: Manchester University Press, 1995.

Brown, Callum G. *Religion and Society in Scotland since 1707*. Edinburgh: Edinburgh University Press, 1997.

———. *The Social History of Religion in Scotland since 1730*. London: Methuen, 1987.

Brown, Homer Obed. *The Institutions of the English Novel: From Defoe to Scott*. Philadelphia: University of Pennsylvania Press, 1997.

Brown, John. *Bunyan's Home*. London: Ernest Nister, n.d.

———. Introduction to *The Pilgrim's Progress*. London: Hodder and Stoughton, 1887.

———. *John Bunyan: His Life Times and Work*. London: Isbister, 1900.

Budden, H. D. *The Story of Marsh Street Congregational Church Walthamstow*. London: Bobby and Co., 1923.

Bunyan, John. *Grace Abounding to the Chief of Sinners*. 1666. Reprint, London: Penguin, 1987.

———. *The Holy War.* 1682. Reprint, London: Religious Tract Society, n.d.

Burbidge, John. *Half-hours with Bunyan's "Pilgrim's Progress."* Liverpool: J. A. Thompson, 1856.

Callaway, Godfrey. *The Pilgrim Path: A Story of an African Childhood.* London: The Society for the Propagation of the Gospel in Foreign Parts, n.d.

Camden Road Baptist Church. *Sunday School Centenary, 1856–1956.* London: Camden Road Baptist Sunday School, n.d.

Camden Road Chapel Jubilee, 1854–1904: A Brief Historical Summary. N.p., n.d.

Carnegie, David. *Among the Matabele.* London: Religious Tract Society, 1894.

Carson Graham, R. H. *Under Seven Kongo Kings.* London: Carey Press, n.d.

Catherell, G. A. "Baptist War and Peace: A Study of British Baptist Involvement in Jamaica, 1783–1865," n.d. Ts. based on M.A. (Liverpool) and Ph.D. (Keele). Housed in the BMS Archives.

Chakrabarty, Dipesh. "Postcoloniality and the Artifice of History: Who Speak for 'Indian' Pasts." *Representations* 37 (1992): 1–26.

———. *Provincializing Europe: Postcolonial Thought and Historical Difference.* Princeton: Princeton University Press, 2000.

Chalmers, John A. *Tiyo Soga: A Page of South African Mission Work.* Edinburgh: Andrew Elliot, 1877.

Chapman, Michael. "South Africa in the Global Neighbourhood: Towards a Method of Cultural Analysis." *Media, Culture and Society* 20 (1998): 669–75.

Cheever, George B. *Lectures on the "Pilgrim's Progress" and on the Life and Times of John Bunyan.* London: William Collins, 1828.

Christian History Institute. "Glimpses: Issue No. 86: John Bunyan." Twenty Centuries of Church History from Christian History Institute. http://www.gospelcom.net/chi/GLIMPSEF/Glimpses/glmps086.shtml, n.d.

———. "November 21, 1866: From English to Xhosa." Twenty Centuries of Church History from Christian History Institute. http://www.gospelcom.net/chi/ARCHIVEF/11/daily-11-21-2001.shtml, n.d.

Church, J. E. *Quest for the Highest: An Autobiographical Account of the East African Revival.* Exeter: Paternoster Press, 1981.

City Land Committee of the Corporation. *History of the Bunhill Fields Burial Grounds: With Some of the Principle Inscriptions.* London: Charles Skipper and East, 1902.

Clanchy, M. T. *From Memory to Written Record: England, 1066–1307.* London: Edward Arnold, 1979.

Clarke, J. A. "What Literature is Most Suitable for Circulation among the Converts?" *The Congo Missionary Conference: A Report of the Fourth Congo General Conference of Protestant Missionaries.* Baptist Missionary Society: Bolobo, n.d.

Clarke, John. *Memoir of Joseph Merrick: Missionary to Africa.* London: Benjamin L. Green, 1850.

———. *Memorials of the Baptist Missionaries in Jamaica, Including a Sketch of the Labours of Early Religious Instructors.* London: Yates and Alexander, 1869.

Clarke, Jonathan. Extract of Letter (recipient unclear). 20 January 1788. In "Letters Showing the Rise and Progress of the Early Negro Churches of Georgia and the West Indies." *Journal of Negro History* 1, no. 1 (1916): 79.

Clingman, Stephen, ed. *Regions and Repertoires: Topics in South African Politics and Culture.* Johannesburg: Ravan Press, 1991.

Cobley, Alan. *Class and Consciousness: The Black Petty Bourgeoisie in South Africa, 1924–1950.* New York: Greenwood Press, 1990.

Cockett, C. Bernard. *Bunyan's England: A Tour with the Camera in the Footsteps of the Immortal Dreamer.* Luton: Leagrave Press, 1948.

———. Foreword to *John Bunyan's England*, by C. Bernard Cockett. London: Homeland Association, 1928.

———. "John Bunyan—The Man." *The Literary Review* 1, no. 2 (1928): 39–45.

———. *John Bunyan's England.* London: Homeland Association, 1928.

[Codner, Elizabeth]. *The Missionary Farewell.* London: Wertheim and Macintosh, 1854.

———. *The Missionary Ship.* London: Wertheim and Macintosh, 1856.

Colenso, John William. "Amazwi ka-Sobantu" ("Words of Sobantu" [Colenso]). In *Inncwadi ka'Bunyane okutiwa ukuhamba kwesihambi* (*The Pilgrim's Progress*, part 1). Translated by John William Colenso. Pietermaritzburg: Vause and Slatter, 1901.

A Colonial Pilgrim. *Footsteps of "The Pilgrim's Progress": A Key of the Allegory.* London: Premier Publishing, n.d.

Comaroff, Jean, and John Comaroff. *Of Revelation and Revolution: Christianity, Colonialism and Consciousness in South Africa.* Vol. 1. Chicago: University of Chicago Press, 1993.

———. *Of Revelation and Revolution: The Dialectics of Modernity on a South African Frontier.* Vol. 2. Chicago: University of Chicago Press, 1997.

Coombes, Annie E. *Reinventing Africa: Museums, Material Culture and Popular Imagination.* New Haven: Yale University Press, 1994.

Cooper, Frederick, and Ann Laura Stoler, eds. *Tensions of Empire: Colonial Cultures in a Bourgeois World.* Berkeley: University of California Press, 1997.

Cooper, Lina Orman. *John Bunyan: The Glorious Dreamer.* London: The National Sunday School Union, n.d.

Coplan, David B. *In the Time of Cannibals: The Word Music of South Africa's Basotho Migrants.* Chicago: University of Chicago Press, 1994.

Corelli, Marie. *The Master Christian.* London: Methuen, 1900.

Court, Franklin. *Institutionalizing English Literature: The Culture and Politics of English Study.* Stanford: Stanford University Press, 1992.

Couzens, Tim. "Widening Horizons of African Literature, 1870–1900." In *Literature and Society in South Africa*, edited by Landeg White and Tim Couzens. Johannesburg: Maskew Miller Longman, 1984.

———. *The New African: A Study of the Life and Work of H. I. E. Dhlomo.* Johannesburg: Ravan Press, 1985.

Couzens, Tim, and Essop Patel, eds. *The Return of the Amasi Bird: Black South African Poetry, 1891–1981.* Johannesburg: Ravan Press, 1982.

Crawford, Anne, Tony Hayter, Ann Hughes, Frank Prochaska, Pauline Stafford, and Elizabeth Vallance, eds. *The European Biographical Dictionary of British Women.* London: Europa, 1983.

Curtin, Philip D. *Two Jamaicas: The Role of Ideas in a Tropical Colony, 1830–1865.* Cambridge: Harvard University Press, 1955.

Cutt, Margaret Nancy. *Ministering Angels: A Study of Nineteenth-Century Evangelical Writing for Children.* Wormley: Five Owls Press, 1979.

Dangarembga, Tsitsi. *Nervous Conditions.* London: Women's Press, 1988.

Danielson, Dennis. "Catechism, "The Pilgrim's Progress," and the pilgrim's progress." *Journal of English and Germanic Philology* 94, no. 1 (1995): 42–59.

Davenport, Rodney. *South Africa: A Modern History.* Johannesburg: Macmillan, 1977.

Davies, W. H. *The Sunday Scholars' Service of Sacred Song, Illustrative of "The Pilgrim's Progress."* London: Sunday School Union, n.d.

Davis, Michael. "'Stout and Valiant Champions for God': The Radical Reformation of Romance in Bunyan's *The Pilgrim's Progress.*" Paper presented to a conference "The Holy War: Ideology, Culture and Dissent in Bunyan's England," University of Stirling, Scotland, August/September 1998.

Davison, Hugh A. *The Pageant of Woman Greatheart.* Leeds: James Broadbent, 1937.

de Kock, Leon. *Civilizing Barbarians: Missionary Narrative and African Textual Response in Nineteenth-Century South Africa.* Johannesburg: Witwatersrand University Press, 1996.

de Mestral, Claude. "Christian Literature for Africa." *The International Review of Mission* 43, no. 172 (1954): 436–42.

———. "What is Christian Literature?" *Books for Africa* 23, no. 3 (1953): 45–46.

Dell, Ethel M. *Greatheart.* New York: Grosset and Dunlap, 1918.

"Devotion to Progress." *Period Garden,* December 1993, 86–91.

Dobson, Austin. *A Handbook of English Literature.* 1874. Reprint, London: C. Lockwood, 1897.

Doyle, Brian. *English and Englishness.* London: Routledge, 1989.

Dramatic Illustrations of Passages from the Second Part of "The Pilgrim's Progress" by John Bunyan, arranged by Mrs. George MacDonald. London: Oxford University Press, 1925.

Du Bois, W.E.B. *The Souls of Black Folk.* 1903. Reprint, New York: Vintage Books, 1990.

Eagleton, Terry. *Literary Theory: An Introduction.* London: Basil Blackwell, 1995.

Edwards, Elizabeth, ed. *Anthropology and Photography, 1860–1920.* New Haven: Yale University Press, 1992.

Elbourne, Elizabeth and Robert Ross. "Combating Spiritual and Social Bondage: Early Missions in the Cape Colony." In *Christianity in South Africa: A Political, Social and Cultural History,* edited by Richard Elphick and Rodney Davenport. Oxford: James Currey, 1997.

Ellis, William. *Faithful unto Death: The Story of the Founding and Preservation of the Martyr Church of Madagascar.* London: John Snow, 1876.

————. *History of Madagascar.* Vol. 2. London: Fisher, n.d.

————. *The Martyr Church: A Narrative of the Introduction, Progress and Triumph of Christianity in Madagascar.* London: John Snow, 1870.

Elphick, Richard, and Hermann Giliomee, eds. *The Shaping of Southern African Society, 1652–1840.* Cape Town: Maskew Miller Longman, 1989.

Elphick, Richard, and Rodney Davenport, eds. *Christianity in South Africa: A Political, Social and Cultural History.* Oxford: James Currey, 1997.

The English Assocation. *English Literature in Schools* (Pamphlet 21). N.p., n.d.

————. *English Papers and Examinations for Pupils of School Age in England and Wales* (Pamphlet 37). N.p., n.d.

————. *John Bunyan* (Pamphlet 19). N.p., n.d.

————. *A Short List of Books on English Literature from the Beginning to 1932 for the Use of Teachers* (Leaflet No. 3). N.p., n.d.

Esking, Erik. English Summary in *John Bunyan i Sverige under 250 år.* Klippan: Skeab Verbum, 1980.

Fagunwa, D. O. "Writing a Novel." In *Loaded Vehicles: Studies in African Literary Media,* by Bernth Lindfors. Trenton: Africa World Press, 1996.

Finnegan, Ruth. *Literacy and Orality: Studies in the Technology of Communication.* Oxford: Basil Blackwell, 1988.

Firth, C. H. Introduction to *The Pilgrim's Progress.* London: Methuen, 1908.

Fish, Stanley E. *Self-Consuming Artifacts: The Experience of Seventeenth-Century Literature.* Berkeley: University of California Press, 1972.

Fitzgerald, W. B. *The Pilgrim Road.* London: Charles H. Kelly, 1915.

Fletcher, Angus. *Allegory: The Theory of a Symbolic Mode.* Ithaca: Cornell University Press, 1964.

Fletcher, Irene M. "*The Pilgrim's Progress* and the London Missionary Society." *Bedfordshire Magazine* 10, no. 77 (1966): 194–96.

Foster, Albert J. *Bunyan's Country: Studies in the Bedford Topography of "The Pilgrim's Progress."* London: H. Virtue, 1901.

Franz, G. H. "The Literature of Lesotho." *Bantu Studies* 4 (1930): 173–74.

Fraser, Donald. *The Autobiography of an African: Retold in Biographical Form and in the Wild African Setting of the Life of Daniel Mtusu.* London: Seeley, Service and Co., 1925.

Freeman J. J. [Joseph John], and David Johns. *A Narrative of the Persecution of Christians in Madagascar with Details of the Escape of the Six Christian Refugees Now in England.* London: John Snow, 1840.

Froude, James Anthony. *Bunyan.* London: Macmillan, 1880.

Fuller, J. J. Preface to *Bedangweri ya balondo* (*The Pilgrim's Progress,* part 1). Translated by J. J. Fuller. London: Alexander and Shepheard, 1888.

Fuller, Joseph Jackson. Testimony in *Report of the Centenary Conference on the Protestant Mission of the World.* Edited by James Johnstone. London: James Nisbet, 1889.

Fullerton, W. Y. *The Christ of the Congo River.* London: The Carey Press, 1929.

————. *The Legacy of Bunyan.* London: Ernest Benn, 1928.

Fussell, Paul. *The Great War and Modern Memory.* New York: Oxford University Press, 1975.

Gayle, Clement. *George Liele: Pioneer Missionary to Jamaica.* Kingston: Jamaica Baptist Union, 1982.

Geary, Christraud M. "Missionary Photography: Private and Public Readings." *African Arts* 4, no. 24 (1991): 48–59.

Gérard, Albert S. *African Language Literatures: An Introduction to the Literary History of Sub-Saharan Africa.* Washington: Three Continents Press, 1981.

———. *Four African Literatures: Xhosa, Zulu, Sotho, Amharic.* Berkeley: University of California Press, 1974.

Girdlestone, R. B. *Suggestions for Translators, Editors and Revisers of the Bible.* London: Hatchards, 1877.

Girouard, Mark. *The Return of Camelot: Chivalry and the English Gentleman.* New Haven: Yale University Press, 1981.

Godby, Michael. "Framing the Colonial Subject: The Photographs of W. F. P. Burton (1886–1971) in the Former Belgian Congo." *Social Dynamics* 19, no. 1 (1993): 11–25.

Golder, Harold. "Bunyan's Giant Despair." *The Journal of English and Germanic Philosophy* 30, no. 3 (1931): 361–78.

Gollock, G. A. Review of *The Traveller of the East* (*Moeti oa Bochabela*), by Thomas Mofolo, translated by H. Ashton. *Africa* 8, no. 3 (1934): 510.

Goody, Jack. "Restricted Literacy in Northern Ghana." In *Literacy in Traditional Societies,* edited by Jack Goody. London: Cambridge, 1968.

———, ed. *Literacy in Traditional Societies.* London: Cambridge, 1968.

Gosse, Edmund. *English Literature: An Illustrated Record: From Milton to Johnson.* Vol. 3. London: W. Heinemann, 1906.

Gow, Bonar A. *Madagascar and the Protestant Impact: The Work of British Missionaries, 1818–1895.* London: Longman and Dalhousie University Press, 1979.

Great Heart of New Guinea: A Missionary Cantata for Boys and Girls. London: London Missionary Society, n.d.

Greaves, Richard L. "Bunyan through the Centuries: Some Reflections." *English Studies* 64 (1983): 113–21.

Green, Samuel G. *The Story of the RTS for 100 Years.* London: Religious Tract Society, 1899.

Grenfell, Jim. Letter to author. 13 October 1998.

Griffiths, Gareth. *African Literature in English: East and West.* London: Longman, 2000.

Griffiths, Gertrude. *The Great Adventure: Three Scenes.* London: London Missionary Society, 1920.

Guillebaud, Rosemary. Interview by author. Cambridge, 3 December 1998.

Gupta, M. G. *Mystic Symbolism in Ramayan, Mahabharat and "The Pilgrim's Progress."* Agra: M. G. Publishers, 1993.

Guy, Jeff. "Class, Imperialism and Literary Criticism: William Ngidi, John Colenso and Matthew Arnold." *Journal of Southern African Studies* 23, no. 2 (1997): 219–43.

———. *The Heretic: A Study of the Life of John William Colenso, 1814–1883*. Pieter-maritzburg: University of Natal Press/Ravan Press, 1983.

Gwynne Daniell, Jessie E. *The Religion of the Hearth*. London: The Sheldon Press, 1928.

Haider, Arwa. "Turning the Tablas." *Time Out*, 12–19 August 1998, 27.

Hancock, Maxine. "Bunyan as Reader: The Record of *Grace Abounding*." *Bunyan Studies* 5 (1999): 68–86.

Hargreaves, Cyril, and M. Greenshields, comps. *Catalogue of the Bunyan Meeting Library and Museum, Bedford*. Bedford: Bunyan Meeting Library and Museum, 1955.

Harries, Patrick. "Photography and the Rise of Anthropology: Henri-Alexandre Junod and the Thonga of Mozambique and South Africa." Encounters with Photography. http://www.museums.org.za/sam/conf/enc/harries.htm, 10 November 2001.

Harrison, Frank Mott. "Some Illustrators of *The Pilgrim's Progress* (part 1) John Bunyan." *The Library* 3, no. 7 (1936): 241–63.

Hatch, Nathan O. *The Democratization of American Christianity*. New Haven: Yale University Press, 1989.

Hawker, George. *An Englishwoman's Twenty-Five Years in Tropical Africa*. London: Hodder and Stoughton, n.d.

Hayashida, Nelson Osamu. *Dreams in the African Church: The Significance of Dreams and Visions among Zambian Baptists*. Amsterdam: Rodopi, 1999.

Headland, A. R. *David Carnegie of Matabeleland*. London: London Missionary Society, n.d.

Hewitt, Gordon. *Let the People Read: A Short History of the United Society for Christian Literature*. London: United Society for Christian Literature, 1949.

———. *The Problems of Success: A History of the Church Missionary Society, 1910–1942*. Vol. 1. London: SCM Press, 1971.

Hill, Christopher. "Bunyan's Contemporary Reputation." In *John Bunyan and his England, 1628–1688*, edited by Anne Laurence, W. R. Owens, and Stuart Sim. London: The Hambledon Press, 1990.

———. *A Tinker and a Poor Man: John Bunyan and his Church, 1628–1688*. New York: W. W. Norton, 1988.

Hilton, Anne. *The Kingdom of the Kongo*. Oxford: Clarendon Press, 1985.

Hilton, Boyd. *The Age of Atonement: The Influence of Evangelicalism on Social and Economic Thought, 1785–1865*. Oxford: Clarendon Press, 1988.

Hodgson, Janet. *Ntsikana's Great Hymn: A Xhosa Expression of Christianity in the Early Nineteenth Century Eastern Cape*. Cape Town: Centre for African Studies, University of Cape Town, 1980.

Hofmeyr, Isabel. "Metaphorical Books." *Current Writing* 13, no. 2 (2001): 100–108.

———. "Portable Landscapes: Thomas Mofolo and John Bunyan in the Broad and Narrow Way." Paper presented at a conference "Space, Place and Identity," University of Perth, Australia, July 2001.

———. *"We Spend our Years as a Tale that is Told": Oral Historical Narrative in a South African Chiefdom.* Portsmouth: Heinemann, 1993.

Holt, Basil. *Greatheart of the Border: A Life of John Brownlee Pioneer Missionary of South Africa.* King Williamstown: The South African Missionary Museum, 1976.

Horne, Silvester C. *The Story of the LMS.* London: London Missionary Society, 1904.

Howard, R. W. *A Greatheart of Africa.* N.p.: Church Mission Society, n.d.

Howkins, Alan. "The Discovery of Rural England." In *Englishness: Politics and Culture, 1880–1920,* edited by Robert Colls and Philip Dodds. London: Croom Helm, 1986.

Howse, Ernest Marshall. *Saints in Politics: The "Clapham Sect" and the Growth of Freedom.* 1953. Reprint, London: George Allen and Unwin, 1971.

Huddleston, Sarah. *George Pemba: Against All Odds.* Johannesburg: Jonathan Ball, n.d.

Hurry, Patricia, and Alan Cirket, comps. *Bunyan Meeting Museum Library Catalogue.* Bedford: Bunyan Meeting House, 1995.

Hutton, W. H. *John Bunyan.* London: Hodder and Stoughton, 1928.

Hyslop, Jonathan. "Food, Authority and Politics: Student Riots in South African Schools, 1945–1976." In *Regions and Repertoires: Topics in South African Politics and Culture,* edited by Stephen Clingman. Johannesburg: Ravan Press, 1991.

"In Praise of Hugh Rowland." *The Chronicle of the London Missionary Society* 43 (1935): 179.

Innis, Alexander. *Cruelties Committed on the West Coast of Africa by an Agent of the Baptist Mission and Others: A Letter to John Cropper, Esq.* London: Arthur Hall, Virtue, 1862.

"'Interpreter's House' in Bemba." *The Chronicle of the London Missionary Society* 37 (1929): 252.

J.H.W. Introductory notice to *The Pilgrim's Progress.* Edinburgh: Andrew Stevenson, n.d.

Jakeman, E. M. [Eva Milton] *Pioneering in Northern Rhodesia.* London: Morgan and Scott, n.d.

Janzen, John M., and Wyatt MacGaffey, eds. *An Anthology of Kongo Religion: Primary Texts from Lower Zaire.* Lawrence, Kansas: University of Kansas, 1974.

Jeater, Diana. *Marriage, Perversion, and Power: The Construction of Moral Discourse in Southern Rhodesia, 1894–1930.* Oxford: Clarendon, 1993.

Johanson, B. "Amazwi esingeniso" (Introduction) to *Uhambo lwesihambi* (*The Pilgrim's Progress,* part 1). Translated by B. Johanson. Sweetwaters: Union Bible Institute, 1956.

Johnson, Galen. "Muhammad and Ideology in Medieval Christian Literature." *Islam and Christian-Muslim Relations* 11, no. 3 (2000): 333–46.

Jordan, Archibald Campbell. *Towards an African Literature: The Emergence of Literary Form in Xhosa.* Berkeley: University of California Press, 1973.

Julien, Eileen. *African Novels and the Question of Orality.* Bloomington: Indiana University Press, 1992.

Kallam, James G. Letter to the author. 29 January 1999.

Kaufmann, U. Milo. *"The Pilgrim's Progress" and Traditions in Puritan Meditation.* New Haven: Yale University Press, 1966.

Kayira, Legson. *I Will Try.* London: Longman, 1966.

Keeble, N. H. "'Of Him Thousands Daily Sing and Talk': Bunyan and His Reputation." In *John Bunyan: Conventicle and Parnassus: Tercentenary Essays,* edited by N. H. Keeble. Oxford: Clarendon Press, 1988.

———. *The Literary Culture of Nonconformity in later Seventeenth-Century England.* Leicester: Leicester University Press, 1987.

———, ed. *John Bunyan: Conventicle and Parnassus: Tercentenary Essays.* Oxford: Clarendon Press, 1988.

Kelman, John. *The Road: The Story of John Bunyan's "The Pilgrim's Progress."* Edinburgh: Oliphant Anderson and Ferrier, n.d.

Kettle, Arnold. *An Introduction to the English Novel.* Vol. 1. London: Hutchinson University Library, 1969.

Kilgour, R. "The Order of First Translation of Scripture in Mission Fields." *The International Review of Mission* 7, no. 28 (1918): 456–69.

Kingsley, Charles. Introduction to *The Pilgrim's Progress.* London: Longman, Green, Longman, and Roberts, 1860.

Knott, John R. "'Thou Must Live Upon my Word': Bunyan and the Bible." In *John Bunyan: Conventicle and Parnassus: Tercentenary Essays,* edited by N. H. Keeble. Oxford: Clarendon Press, 1988.

Knox, Christina. Introduction to *The Pilgrim's Progress.* London: Macmillan, 1923.

Kunene, Daniel P. *Thomas Mofolo and the Emergence of Sesotho Prose.* Johannesburg: Ravan Press, 1989.

Labou Tansi, Sony. *The Seven Solitudes of Lorsa Lopez.* Translated by Clive Wake. Oxford: Heinemann, 1995.

Landau, Paul. "The Illumination of Christ in the Kalahari Desert." *Representations* 45 (1994): 26–40.

———. "Photography and Colonial Vision." H-AFRICA Africa Forum. http://www2. h-net.msu.edu/~africa/africaforum/Landua.html, 10 November 2001.

———. *The Realm of the Word: Language, Gender and Christianity in Southern Africa.* Portsmouth: Heinemann, 1995.

Large, James. *Evenings with John Bunyan, or The Dream Interpreted.* London: James Nisbet and Co., 1861.

Larson, Piers M. "'Capacities and Modes of Thinking': Intellectual Engagements and

Subaltern Hegemony in the Early History of Malagasy Christianity." *American Historical Review* 102, no. 4 (1997): 969–1002.

Laurence, Anne, W. R. Owens, and Stuart Sim, eds. *John Bunyan and his England, 1628–1688*. London: The Hambledon Press, 1990.

Law, Alice. "Some Aspects of *The Pilgrim's Progress.*" *The Empire Review* 46, no. 318, (1927):48–55.

Leavis, F. R. "Bunyan through Modern Eyes." In *The Common Pursuit*, by F. R. Leavis. London: Penguin, 1952.

Leavis, Q. D. *Fiction and the Reading Public*. London: Chatto and Windus, 1939.

Lee, Sidney. Introduction to *The Pilgrim's Progress*. London: Methuen, 1905.

Legassick, Martin. "The Northern Frontier to c. 1940: The Rise and Decline of the Griqua People." In *The Shaping of Southern African Society, 1652–1840*, edited by Richard Elphick and Hermann Giliomee. Cape Town: Maskew Miller Longman, 1989.

Leslie, Omolara. "*The Palm-Wine Drinkard*: A Reassessment of Amos Tutuola." *Journal of Commonwealth Literature* 9 (1970): 48–55.

"Letters Showing the Rise and Progress of the Early Negro Churches of Georgia and the West Indies." *Journal of Negro History* 1, no. 1 (1916): 69–75.

Lewis, Thomas. *These Seventy Years: An Autobiography*. London: The Carey Press, 1930.

Light, Alfred W. *Bunhill Fields*. London: Farncombe, 1915.

Lindfors, Bernth. "Amos Tutuola." In *Twentieth-Century Caribbean and Black African Writers*, edited by Bernth Lindfors and Reinhard Sander. Detroit: Bruccoli Clark Layman, 1993.

———. "Amos Tutuola and D. O. Fagunwa." *Journal of Commonwealth Literature* 9 (1970): 57–65.

———. *Loaded Vehicles: Studies in African Literary Media*. Trenton: Africa World Press, 1996.

Lindfors, Bernth and Reinhard Sander, eds. *Twentieth-Century Caribbean and Black African Writers*. Detroit: Bruccoli Clark Layman, 1993.

Lindsay, Jack. *John Bunyan: Maker of Myths*. London: Methuen, 1937.

Liu, Lydia H. Introduction to *Tokens of Exchange: The Problem of Translation in Global Circulations*, edited by Lydia H. Liu. Durham: Duke University Press, 1999.

———. "The Question of Meaning-Value in the Political Economy of the Sign." In *Tokens of Exchange: The Problem of Translation in Global Circulations*, edited by Lydia H. Liu. Durham: Duke University Press, 1999.

———, ed. *Tokens of Exchange: The Problem of Translation in Global Circulations*. Durham: Duke University Press, 1999.

London Missionary Society, *Fifty-Third Annual Report of the London Missionary Society*. London: London Missionary Society, 1847.

MacGaffey, Wyatt. "*The Beloved City*: Commentary on a Kimbanguist Text." *Journal of Religion in Africa* 2, no. 2 (1969): 129–47.

Mackail, J. W. *"The Pilgrim's Progress": A Lecture Delivered at the Royal Institution of Great Britain.* London: Longmans, Green and Co., 1924.

Mackay, Donald J. "Simon Kimbangu and the B.M.S. Tradition." *Journal of Religion in Africa* 17, no. 2 (1987): 113–71.

Mackay, Donald J., and Daniel Ntoni-Nzinga. "Kimbangu's Interlocutor: Nyuvudi's *Nsamu Miangunza (The Story of the Prophets)." Journal of Religion in Africa* 22, no. 3 (1993): 233–65.

Mahood, M. M. "Marie Corelli in West Africa." *Ibadan*, February 1959, 19–21.

Mair, J. H. *Books in their Hand: A Short History of the United Society for Christian Literature.* London: United Society for Christian Literature, 1960.

Malibongwe ANC Women: Poetry is Also Their Weapon. N.p.: ANC, n.d.

Manning, H. S. "Bedford's Historic Mile." *Bedfordshire Magazine* 5, no. 36 (1956): 190–96.

Marcum, John. *The Angolan Revolution: The Anatomy of an Explosion (1950–1962).* Vol. 1. Cambridge: The M.I.T. Press, n.d.

Martin, Marie-Louise. *The Biblical Concept of Messianism and Messianism in Southern Africa.* Morija: Morija Sesuto Book Depot, 1964.

Martin, Roger H. *Evangelicals United: Ecumenical Stirrings in Pre-Victorian Britain, 1795–1830.* Metuchen: The Scarecrow Press, 1983.

Martin, W. Stanley, and David Catt. *Pictures and Portraits from "The Pilgrim's Progress."* London: Stanley Martin, n.d.

Mason, William. Preface to *The Pilgrim's Progress.* London: Hogg and Co., 1790.

Massing, Jean Michel. "From Greek Powder to Soap Advert: Washing the Ethiopian." *Journal of the Warburg and Courtauld Institutes* 58 (1995): 180–201.

Maughan, Steven. "'Mighty England do Good': The Major English Denominations and Organisations for the Support of Foreign Missions in the Nineteenth Century." In *Missionary Encounters: Sources and Issues*, edited by Robert A. Bickers and Rosemary Seton. London: Curzon, 1996.

Mbembe, Achille. *On the Postcolony.* Berkeley: University of California Press, 2001.

McClintock, Anne. *Imperial Leather: Race, Gender and Sexuality in the Colonial Contest.* New York: Routledge, 1995.

McGown, G.W.T. *Ten Bunyan Talks.* Paisley: Alexander Gardner, 1906.

McKeon, Michael. *The Origins of the English Novel, 1600–1740.* Baltimore: The Johns Hopkins University Press, 1987.

McLeod, Hugh. *Religion and Society in England, 1850–1914.* New York: St Martin's Press, 1996.

McWilliams, Sally. "Tsitsi Dangarembga's *Nervous Conditions*: At the Crossroads of Feminism and Post-colonialism." *World Literature Written in English* 31, no. 1 (1991): 103–12.

Mee, Arthur. *The Children's John Bunyan.* London: Hodder and Stoughton, n.d.

Meyer, Birgit. *Translating the Devil: Religion and Modernity Among the Ewe in Ghana.* Edinburgh: Edinburgh University Press, 1999.

Michaeli, F. "Bible Problems in Central Africa." *Congo Mission News*, July 1954, 17.

Micheletti, Ellen. "Tiger Skins, Sheiks and Passionate Kisses." All about Romance. http://www.likesbooks.com/hist1.html, 10 September 2001.

Miller, Ethel. *Change Here for Kano: Reminiscences of Fifty Years in Nigeria*. Zaria: Gaskiya Corporation, n.d.

Miller, Joseph Calder. *Way of Death: Merchant Capitalism and the Angolan Slave Trade, 1730–1830*. London: James Currey, 1988.

Miller, Robert Strang. "Greatheart of China." In *Five Pioneer Missionaries*, by Stephen M. Houghton. London: Banner of Truth Trust, n.d.

The Missionary Ship John Williams. London: John Snow, 1844.

Mofolo, Thomas. *Moeti wa Botjhabela* [*Moeti oa Bochabela*]. 1906. Reprint, Morija: Morija Sesuto Book Depot, 1961.

Molema, Leloba Sefetogi. *The Image of Christianity in Sesotho Literature*. Hamburg: Helmut Buske, 1984.

Montague, C. J. "Bunyan for the Matabele." *The Chronicle of the London Missionary Society* 11 (1902): 252–54.

"The Month's Mail: South Africa." *The Chronicle of the London Missionary Society* 11 (1902): 41–42.

"Monument to John Bunyan." In *Works of the English Puritan Divines: Bunyan*. London: Thomas Nelson, 1845.

Morton, Chris. "'Interesting and Picturesque': Staging Encounters for the British Association in South Africa, 1905." Encounters with Photography. http://www.museums.org.za/sam/conf/enc/morton.htm, 10 November 2001.

Mostert, Noël. *Frontiers: The Epic of South Africa's Creation and the Tragedy of the Xhosa People*. London: Pimlico, 1992.

Mpiku, Mbelolo ya. "Introduction à la littérature Kikongo." *Research in African Literatures* 3, no. 2 (1972): 117–61.

Mrs. King. "The Narrow Way." *Young Africa* 78, no. 17 (1938): 11.

Mugambi, J.N.K. "Christological Paradigms in African Christianity." In *Jesus in African Christianity*, edited by J.N.K. Mugambi and Laurenti Magesa. Nairobi: Initiatives, 1989.

Mugambi, J.N.K., and Laurenti Magesa, eds. *Jesus in African Christianity*. Nairobi: Initiatives, 1989.

Mwase, Simeon. "Dialogue of Nyasaland Record of Past Events, Environments and the Present Outlook within the Protectorate." MS published as *Strike a Blow and Die: A Narrative of Race Relations in Colonial Africa*, by George Simeon Mwase. Edited by Robert Rotberg. Cambridge: Harvard University Press, 1967.

Nairne, W. P. *Greatheart of Papua*. Oxford: Oxford University Press, n.d.

National Sunday School Union. *Bunyan: The Dreamer—A Cantata for Young People*. London: The National Sunday School Union, n.d.

Newbolt, Margaret, ed., *The Later Life and Letters of Sir Henry Newbolt.* London: Faber, 1942.

Nettleton, Anitra, ed. *'Of Course you Would not Want a Canoe': The Collection of W.F.P. Burton.* Johannesburg: University of the Witwatersrand, 1992.

Newell, Stephanie. *Ghanaian Popular Fiction: 'Thrilling Discoveries in Conjugal Life and Other Tales.'* Oxford: James Currey, 2000.

———. *Literary Culture of Colonial Ghana: 'How to Play the Game of Life.'* Manchester: Manchester University Press, 2002.

Newey, Vincent, ed. *"The Pilgrim's Progress": Critical and Historical Views.* Liverpool: Liverpool University Press, 1980.

Ngũgĩ wa Thiong'o. *Decolonising the Mind: The Politics of Language in African Literature.* London: James Currey, 1987.

———. *Devil on the Cross.* Translated from Kikuyu by the Author. Oxford: Heinemann, 1987.

Nida, Eugene A. "Congo and the Bible." *Congo Mission News*, January 1955, 10–11.

———. "Some Language Problems in the Congo." *Congo Mission News*, January 1949, 14–16.

Niranjana, Tejaswini. *Siting Translation: History, Post-structuralism and the Colonial Context.* Berkeley: University of California Press, 1992.

Nishimura, Kazuko. "John Bunyan's Reception in Japan." *Bunyan Studies* 1, no. 2 (1989): 49–62.

Nkondo, Sankie Dolly. *Flames of Fury and Other Poems.* Johannesburg: Congress of South African Writers, 1990.

Norvig, Gerda S. *Dark Figures in the Desired Country: Blake's Illustrations of "The Pilgrim's Progress."* Berkeley: University of California Press, 1993.

Noyes, Alfred. "Bunyan—A Re-evaluation." *The Bookman* 445, no. 75 (1928): 13–17.

———. "Mr. Alfred Noyes' Rejoinder." *The Bookman* 445, no. 76 (1928): 104–106.

Offor, George, ed. Introduction to *The Pilgrim's Progress.* London: Hanserd Knollys Society, 1847.

———. Introductory memoir to *The Pilgrim's Progress and other Works of John Bunyan.* Edinburgh: William Mackenzie, n.d.

———. *The Pilgrim's Progress and other Works of John Bunyan.* Edinburgh: William Mackenzie, n.d.

Opland, Jeff. "The Image of the Book in Xhosa Oral Poetry." In *Oral Literature and Performance in Southern Africa*, edited by Duncan Brown. Oxford: James Currey, 1999.

Overtone, Charles. *"The Pilgrim's Progress" Practically Explained in a Series of Lectures.* London: Seeley Jackson and Halliday, 1864.

Owens, W. R. Introduction to *Grace Abounding to the Chief of Sinners*, by John Bunyan. 1666. Reprint, London: Penguin, 1987.

Palmer, D. J. *The Rise of English Studies: An Account of the Study of English Language* and Literature from its Origins to the Making of the Oxford English School. London: Oxford University Press, 1965.

Patten, John A., and Edward Shillito. *The Martyr Church and its Book*. London: British and Foreign Bible Society and London Missionary Society, n.d.

Patton, Cornelius H. "A World Program of Christian Literature." *The International Review of Mission* 11, no. 44 (1922): 572–85.

Peel, J.D.Y. "'For Who Hath Despised the Day of Small Things': Missionary Narratives and Historical Anthropology." *Comparative Studies in Society and History* 37, no. 3 (1995): 581–607.

Peires, J. B. *The Dead Will Arise: Nongqawuse and the Great Xhosa Cattle-Killing Movement of 1856–1857*. Johannesburg: Ravan Press, 1989.

Pelling, Henry. *Origins of the Labour Party, 1880–1900*. Oxford: Clarendon Press, 1974.

Pemberton, Jeremy. "The History of Simon Kimbangu, Prophet, by the Writers Nfinangani and Nzungu, 1921: An Introduction and Annotated Translation." *Journal of Religion in Africa* 23, no. 3 (1993): 194–231.

Persson, J. A. "Preparation, Production and Distribution of Literature in African Languages." *Congo Mission News*, April 1947, 11–13.

Peterson, Bhekizizwe. *Monarchs, Missionaries and African Intellectuals: African Theatre and the Unmaking of Colonial Marginality*. Johannesburg: Witwatersrand University Press, 2000.

Pettifer, Julian, and Richard Bradley. *Missionaries*. London: British Broadcasting Corporation, 1990.

Phillippo, James Mursell. *Jamaica: Past and Present*. London: John Snow, 1843.

Pietz, William. "The Problem of the Fetish." Parts 1–3a. *Res* 9 (1985): 5–17; 13 (1987): 23–45; 16 (1988): 105–23.

Pietz, William, and Emily Apter. Introduction to *Fetishism as Cultural Discourse*, edited by William Pietz and Emily Apter. Ithaca: Cornell University Press, 1993.

———, eds. *Fetishism as Cultural Discourse*. Ithaca: Cornell University Press, 1993.

Pigafetta, Filippo. *A Representation of the Kingdom of Congo and of the Surrounding Countries Drawn out of the Writing and Discourses of the Portuguese Duarte Lopez*. Translated by Margarite Hutchinson. 1591. Reprint, London: John Murray, 1881.

Piggin, Stuart. *Making Evangelical Missionaries, 1789–1858: The Social Background, Motives and Training of British Protestant Missionaries to India*. Abingdon: Sutton Courtenay Press, 1984.

A Pilgrim. *Greatheart: Some Talks with Him*. London: Macmillan, 1905.

———. *Some Daily Thoughts on "The Pilgrim's Progress."* London: Churchman Publishing Company, 1917.

Pirouet, M. Louise. *Black Evangelists: The Spread of Christianity in Uganda, 1891–1914*. London: Rex Collings, 1978.

Pitts, Walter F. *Old Ship of Zion: The Afro-Baptist Ritual in the African Diaspora.* New York: Oxford University Press, 1993.

Porter, Andrew N., ed. *Atlas of British Overseas Expansion.* London: Routledge, 1991.

Porter, Roy. *London: A Social History.* London: Penguin, 1994.

Poteat, Gordon. *A Greatheart of the South: John T. Anderson Medical Missionary.* New York: George H. Doran, n.d.

Potter, Sarah Caroline. "The Social Origins and Recruitment of English Protest Missionaries in the Nineteenth Century." Ph.D. diss., University of London, 1974.

Poynter, R. H. *Syllabus of Bunyan Lectures.* Bedford: Robinson, 1912.

Prakash, Gyan. "Introduction: After Colonialism." In *After Colonialism: Imperial Histories and Postcolonial Displacements,* edited by Gyan Prakash. Princeton: Princeton University Press, 1995.

——, ed. *After Colonialism: Imperial Histories and Postcolonial Displacements.* Princeton: Princeton University Press, 1995.

Pugh, Charles E. Foreword in *Lokendo loa bokendi* (*The Pilgrim's Progress,* part 1). Translated and compiled by Charles E. Pugh. London: Religious Tract Society, 1916.

Punshon, W. Morley. Lectures in *John Bunyan,* by W. Morley Punshon. London: T. Woolmer, 1882.

Raboteau, Albert J. *Slave Religion: The "Invisible Institution" in the Antebellum South.* New York: Oxford University Press, 1978.

Rafael, Vicente. *Contracting Colonialism: Translation and Christian Conversion in Tagalog Society under Early Spanish Rule.* Ithaca: Cornell University Press, 1988.

Ranger, Terence O. *Revolt in Southern Rhodesia, 1896–1897.* London: Heinemann, 1979.

——. "Missionaries, Migrants and Manyika: The Invention of Ethnicity in Zimbabwe." In *The Creation of Tribalism in Southern Africa,* edited by Leroy Vail. London: James Currey, 1989.

Ransome, Arthur. *A History of Story-telling: Studies in the Development of Narrative.* London: T. C. and E. C. Jack, 1909.

Read, Alfred Hamish. *Samuel Marsden: Great Heart of Maoriland.* London: Pickering and Inglis, n.d.

Reason, J., ed. *The Ship Book: Stories, Games, Poems, Models etc.* London: Livingstone Press, 1944.

Report. *The Female Missionary Intelligencer,* January 1899.

"Report from Old Calabar." *Missionary Record of the United Presbyterian Church,* June 1868, 120.

The Return to England of the Missionary Ship John Williams. London: John Snow, 1847.

Reviews of *Uhambo lo Mhambi* (*The Pilgrim's Progress,* part 1), translated by Tiyo Soga. *United Presbyterian Missionary Record,* July 1869, 400–401.

Ridgwell, Harold A. *Heroes in Madagascar*. London: Marshall, Morgan and Scott, n.d.

Ritson, John H. "Christian Literature in the Mission Field." *International Review of Mission* 4, no. 14 (1915): 200–20.

Rivers, Isabel. "Grace, Holiness, and the Pursuit of Happiness: Bunyan and Restoration Latitudinarianism." In *John Bunyan: Conventicle and Parnassus: Tercentenary Essays*, edited by N. H. Keeble. Oxford: Clarendon Press, 1988.

Robb, Alex. *A Narrative of the Life and Labours of the Rev. William Jameson in Jamaica and Old Calabar*. Edinburgh: Andrew Elliot, n.d.

Robert, Dana R. "The First Globalization: The Internationalization of the Protestant Missionary Movement between the World Wars." Abstract in "Interpreting Contemporary Christianity: Global Processes and Local Identities: Conference Programme." Hammanskraal Campus, University of Pretoria, July 2001.

Rotberg, Robert I., ed. Introduction to *Strike a Blow and Die: A Narrative of Race Relations in Colonial Africa*, by George Simeon Mwase. Cambridge: Harvard University Press, 1967.

Rowling, Frank, and C. E. Wilson, comps. *A Bibliography of African Christian Literature*. London: Conference of Missionary Societies of Great Britain and Ireland, 1923.

Rutherford, Mark [William Hale White]. *John Bunyan*. London: Hodder and Stoughton, n.d.

Saintsbury, George. *A Short History of English Literature*. 1898. Reprint, London: Macmillan, 1907.

Samarin, William J. "Protestant Missions and the History of Lingala." *Journal of Religion in Africa* 16, no. 2 (1986): 138–63.

Samuel, Raphael. *Island Stories: Unravelling Britain Theatres of Memory*. Vol. 2. London: Verso, 1998.

Sann, Auguste. *Bunyan in Deutschland*. Giessen: Wilhelm Schmitz, 1951.

Sanneh, Lamin. *Translating the Message: The Missionary Impact on Culture*. Maryknoll: Orbis Books, 1991.

Sayer, Derek. *Capitalism and Modernity: An Excursus on Marx and Weber*. London: Routledge, 1991.

Scheub, Harold. *The Xhosa Ntsomi*. Oxford: Clarendon Press, 1975.

Schneider, Jane. "Dressing for the Next Life: Raffia Textile Production and Use among the Kuba of Zaire." In *Cloth and Human Experience*, edited by Annette B. Weiner and Jane Schneider. Washington: Smithsonian Institution Press, 1988.

Schutte, G. J. *Bunyan in Nederland*. Houten: Den Hertog, 1989.

Segoete, Everitt. *Monono ke moholi ke mouoane*. Morija: Sesuto Book Depot, 1926.

———. *Moya oa bolisa*. Morija: Sesuto Book Depot, 1915.

Sharrock, Roger. "Bunyan and the English Emblem Writers." *The Review of English Studies* 21, no. 82 (1945): 105–16.

———. Introduction to *The Pilgrim's Progress*. London: Penguin, 1987.

———. "Life and Story in *The Pilgrim's Progress.*" In *"The Pilgrim's Progress": Critical and Historical Views*, edited by Vincent Newey. Liverpool: Liverpool University Press, 1980.

———. Notes in *The Pilgrim's Progress*. London: Penguin, 1987.

———, ed. *Bunyan, "The Pilgrim's Progress": A Casebook*. London: Macmillan, 1976.

Sherry, Norman. *Conrad's Western World*. Cambridge: Cambridge University Press, 1971.

Smit, M.T.R. *African Greatheart: The Story of Cornelius Sejosing*. London: Religious Tract Society/Lutterworth, n.d.

Smith, David E. *John Bunyan in America*. Bloomington: Indiana University Press, 1966.

Smith, Herbert. "The Need for Union Literature in Congo." In *The Congo Missionary Conference: A Report of the Eighth Congo General Conference of Protestant Missionaries*. Baptist Missionary Society: Bolobo, n.d.

Smith, Nigel. "Bunyan and the Language of the Body in Seventeenth-Century England." In *John Bunyan and his England, 1628–1688*, edited by Anne Laurence, W. R. Owens, and Stuart Sim. London: The Hambledon Press, 1990.

Smout, T. Christopher. *A Century of the Scottish People, 1830–1950*. London: Collins, 1986.

Soga, Tiyo. "Intshayelelo" (Introduction) to *Uhambo lo Mhambi* (*The Pilgrim's Progress*, part 1), translated by Tiyo Soga. 1868. Reprint, Lovedale: Lovedale Press, 1965.

———. "The Journal." In *The Journals and Selected Writings of the Reverend Tiyo Soga*, edited by Donovan Williams. Cape Town: A. A. Balkema, 1983.

———. "A National Newspaper." In *The Journals and Selected Writings of the Reverend Tiyo Soga*, edited by Donovan Williams. Cape Town: A. A. Balkema, 1983.

———. "What is the Destiny of the Kaffir Race?" In *The Journals and Selected Writings of the Reverend Tiyo Soga*, edited by Donovan Williams. Cape Town: A. A. Balkema, 1983.

Souvenir of the Centenary of Camden Road Baptist Church, 1854–1954. N.p., n.d.

Soyinka, Wole, trans. *The Forest of a Thousand Daemons: A Hunter's Saga*, translation of *Ògbójú Ọdẹ Nínú Igbó Irúnmalẹ*, by D. O. Fagunwa. London: Nelson, 1968.

Spargo, Tamsin. *The Writing of John Bunyan*. Aldershot: Ashgate, 1997.

Spufford, Margaret. *Small Books and Pleasant Histories: Popular Fiction and its Readership in Seventeenth-Century England*. Cambridge: Cambridge University Press, 1981.

Spyer, Patricia, ed. *Border Fetishisms: Material Objects in Unstable Spaces*. New York: Routledge, 1998.

Stanley, A. P. "The Character of John Bunyan: Local, Ecclesiastical, Universal." In *The Book of the Bunyan Festival: A Complete Record of the Proceedings at the Unveiling of the Statue*, edited by W. H. Wylie. London: James Clarke and Christian World Office, 1874.

Stanley, Brian. *The History of the Baptist Missionary Society, 1792–1992*. Edinburgh: T. and T. Clark, 1992.

Starr, Frederick. *A Bibliography of Congo Languages*. Chicago: Chicago University Press, 1908.

Stevenson, J. Sinclair. *Robert Henderson: The Story of a Missionary Greatheart in India*. London: James Clarke, 1922.

Stevenson, Robert. *Expositions of "The Pilgrim's Progress" with Illustrative Quotations from Bunyan's Minor Works*. London: A. and C. Black, 1912.

Stewart, Robert J. *Religion and Society in Post-Emancipation Jamaica*. Knoxville: University of Tennessee Press, 1992.

Stock, Brian. *The Implications of Literacy: Written Language and Models of Interpretation in the Eleventh and Twelfth Centuries*. Princeton: Princeton University Press, 1983.

Stones, Rob. *Key Sociological Thinkers*. Basingstoke: Macmillan, 1998.

Stratton, Florence. *Contemporary African Literature and the Politics of Gender*. London: Routledge, 1994.

Struyf, Ivo. *Uit den Kunstschat der Bakongos*. Vol. 1. Amsterdam: Van Langenhuysen, 1908.

Sundkler, Bengt G. M. *Bantu Prophets in South Africa*. London: Oxford University Press, 1948.

Sutton Smith, Herbert. *Yakusu: The Very Heart of Africa*. London: Marshall Brothers, n.d.

Swaim, Kathleen M. "Mercy and the Feminine Heroic in the Second Part of *Pilgrim's Progress*." *Studies in English Literature, 1500–1900* 30 (1990): 387–409.

Thickstun, Margaret Olofson. "From Christiana to Stand-fast: Subsuming the Feminine in *The Pilgrim's Progress*." *Studies in English Literature, 1500–1900* 26 (1986): 439–53.

Thompson, Douglas. *Talks with Bunyan: Discourses on Bunyan's "Pilgrim's Progress" and "The Holy War."* London: Elliott Stock, 1859.

Thompson, E. P. *The Making of the English Working Class*. Middlesex: Penguin, 1968.

Thompson, John, and Sidney Robjohns. *Bunyan Home Scenes*. Bedford: J. Thompson, 1900.

Thompson, T. Jack. *Christianity in Northern Malawi: Donald Fraser's Missionary Methods and Ngoni Culture*. Leiden: E. J. Brill, 1995.

Thorne, Susan. *Congregational Missions and the Making of an Imperial Culture in Nineteenth-Century England*. Stanford: Stanford University Press, 1999.

———. "'The Conversion of Englishmen and the Conversion of the World Inseparable': Missionary Imperialism and the Language of Class in Early Industrial Britain." In *Tensions of Empire: Colonial Cultures in a Bourgeois*

World, edited by Frederick Cooper and Ann Laura Stoler. Berkeley: University of California Press, 1997.

Thornton, John. *Africa and the Africans in the Making of the Atlantic World, 1440–1800*. Cambridge: Cambridge University Press, 1998.

———. *The Kingdom of Kongo: Civil War and Transition, 1641–1718*. Madison: University of Wisconsin Press, 1983.

Tibbutt, H. G. *Bunyan's Meeting Bedford, 1650–1950*. Bedford: Trustees of Bunyan Meeting House, n.d.

———. *Bunyan's Standing Today*. Bedford: Elstow Moot Hall, 1966.

———. "The Pilgrim's Route." *Bedfordshire Magazine* 7, no. 49 (1959): 66–68.

Tidmarsh, Alan. *Sale of the Century: An Illustrated History and Souvenir of the Centenary Church and Missionary Sale*. London: Camden Road Baptist Church, 1978.

Tobias, Steven M. "Amos Tutuola and the Colonial Carnival." *Research in African Literatures* 30, no. 2 (1999): 66–74.

Trevelyan, G. M. "Bunyan's England." *The Review of the Churches* 5, no. 3 (1928): 319–24.

Turner, James. "Bunyan's Sense of Place." In *"The Pilgrim's Progress": Critical and Historical Views*, edited by Vincent Newey. Liverpool: Liverpool University Press, 1980.

Tutuola, Amos. *The Wild Hunter in the Bush of Ghosts*, edited by Bernth Lindfors. Washington: Three Continents Press, 1989.

Underhill, Edward Bean. *Life of James Mursell Phillipo: Missionary in Jamaica*. London: Yates and Alexander, 1831.

Uwakheh, Pauline Ada. "Debunking Patriarchy: The Liberational Quality of Voicing in Tsitsi Dangarembga's *Nervous Conditions*." *Research in African Literatures* 26, no. 1 (1995): 75–84.

Vail, Leroy ed. *The Creation of Tribalism in Southern Africa*. London: James Currey, 1989.

Van 't Veld, H. "A New Thesis on Luyken as Illustrator of Bunyan." *The Recorder* 7 (2001): 8–11.

Vassady, Bela. "The Role of the Black West Indian Missionary in West Africa, 1840–1890." Ph.D. diss., Temple University, 1972.

Veit-Wild, Flora. *Teachers, Preachers and Non-Believers: A Social History of Zimbabwean Literature*. London: Hans Zell, 1992.

Venables, Edmund. Introduction to *The Pilgrim's Progress*. London: Oxford University Press, 1903.

———. *Life of John Bunyan*. London: Walter Scott, 1888.

Victor, Osmund. *The Salient of South Africa*. London: The Society for the Propagation of the Gospel in Foreign Parts, 1931.

Vincent, David. *Literacy and Popular Culture: England, 1750–1914*. Cambridge: Cambridge University Press, 1989.

Viswanathan, Gauri. *Masks of Conquest: Literary Study and British Rule in India.* New York: Columbia University Press, 1989.

—. *Outside the Fold: Conversion, Modernity, and Belief.* Princeton: Princeton University Press, 1998.

"The Voice of Africa: A Bit of Bunyan by Moses Mubitana." *Africa* 16, no. 3 (1946): 179–82.

Waddell, Hope Masterton. *Twenty-Nine Years in the West Indies and Central Africa: A Review of Missionary Work and Adventure, 1829–1858.* London: Nelson, 1863.

Warner, Michael. "Publics and Counterpublics." *Public Culture* 14, no. 1 (2002): 49–90.

Warr, Daniel. *A Course of Lectures, Illustrative of "The Pilgrim's Progress."* London: Richard Baynes, 1832.

Werner, Alice. "A Mosuto Novelist." *International Review of Mission* 14, no. 55 (1925): 428–36.

Wharey, James Blunton. Introduction to *The Pilgrim's Progress.* 1928. Reprint, Oxford: Clarendon Press, 1960.

White, Alexander. *Bunyan Characters in "The Pilgrim's Progress."* Edinburgh: Oliphant Anderson and Ferrier, n.d.

Willan, Brian. *Sol Plaatje: A Biography.* Johannesburg: Ravan Press, 1984.

Williams, Charles. *A Bi-Centenary Memorial of John Bunyan who Died A.D. 1688.* London: Baptist Tract and Book Society, 1888.

Williams, Donovan. *Umfundisi: A Biography of Tiyo Soga, 1928–1871.* Lovedale: Lovedale Press, 1978.

—, ed. *The Journals and Selected Writings of the Reverend Tiyo Soga.* Cape Town: A. A. Balkema, 1983.

Wilson, C. E. "The Provision of a Christian Literature for Africa." *International Review of Mission* 15, no. 59 (1926): 506–14.

—. "A Survey of Christian Literature in African Languages." *International Review of Mission* 10, no. 39 (1926): 376–84.

Wylie, W. H., ed. *The Book of the Bunyan Festival: A Complete Record of the Proceedings at the Unveiling of the Statue.* London: James Clarke and Christian World Office, 1874.

Boy Scout movement, 161
Boys' Brigade, 161
Brathwaite, Edward, 90
Breen, Margaret Soenser, 143
British Baptists, 109; as active propagators of *The Pilgrim's Progress,* 89–90; in Jamaica, 90
Brown, John, 62
Bunn, David, 274n. 34
Bunyan, John, 56, 58–59, 70–71, 148, 192, 256n. 85; attempts to "Bedfordize," 234–37; as "Caliban-Bunyan," 225–26; and commodities concerning, 60; conversion of, 74; as English, 11–12, 58; Englishness of, 11–12, 217–18, 220–26; historiography, 31–41; jailing of, 88; language of, 220; manliness of, 162; and slave Christianity, 88, 260n. 57; tercentenary of, 217, 222; tomb of, 69–70, 256n. 79; translators of, 35, 244–45; transnational presence of, 1–2, 11–12, 71; universality of, 15, 217–18, 225–27, 228–29, 238–39
Bunyan in America (Smith), 12
Burnside, Janet, 118
Burton, W.F.P., 178, 273n. 35
Buta War, 182–83, 187

Cabinda, 183
Caitaani Mūthabaranī (Devil on the Cross/ Ngũgĩ), 203–8; depiction of hell, 206–7; plot of, 204; references to *The Pilgrim's Progress* in, 204–6; as subverting text of *The Pilgrim's Progress,* 203–4; Warĩĩnga in, 204–6
Calvinism: and covenanting, 120; and the doctrine of election, 150
Camden Road Baptist Chapel, 45–47, 50, 160
Cameroon, 93, 261–62n. 97
Cannell, W. M., 244
Cape Colony, 128, 129; and the Eastern Cape elite, 116–17; and the Native Affairs Department (NAD) Bunga (Council of Chiefs), 130
Carnegie, David, 104–5, 137, 245
Carnegie, Mary, 137, 245
Cassell's History of English Literature (Cassell), 219

Chaka (Mofolo), 151
Chakrabarty, Dipesh, 24, 232, 249n. 29
Chalmers, James, 162
Chief Tulante Alvaro Buta, 183
Chilembwe, John, 146–47
Chinula, Charles, 244
Christ of the Congo River, The (Fullerton), 57
Christian (character in *The Pilgrim's Progress*), 89, 91, 99–101, 103, 107, 137, 138, 141–43, 169, 184, 185, 198, 205–6, 235; and alternative forms of manliness, 152–53; and the burden of original sin, 84–85; and the ideology of resistance, 229; manliness of, 162, 169, 171
Christianity, 16, 17, 64, 78, 120–21, 131, 167, 213, 230; Creole, 90–91; "de-Westernizing," 108; and literary forms, 171–72; shepherding as metaphor of, 169–70; slave, 88, 91, 260n. 57. *See also* African Christianity; African American Christianity; evangelicalism
Chronicle of the LMS, 188
Church of the Nazarites, 139–40
Cindi, Andrew, 143–44
Civil Service of East India Company Report, 218
Clarion, The, 59
Clark, J. A., 83
Cockett, Bernard, 78, 222
Colenso, Harriet, 189
Colenso, John William, 80–81, 245
colonialism, and the "pleasures" of chronology, 232–33
Comber, Thomas, 47, 50, 54
Congo (Kongo Kingdom), 50–51, 76; Catholicism in, 51; death rates in, 51–52; Islam in, 51. *See also* Baptist missions, in the Congo
Congo Balolo Mission, 83
Congo boat songs, 53–54
Congo Exhibition, 56
"Congo mimicry," 53
Congo Mission Conference, 83
"Congo parable, the," 106, 108–9
Congo River, 52, 56
Conrad, Joseph, 52, 191

McClintock, Anne, 164

McKeon, Michael, 237

Mee, Arthur, 221, 236

Mellor, James, 60–61

Mensah, Marjorie. *See* Danquah, Mabel Dove

Merrick, Richard, 92

"methodological fetishism," 14

Meyer, Birgit, 16–17

Miller, Ethel, 245

Millman, William, 108

Milton, Eva, 245, 279–80n. 3

mimicry, 108. *See also* "Congo mimicry"

Minsamu Miayenga, 106

mission translation, 19–20, 77–78, 82, 118, 250n. 45; and African Christian thinking, 21; constraints on, 20–21; as done by "couples," 21–22; and "embezzlement" of African folktales, 105–9; key features of, 77; and recording of dreams, 106; unstable nature of, 258–59n. 34

Missionary Herald, 52, 109, 182, 257n. 99

missions/missionaries, 16–17, 61–63, 73, 82, 105, 108, 197, 248n. 14; and African/Protestant masculinities, 153, 161–63; Dutch, 118–19; and the imperatives of proselytization, 19–20; and imperialism, 46; in Jamaica, 87, 92–94; missionary exhibitions, 65, 70; and photography, 183–86; use of illustrations in proselytization ("visual evangelism"), 174–75; and women, 163–64. *See also* Baptist Missionary Society; Baptist missions, in Angola; Baptist missions, in the Congo; Lovedale Missionary Institution

Moeti oa Bochabela (*The Traveller to the East*/Mofolo), 151–52, 160, 176, 270n. 1; critical reaction to, 166; Fekisi in, 167–71, 271n. 61; importance of cattle herding in, 169–70; literary forms in, 171–72; masculinity issues in, 169–71; Phakoane in, 271n. 61; plot outline, 167–68; similarities to *The Pilgrim's Progress,* 168–69; and the "two cultures," 166–67

Moffat, Robert, 245

Mofolo, Thomas, 24, 151–52, 153, 166–67, 231; Christianity of, 167, 271n. 57; ideas on masculinity, 171

Moholo, 137, 245

Monono ke moholi ke mouoane (*Wealth is a Haze, a Mist*/Segote), 138–39

Montague, C. J., 137, 152, 188–90, 223–24, 274n. 44

Morley, Henry, 70

Moule, Handley Carr Glen (Bishop of Durham), 217, 218, 224

Mpambu, 147

Mpiku, Mbelolo ya, 105–6

Mqhayi, S.E.K., 123, 126

Mthembi-Mahanyele, Sankie. *See* Nkondo, Sankie

Mubitana, Moses, 244

Mwakasungula, A.B.M., 244

Mwase, Simeon, 146–47

Naipaul, V. S., 191

"Named for Victoria, Queen of England" (Achebe), 173

Ndebele society, 152; and concern with masculinity, 153

Nekaka, Miguel, 182, 183

Nervous Conditions (Dangarembga), 207–13; and the African elite, 210; and gender roles, 210–13; references to *The Pilgrim's Progress* in, 209–12; Tambudzai in, 209–11

New Imperialism, 222

Newbolt report, 219

Newell, Stephanie, 27, 212

Ngidi, William, 259n. 24

Ngũgĩ wa Thiong'o, 203–4, 212; on documents, 206

Nida, Eugene, 82

Nkondo, Sankie ("Rebecca Matlou"), 134–36

Nonconformists, 45, 57, 69–70, 153, 160; importance of *The Pilgrim's Progress* to, 58–59, 61; and the Liberal Party, 221–22; and preparations for dying, 98–99

Nongqawuse, 119

Nontsizi, 132, 134

Noyes, Alfred, 74–75; criticism of Bunyan, 225–26

Ntsikana, 119

Nyasaland, 146

Ògbójú Ọdẹ Nínú Igbó Irúnalẹ (*The Forest of a Thousand Daemons*/Fagunwa), 200–201; depictions of heaven and hell, 195, 197–99; elements of Bunyan in, 195; as extended folktale, 194; religious world of, 194–95

Old Soga, 117–18

Ouless, E. U., 123

Pageant of Woman Greatheart, The, 160

Pamela (Richardson), 233

Paris Evangelical Mission Society (PEMS), 36

"passports to heaven," 91–92, 261n. 80

Peace, 52

Peires, Jeff, 119

Pemba, George, 175

Phillipo, James Mursell, 90

philology, 219

photography, 273n. 34; ethnographic, 184, 186–87; "fictional," 183–84, 186; and the mission station landmark, 184–85; and the religious tableau, 185–87

Pilgrim's Progress, The (Bunyan), 1–2, 56, 88, 150; as abolitionist tract, 88; abridgement of, 173, 230–31; and abridgement of theology by African readers, 107–8; and African folktales, 106–7, 238; binding of, 72, 79; and colonialism, 230, 233–34; description of landscape in, 220–21; as devotional text, 58–62; and different forms of reading, 59–60, 92, 100–101, 103, 104, 123; dissemination of "at home," 61–62, 221, 224–25; dissemination across languages and cultures, 12–13; in an educational setting, 122–24; as fetish, 72–75, 232; and geographical realism, 236–37; and imperialism, 16; as international text, 23, 230–31; and "magical" reading practices, 72–73, 232–33; as a material object, 37–39; and metaphors of religious melancholy, 107; Old Testament characters in, 233; and original sin, 84–85; and pageants, 103–4; plot synopsis, 3–5; and political debate, 131–32, 134–36; political radicalism of, 15; as a portmanteau text, 28; as protonovel, 237;

and realism, 237–38; relationship to the Bible, 77–80, 83, 91–92; reviews of, 70; as a "second Bible," 73, 77, 78–79, 11, 229; setting of in Bedfordshire, 234–37; and slide shows/magic lantern slides, 103, 104, 182. *See also* documents; Ndebele society; *Pilgrim's Progress, The,* characters in; *Pilgrim's Progress, The,* illustration of; *Pilgrim's Progress, The,* and missions; *Pilgrim's Progress, The,* places in; *Pilgrim's Progress, The,* specific translations of; *Pilgrim's Progress, The,* translation issues

Pilgrim's Progress, The, characters in: Apollyon, 89; Christiana, 98–99, 140–41, 164, 198; Discretion, 209; Evangelist, 90, 189, 204; Faithful, 142, 184; Fool, 95; Giant Despair, 107, 128–30, 185; Hopeful, 91, 107, 137, 138, 142; Ignorance, 137, 138; Mistrust, 188; Obstinate, 148–49; Pliable, 101, 102, 149; Presumption, 170; Mr. Talkative, 102, 107; Want-Wit, 94; Watchful, 209. *See also* Christian; Great-heart

Pilgrim's Progress, The, illustration of, 60, 69, 79, 104–5, 173–74, 273n. 34; and the Austin photographs, 177–78, 181–84, 187–88, 271n. 1; Burton-Lingala sketches, 177, 178, 180; and "canonical" Africanized illustrations, 176–79; Kamba illustrations, 177, 180, 224; Montague/ Burton drawings, 177–78; racial character of, 223–24; and rescripting of martial ideals, 152–53; stick figure illustrations, 175, 272n. 12; use of African characters in, 175–81; as visual evangelism, 174–75

Pilgrim's Progress, The, and missions, 18–20; and mission exhibitions, 65; and mission magazines, 65, 106; as a mission parable, 57–58; and missionary work in Jamaica, 87–88, 92–93

Pilgrim's Progress, The, places in: Delectable Mountains, 5, 142, 197, 205; Doubting Castle, 185; Hill Difficulty, 134, 141, 188, 266n. 65; House of the Interpreter, 196, 197, 198, 211–12; Palace Beautiful, 197, 209, 211, 235–36; Slough of Despond, 4, 102; Vanity Fair, 141–42, 184